TOBIAS SMOLLETT

Portrait of Smollett. About 1750
Attributed to Gainsborough

Tobias Smollett

DOCTOR
OF MEN AND MANNERS

By Lewis Mansfield Knapp

NEW YORK

RUSSELL & RUSSELL · INC

1963

TO MY MOTHER

PREFACE

THERE are abundant indications today of a steadily surging tide of interest in the Age of Johnson. With the single exception of the great Cham of Literature, there was from 1745 to 1771 no literary personality as independent, colorful, and versatile as Dr. Tobias Smollett. Before his untimely death, this Scottish doctor of men and manners had won wide acclaim as translator, historian, book reviewer, writer of travel literature, social satirist, and, above all, as one of the four leading novelists of his period.

During the turbulent half-century after Smollett died in Italy, he was very widely read, not only in the British Isles, but also on the Continent and in America. In the Victorian era, of course, his vogue declined, along with that of other eighteenth-century luminaries. But in the past few decades, his reputation has increased. This is not to be wondered at, for all who enjoy the spirit of a dynamic personality and relish hilarious comedy, memorable characters, and incisive satire, may find in Smollett a goodly realm of gold.

Moved by these considerations, I was attracted some twenty years ago by the challenge of building a definitive biography commensurate with Smollett's stature as a man and as a writer. I shall not detail here my adventures in this exacting undertaking. I must only assert that the vexations and drudgery involved in it have been far outweighed by the satisfactions with which I have been rewarded.

In this preface, it is proper to summarize the central objectives and contributions of this biography. One obvious purpose has been to rectify factual and interpretative inaccuracies in former accounts of Smollett. What is more important, I have tried to be accurate in presenting and evaluating whatever new material is brought to light. Furthermore, I have made every effort to project a living personality vitalized by facts rather than by specious fictions. In significant respects a new portrait of Smollett is here unveiled, one considerably more complete, and, I believe, more pleasing than former sketches have been. I have sought the truth about Smollett, an activity which necessitates the avoiding, as far as possible, of partial prepossessions and wishful thinking. The result is, I hope, what constitutes a more reliable likeness and a portrait freed from Victorian distortions. In general, the result is a rehabilitation of Smollett's personality. Finally, in the concluding chapter devoted to his contribution to the English novel, I have stressed what I consider to be his most enduring merits as a creative writer.

To write this book would have been utterly impossible without the courteous assistance and the warm encouragement of many helpers: booksellers, collectors, librarians, authorities in eighteenth-century life and literature, and other assistants, including devoted relatives, have all had a hand visible or invisible in the pages that follow. To some of these I owe an especial debt. For financial aid I thank The American Council of Learned Societies for four substantial grants in the 1930's for research in England and Scotland. I also acknowledge with gratitude a research grant made available in 1937 by former President Tyler Dennett and the trustees of Williams College.

I am greatly indebted to Professor Chauncey Brewster Tinker for revealing to me the mysteries and the pleasures of research, for helping me in my original dissertation, and for remaining through the years a loyal and inspiring friend.

For invariable courtesies, including the permission to print unpublished material, I wish to thank the librarians and staffs of the following institutions: Yale University Library, Harvard University Library, The Library of Congress, Columbia University Library, The J. Pierpont Morgan Library, Boston Public Library, The Boston Athenaeum, The University of Rochester Library, The New York State Library, Williams College Library, Coburn Library of Colorado College, University of Colorado Library, The Huntington Library, The Bibliographical Center of Denver, Colorado, and The Ridgway Library of Philadelphia. For similar services I thank The Pennsylvania Historical Society, The Massachusetts Historical Society, and The Maine Historical Society. For unfailing courtesies and invaluable services rendered me as a visiting American student, I thank the various officials at the following libraries or repositories of documents: The British Museum, The National Library of Scotland, The Bodleian Library, The

PREFACE

Public Record Office, The Admiralty Library, The Stationers' Company, The Victoria and Albert Museum, The East India Office, The Guildhall Library, Trinity College Library of Dublin University, The National Library of Ireland, The Chelsea Public Library, The Central Library of Bristol, The Bath Municipal Reference Library, The Glasgow University Library, The Public Library of Nice, and The Biblioteca Riccardiana of Florence.

In the considerable list of individuals who have assisted me, I am very grateful to the following: the late R. B. Cunninghame Graham, the late Victor Plarr, the late Reginald Blunt, the late J. Paul De Castro, Mr. R. A. Austen-Leigh, the Reverend R. Langton Douglas, Mrs. Helen Margaret Home-Robertson, Mr. Henry W. Meikle, and Major-General Alexander P. D. Telfer-Smollett. To the following who have been especially generous in sharing with me their knowledge of Smollett I record my thanks: Professors Edward S. Noyes, Eugène Joliat, George M. Kahrl, Louis L. Martz, Howard P. Vincent, and Alan D. McKillop. I wish also to acknowledge the valuable assistance of the following colleagues and friends in Colorado Springs: the late Albert H. Daehler, Professor Charles T. Latimer, Professor and Mrs. George S. McCue, Professor Frank A. Krutzke, Miss Louise F. Kampf, and Mr. and Mrs. Frank V. Henry.

For devoted personal aid and encouragement, words fail to express my obligations to the late Louise Ansley Knapp and to the late Flora Robinson Heath. Similarly I owe more than can be conveyed by conventional phrases to my wife, Helen June Knapp, for her loyal interest and help.

LEWIS MANSFIELD KNAPP

Colorado College
April 8, 1948

CONTENTS

ILLUSTRATIONS

ERRATA

p. 60, n. 53, for *Kitson* read *Kidson* (twice)

p. 103, line 19, for *T. Osborne's*, read *J. Osborne's*

p. 104, line 15, for *T. Osborne*, read *J. Osborne*

p. 124, n. 80, for *Smolett*, read *Smollett*

for *Lady Vane was* read *Lady Vane were*

p. 342, Battle of the Reviews, The, this title should be in italics.

p. 355, In the Entry, Scott, James, D. D. ("Old Slyboots"), for *293 n.*, read *292 n.*

p. 362, The entry, *Williams, Ralph*, should not be in italics.

TOBIAS SMOLLETT

CHAPTER I

Youth and Education in Scotland,
1721-1739

ON Sunday, March 19, 1721, in the parish church of Cardross, Dumbartonshire, Mr. Archibald Smollett and his wife, Barbara Cunningham Smollett, presented their third child for baptism.[1] This infant in arms, christened Tobias George Smollett, was destined to become celebrated as a man of letters far beyond the banks of the Leven and the wider confines of the British Isles.

Only a few miles from Cardross kirk lay Dumbarton, Ardoch, Bonhill, and the area later called Renton. Overlooking the Leven valley in the ancient acres of Dalquhurn near the mansion of Smollett's grandfather at Bonhill stood the old house of Dalquhurn in which Smollett was born. From local accounts[2] and from old prints[3] Smollett's birthplace appears to have been a severe, unadorned, three-storyed building with a low wing on its west end. Though not pretentious or beautiful, it stood on high ground above the Leven and afforded a view of romantic Dumbarton Castle and a valley rich in natural beauty and in the stirring associations of Bruce and Wallace. In this delightful scene had lived and died many generations in the long line of Smollett's forefathers.

[1] The baptismal record reads: "March 19, 1721, Tobias George, son to Mr Ard. Smollet and Barbra Cunningham, Dalquhurn, was baptised." Cited from Robert Chambers, *Smollett* (London and Edinburgh, 1867), p. 6n.

[2] See Joseph Irving, *The History of Dumbartonshire* (Dumbarton, second edition, Printed for the Author, 1860), p. 433; and William C. Maughan, *Annals of Garelochside* (Paisley and London, 1897), p. 269. Robert Anderson declared in his biography of Smollett that when he visited the Dalquhurn house in 1809, it was uninhabited and "hastening to decay." See Smollett's *Miscellaneous Works*, ed. Robert Anderson, 6 vols. (Edinburgh, 1820), I, 5n.

[3] In my possession is a print entitled, "Dr Smollett's House and Monument" drawn by W. H. Watts, engraved by Wm Green, and published January 2, 1800 by Cadell and Davies, Strand [London]. I have another and smaller print drawn by Miss Cochran entitled, "Column to the Memory of Smollett, and the House in which He Was Born." The name of the engraver has been erased. Dalquhurn has long since disappeared.

Young Smollett had very good reasons to be proud of his ancestors.[4] For generations before the birth of the novelist, the Smolletts representing the *noblesse de robe* of Scotland had kept alive an admirable tradition of public service in the law and in military affairs. Sir James Smollett (*ca.* 1648-1731), grandfather of Tobias, was an excellent example of ancestral virtues: he played an active part in the Revolution, was knighted by King William in 1698, and subsequently held important offices in Dumbarton, Glasgow, and Edinburgh. Three of his sons, including Archibald, father of Tobias, he sent to Leyden for education in law and business, and in his old age he became a patriarch of power and property. It is unlikely that Smollett drew a detailed likeness of him in the person of Roderick's grandfather, the old judge in *Roderick Random*, although a partial portrait has been detected.

Archibald Smollett, father of Tobias, contracted an ague at Leyden and returned with a weakened constitution. Then, to make things worse, he married without paternal consent a woman with no money. However, his wife, Barbara Cunningham, seems to have been an accomplished person, "a woman of distinguished understanding, taste and elegance, but no fortune," in the words of an anonymous contemporary.[5] Of this union three children were born—James, Jane, and Tobias—all left without income upon their father's untimely death, not long after the birth of Tobias, the youngest.

James, brother of Tobias, became a captain in the army and was lost at sea off the coast of America; a passing reference to him was made by Dr. Moore,[6] author of the first important memoir of Smollett, who recalled that Tobias always retained a deep affection for him. Such was the feeling expressed in Smollett's letter to

[4] For details of the family history and the family pedigree see Joseph Irving, *Some Account of the Family of Smollett of Bonhill*, privately printed, Dumbarton, 1859. The material of this scarce book was reprinted in Irving's *History of Dumbartonshire* (Dumbarton, 1860), 2nd ed., pp. 334ff. For what appears to be the same text see Irving's *The Book of Dumbartonshire*, 3 vols. (Edinburgh and London, 1879), II, 175ff.

[5] This characterization was cited by James Alexander Wilson in his *History of Cambuslang* (Glasgow, 1929), pp. 130-31.

[6] *The Works of Tobias Smollett, M.D.*, ed. John Moore, M.D. (London, 1797), I, xcix. An earlier tribute to his memory was written by the Rev. Alexander McAulay in his account of the parish of Cardross in *The Statistical Account of Scotland*, XVII (1796), 221: James "was distinguished for his address, and those talents of wit and humour, which afterwards characterised Tobias."

Alexander Carlyle, April 15, 1754, wherein he conveyed his sympathy for John Home, who had recently lost his brother. "I know," he wrote, "what a man of Jack's sensibility must feel upon such an occasion: for I once sustained the same Calamity, in the death of a brother whom I loved and honoured."[7]

Jane, sister of Tobias, married Alexander Telfer of Scotstoun from whom is descended the present owner of Cameron House,[8] Major General Alexander P. D. Telfer-Smollett. Of Jane there was a tradition, passed on to Robert Chambers by Charles Kirkpatrick Sharpe in 1824, that "she was very fond of cards—ill-natured looking, with a high nose—but not of a bad temper."[9] Chambers printed the following anecdote and comment:

> She was enthusiastically devoted to cards. One of the magistrates of Edinburgh, who was a tallow-chandler, paying her a visit one evening, she saluted him with, "Come awa', bailie, and tak' a trick at the cartes." —"Troth, madam," says he, "I ha' na a bawbee i' my pouch."—"Tut, man, ne'er mind that; let us play for a pund o' can'le!" She was a shrewd, intelligent, and what one might call a clever old lady. She had a very high nose.[10]

This sketch of Smollett's immediate relatives comprises all that is well-known of them through documented fact or tradition, except for two anecdotes about his mother. One of these is an account of how Smollett disguised himself on visiting her in 1753 and of her joy on recognizing him;[11] the other has no certain origin but reveals her stoicism:

> Ten years afterwards he [Smollett] again went north, and again saw his mother; he told her that he was very ill and that he was dying. "We'll no' be very lang pairted onie way. If you gang first, I'll be close on your heels. If I lead the way, you'll no' be far ahint me, I'm thinking," said this more than Spartan parent.[12]

Although our information about Smollett's immediate relatives and ancestors is limited, what we know suggests that as a group

[7] See the *Times Literary Supplement* (London), July 31, 1943, p. 372.
[8] This beautiful estate on Loch Lomond belonged in Smollett's time to his cousin, Commissary James Smollett, who was host to Johnson and Boswell.
[9] Robert Chambers, *Smollett* (London and Edinburgh, 1867), 127n.
[10] Robert Chambers, *Traditions of Edinburgh*, 2 vols. (Edinburgh, 1825), I, 271. This anecdote was attributed inaccurately to Smollett's mother, but Chambers corrected the error in his "Corrections and Additions" at the end of Vol. I.
[11] Smollett's *Works*, ed. Moore, 1797, I, cxxxvi.
[12] Francis Watt, *The Book of Edinburgh Anecdote* (London and Edinburgh, 1913), p. 153. Watt's source may have been Oliphant Smeaton's *Tobias Smollett* (Edinburgh and London [1897]), p. 116.

they were proud, resourceful, independent, and gifted. Whigs in politics, Presbyterians in religious persuasion, they maintained a secure position among the lawyers and landed gentry of Dumbartonshire. Appropriately enough on their family crest was an oak tree with the motto, *Viresco*.[13]

Favored by ancestry, Smollett was also very fortunate in the environment of his youth. Much has been written of the pastoral beauties of Loch Lomond and Leven-Water as they existed two centuries ago, before modern industry despoiled their bloom. Today it is difficult, but not impossible, to recapture in imagination something of their pristine charm. Upon young Smollett they made an indelible impression. *O Rus, quando te aspiciam*! exclaimed Bramble in *Humphry Clinker*,[14] who, while in Scotland, waxed enthusiastic over Loch Lomond:

> I have seen the Lago di Gardi, Albano, De Vico, Bolsena, and Geneva, and, upon my honour I prefer Loch Lomond to them all. . . . Every thing here is romantic beyond imagination. This country is justly styled the Arcadia of Scotland; and I don't doubt but it may vie with Arcadia in every thing but climate.[15]

A similar feeling dictated the still-pleasing "Ode to Leven-Water":

> On Leven's banks, while free to rove,
> And tune the rural pipe to love;
> I envied not the happiest swain
> That ever trod th' Arcadian plain.
>
> Pure stream! in whose transparent wave
> My youthful limbs I wont to lave;
> No torrents stain thy limpid source;
> No rocks impede thy dimpling course,
> That sweetly warbles o'er its bed,
> With white, round, polished pebbles spread;
> While lightly pois'd, the scaly brood
> In myriads cleave thy crystal flood;
> The springing trout in speckled pride;

[13] For a print of the family arms (uncolored) see Irving's genealogical account. The early armorial bookplate (Smollett of Bonhill) is reproduced in the *Catalogue of British and American Book Plates Bequeathed to the Trustees of the British Museum by Sir Augustus Wollaston Franks* . . . by E. R. J. Gambier Howe, 3 vols. ([London], 1903-04), III, 54.

[14] Letter to Dr. Lewis, Bath, May 8.

[15] Letter to Dr. Lewis, Cameron, August 28.

The salmon, monarch of the tide;
The ruthless pike, intent on war;
The silver eel, and motled par.

Devolving from thy parent lake,
A charming maze thy waters make,
By bow'rs of birch, and groves of pine,
And edges flow'r'd with eglantine.

Still on thy banks so gayly green,
May num'rous herds and flocks be seen,
And lasses chanting o'er the pail,
And shepherd's piping in the dale,
And ancient faith that knows no guile,
And industry imbrown'd with toil,
And hearts resolv'd, and hands prepar'd,
The blessings they enjoy to guard.[16]

Such idyllic scenes may well have been sentimentalized to a certain extent by Smollett as he grew older and frailer and exiled from them, but the vivid memory of that Scottish valley always kept alive his dislike for cities and for urban vices. It would be misleading to imply that Smollett's youth was one of unshadowed bliss. As a boy he doubtless had a very limited diet, and endured the disciplines and deprivations of Scottish farm-life in the 1720's. Moreover his father's loss of favor with Sir James, his father's untimely death, and the fact that his cousins had more money than he did—all these matters must be remembered. But upon Smollett's sensitive temperament, the daily impact of scenic beauty made a profound impression. Hence when he arrived at London in 1739, how acutely he must have felt the contrast between his rustic environment and the relative ugliness and artificiality of the English metropolis.

Of his grammar-school days, and of his university training and activities there are relatively few documented facts, but some reconstruction of this period can be offered. Smollett entered the Dumbarton grammar school about 1727 or 1728, and in the normal course of events he would have remained there some five years. According to Robert Anderson, who wrote early memoirs of Smol-

[16] This poem first appeared in 1771 in *The Expedition of Humphry Clinker*, following Bramble's letter to Dr. Lewis, August 28. The above text follows an edition of *Humphry Clinker* printed in 1771. Some of these stanzas are printed in *The Oxford Book of English Verse*.

lett, this burgh school was then "kept in that part of the church which is now [1820] the session-house."[17] Like all grammar schools of the time it was under the close surveillance of the clerical and burgh authorities. It should be remembered that Smollett's grandfather, Sir James, was one of the commissioners having supervision over Scottish universities and schools.[18] The headmaster of Dumbarton's school was John Love[19] (1695-1750), celebrated controversialist and grammarian, and also clerk of the presbytery of Dumbarton. He was, in the 1730's, an outstanding teacher of boys; and after his death, Thomas Ruddiman,[20] his former antagonist in scholastic controversy, eulogized him in *The Caledonian Mercury*:

> For his uncommon knowledge in classical learning, his indefatigable diligence, and strictness of discipline, without severity, he was justly accounted one of the most sufficient masters in this country.[21]

Smollett owed much to John Love and was not ungrateful, as is clear from his attempt in 1761 to help Love's son, in whom he was "remarkably interested."[22]

Under this excellent schoolmaster Smollett spent his most impressionable years in the typical activities of Scottish grammar schools[23] two centuries ago, when the Renaissance emphasis on the classics was still dominant. There he studied plenty of Latin,[24] and an uncertain amount of Greek. All, or nearly all, the lectures and schoolroom dialogues were in Latin. On Sundays he was shepherded to church and questioned later on the sermon. If found

[17] *Works of Smollett*, ed. Anderson, 1820, I, 12n.

[18] See Joseph Irving, *History of Dumbartonshire*, 1860, p. 341.

[19] See *DNB*.

[20] Thomas Ruddiman's *Rudiments of the Latin Tongue* (1714) was the standard Latin grammar of the time.

[21] Smollett's *Works*, ed. Anderson, 1820, I, 12n.

[22] *Letters of Tobias Smollett, M.D.*, ed. by Edward S. Noyes (Harvard University Press, 1926), p. 70. Writing to Wilkes in 1761, Smollett asked a favor for "Robert Love, son of the man from whose Instruction I imbibed the first Principles of my Education."

[23] For information on this subject see James Grant, *History of the Burgh Schools of Scotland*, 1876; John Kerr, *Scottish Education, School and University*, 1910; and George Stewart, *The Story of Scottish Education*, 1927.

[24] James Grant in his *History of the Burgh Schools of Scotland*, 1876, cites from the Burgh Records of Edinburgh a list of Latin authors read in the Edinburgh schools about 1710. The reading in the second class included Virgil's *Pastorals*, Claudian, Ovid, Buchanan's *Psalms*, and Caesar; in the third class were read Phaedrus, Ovid, Cicero, and Nepos; in the fourth class, Sulpicius, Cato, Erasmus, etc. The highest class read, among others, Virgil, Horace, Juvenal, Cicero, Livy, and Sallust.

guilty of falsehood, swearing, Sabbath-breaking, or speaking in the vernacular, he could have been publicly whipped or flogged. Besides the classical languages, Smollett studied, presumably, English, arithmetic, penmanship, and music, all a part of the curriculum, in his boyhood.[25] Whether or not he was offered French and bookkeeping, which were among the list of courses by 1747,[26] is uncertain.

Judging from Smollett's literary partiality for picaresque adventure and practical jokes, it is very likely that as a boy he enjoyed all opportunities available for sports and games. On this subject the historians of Scottish education contribute little, but the burgh records of Dumbarton might reveal whether or not the local schoolboys enjoyed an annual cock-fight[27] on Shrove Tuesday. They probably did, as this custom was widespread in Scotland until the middle of the eighteenth century. Moreover, in most schools of the time, handball was a common game, and rough-and-tumble fights were frequent. The game of nine-pins is alluded to in *Roderick Random* (Chapter 2). Roderick was the leader of a "faction consisting of thirty boys" possibly because he was unusually accurate at throwing stones.

Smollett's spare time at grammar school was sometimes devoted to writing verses, as "an old schoolfellow of his" told Dr. John Moore.[28] This juvenile poetry, supposedly written to the memory of the heroic Wallace, has disappeared.

Certain other allusions to school life are found in *Roderick Random* (Chapter 2). Smollett, like Roderick, "became a good proficient in the Latin tongue," and possibly, like his hero, he was "allowed by everybody to be the best scholar in the school."

Is the second chapter of *Roderick Random* true to the facts of Smollett's school experience? If so, he was "very ragged and contemptible" and often scourged; and he hated an "arbitrary pedagogue" who treated him cruelly, even as he felt deeply injured by his grandfather, who sent him to school "at a village hard by, of which he had been dictator time out of mind," without paying for his board, clothes, books, and "other necessaries." The "schoolmaster," asserted Roderick, "through fear of my grandfather,

[25] See Irving, *op. cit.*, p. 288n.   [26] James Grant, *op. cit.*, p. 542.
[27] *Ibid.*, pp. 478ff., for documented details on this custom.
[28] See *Works*, ed. Moore, 1797, I, cviii. Moore is characteristically vague in failing to mention the name of Smollett's schoolfellow.

taught me *gratis*" and "gave himself no concern about the progress I made under his instruction." The schoolmaster is obviously not a portrait of John Love, but rather of the typical flogging pedant; but the village dictator was perhaps suggested by Sir James Smollett, powerful for decades in Dumbarton councils, as well as on the school committee, so that any local teacher might fear him. To accept this identification is not to assume that most of the detail in the earlier chapters of Smollett's first novel is exact autobiography. Smollett insisted years later: "The low situations in which I have exhibited Roderick, I never experienced in my own Person."[29] I know of no reason to doubt Smollett's veracity. But the situations in the second chapter are not necessarily "low" situations, as Smollett used that term.

Whether generally true to fact or not, the second chapter of *Roderick Random* reveals very convincingly the fierce pride, resentment, and indignation which tormented Smollett all his life. The novelist, like his schoolboy hero, was in frequent temperamental difficulties, and the essential spirit of an important phase of Smollett's personality is felt in Roderick's complaint:

> I was often inhumanly scourged for crimes I did not commit; because, having the character of a vagabond in the village, every piece of mischief, whose author lay unknown, was charged upon me. I have been found guilty of robbing orchards I never entered, of killing cats I never hurted, of stealing gingerbread I never touched, and of abusing old women I never saw.

Compare this with the following grievance expressed some ten years later in an intimate letter:

> [I have] been baited like a bear by all the hounds of Grub-street. . . . I have been abused, reviled, and calumniated, for satires I never saw; I have been censured for absurdities of which I could not possibly be guilty.[30]

How curiously similar these passages are in sentiment and in style!

Just when Smollett arrived at Glasgow University or when he left is not known. He neither entered his name on the matriculation albums[31] nor was graduated. It appears that he was working in a

---

[29] *Letters*, p. 80.

[30] See L. M. Knapp, "An Important Smollett Letter," *Review of English Studies*, XII (1936), 76.

[31] The absence of Smollett's name is not surprising because matriculation was compulsory only for "gown" students in Arts planning to graduate, or for students voting in Rectorial elections, and this requirement was not rigidly enforced for either group. See *The Matriculation Albums of the University of Glasgow*, transcribed and annotated by the late W. Innes Addison (Glasgow, 1913), p. xi.

dispensatory in Glasgow in November 1735 at which time he possibly wrote, and was certainly the subject of, some doggerel to a fellow apprentice, John Armstrong.[32] These hitherto unpublished verses run as follows:

Tobie Smalet to Jö Armstrong both prentice[s]
in ye Dyspensitory Novr 24, 1735

John Armstrong to you I send
these lines wch I have lately pen'd
I'll my sad case to you relate [.]
perhaps you will amend my state
These fellows whom you did remind
And told them lately to be kind
To me who am but strange to them
And bad them danger from me fen
Instead of taking your advice
They turned saucy proud & nice
Against me now they do Conspire
And makes [sic] me alwayes mend y[e] fire
And likwise [sic] all the earands run
Which when its spocke must ay be done
Therfore wise John I pray you speak
Unto the people* couple when you meet
And see if they will ease my life
And free themselves from all this strife
Which if you do & end this strife
I wish you may get a good wife
but if it do last ay for good
Great Sorrow to you do, wish aden[33] [.][34]

* This word crossed out in original.

[32] This was not Smollett's friend, Dr. John Armstrong, who had obtained his M.D. from Edinburgh in 1732.

[33] As "aden" meant a glandular swelling or bubo, this last sentence may be translated: A plague on you to your great sorrow!

[34] These verses are printed by the kind permission of the librarian of Yale University. The manuscript of this verse epistle was purchased from the collections of Walter T. Spencer, 27 New Oxford Street, London, about 1936. Mr. Spencer seems to have acquired it in 1918. (See *Letters*, pp. 3, 113). Where it had been before 1918 I do not know. The document consists of a small single sheet apparently torn from a large one. In the upper left-hand corner on the side containing the verses there is written in manuscript differing from that of the verses the following: "Comms[r] Smolet is his Uncle [?] Puine lc." By a third hand near the title was written "Glasgow" and "Jajoy &." On the other side of the sheet there appears the following: "To The Honour[ble]. Commiss off Excise, att [?] their [?] Edinb." and also the following: "Tobie Smolet a new Prentic at y[e] Dyspensitory; to John Armstrong Glasgow. 9[br] 24 1735 or, Rodre[i]ck [sic] Random [.]"

It is difficult to believe that Smollett at the age of fourteen penned this doggerel; it contains no suggestion whatever of his mature style, and other considerations are against it. The first is the fact that the title contains the nickname Tobie, which we know he always detested in later life. Furthermore, the handwriting of the verse epistle is not similar to the earliest known specimen of Smollett's script, found, as will appear later, at the bottom of a tailor's bill in 1739, where he signed himself "Tobias Smollett." It is likely, then, that these verses were composed by another apprentice, who in an idle hour amused himself by recording Smollett's juvenile reaction to what he felt was more than his share of running errands and mending the fire. What is important, however, is that this doggerel does express a central emotional pattern in Smollett's life—an irritating obsession of persecution, and the quick, instinctive reaction, so often repeated, of revenge, not only threatened but usually executed with the weapons of satire or even with a cudgel.

In 1736, Smollett was continuing his study of medicine and surgery, influenced in that direction, according to Dr. Moore, because he became friendly with a group of medical students, rather than from any natural taste for these subjects. The need of preparing himself to earn his living must have influenced him also, as his father had been dead for some years, and Sir James, his grandfather, died in 1731. And his relatives may have urged him on.[35] At any rate he became apprenticed to William Stirling and John Gordon, well-known surgeons of Glasgow. The following is the entry of his apprenticeship taken from the faculty records of the Physicians and Surgeons of Glasgow as of May 30, 1736:

> The which Day Tobias Smollett, son of the deceased Mr. Archd Smollett in Dumbarton, is booked apprentice with Mr. William Stirling and John Gordon, freemen, for five years from the date of the Indenture produced, dated the Sixteenth and Nineteenth days of Aprill last, and he payed the Collector ten shillings ster. of Booking money with the Clerk and Officer their dues.[36]

Stirling and Gordon[37] were influential and reputable surgeons and

[35] See *Works*, ed. Moore, I, cx.

[36] Cited from Alexander Duncan, *Memorials of the Faculty of Physicians and Surgeons of Glasgow 1599-1850* (Glasgow, 1896), p. 120.

[37] There are revealing references to Stirling and Gordon in *Extracts from the Records of the Burgh of Glasgow . . . 1718-38, with Charters and other Documents . . .*

probably treated young Smollett very well. There is the tradition, first publicized by Sir Walter Scott, that "keensighted Mr. Gordon" foresaw the brilliant future of his apprentice, preferring to all other students his "own bubbly-nosed callant, with the stane in his pouch."[38] Proof that Smollett admired Gordon when he wrote *Humphry Clinker* is clearly revealed in Bramble's tribute:

> I was introduced to Dr. Gordon, a patriot of a truly noble spirit, who is father of the linen manufactory in that place, and was the promoter of the city workhouse, infirmary, and other works of public utility. Had he lived in ancient Rome, he would have been honoured with a statue at the public expence.[39]

The eighteenth-century rumor that Smollett satirized Gordon as Potion in *Roderick Random* may have some truth in it; nevertheless, the all-but-certain reunion in Glasgow in 1766 of the elderly physician[40] and his then celebrated pupil should have been most pleasant for both.

According to the terms of his apprenticeship, Smollett was bound to assist Gordon and Stirling for five years, beginning in April 1736. Being sometimes troubled with a cough, Smollett was granted in 1738 what amounted to an extra holiday in the country,[41] and was released from his contract in order to go to London in the fall of 1739. Clearly enough during this period he was torn between his medical tasks and his literary interests. There must be truth in the Glasgow tradition that he was a "restless apprentice

---

1708-38, ed. Robert Renwick (Glasgow, 1909), and in *Extracts from the Records of the Burgh of Glasgow . . . 1739-59* [Vol. VI] (Glasgow, 1911). In 1736, Stirling and Gordon were appointed "touns surgeons" to look after the poor, their salary being £10 (*Extracts 1708-38*, p. 468). As early as 1720 they had petitioned the borough council to appropriate money for the destitute (*Extracts 1708-38*, p. 92). In 1743, they were exempted for life from the rent "for their seats they possess in the Northwest church" as payment for medical services rendered to the deceased Mr. John Anderson, minister. (*Extracts from the Records . . . 1739-59*, VI, 137). For the best short accounts of Stirling and Gordon, see Alexander Duncan, *op. cit.*, pp. 250-51.

[38] Sir Walter Scott, *Lives of the Novelists* (New York, 1872), p. 111.

[39] *Humphry Clinker*, Letter of Bramble from Cameron, August 8, [28].

[40] Dr. John Gordon died July 17, 1772. For his obituary see *Scots Magazine*, XXXIV (1772), 399.

[41] It appears that Gordon did not hold Smollett very strictly to his apprenticeship, for on September 15, 1738, he wrote to James Smollett of Bonhill, "There is no matter of Tobias staying, for as he is sometimes troubled with a cough, I was satisfied that he got a week or two in the country. I hope he will do very well." Quoted Joseph Irving, *The History of Dumbartonshire*, second edition (Dumbarton: Printed for the Author, 1860), p. 345n.

and a mischievous stripling."[42] Such an impression is borne out by the following anecdote:

> On a winter evening, when the streets were covered with snow, Smollett happened to be engaged in a snow-ball fight with a few boys of his own age. Among his associates was the apprentice of that surgeon who is supposed to have been delineated under the name of *Crab* in Roderick Random. He entered his shop while his apprentice was in the heat of the engagement. On the return of the latter, the master remonstrated severely with him for his negligence in quitting the shop. The youth excused himself by saying, that while he was employed in making up a prescription, a fellow had hit him with a snow-ball, and that he had been in pursuit of the delinquent.
>
> "A mighty probable story, truly," said the master, in an ironical tone. "I wonder how long I should stand here," added he, "before it would enter any mortal's head to throw a snow-ball at me."
>
> While he was holding his head erect with a most scornful air, he received a very severe blow in the face by a snow-ball.
>
> Smollett, who stood concealed behind the pillar at the shop-door, had heard the dialogue, and perceiving that his companion was puzzled for an answer, he extricated him by a repartee equally smart and a-propos.[43]

In another version of this story, printed some thirty years later in a Glasgow periodical called *The Emmet*, the surgeon hit by Smollett's snowball was said to be Crab in *Roderick Random*, and was identified as one Dr. Crawford, whose shop was the corner one of Gibson's land, fronting on Prince's Street. The contributor to *The Emmet* also asserted that Smollett was an apprentice to Dr. Crawford after serving Dr. Gordon in that capacity,[44] but the period of Smollett's service with Crawford is undetermined.

It is fairly certain that a sense of inferiority (reflected in *Roderick Random*) was tormenting young Smollett when he walked from Stirling's shop,[45] or from Crawford's, to the University library and gardens, where red-gowned students strolled in relative leisure.

As to what university program Smollett followed, there is no precise information. Dr. Moore merely ventured that he "attended

[42] This tradition was written down by Thomas Campbell in his memoir of Smollett in *Specimens of the British Poets* (London, 1819), VI, 219.

[43] *Works*, ed. Moore, I, cxii-cxiii.

[44] See *The Emmet; A Selection of Original Essays, Tales, Anecdotes, Bon Mots, Choice Sayings, &c.*, 2 vols. (Glasgow, 1824), I, 5. For a complete transcript of this essay in *The Emmet*, see Appendix, p. 325.

[45] Located in Dispensary Close, High Street, near the University. See Alexander Duncan, *op. cit.*, p. 250.

the anatomical and medical lectures."[46] Dr. Anderson, however, scenting autobiography in *Roderick Random*, quoted a passage from Chapter 6:

> he was sent to the university of Glasgow, where he prosecuted his studies with such success, that, in three years, it is said, "he understood Greek very well, was pretty far advanced in the mathematics, and no stranger to moral and natural philosophy: Logic, he made no account of; but he took much delight in the *Belles Lettres* and poetry, and had already produced some verses that met with a very favourable reception."[47]

But Anderson's extract differs from the text of the first edition of the novel, where Smollett wrote as follows:

> . . . in the space of three years, I understood Greek very well, was pretty far advanced in the mathematics, and no stranger to moral and natural philosophy: logick I made no account of; but above all things, I valued myself on my taste in the *Belle Lettre*, and a talent for poetry, which had already produced some morceaus, that brought me a great deal of reputation.[48]

When these two versions are compared, it is clear that the revised text is better grammatically. It is also slightly more modest in its statement of Roderick's interest and achievement in poetry. The revision in grammar was a routine matter, but why was the conception of Roderick's poetical gifts altered? Possibly it was to make the hero more truly symbolic of that "modest merit" claimed for him in the author's "Preface." It is much more likely, however, that Smollett at the time of the revision was disturbed by the youthfully naive and egotistic portrait of Roderick (already recognized by the public as the image of his own adolescent pride) and retouched it for personal rather than for artistic reasons. If this is true, it is practically certain that the sketch of Roderick's literary talents was largely autobiographical. This granted, we may accept the whole passage as an essentially accurate account of Smollett's studies at Glasgow.

Had Smollett matriculated as a gown-student and met the conventional requirements for a degree, we could determine fairly exactly what his courses were from data on the University of Glasgow available in Chamberlayne's *Present State of Great Britain*.[49]

[46] *Works*, ed. Moore, I, cx.   [47] Anderson's *Life* (London, 1796), p. 5.
[48] *Roderick Random*, first edition, 1748, I, 30-31.
[49] John Chamberlayne, *Magnae Britanniae Notitia* (London, 1737), Part II, Book III, "A List of all the Offices and Officers in North-Britain," 12ff.

Abstracted from this source, a brief outline of the five-year course, about 1737, is useful in reconstructing, on the basis of limited evidence, something of the program of lectures available to him. An entering student with his average grammar-school grounding in Latin, Greek grammar, and the Gospels, would have been placed under the professor of Humanity with a program in Latin (Horace, Juvenal, Livy, and Cicero) taught three hours daily, and Greek for one-half hour daily. For the second year the usual routine was Greek (Homer, Theocritus, Euripides, Sophocles, Demosthenes, Longinus, and Aristotle's *Poetics*) taught two hours daily, and Latin for one-half hour daily. During the third year, according to Chamberlayne,

they read two Hours each Day Logicks, Metaphysics, and Pneumaticks with the Professors of these Branches of Philosophy; and this year begin the Study of Geometry.

In the fourth year

they are taught two Hours each Day by the Professor of Moral Philosophy . . . [and] continue to attend the Lessons of Geometry, and perhaps attend a Lecture of Humanity.

The fifth year

they are taught two Hours at least by the Professor of Natural Philosophy, as that Science is improved by Sir Isaac Newton, and attend two Hours in the Week a Course of Experiments. Some continue to attend Lessons of Mathematics, or the Lessons of the Law of Nature and Nations, or of Greek, or Latin.

In his outline of the curriculum, Chamberlayne included this important statement:

And all who have studied well the Latin Tongue at School, and have got the Rudiments of the Greek are admitted to enter as of the Bajan Class [i.e. the second-year class] nay, may enter the Logick Class [i.e. the third-year class].

Such was the university program at Glasgow in 1737. Now what can be proved or inferred as to Smollett's studies? Fortunately we have Smollett's own word that he learned logic in his youth,[50]

[50] See Smollett's own review of Archibald Bowyer's *History of the Popes* (*Critical Review*, XI [March, 1761], 225-26), where he wrote: "His digesting some part of his defence into syllogisms is diverting enough, and puts us in mind of what we learned in our youth, concerning Aristotle's Categories, and the opposition and conversion of propositions. . . . The art of logic has been transformed into a kind of legerdemain, by which boys can syllogize."

even though his Roderick "made no account of" it.[51] Because he was excellently trained by John Love, young Smollett was presumably allowed to enter at the age of fourteen or fifteen the so-called Logick Class. Furthermore, we may assume the essential truth of the statement in *Roderick Random* (Chapter 6), where we see that Roderick, after applying himself "with great care . . . in the space of three years . . . understood Greek very well, was pretty far advanced in the mathematics, [and] was no stranger to moral and natural philosophy." This all suggests very strongly that Smollett's studies at Glasgow, from about 1735 to 1739, comprised the subjects of the fourth and fifth year in the university program. Hence it is reasonable to believe that he was instructed in Greek by Mr. Alexander Dunlop; in Mathematics, by Mr. Robert Simson; in Moral Philosophy, by the celebrated Francis Hutcheson; and in Natural Philosophy, by Mr. Robert Dick, who was dean of the faculty in 1737. Of these professors the latter was alluded to with friendliness by Smollett in his letter to Dr. Moore in 1754.[52] Whose lectures in Anatomy he followed is not certain. Concerning his opinion of his professors we are left in the dark, but he surely admired the independent spirit of Hutcheson's vigorous *Considerations on Patronages addressed to the Gentlemen of Scotland* (London, 1735).

Associated with these suggestions as to what Smollett studied is the question of how he spent whatever leisure hours he could steal from classroom and dispensary. The sad fact is that there are practically no records[53] available on the basis of which we can reconstruct student life at Glasgow in the 1730's. Quite possibly there were student clubs[54] devoted to literature, public speaking, and drama, in which Smollett may have exercised his literary powers. At any rate it is evident that while in Glasgow he wrote satires

[51] See *supra*, footnote 48.

[52] *Letters*, p. 29. Professor Noyes printed "Deck (?) & Hamilton," but after carefully studying the facsimile of the letter, published in John Glaister's *Dr. William Smellie and His Contemporaries* (Glasgow, 1894, p. 118), I am convinced that Smollett wrote "Dick."

[53] Here I merely echo the opinion of the recent biographer of Adam Smith, who was a student at Glasgow University presumably during Smollett's final year. (William Robert Scott, *Adam Smith as Student and Professor*, Glasgow, 1937, p. 36.)

[54] Clubs or societies were active in 1743, while Alexander Carlyle was following lectures at Glasgow. (*Autobiography*, 1910, pp. 85ff.) There were attempts to produce plays in 1722 and in 1744. (David Murray, *Memories of the Old College of Glasgow*, 1927, pp. 365, 448.)

(long since lost) "against such green and scanty shoots of affectation and ridicule as the soil produced," in the words of his biographer, Dr. Moore. The butts of these satires were, according to Moore, persons whom Smollett considered to be excessively smug businessmen or religious hypocrites. Moore had been told that these compositions, though full of humor, offended some of the respectable citizens of Glasgow.[55] There is another tradition that Smollett, while at the university, satirized his neighbors, the Colquhouns.

That he made lasting friendships, however, in Glasgow is abundantly clear from his correspondence. As a final approach, therefore, to his student days we shall deal with a group of obscure but early acquaintances, fellow students, and intimate friends, some of whom may be readily identified.

Among those matriculating at Glasgow in 1737 was Allan McLean[56] of Brollos in the Isle of Mull, later Sir Allan McLean, the host of Boswell and Johnson in 1773. That Smollett knew him and corresponded with him or with members of his family is suggested by the following communication from William Richardson, professor of Humanity in the University of Glasgow, to Robert Anderson, Smollett's biographer, under date of February 27, 1807:

> Not later than two or three days ago, speaking . . . to a friend, I learned from him, that a Mr Maclean of Pennycross in the Isle of Mull is in possossion [sic] of some original letters by Smollett; and as that Gentleman has two sons in my class I will endeavor to inform myself of the fact, and whether he will indulge you, or me with a perusal of them.[57]

Whatever effort Richardson made to see these letters apparently failed. The Maclean of Pennycross alluded to by Professor Richardson may have been connected with the McLean mentioned by Smollett in several of his published letters.[58]

Another student perhaps known by Smollett was James Louttit,[59] who matriculated in 1737. The surname Louttit is so extremely uncommon that the chances are good that it was this same James Louttit who appealed to Smollett for aid in getting his sick son

---

[55] See *Works*, ed. Moore, I, cxi-cxii.
[56] *Matriculation Albums of the University of Glasgow*, 1913, No. 630, p. 18.
[57] National Library of Scotland, MS 22.4.13, f. 161, v.
[58] *Letters*, pp. 8, 42, 43, 64.
[59] *Matriculation Albums*, No. 639, p. 19: "Jacobus Louttit filius Jacobi Louttit civis Glasguensis."

admitted to Bartholomew's Hospital, which appeal occasioned Smollett's letter to Mr. Hunter, surgeon, written about 1750.[60] Furthermore, it is worth noting that in a communication to the *Philosophical Transactions*[61] dated London, November 5, 1745, the writer, one Andr. [Andrew] Reid, alluded to his apothecary, Mr. Louttit. A letter written by Smollett in 1763[62] to Dr. Alexander Reid[63] shows that the novelist was on very friendly terms with Reid, who had been his neighbor for years in Chelsea. Did Smollett also know Andrew Reid, perhaps a relative of Dr. Alexander Reid? At any rate, it is likely that in aiding Louttit, Smollett was doing a favor for an old fellow medical student of Glasgow.

Among the most obscure of Smollett's acquaintances in 1756 were the Harvies,[64] from whom on one occasion he was expecting money. It may be that these persons were of the same family as the Harvie brothers, Joa [John] and Alexander,[65] who matriculated at Glasgow in 1735 and 1736. According to the data of matriculation,[66] they were sons of "Thomas Harvey A.M. ex praeceptoribus Schola Grammaticorum Glasguae." One Thomas Harvie was recorded[67] as "one of the doctors in the Grammar School" at Glasgow in 1737.

In a highly important letter to a Mr. Barclay of Glasgow, written May 22, 1744, Smollett concluded by way of a postscript: "Willy Wood, who is just now drinking a glass with me, offers you his good wishes, and desires you to present his compliments to Miss Becky Bogle." This Willy Wood with whom Smollett was surely reminiscing about Glasgow may well have been a William Wood, who, according to contemporaneous Glasgow records,[68] was factor to the college in 1729 and in 1737-1738. Miss Becky Bogle

[60] See "More Smollett Letters," published by the writer in *MLN*, XLVIII (1933), 246.

[61] Vol. XLIII (for the years 1744-1745), London, 1750, pp. 225-34. The "Letter," signed "Andr Reid," is indexed erroneously under Alex. Reid.

[62] *Letters*, p. 84.

[63] For a brief account of Alexander Reid, see Thomas Faulkner, *An Historical and Topographical Description of Chelsea* (London, 1810), p. 192. Smollett's letter to Reid was first printed in the second edition of Faulkner's *Chelsea*, 2 vols., 1829, I, 271. For permission to publish the letter, Faulkner thanked Reid's grandson, C. W. Reid, Esq., of Durham Place.

[64] *Letters*, p. 42.   [65] *Matriculation Albums*, Nos. 519 and 559.

[66] *Ibid.*, p. 15.

[67] *Extracts from the Records of the Burgh of Glasgow, A.D. 1708-38* (Glasgow, 1909), p. 485.

[68] *Ibid.*, pp. 315, 518.

was doubtless one of the numerous and prominent Bogles of Glasgow, possibly related to Patrick Bogle, who matriculated at Glasgow in 1735, or to Robin Bogle, the friend of Alexander Carlyle.

In several letters to friends in Glasgow, extending over a considerable period of time, Smollett sent his greetings to "honest Robin Urie,"[69] whom he seems to have known well, and who kept an eye on Smollett's productions.[70] Robert Urie[71] (*ca.* 1711-1771), called by Bishop Pococke in 1747 a "learned bookseller,"[72] was a pioneer printer and publisher of Glasgow before the era of the Foulis brothers. There is reason to assume that he was doing good printing as early as 1735, although his earliest extant imprints are dated 1740, at which time he had his printing shop in the Gallow-gate very close to the University. In Urie, Smollett met and liked a person of scholarly achievement and a man interested in printing as a fine art. It is not fantastic to suggest that Urie printed occasional sheets, now lost, for students burning to see their verses in print, and that Smollett's student satires were among them. Or if Urie did not print such material, there were other printers available for Glasgow students of the 1730's.[73] At any rate, Urie's friendship was a humanizing influence in the Glasgow environment where Smollett mixed potions and measured out the ingredients of *The Regicide.*

For more light on Smollett's fellow collegians, we are indebted to one of the Colquhouns, presumably Alexander,[74] who matriculated in 1735 and was graduated as M.A. in 1744, for a tradition in his family concerning the satirical propensities of young Tobias—a tradition put on record by Robert Anderson, who first received it in a letter from John Ramsay of Ochtertyre, September 24, 1796:

[69] *Letters*, p. 100 and *passim.*

[70] *Ibid.*, p. 28.

[71] For the best account see "Robert Urie, Printer in Glasgow" by Hugh A. McLean, M.B. in *Records of the Glasgow Bibliographical Society*, III (session 1913-1914), Glasgow, 1915, pp. 89ff. This article includes a hand-list of books printed by or for Robert Urie. See also *A Dictionary of the Printers and Booksellers . . . from 1726 to 1775*, eds. Plomer, Bushnell and Dix (Oxford University Press, 1932), p. 362.

[72] Richard Pococke, *Tours in Scotland, 1747, 1750, 1760*, ed. Daniel W. Kemp (Edinburgh, Scottish History Society, 1887), p. 4.

[73] Alexander Carmichael and Andrew Stalker were printing within the University at about the same period.

[74] *Matriculation Albums*, 1913, p. 14 (No. 492). See also an account of the career of Lord Provost Patrick Colquhoun, LL.D., in the *Annual Biography and Obituary*, V (1821), 149ff. where it is stated that "Mr. Colquhoun's father was a classfellow of the celebrated Dr. Smollett."

Mr Colquhoun [of] Camstraddam, a neighbor of the Smolletts promised me copies of the Satyrs[75] by our author while at college on his Cousins, but could not find them. . . . The same gentleman told me that Smollett's conversation though lively was one continued series of epigrammatical sarcasms against one or other of the Company, for which no talents could compensate.[76]

If this testimony accurately conveyed Colquhoun's impressions, it must be accepted as essentially true, especially if Mr. Colquhoun of Camstraddam was the Alexander Colquhoun, who, as a student, felt the sharp edge of Smollett's sarcasm.

Finally, we must do full justice to Smollett's youthfully ardent friendship with a student named Ritchie, of whose death he learned in May 1744 and lamented in a prose elegy couched in the form of a letter dispatched to their mutual friend, Mr. Barclay of Glasgow:

All those (as well as my dear Barclay) who knew the intimacy betwixt us, must imagine that no stroke of fate could make a deeper impression on my soul than that which severs me forever from one I so entirely loved! from one who merited universal esteem; and who, had he not been cut off in the very blossom of his being, would have been an ornament to society, the pride and joy of his parents, and a most inestimable jewel to such as were attached to him, as we were, by the sacred ties of love and friendship. O my dear Ritchie, little did I think, at our last parting, we should never meet again! How many hours, days, nay years, of enjoyment did I promise myself on the prospect of seeing thee again! How has my heart throbbed at thy imaginary presence! And how oft have I conversed with thee by the indulgence of a dream! Even when I waked to my disappointment, I flew to pleasing hope for refuge, and reflected on the probability of real gratification! But now, alas! even that forsakes me. Hope itself lies buried with its object, and remembrance strives to soothe itself by recalling the delightful scenes of past intercourse! Dear brother, this is a theme I scarce can quit; my imagination broods o'er my melancholy, and teems with endless sentiments of grief and tenderness. My weeping muse would fain pay a tribute to his manes; and were I vain enough to think my verse would last, I would perpetuate his friendship and his virtue.[77]

These fervid lines throw much light on young Smollett's imagina-

---

[75] These youthful satires would be of much interest, but recent searching has failed to bring them to light. Anderson's "editing" is nicely illustrated by the fact that he preserved Colquhoun's appraisal in his "Life" as late as 1817 (*Miscellaneous Works*, Edinburgh, 1817, I, 13n.). But in the version of 1820 (*Works*, 1820, I, 15n.) Anderson tampered with the evidence to make it read: "He [Colquhoun] told Mr. Ramsay that Smollett's conversation was distinguished by vivacity, sarcasm, and epigrammatic facility."

[76] National Library of Scotland, MS, 22.4.13.   [77] *Letters*, pp. 4-6.

tive and sentimental spirit and reveal his capacity for the most intimate friendship with congenial friends. This characteristic of Smollett is certainly as important as his alleged accuracy in hurling snowballs or his disturbing with darts of sarcasm certain relatives or citizens in Glasgow. As we read this remarkable letter, it is natural to wonder who Barclay and Ritchie were, and, fortunately, more than the shadowy ghosts of what they represented to Smollett may be restored.

There matriculated at the University of Glasgow in 1732 a certain Robert Barclay,[78] who appears to have been Smollett's correspondent. This Robert Barclay became eminent as a lawyer in Glasgow, was a member of the firm of Barclay and Grahame, writers,[79] and eventually bought the estate of Capelrig in the parish of Mearns, Renfrewshire. In George Crawfurd's *History of the Shire of Renfrew*, published a year before Barclay's death, he is mentioned as "now of Capelrig, late writer in Glasgow, married to Susan Wood, second daughter of the late Mr. William Wood,[80] factor for the Duke of Hamilton."[81] This Robert Barclay, Smollett's fellow student, was, undoubtedly, the recipient of Smollett's letter of impassioned grief over the death of their mutual friend Ritchie. But who was the gifted young Ritchie?

In the *Matriculation Albums* we find that three sons of John Ritchie, merchant of Glasgow, entered the University, two of them while Smollett presumably was there. Joannes [John] Ritchie[82] matriculated in 1733, his brother Jacobus [James] in 1735, and a younger brother Henry in 1748. James and Henry, according to the *Albums*, later resided in Busbie, Lanark. Concerning the career of John, the eldest son, the editors of the *Album* had no data to offer. This lack of information suggests that he died at an early age. Might his death have occurred in 1744? If so, he was almost cer-

---

[78] The entry, according to the *Matriculation Albums*, p. 10, No. 329, was "Rob: Barclay F: Davidis Barclay Mercatoris quondam in Urbe Largs in Com: Air," i.e. Robert Barclay, son of David Barclay, formerly merchant in the city of Largs, Ayrshire. To this the editors of the *Albums* added, "Of Capelrig. Writer [lawyer] in Glasgow. Died at Southampton 4th December, 1783."

[79] See George Stewart, *Curiosities of Glasgow Citizenship* (Glasgow, 1881), p. 179.

[80] Was this the William Wood, Smollett's friend, identified above as at one time factor of Glasgow University?

[81] George Crawfurd and William Semple, *The History of the Shire of Renfrew* (Paisley, 1782), p. 211.

[82] The entry reads, "Joannes Ritchie F. Natu Max Johannis Ritchie Mercatoris Glasguensis."

tainly the very dear friend of Smollett. Substantial proof of this is found in the following record from the "List of Benefactions to the Merchants House of Glasgow" under the year 1744:

> John Ritchie, Merch[t] in Glasgow, at the death of his son John, gave to the Poor of this House 100 Scots. He died the 13th of April, 1744, in the 23 year of his age . . . [£] 8.6.8.[83]

It is clear that John Ritchie was born in 1721, matriculated at Glasgow in 1733, and died April 13, 1744. Now on May 22, 1744, Smollett began his letter to Barclay:

> I am this minute happy in yours, which affords me all the satisfaction of hearing from you, without the anxiety naturally flowing from its melancholy occasion; for I was informed of the decease of our late friend by a letter from Mr. Gordon,[84] dated the day after his death.

To detect what happened is easy: Barclay had written Smollett of Ritchie's grave illness; upon his death Gordon wrote immediately to notify him of the sad fact. This means that the friendship between Smollett and John Ritchie was well-known to Dr. Gordon in Glasgow, even eight years after Smollett had bade farewell to his university friends when he set out for London in 1739. John Ritchie's character must be inferred from what we know of his family. His father[85] appears to have been a man of property with a sense of civic responsibility, and his brother James[86] had a brilliant career as a tobacco lord in Glasgow, being among the leading financiers of eighteenth-century Scotland.

Smollett's friendship with John Ritchie and Robert Barclay was doubtless of real advantage to him at Glasgow. Through them and their families he may well have started to develop his broad interest in economics and trade, and surely he felt a certain pride in associating with these two prominent and respected families. Through them, Smollett could have met Hugh Blackburn, another Glasgow merchant, to whom he alluded in his correspondence with John Moore.[87]

Turning now from Smollett's youth in Scotland, we may visual-

---

[83] See *View of the Merchants House of Glasgow* (Glasgow, 1866), p. 583.
[84] Presumably Dr. John Gordon.
[85] John Ritchie, Senior, belonged to Donaldson's Club, and at his death in 1755 left a legacy to the Merchants House. (See *View of the Merchants House of Glasgow*, 1866, pp. 586, 614.)
[86] For James Ritchie (1722-1799) of Craighton and Busbie, see David Murray, *Early Burgh Organization in Scotland* (Glasgow, 1924), I, 448-51.
[87] *Letters*, p. 29 and *passim*.

ize the circumstances under which he departed for London. In June 1739 he was preparing to leave, as is evident from the following bill, which pictures the kind of clothing he was then ordering:

Tobias Smollett .. 1738   Glasgow 2^d May 1738

Mr John Gordon Surgeon in Glasgow for the use of Mr Tobias Smallet

Bought of Arch. & John Hamiltons

(154)

4½ yards of fine broad Cloth ....13/6.	3.	–.	9.
6½ yards blue Shaloon ....18^d	–.	9.	9
2½ yards broad buckrum & Canvas ....10^d	–.	1.	10½
2 oz. 10 drop thread	–.	–.	8
4½ yards fustian .... 1/.	–.	4.	6.
2 sheep skins 14^d 4 p^s binding 2^d	–	1.	4.
8 drop Silk 1/. 1 oz Silk twist ....1.8^d	–	2.	6.
3 doz. big 5 doz. small buttons ....10^d	–	4.	7.
1½ yard plying 6^d 1/16 yard velvet .....14^d	–.	1.	8
a [sic] pair 3^d gray Stockings..................	–.	4.	6.
4¾ yards fine broad Cloth....................14/.	3.	6.	6
3¼ yards fine drab Cloth ....10/.	1.	12.	6
⅜ yard velvet ....16/..	–.	6.	–
½ oz: thread 2 drop Silk	–.	–.	4½
7½ yards Superfine Shaloon ....22^d	–.	13.	9
1 oz: fine Scarf twist	–.	2.	–
3 oz: thread 9^d 11½ drop silk ....17^d	–	2.	2¼
3½ doz. big & 5 doz. small buttons ....14^d	–	7.	–
2¼ yards broad buckrum & Canvas ....10^d	–	1	10½
4½ yards fine fustian ....15^d	–	5	– 7½
2 Sheep Skins 14^d 4 p^s binding .... 2^d	–	1	– 4
3/32 p^{ts} cloth coloured velvet ....16/.	–	1	– 6.
3 doz: big basket buttons ....10^d	–	2	– 6.
½ doz: small D° .... 5^d	–.	–.	2½
½ oz: twist ....18^d	–.	–.	9.
1 yard green Sarge	–.	1.	6
⅝ yard col° D° ¼ yard Canvas	–.	1.	1-¾

In the left margin: 1739 June 6

£11.   18.   10¼

I acknowledge the contents of the above Acco^t to be justly owing by me

TOBIAS SMOLLETT[88]

On the verso of this document is written "Acco^t Mr Tobias Smallet To Arch^d & John Hamilton 1741."

[88] Printed from a photostat of the document with the kind permission of Henry W. Paton, Esq., Curator of Historical Records, General Register House, Edinburgh. I wish to thank Mr. A. F. Falconer for information about this document.

This record illuminates in several ways Smollett's status in 1738-1739. It seems that, under the terms of his apprenticeship, he ran up part or all of the bill as charged to Gordon, and that after he left Gordon and Stirling, presumably in 1738,[89] he assumed personal responsibility for it. It also discloses the fact that he lacked funds to pay for it, even as late as 1741. What is more important, it shows the kind of clothing he wore at the age of eighteen on his venturesome trip to London. He was no Roderick Random, limited to "one suit of clothes, half a dozen ruffled shirts, as many plain, two pair of worsted, and a like number of thread stockings."[90] On the contrary, his suits were made of fine broadcloth, lined with superfine shalloon, and adorned with big basket-buttons. Smollett never hesitated to part with his money and was, we may be sure, proud of such attire.

Thus equipped with newly tailored and expensive clothes, the style of which was doubtless appropriate to the material, Smollett was ready to depart for London sometime after June 1739. Like his Roderick, he probably carried along a few books, both medical and literary. Roderick treasured his "Wiseman's Surgery"[91] and "a small edition of Horace." Just why he decided to discontinue his medical apprenticeship (due to run until April 1741) and to depart at this time is not known, but three conjectures may be advanced.[92] The first is that in 1738 his mother realized that she could in the future be of less financial help to him owing to the death that year of his cousin James Smollett of Bonhill,[93] from whom she had per-

[89] Whatever settlement Smollett made with his masters, Stirling and Gordon, he did not forfeit the friendship of the latter. However, the fact that his apprenticeship was not served out was unfairly exploited by Andrew Henderson in a scurrilous attack on Smollett in his *A Second Letter to Dr. Samuel Johnson . . . with an impartial Character of Doctor Smollett* (London, ca. 1775), pp. 12ff., where he asserted that Smollett "was a man of very little learning, and always remarkable for perverseness, obstinacy, and revenge," and that being "an apprentice to a surgeon at Glasgow, he eloped from his master."

[90] *Roderick Random*, Chap. 7.

[91] The best known work of Richard Wiseman, prominent seventeenth-century surgeon, was his *Eight Chirurgical Treatises*, which was reprinted from 1672 to 1734. Smollett may have carried along the 6th edition in two volumes, London, 1734.

[92] On this problem see Robert Chambers, *Smollett*, pp. 15-16.

[93] Tobias Smollett's cousin, James Smollett of Bonhill, heir of Sir James Smollett the first of Bonhill, died in 1738 and was succeeded as head of the family by his cousin James, later Commissary Smollett, who appears in *Humphry Clinker*. With his cousin James of Bonhill, Tobias had been on friendly terms, judging from his letter to him in 1737 (*Letters*, p. 3). Smollett may have been disappointed, however, because he was not a beneficiary in James's will, according to information kindly sent me by Henry M. Paton, Esq., Curator of Historical Records, General Register House, Edinburgh.

haps received some regular assistance. Another conjecture is that Smollett's relatives felt that the expected conflict between England and Spain would provide him with an opportunity for self-supporting medical experience. Finally, it may be that Smollett, having completed his *Regicide*, was impatient to reach London, especially now that in 1739 his brother James was in the army, and his sister Jane, recently married, was able to provide a home for their mother. Whatever the most compelling reasons were, Smollett set out for London, enduring the hardships of the road and gathering data for his first novel.

Remembering the proud family traditions into which he was born, the beauty of his rural surroundings, the exceptional merits of his teachers, both in grammar school and at the University of Glasgow, and the kindly regard of Dr. Gordon, we must revise the long established concept of young Smollett as primarily an uncouth, sarcastic, quarrelsome cub, quick to make enemies and to satirize his acquaintances at the least provocation. The undeniable fact is that he had a large capacity for significant friendships, and that he was also more widely educated, and more sophisticated, resourceful, and mature than has generally been assumed. Such qualities are visible in two paintings,[94] both done presumably before he left Glasgow. In both of them he appears as a sensitive, and self-consciously proud young man. There is, besides, a suggestion of physical frailty,[95] reflected, perhaps, in Roderick's excessive fatigue after walking twenty miles.[96] This more accurate view of the adolescent Smollett will be borne out and strengthened as we scrutinize the later phases of his personality.

[94] An engraving of what appears to be the earlier of these portraits forms the frontispiece of Robert Chambers' *Smollett*, London and Edinburgh, 1867. This is said to be "copied from an original oil painting in the possession of W. F. Watson, Esqr Edinburgh." The original oil painting of young Smollett in the University of Glasgow (Hunterian Museum) was supposedly done by William Cochrane. This is poorly reproduced in Henry Grey Graham's *Scottish Men of Letters in the Eighteenth Century* (London, 1901), opposite p. 298.

[95] See footnote 41.

[96] *Roderick Random*, Chap. 10.

CHAPTER II
Naval Service and Marriage,
1739-1743

FROM 1739 to 1743 Smollett came into contact with three new types of experience, each of which made an indelible impression upon him: the melee of London, the roaring life of the navy, and romantic love in the West Indies. Upon a limited framework of fact for these years[1] it is possible to reconstruct some of his activities and to paint the colorful scenery before which he enacted his still youthful roles.

Smollett reached London with more letters of introduction than money in his pockets. Moore asserted, seemingly from Smollett's own reminiscences, that he had "a small sum of money and a very large assortment of letters of recommendation: whether his relations intended to compensate for the scantiness of the one by their profusion in the other, is uncertain; but he has been often heard to declare, that their liberality in the last article was prodigious."[2] It was like Smollett to be jocular about this matter, and yet some of these letters must have been very useful. As we have seen, he represented a prominent family and had come to know at Glasgow a circle possessing plenty of influential connections both in London and in the West Indies. Hence it is quite naive to visualize him as ever penniless or friendless in London or anywhere else. He was attractive, entertaining as a *raconteur*, and blessed with self-assurance and *savoir faire*. Naturally, therefore, there were not a few Scotsmen in London ready to help him. In fact there are clear indications as to the identity of some of them.

Prominent among these was Sir Andrew Mitchell,[3] whose mother was sister to the mother of James Smollett of Bonhill, Tobias' cousin. In 1739 Sir Andrew was a member of the Royal

---

[1] I refer to the musters of H.M.S. *Chichester*, and the manuscript journals of Lieut. Robert Watkins, who served on that ship. Photostats of the latter from the Public Record Office, London (P.R.O., Ad. 51/4147) are in my possession.
[2] See *Works*, ed. Moore, I, cxv.   [3] See *DNB*.

Society, an acquaintance of Quin, and an intimate friend of the poet Thomson, and hence in a position to introduce his relative to that literary group so loyal to the author of *The Seasons*, a circle containing Dr. John Armstrong, Mallet, and Andrew Millar, the publisher. Mitchell, indeed, because of his political connections,[4] may have helped Smollett obtain his warrant from the Navy Board in March 1740, although there is no record of such assistance.[5]

To medical circles in London Smollett must have had an immediate and easy *entree*. As evidence of this, we may recall the analogous experience of Dr. William Hunter, who, on arriving in London about 1740, appears to have been armed with a letter of introduction from Robert Foulis of Glasgow to Dr. James Douglas[6] in Red Lion Square, one of the best known physicians of that day. We take it for granted that Smollett had a letter to Douglas from Foulis,[7] whom he surely had met in Glasgow. Assuming that Smollett met Dr. James Douglas in the winter of 1739-1740, he could scarcely have missed knowing his well-known brother, the surgeon, John Douglas,[8] who eventually lived in Downing Street in the same house where Smollett was to set up as surgeon in 1744.[9] That he occupied this house certainly suggests more than a casual acquaintance with the Douglas brothers, and one which began before he served in the navy. Their libraries and their advice were perhaps at his disposal before he received his warrant from the Navy Board, March 10, 1740, and served for a time on the *Chichester*.[10]

[4] See Robert Chambers' *Smollett*, p. 39.

[5] There is nothing on Smollett in Andrew Bisset's *Memoirs and Papers of Sir Andrew Mitchell, K.B.*, London, 1850.

[6] Dr. James Douglas, member of the Society for the Encouragement of Learning, collector of Horace (thanks in part to Robert Foulis), was a prominent anatomist and obstetrician, who died in April 1742. Many of his MSS are described in *A Catalogue of the Manuscripts in the Library of the Hunterian Museum in the University of Glasgow* (Glasgow, 1908), *passim*.

[7] David Murray, authority on the Foulis brothers, suggested in his *Robert & Andrew Foulis and the Glasgow Press* (Glasgow, 1913), pp. 4-6, that Smollett may have portrayed Robert Foulis in Strap.

[8] John Douglas, F.R.S., engaged in controversies over the employment of male midwives. He died in June 1743, and a highly laudatory account of him appeared in the *Daily Advertiser*, June 28, 1743, stressing particularly the great value of his method of curing venereal disease. In the same newspaper (September 20, 1743) we find it stated that his widow was making his medicines and carrying on his work in Downing Street. Apparently he had a large library, as it was disposed of in January 1744 in a seven-day sale. (*Daily Advertiser*, January 31, 1744.)

[9] *Letters*, p. 6.

[10] For details of Smollett's naval record, see George M. Kahrl, *Tobias Smollett Traveler-Novelist* (University of Chicago Press, 1945), Chaps. I and II.

During the very severe winter of 1739-1740[11] Smollett had his first view of London (which Strap in *Roderick Random* so often called the devil's drawing room), sensing its ostentatious wealth, its abject poverty, its lawlessness and violence, and its scorn of the Scots. He heard talk of the riot in the Drury Lane Theatre[12] where he hoped that some day his *Regicide* would be applauded. He had access to journals and pamphlets of the day, such as the *Craftsman* and Fielding's first newspaper, the *Champion*. He became aware of how contributors to, and editors of, such sheets were frequently arrested on political grounds. He dreamed of his future naval service, war with Spain having been declared in October. Having literary as well as medical interests, he read, perhaps, Johnson's *London*, 1738, Fielding's *Pasquin*, 1736, Shenstone's *Poems*, 1737, Thomson's *Liberty*, 1736, and looked into the *Scots Magazine*, then in its first year. During that winter or spring, he passed his examination for naval service, presented his credentials to the Navy Office, and, like Roderick, was "mightily pleased" to find himself "qualified for second mate of a third rate."

Smollett's naval experience in the tragic expedition to Carthagena, 1740-1741, was of signal importance in his own life, and his story of naval conditions in Chapters 24-38 of *Roderick Random* has long been recognized as the most accurate and graphic account available anywhere. These chapters, moreover, constitute an original contribution to social history and to the materials of the English novel. Hence arises the importance of knowing as much as possible about his actual experience in the navy. In this matter, the early biographers had little to offer. Moore certainly heard and enjoyed Smollett's yarns about his naval service, but without reference to any dates or ships he recorded merely that Smollett was "soon disgusted with his situation; and although he had a certainty of being promoted, he quitted the service in the West Indies, and resided some time in the island of Jamaica."[13] Anderson, however, tried to be specific: Smollett, he declared, served "on board the

[11] For repeated references to the extreme rigor of the winter, see *The Political State of Great-Britain*, Vols. 58 and 59 (1739, 1740).

[12] See *The Political State of Great-Britain*, Vol. 59 (February 1740), 95-96 for an account. The estimated damage was about £400.

[13] *Works*, ed. Moore, I, cxvi. Moore's statement, however, may well be merely an echo of the anonymous biographer of Smollett in *The Miscellaneous Works of Tobias Smollett*, 6 vols. (Edinburgh, 1790), I, [i]: ". . . he continued only a short time in this line [the navy], being disgusted at the service."

Cumberland, one of the largest ships of the armament," and in a footnote he added that "the name of Smollett, cut by himself in the timber of the Cumberland, was shewn long after as a memorial of his service."[14] This story was accepted by Smollett's careful biographer, Robert Chambers,[15] but David Hannay, in an attempt to find proof, asserted that there was no record of Smollett's name "on her [the Cumberland's] paybook."[16] More recently Mr. W. G. Perrin confirmed Hannay and then proceeded to reveal a few facts of Smollett's service on H.M.S. Chichester.[17]

Neither Hannay nor Perrin seems to have considered that there were two ships in 1739 named the Cumberland. There was in 1739 the large Cumberland, carrying 80 guns and commanded by Capt. James Steuart, and there was a fireship, Cumberland, carrying 10 guns, commanded by Capt. Robert Maynard, and stationed around Jamaica.[18] The tradition that Smollett served on a ship called the Cumberland cannot be wholly discredited, therefore, until the records of the fireship Cumberland are examined.

It was on the Chichester, however, that Smollett saw most of his naval service, the most complete account of which is found in Professor Kahrl's recent book, Smollett, Traveler-Novelist. Although classified as a third-rate ship, the Chichester was one of the largest men-of-war afloat in 1739. Built in 1694 at Chatham,[19] she mounted 80 guns, carried 600 men (sometimes more) and had seen much service.[20] In design, dimensions, and tonnage, she was not very different from a Restoration first-rate.[21] The Chichester, like

[14] Robert Anderson, M.D., *The Life of Tobias Smollett, M.D.*, 5th edition (Edinburgh, 1806), p. 19.

[15] Robert Chambers, *Smollett*, p. 40.

[16] David Hannay, *Life of Tobias George Smollett* (London, 1887), p. 29.

[17] *Mariner's Mirror* (London, Cambridge University Press), x (1924), 94.

[18] See *The Political State of Great-Britain*, LVIII (December 1739), 511, 517.

[19] See the *Mariner's Mirror*, II (1912), 265.

[20] For a few records of the *Chichester's* service, see *The Political State of Great-Britain*, London, XXI (1721), 325; and W. L. Clowes, *The Royal Navy*, 5 vols. (Boston and London, 1898), II, 377n. See also *The Mariner's Mirror*, XXVI (1940), 266.

[21] The following data on the *Chichester* from *The Mariner's Mirror* (Vol. II, 1912, p. 265), should be reliable:

Builder, Lee at Chatham
Date, 1694
Gun Deck, 157' 3"
Keel, 130' 5"
Beam, 41' 9½"
Tonnage, 1210

For a cross-section and colored illustration of a Restoration first-rate, see the *Illustrated London News*, August 6, 1932, pp. 204-205 and pp. II-III of the section in color.

many ships of that period, rolled badly; Admiral Mathews, Commander-in-Chief in the Mediterranean, reported in 1743: "They can scarce haul up a port; the 'Chichester' hauled up but her two aftermost, but was obliged soon to lower them; as for the rest of her ports, they were caulked in when she was first fitted out, and have never been opened since, nor will they ever be, except in a Mill Pond."[22] Below the lower gun-deck in this type of ship was the orlop deck, containing the cockpit with quarters for surgeons and their mates, and the orlop platform where the wounded were received. On the quarter deck and upper deck were officers' cabins. Above the upper deck swayed the great masts and sails. Color streamed in flags and pennants. Past the guns on the decks trooped hundreds of men, some of them seasoned tars, others newly impressed sailors. None of them wore naval uniforms. Shouts, dialects, and oaths filled the air. At sea, in a hurricane, Smollett from the orlop deck heard "a most horrible din, occasioned by the play of the gun carriages upon the deck above, the cracking of cabins, the howling of the wind through the shrouds, the confused noise of the ship's crew, the pipes of the boatswain and his mates, the trumpets of the lieutenants, and the clanking of the chain pumps."[23] Even in a calm sea there was always the creaking of rope and canvas as the ship rolled in the seas. At night a group of sailors might "chaunt a few ballads to keep the hands awake in the night-watch" (*Launcelot Greaves*, Chapter 7).

Into such scenes Smollett plunged shortly after his nineteenth birthday. Having received his warrant as surgeon's second mate, March 10, 1740, he went aboard the *Chichester* at Blackstakes (in the river Medway above Sheerness) on April 3. The first of June the *Chichester* was ordered to Spithead[24] (near Portsmouth) where Smollett appears to have had a short shore-leave[25] from June 5 to June 30. A month later his ship moved to Tor Bay (near Dartmouth), but after October first returned to Spithead until the fleet assembled at Start Point and sailed southwest from St. Helen's on October 26, 1740.[26] Some eleven weeks later, January 10, 1741, the *Chichester* anchored at Port Royal, Jamaica.

[22] See Romola and R. C. Anderson, *The Sailing Ship* (London [1927]), p. 178.
[23] *Roderick Random*, Chap. 28.   [24] P.R.O., Ad. 8.21 (Monthly Lists).
[25] See Kahrl, *op. cit.*, p. 4.
[26] In the journal of Lieutenant Robert Watkins on board the *Chichester* there is the following in the entry for October 26, 1740: "at 9 weigh'd in Company W:th the

Smollett's experiences on this first lap of the expedition can only be surmised. We learn from the journal kept on board the *Chichester* by Lieutenant Robert Watkins of gales early in November so severe that the *Superb* lost all three of her masts, and the *Chichester* had her mainsail split and two men lost overboard. The following entries made by Watkins are of interest:

1740	Nov. 19	Began to serve Wine to the Sick men.[27]
——	Nov. 20	Sold some of Our Dead Mens Cloths at the Mast.
——	Dec. 18	Samuel Murray was whipt for mutiny because the Stewart would not give him his meat raw & for beating the cooper.
——	Dec. 22	Had a Survey and condemd Eighteen Hundred and Ninety five pounds of cheese.

Smollett's criticism of putrefied cheese was conveyed through his character Morgan (*Roderick Random*, Chapter 26), but there is no whipping of a mutineer in the novel, though Smollett, if not ill, must have witnessed the punishment of Samuel Murray. As the *Chichester* plunged south through heavy weather, Smollett learned much about bad food, banyan-days, foul quarters, sick soldiers and tars, and the brutalities of men in such surroundings. As second mate to the surgeon, he thought of himself as an officer, no doubt, as did Roderick (*Roderick Random*, Chapter 27), and consequently bore himself with proud dignity. A part of his daily schedule may be inferred from these lines in *Roderick Random* (end of Chapter 26):

> At a certain hour in the morning, the boy of the mess went round all the decks, ringing a small hand-bell, and, in rhymes composed for the occasion, invited all those who had sores to repair before the mast, where one of the doctor's mates attended, with applications to dress them.

And down on the orlop deck, near the gloomy and unventilated cockpit below the water line, there were sick men in growing numbers to be treated. Smollett, as might be expected, fell ill, either on the southward trip, or later, and ran up a considerable hospital bill (10s. 8d.). It was his own illness, perhaps, as well as the general epidemic, which he had in mind in describing Roderick's

---

Russell S:ʳ Chaloner & Twenty four Sails of the Line and with Six Fireships, two hospitall Ships & Sixty or Seventy Trans.[ports]."

[27] Almost daily Watkins recorded deaths. In *Roderick Random* (Chap. 27), Captain Oakum found, on taking command of the *Thunder*, "sixty-one sick people on board."

desperate fight with tropical fever (*Roderick Random,* Chapter 34). But apart from this enforced period in sick-bay, Smollett must have been extremely busy caring for the sick. Some idea of the number of incapacitated men in the fleet can be gained from the records of illness on board the *Torbay.* Captain Gascoigne, when his ship reached Dominica, December 1740 (where the *Chichester* also stopped), had to send ashore 110 sick men,[28] about one-sixth of its normal complement. The *Chichester,* however, had a somewhat better bill of health, according to Watkins' journal.

On the outgoing trip Smollett had some association with the Captain and with other officers and mates, whose names, as taken from the musters of the *Chichester,* are here recorded:

> Rd. Girlington, Captain from March 1740- *ca.* October 1740.
> Robert Trevor, Captain from *ca.* October 1740-April 1741.
> Rob. Mason, third Lieut., promoted to second Lieut.
> Robert Watkins, second Lieut., promoted to first Lieut.
> Edm. Horne, fourth Lieut., promoted to third Lieut.
> Jn Atkinson, Surgeon
> Jn Ker, Surgeon's mate
> R. J. Hadsor, Surgeon's first mate
> Jacob Tayler, Surgeon's third mate
> Ben: Baxter, Surgeon's third mate
> John Bellew, purser

The Lieut. Edm. Horne here listed may have been the "late general Horn," who, according to trustworthy information, "knew Smollett well" and "thought his account of the expedition, given in *Roderick Random,* very accurate and faithful in every particular."[29] But these actual persons should not be considered as specific prototypes of any of the brilliant character-creations in the novel.

The *Chichester* anchored at Port Royal January 10, 1741. For the next six months the whereabouts of Smollett can only be surmised. Professor Kahrl has reported the lack of *Chichester* musters from February 1 to April 13, 1741, and the fact that Smollett's name is not in the muster records from April 20 to June 18, 1741,

---

[28] See Frank R. Lewis, "John Morris and the Carthagena Expedition, 1739-1740" in *The Mariner's Mirror* (Cambridge University Press), XXVI (1940), 265.

[29] Smollett's *Works,* ed. Anderson, I, 19n. Anderson cited Kirkpatrick Williamson Burnet of Monboddo as the authority for Horn's endorsement of Smollett's accuracy. The identification of General Horn remains in doubt. Perhaps he was the subject of the following obituary in the *Gentleman's Magazine,* LII (1790), 258: "July 28, 1789. In the East Indies General Horne, Commander-in-chief of The Company's Forces at Fort St. George."

which means that we have no proof that he was or was not on the *Chichester* during the naval bombardment of Carthagena. The chances are, however, as Professor Kahrl has shown, that Smollett saw some detached service; he could have been on another man-of-war,[30] or on a hospital ship, or on land duty in Jamaica, or even for a short time with the troops before Carthagena, supplementing the work of other medical officers where the need was most pressing. Wherever he was, he won the regard of a Scottish surgeon, M'Callum, whose obituary in 1810 occasioned the following reference to Smollett:

> At Queensferry, Scotland, aged 90, Mr M Callum [*sic*], surgeon. The early part of his life was spent in the naval service of his country. At the unsuccessful attack on Carthagena in 1741, he was landed to do duty as an assistant surgeon to the troops, along with the celebrated Dr. Smollet, then also an assistant naval surgeon, of whom he always spoke in terms of high esteem.[31]

On some sort of service away from the *Chichester* in 1741, Smollett may have taken orders from Commodore (later Admiral) Knowles, who commanded the *Weymouth* at the attack on Carthagena, and the *Litchfield*,[32] shortly after, in patrol duty. But there is no document which shows that Smollett ever set foot on either ship or met Knowles in 1741. If it could be proved that Smollett remained on the *Chichester* while the fleet attacked Carthagena, then it would be possible to assume that the novelist observed or even met Knowles in 1741. Again, only if it were certain that Smollett never left the *Chichester* during the naval operations around Carthagena, could we make fruitful comparisons between Watkins' records of the location and movements of that ship[33] and the naval episodes in *Roderick Random*.[34]

[30] As Professor Kahrl suggested, Smollett may have served on the *Prince Frederick*, even though his name cannot be found on her musters.

[31] *Gentleman's Magazine*, LXXX (June 1810), 597; and *Scots Magazine*, LXXII (June 1810), 479. In the latter, McCallum's name is correctly printed. See also Chambers' *Smollett*, p. 41n.

[32] See *Naval Chronicle*, I (1799), 100.

[33] For the activities of the *Chichester* around Carthagena, see Kahrl, *op. cit.*, p. 20 and *passim*. It is true that there are no entries in Watkins' journal to prove that the *Chichester* ever fired a broadside or was under fire. And yet the *Chichester* was one of the first ships to reach the inner harbor at Carthagena, and may have been under fire. This is suggested by a sentence in Admiral Vernon's letter to Newcastle, April 1, 1741: "The *Torbay*, and two Fireships of my Division, have got through, and go up to me the 30th in the Morning; as did the Evening of the same Day, the *Chichester*, of my

The captain of the *Chichester*, Robert Trevor, died on April 18, 1741, and on the 20th the ship moved out of the harbor. The next day, the new commander, Captain Stapilton, assumed his formal duties and mustered the ship's company,[35] but according to the records of the ship, Smollett was not present.[36] On June 18, the *Chichester* moored at Port Royal, Jamaica, on which day Smollett was present at musters,[37] and sailed back to England, appearing on her musters until the ship reached Tarr Point, September 21, 1741.[38] Where Smollett spent his days from this time until May 1744, when he set up as surgeon in London, cannot be precisely determined. We have to admit the possibility of further naval service and the certainty of further residence in Jamaica.

Although Smollett's name has not been found on the *Chichester's* musters after September 1741, he remained on her payroll until February 1742, when she was placed in reserve.[39] But on pay-day, February 17, 1742, Smollett was not present at Plymouth to receive the sum of £38/5/11 which was due him. Instead he arranged to have it paid to one James Henshaw, attorney, probably the James Henshaw of Tower Hill, listed in *A Compleat Guide to . . . Lon-*

Division." (From *Authentic Papers Relating to the Expedition against Carthagena*, London, second edition, 1744, p. 11.)

[34] Such comparisons as I made in my article, "The Naval Scenes in *Roderick Random*" (*PMLA*, XLIX [1934], 593ff.), before Professor Kahrl's data on the musters of the *Chichester* came to my attention, are of relatively little value.

[35] Recorded in Watkins' journal.

[36] See Kahrl, *op. cit.*, p. 4.

[37] *Ibid.* It is possible that prior to this time Smollett first met Anne Lassells.

[38] Kahrl, *op. cit.*, p. 5.

[39] I reach this conclusion by simple arithmetic. Smollett's first pay he received at Spithead, September 30, 1740, for the period April 3 to June 30 of that year. This is the entry from P.R.O., Ad. 33/354, No. 188, Tobias Smollet: "Chest 33 (i.e. 3/3) Hospital 18 (i.e. 1/8) Full Wages 6.7.1 Neat Wages 6.2.2." For about 84 days' service, then, Smollett received just about 1/6 per day, or £2/5/0 per month. This sum equals approximately the wage of £2/0/0 per month for second mates to the surgeon of a third-rate ship as specified in *Regulations and Instructions Relating to His Majesty's Service at Sea*, London, 4th Ed., 1743, p. 148. These *Regulations* (see "Appendix," following p. 158) appear to have been in force in 1740. The only other record of Smollett's pay on the *Chichester* is from P.R.O., Ad. 33/410: "No. 188 Tobias Smollett. Surg[ns] 2 m[te]: Time of Discharge (blank); Dead Men's Cloaths 2:15:0; Beds (blank); Chest, 1:1:3; Hospital 10:8; Full Wages, 42:12:10; Neat Wages, 38:5:11; When Paid, 15 May To Whom Paid, James Henshaw. Att." The full wages, £42/12/10, was the sum due to Smollett from July 1, 1740, to February 17, 1742, when the men were paid off at Plymouth. On the basis of two pounds per month this represents a service of approximately twenty months, or for all practical purposes, the period July 1740 to February 1742.

don, London, 1740. This suggests that Smollett, early in February 1742, had sailed as a medical assistant on a merchant ship or man-of-war for the West Indies, where it is likely that he lived the next year or so. Professor Buck conjectured on circumstantial evidence that he returned to England "in the last months of 1742 or the first months of 1743."[40] How did he spend his time from 1742 to 1743?

There is the possibility that he served under Captain (later Admiral) Knowles at La Guaira, though Smollett never referred to any such service and though his name has not yet been found on the musters of Knowles' ship or accompanying craft.[41] Yet it was asserted in an anonymous memoir of Knowles in the *Naval Chronicle* of 1799 that Smollett served under the Admiral, whom he later libeled in the *Critical Review*. The statement is worth recording:

> In 1757, Vice Admiral Knowles, being appointed second in the armament that was sent against Rochfort, under the command of Sir E. Hawke, hoisted his flag on board the Neptune. . . . The present Sir Charles Henry Knowles accompanied his father on this expedition. . . . This expedition, owing to the superficial knowledge of Thierry the French pilot . . . did not succeed.
>
> As Mr. Smollet was at that time an active writer in support of any party, and treated the account which Admiral Knowles published of the transaction, with much harshness in the Critical Review, it may be of service to the public, who already have been acquainted with some particulars of Mr. Smollet's history, to know the real motives of this writer's conduct. We state them with undoubted authority, and claim that credit we are confident they deserve.
>
> Dr. Smollet was originally what is termed a loblolly boy,[42] an inferior attendant on the surgeon, on board Commodore Knowles' ship at La Guira. Mr. Knowles gave him his first warrant as surgeon's mate, and in many instances behaved toward him with paternal kindness. Mr. Smollet afterwards published a libel on his patron. The admiral sent and requested to know in what particular he had ever injured him. At length after much prevarication it appeared, that some favour had been refused him by the admiral's secretary, of which Mr. Knowles was perfectly ignorant. Smollet made his apologies for what had happened, and retired. The worthy admiral, who with surprise beheld the insignificance of the man, who under an apparent zeal for literature, had attacked and sullied

[40] Howard S. Buck, *A Study in Smollett* (New Haven, 1925), p. 59.
[41] See Kahrl, *op. cit.*, p. 10.
[42] In the *NED*, a loblolly boy is defined as "an attendant who assists a ship's surgeon and his mates in their duties."

the fame of a naval officer, wished and intended to pardon him; *but the Earl of Mansfield, then Mr. Murray, and Hume Campbell, afterwards Lord Register of Scotland, would not suffer it to be done. Mr.* Smollet was therefore prosecuted and fined 100£., was imprisoned a year in the Marshalsea, and obliged to find securities for his good behavior. Mr. Smollet afterwards published a continuation of his History of England, and industriously suppressed, or sedulously distorted every circumstance that tended to the honour of Admiral Knowles.[43]

This passage is a mixture of statements, some false, some unproved, and some true. That Knowles gave Smollett his *first warrant* must be false,[44] though he might have had something to do with promoting Smollett to the status of a surgeon's *first mate*. That Smollett served on Knowles' ship, the *Suffolk*, in February 1743 is still to be proved.[45] That Smollett was prosecuted and imprisoned for his libel on Knowles is true, though the account of it as given above is not wholly accurate in details.[46] Considering the passage *in toto* it is very possible that Smollett served under Knowles at La Guaira, and it may well be that it was Knowles' ship or naval unit which Smollett left, when, according to Dr. John Moore, "he quitted the service in the West Indies, and resided some time in the island of Jamaica." Moore, the only biographer of Smollett who knew him personally, should have had the facts, and there is nothing to prove that Smollett did not leave the navy in the West Indies. To assume that he met Knowles in the West Indies is fairly safe, and in that contact may have originated the bad feeling on Smollett's part which erupted so violently many years later in 1758. This early dislike (if it existed) was possibly nourished by the fact that both men lived in the parish of St. George, Hanover Square, in 1748,[47] Smollett going about in his medical garb, and the admiral resplendent, presumably, in a new blue-and-white uniform.[48] Could the Admiral have protested one day about Oakum in *Roderick Ran-*

[43] *The Naval Chronicle*, 1 (1799), 120-21.
[44] When Smollett received his first warrant in London, in March 1740, Knowles was around Jamaica in command of the *Diamond*. (P.R.O., Ad. 8/21, f. 1).
[45] See Kahrl, *op. cit.*, p. 10.
[46] For an account of Smollett's trial, see my article, "Rex versus Smollett: More Data on the Smollett-Knowles Libel Case," *Modern Philology*, XLI (May 1944), 221-27.
[47] In 1748 Smollett paid a rental of £8 in Chapel Street, while Knowles paid a rental of £25 in Audley Street. For Chapel Street and Audley Street, see *The Environs of London* (London, 1761).
[48] For the introduction of uniforms for the navy in 1748, see Lieut. Comdr. R. G. Lowery, *The Origins of Some Naval Terms and Customs* (London, n.d.), p. 74.

dom? And did the sight of the Admiral evoke in Smollett his old disgust of days below deck?

More important than just where, when, and with whom Smollett saw naval service is the fact that he wrote about it in unforgettable prose and that his account may be trusted as essentially accurate. In so doing he made a lasting contribution both to literature and to the social history of England. This achievement was first justly appraised by Carlyle in his biography of Frederick the Great:

> Most obscure among the other items in that Armada of Sir Chaloner's, just taking leave of England; most obscure of the items then, but now most noticeable, or almost alone noticeable, is a young Surgeon's-Mate,— one Tobias Smollett; looking over the waters there and the fading coasts, not without thoughts. A proud, soft-hearted, though somewhat stern-visaged, caustic and indignant young gentleman. Apt to be caustic in speech, having sorrows of his own under lock and key, on this and subsequent occasions. Excellent Tobias; he has, little as he hopes it, something considerable by way of mission in this Expedition, and in this Universe generally. Mission to take Portraiture of English Seamanhood, with due grimness, due fidelity; and convey the same to remote generations, before it vanish. Courage, my brave young Tobias; through endless sorrows, contradictions, toils and confusions, you will do your errand in some measure; and that will be something.[49]

After sorrows, toils, and confusions experienced while battling on ship and shore for the lives of dying men, Smollett at an uncertain time in Jamaica[50] wooed and won an heiress, Anne Lassells.[51] They were both twenty in 1741, Anne having been baptised January 4, 1722, when ten days old.[52] The Lassells family was an old one in the hierarchy of planters and settlers in Jamaica, being represented there in the seventeenth century in the parish of St. Andrews,[53] but whether this family was closely connected with the Lassells of Yorkshire is not certain. An examination of Jamaica

[49] Thomas Carlyle, *History of Friedrich II. of Prussia called Frederick the Great*, 8 vols. (London, Chapman and Hall Ltd., 1898), IV, 187-88.

[50] It is clear from the muster of the *Chichester* that Smollett returned to England in 1742. He may have been in London in the winter of 1742-1743. (See Howard S. Buck, *op. cit.*, pp. 58ff.). He doubtless returned to Jamaica between 1742 and 1744.

[51] See my article, "Ann Smollett, Wife of Tobias Smollett," in *PMLA*, XLV (1930), 1035-49.

[52] Parish Register, St. Thomas-in-the-East, f. 15. (Island Record Office, Spanish Town, Jamaica, B.W.I.). Information from John M. Lynch.

[53] See [Charles Long], *Names of the principal Planters and Settlers in Jamaica 1633 (From a MS of Charles Long Esq.)* . . . Reprint of the Middle Hill private press (? 1840). The name Lascelles appears under the parish of St. Andrews.

wills, powers of attorney, deeds, indentures, and inventories[54] of the families of Lassells and Leaver clarifies somewhat the economic background of Smollett's relations-in-law. Anne Lassells' father, Charles Lassells,[55] was a planter of the parish of St. Thomas-in-the-East, who died when Anne was about two years old, leaving besides Anne, his widow Elizabeth and two sons, Charles and Edward. Anne's mother later married a William Leaver,[56] merchant of Kingston, who died about 1736. By the terms of his will[57] he left all his estate real and personal to "my present wife," Elizabeth and his son Edward (i.e. Edward Leaver) "in joint tenancy," with the further stipulation that if his son should die without heirs all his property should go eventually to "my said wife Elizabeth's Two Sons and her Daughter Viz.^t Charles Lassells Edward Lassells and Ann Lassells" and to the survivor. Judging from the inventory[58] of William Leaver's personal property, he was a man of considerable wealth, and hence Anne was in a position to inherit money from the estates of both her father and her step-father when Smollett met her. At this time, presumably, she was living with her twice-widowed mother in Kingston. How Smollett happened to be introduced to her we do not know. Gently bred[59] she must have been, and beautiful too, according to Smollett's biographer, Robert Anderson, who also stressed the tradition of her "affectionate disposition and elegant mind." Somewhere in Italy, perhaps, is a painting or miniature of her, treasured after her death in Leghorn in 1791.

[54] For the details, see Appendix, pp. 326ff.

[55] His will, dated April 6, 1723, was proved January 21, 1724. His inventory, not including real estate (as by Jamaican law, only personal property was included), amounted to £782. Included in this were four slaves, and a rather ordinary lot of furniture. His real estate cannot be determined. He may well have been the Ch. Lassells listed as having property on Mark Lane in Kingston in 1702. On this point, see Frank Cundall, *The Governors of Jamaica in the First Half of the Eighteenth Century* (London, 1937), p. 50.

[56] William Leaver was presumably Member of the Assembly for St. Thomas-in-the-East, who, being imprisoned on a writ of *ne exeat insula*, caused a crisis in that legislative body in 1727. See Frank Cundall, *op. cit.*, p. 122.

[57] His will was dated May 20, 1735, and proved January 31, 1735/6.

[58] Inventories 18/136. The total value was £19,948. Included among the items were 30 pictures at 3/9 each, a large quantity of furniture, china, pewter, £100 worth of silver plate, a wherry, and 24 slaves (£734).

[59] Her father stipulated in his will that she should be maintained at the expense of his estate "in decent manner and in proportion with my other children." Smollett in his *Travels* (Letter 34) referred to her as "a delicate creature, who had scarce ever walked a mile in her life."

Smollett's residence[60] in Jamaica, courting Anne, getting acquainted with her mother, her brothers, and their circle, and living in something like affluence for the first time, was like honey in the mouth after the bitter bolus of life on the *Chichester*. The colorful, brawling town of Kingston,[61] (its harbor known as Port Royal) crowded with ships from all over the world, and with its slave-markets, its luxury and barbarity are, curiously enough, never reflected in his novels. The chief city of the island, Spanish Town,[62] a few miles away, boasted a theater, which Smollett and his blue-eyed Nancy undoubtedly attended, Tobias yearning increasingly to see his *Regicide* on the boards and assuring Anne that she would see it acclaimed some day in London.

Because no official record of Smollett's marriage has ever been found either in Jamaica or in England, the date and place of his wedding have long been undetermined. Moore was completely vague.[63] Anderson at first ignored the problem[64] but in later versions of his memoir[65] asserted that the wedding ceremony took place about 1747,[66] this being a sheer guess. Moreover he declared without any ascertainable proof that the "ceremony was performed in London."[67] In 1887, David Hannay suggested that Smollett was "in possession of his wife and her fortune before he left Jamaica in 1744."[68] For this conjecture there is circumstantial evidence in Smollett's letter to Barclay, May 22, 1744:

[60] It was stated by W. J. Gardner (in his *History of Jamaica*, London, 1909, p. 128n.) that "Smollett resided in different parts of Jamaica, and for some time in Kingston, where he lodged in a house now occupied as a Store in Harbour Street." This undocumented statement may be true: Anne Smollett subsequently rented property in Harbour Street, Kingston. (See Appendix, p. 328, 332.) Smollett perhaps occupied quarters owned by Anne's family.

[61] For a satisfactory account of Kingston, see [Charles Leslie], *A New History of Jamaica from the Earliest Accounts, to the Taking of Porto Bello by Vice-Admiral Vernon*, Second Edition (London, 1740), *passim*.

[62] Leslie, in describing Spanish Town, declared: " 'Tis surprising to see the Number of Coaches and Chariots which are perpetually plying, besides those which belong to private Persons: They have frequent Balls, and lately have got a Play-house, where they retain a Set of extraordinary good Actors." *op. cit.*, p. 27.

[63] Smollett's *Works*, ed. Moore, I, cxvi.

[64] There is no reference to Smollett's marriage in Anderson's *Life* (London, 1796).

[65] From 1796 to 1820 Anderson tinkered constantly with his evolving biography of Smollett, making large additions and occasional deletions. His assertions are often undocumented.

[66] Anderson's *Life*, Fourth Edition (Edinburgh, 1803), pp. 34-35; and Anderson's "Memoirs" in Smollett's *Miscellaneous Works* (Edinburgh, 1820), I, 25.

[67] *Ibid.*

[68] David Hannay, *Life of Tobias George Smollett* (London, 1887), p. 41.

As for the particulars you expect from me, you must wait until I shall be better informed myself: for, to tell you an extraordinary truth, I do not know, as yet, whether you had better congratulate or condole with me. I wish I was near you, that I might pour forth my heart before you, and make you judge of its dictates, and the several steps I have lately taken; in which case, I am confident you and all honest men would acquit my principles, howsoever my prudentials might be condemned. However, I have moved into the house where the late John Douglas, surgeon, died, and you may henceforth direct for Mr Smollett, surgeon in Downing Street, West.[69]

Now Hannay pointed out with some reason that this statement "sounds like a reference to a not very wise marriage, though to be sure it is not easy to see why 'the prudentials' of a penniless Scotch gentleman should be condemned for marrying a West Indian heiress."[70] Smollett's confession is curiously noncommittal and obscure in view of the fact that it was written to an old friend who was expecting "particulars" rather than guarded generalities, and it raises vexing questions. What principles were involved? Could it be that Smollett, having married Anne on a return visit to Jamaica in 1743, and having been financially assisted by her mother, felt morally obligated to return to London to win economic independence by practicing surgery? Possibly. And could Smollett have felt himself imprudent in moving into the Downing Street house, where the annual rent, £26, was high even for that fashionable section of London? Possibly. His phrasing, "I have moved," suggests that Anne was not in London with him in May 1744. Whatever the letter implied, it is tolerably certain that Smollett was receiving funds from his wife's relatives at this time.

That Smollett married Anne Lassells in 1747 is definitely disproved by the following clause in the will of her brother Charles, dated October 28, 1746: to "my well beloved Sister Anne the wife of Tobias Smollett, £250 cur."[71] It follows, then, that the marriage certainly took place before October 28, 1746. We may now suggest what seems to have been the most probable time, keeping in mind the following outline of Smollett's known or conjectured whereabouts from 1742-1746:

[69] Robert Chambers, *A Biographical Dictionary of Eminent Scotsmen* (Glasgow, 1835), IV, 271. See also *Letters*, pp. 5-6; 114-16.
[70] Hannay, *op. cit.*, p. 43.
[71] Jamaica Wills, 28/193.

1742, *ca*. February, Smollett reached England on the *Chichester*.

1742, *ca*. February-May 1744: For these years there is no certain information of Smollett's whereabouts.

1744, May-*ca*. March 1745: Smollett was in Downing Street.

1745, *ca*. March-*ca*. January 1746: There are no data on his residence.

1746, *ca*. January-*ca*. July 1748: Smollett lived in Chapel Street.[72]

In the light of this chronological outline, it is evident that the most likely times for Smollett's return visit or visits to Jamaica were in 1742-1743, or in 1745. As there is little chance that the marriage occurred during his first stay in Jamaica in 1741, we are left to choose between the years 1742-1743 and 1745. Because of the implications in Smollett's letter to Barclay, the earlier period is much more acceptable, and for dating the wedding 1742-1743 there are two additional considerations. The first is found in Smollett's letter to Richard Smith in 1763, where he declared: "I married, very young, a native of Jamaica, a young lady well known and universally respected, under the name of Miss Nancy Lassells; and by her I enjoy a comfortable tho' moderate estate in that Island."[73] The words, "very young," are fairly accurate for Smollett's age in 1742-1743, but less appropriate for him two or three years later. The second and fairly conclusive piece of evidence bearing on the date of Smollett's marriage is found in the manuscript diary kept at the time of his death by his Italian doctor, Giovanni Gentili, whose entry began as follows: "M. Smollet di a.[nni] 50 uomo di talento—Istorico 1772," i.e. M. Smollet aged 50 a man of historical talent 1772. Gentili added, among other details, that Smollett "vissuto con la moglie 18 [anni] in perfetta armonia dalla quale ottena una figlia che poetava,"[74] i.e. he lived 18 years in perfect harmony with his wife by whom he had a daughter who wrote poetry. It is clear that Gentili intended to write 1771 instead of "1772": his manuscript is very difficult to read. Similarly it must be that his "18" is a slip for 28. Now Gentili's vivid portrait contains intimate details which he could have obtained only from the Smolletts or from their English physician, Dr. Garden, mentioned

[72] The documents showing Smollett's residences will be presented in Chap. III.

[73] *Letters*, p. 80.

[74] Gentili's entries concerning Smollett were printed by Francesco Pera in his *Curiosità Livornesi Inedite o Rare* (Livorno, 1888), p. 316. My citations, however, follow an exact transcript sent me by the Directress of the Biblioteca Riccardiana, Florence, whose kindness I hereby acknowledge. For the complete transcript, see my account of Smollett's death in this volume, Chap. XIV.

as the consulting doctor in Gentili's complete diagnosis of Smollett's illness. Hence there is no reason to question Gentili's accuracy, and we are convinced that the Smolletts were married, presumably in Jamaica, twenty-eight years before 1771, that is, in 1743. A later ceremony, ratifying their Jamaican marriage, .may have occurred in England.[75] The upshot of the whole matter is that Smollett, with characteristic impetuosity, seems to have married at the age of twenty-two without possessing any economic security of his own. As the result of the advice of Anne's family, perhaps, or of his own considerable pride, Smollett was to travel and to work alone, as far as we know, from 1744 to 1747. The cruel strain of this unhappy isolation must have accounted for some of the furious temper and fierce irritability that characterized him in the years that lay ahead.

[75] In Oliphant Smeaton, *Tobias Smollett* (Famous Scots Series), Edinburgh and London (1897), p. 43, is the following statement: "When he [Smollett] returned to London, he returned as an engaged man. In one of his unpublished letters, he expressly states that he was not married until 1747, when Miss Lascelles came to England. But, on the other hand, there is evidence in Jamaica that some sort of ceremony was performed before Smollett left the island in the end of 1743." This unpublished letter still remains hidden, and the evidence in Jamaica of "some sort of ceremony" has not been found.

CHAPTER III
Surgery and Literary Apprenticeship,
1747-1750

ON May 22, 1744, Smollett, in his twenty-third year, wrote to his Glasgow friend, Barclay: "You may henceforth direct for Mr. Smollett, surgeon, in Downing Street, West."[1] Maturing experiences lay behind him: service in the navy, residence in Jamaica, the winning of an heiress, and, according to his own statement, travel "in France and other foreign countries"[2] for the purpose of self-improvement. This short trip to the Continent may have been a means of advancing his knowledge of French and Spanish before 1744. There must be some truth in Dr. John Shebbeare's sneering reference to Smollett's brief residence in Brussels to study Spanish:

> A Millar, solliciting Subscriptions to this [Smollett's] Edition of *Don Quixote*, when it was objected by one of his own countrymen; that the Translator did not understand *Spanish*, assured him that the Author had been full six weeks to study that Language amongst the native *Spaniards*, at *Brussels*.[3]

An early enthusiasm for Cervantes may have inspired Smollett in 1744 to work on Spanish: by 1748 he was well into translating *Don Quixote*, judging from his correspondence with Carlyle and the announcement in the *General Advertiser*, November 21, 1748.[4]

In 1744 or 1745, as Mr. Otto Deutsch demonstrates in his recent article (*MLN*, February, 1948), Smollett viewed his first publication, *A New Song*, issued with music by James Oswald.

---

[1] *Letters*, p. 5.   [2] *Ibid.*, p. 80.

[3] [Shebbeare, Dr. John], *The Occasional Critic or the Decrees of the Scotch Tribunal in the Critical Review Rejudged* (London, 1757), p. 61n.

[4] "Preparing for the Press, a new Translation of 'The Life and Achievements of the Ingenious Knight Don Quixote De La Mancha,' from the original Spanish of Miguel Cervantes de Saavedra. By the author of Roderick Random. With a new set of cuts design'd by Hayman, and engrav'd by the best masters. Printed for J. Osborn, at the Golden-Ball in Pater-noster Row." This same notice appeared again on September 7, 1749. On June 7, 1748, Smollett informed Carlyle that he was "fairly engaged" with the translation.

This lyric appeared in altered form in *Roderick Random*, 1748.

Where Smollett lived in London before 1744 is not known, but from that year on, his residences have been determined from data in the London Rate Books.[5] Records of his rental in fashionable Downing Street are found in the Rate Book of the Parish of St. Margaret and St. John for 1744 under the heading of a "new Assessment made on such Houses as were empty or Omitted at making of the first assessment [for 1744] for the Relief of the poor" for that parish. The entry is as follows:

Downing Street

	Entered at	Rent	Tax[6]
Mr. Smallett	midsummer	[£]26	[£]1/1/8

Since Smollett's letter was written in May, the term, midsummer, was hardly accurate, but the entry proves that he was taxed for the latter half of 1744 and that his rent was £26 per year. Under the assessment of the same parish for 1745, all that appears is the following:

	Rent	Tax[7]
Smallet	[£]26	£-10-10

As this tax was based on a residence for a period of three months,[8] we must infer that Smollett left Downing Street about the end of March 1745. For the remainder of that year the place of his residence in London, or elsewhere, is not established.

Two clues proved invaluable in finding his next residence. The first was a statement by Dr. Carlyle in his delightful *Autobiography* that Smollett lived in May Fair in 1746.[9] The second hint came from a reference by Charles Bucke in his biography of Akenside to Smollett's abode "in a court leading out of Dean-street

[5] See my article, "Smollett's Early Years in London," in *JEGP*, XXXI (1932), 220-27. The data in eighteenth-century Rate Books are sometimes difficult to interpret because the percentage rate, in terms of a certain number of pence per pound, changed constantly, and because the "Rate" (tax) was levied in some sections of London quarterly, and in other sections, semiannually. Moreover, the data are sometimes incomplete. In interpreting the data on Smollett's residences I was kindly assisted by the custodian of the Record Department at the City Hall, Westminster.

[6] Rate Book 367, f. 22.

[7] Rate Book 368, f. 22.

[8] The tax of ten shillings, ten pence, was based, obviously, on the rate of five pence in the pound. We see that the tax for 1744, representing, apparently, a residence of six months, was just twice as much.

[9] See *The Autobiography of Dr. Alexander Carlyle of Inveresk*, ed. John Hill Burton (London and Edinburgh, 1910), p. 199.

Soho."[10] The Rate Books of the Parish of St. George, Hanover Sq. Grosvenor St. Ward for Chapel Street contain the records of Smollett's taxes for 1746, 1747, and the first half of 1748. The first Rate Book for 1746 has the following on folio 32:

			Rent	(Tax)
[No.]	11	Mr. Smollett	[£]8	.. 2 .. 8

In the other Rate Book, recording the Second Rate for 1746, we find (folio 32) an entry identical with the above. For the year 1747 there are entries of two rates (folio 32) the tax having been increased to three shillings, four pence, for each rate. In the Rate Book for 1748 (folio 32), there is an entry identical with those of 1747. In the book showing the Second Rate for 1748 Smollett's name in the list of residents was replaced by that of one Captain Richardson.

The Chapel Street in which Smollett lived and where the rent was £8 (instead of the £26 which he had paid in Downing Street) was located south of Grosvenor Square not far from Dean Street, and just to the east of Hyde Park. This section was called May Fair because a fair was held in the vicinity annually in the month of May.[11] Chapel Street was also close to Audley Street.[12] From this modest environment Smollett moved next to an expensive rent in Beaufort Buildings, Beaufort Street, as will appear later.

Downing Street, Chapel Street, and Beaufort Street—such was the chain of residences, the first link of which is especially interesting. Smollett's expensive Downing Street medical quarters must have been financed by Anne, for it is impossible to comprehend how, without her financial assistance, Smollett could have accumulated enough funds before 1744 to establish himself where the late John Douglas, surgeon, had lived until his death, June 28, 1743.

Illuminating side-lights on Smollett's medical circle and professional environment radiate from some knowledge of John

[10] See Charles Bucke, *On the Life, Writings and Genius of Akenside* (London, 1832), p. 42.

[11] See *London and its Environs Described*, 6 vols. (London, 1761), IV.

[12] I am told by Professor Howard P. Vincent that documents in an unexplored legal case in which Smollett was involved in 1746 give Smollett's address as Audley St., St. George's, Hanover Square. In *London and its Environs Described*, Vol. I, we find both *Chapel Court* and *Chapel Street* described as bordering on Audley Street. My map of London [1770] has Chapel Street intersecting South Audley Street. This explains the apparent discrepancy in Smollett's address in 1746.

Douglas and his brother Dr. James Douglas (1675-1742). The obituary notice of John Douglas is revealing:

> On Sat. last died in Downing-Street after a tedious Illness, that excellent Surgeon, Mr. John Douglas, (Brother to the late Dr. James Douglas, of Red-Lyon-Square) a Man of Such Consequence to Mankind that the celebrated Dr. Boerhaave writes to him. What a loss would it be to have buried with its Author so easy and effectual a Cure, for many Diseases as well as the Venereal! Which must inevitably [have] been done, had not the Welfare of the Publick lain so much at his Heart, as to communicate it to one, to be practised as usual, at his late House in Downing-Street, Westminster.[13]

The recipient of John Douglas' medical formula was probably his widow, who, according to a newspaper notice[14] in the fall of 1743, was making his medicines and carrying on his work in Downing Street. John Douglas was a prominent London surgeon. He was described in *An Account of the Life . . . of William Cullen, M.D.*, as follows: "Mr. John Douglas, Surgeon to Westminster Hospital, a man of eminence as a surgeon, and particularly as a lithotomist, in which character he was a great patron and practitioner of the High Operation."[15] When Dr. John Douglas died, William Hunter, later an intimate friend of Smollett, wrote to his brother that he considered going into partnership with Douglas' son-in-law Dr. Owen, who had been told by his father-in-law that he had made £4,000 in three years.[16] Further evidence of John Douglas' success is perhaps indicated by a seven-day sale of his library, in January 1744.[17]

John Douglas' brother, Dr. James, was even more distinguished, being a Fellow of the Royal Society, and a member of the Society for the Encouragement of Learning. He was aided by Robert Foulis in building up his famous collection of Horace. As a physician, obstetrician, and lecturer on anatomy, he was praised by Pope in *The Dunciad*:

> There all the Learned shall at the labour stand,
> And Douglas lend his soft obstetric hand.
>
> (BOOK IV, ll. 393-94)

---

[13] *London Daily Advertiser*, June 28, 1743.
[14] *London Daily Advertiser*, September 20, 1743.
[15] John Thomson, M.D., F.R.S.L. & E., *An Account of the Life, Lectures, and Writings of William Cullen, M.D.*, 2 vols. (Edinburgh and London, 1859), II, 734.
[16] See George C. Peachey, *Memoir of William and John Hunter* (Plymouth, 1924), p. 76.
[17] *London Daily Advertiser*, January 31, 1744.

His assistant in 1741-1742 was the eminent William Hunter,[18] who, after the death of Dr. Douglas in 1742, acted as tutor to his son, and became the suitor of his daughter.

It is abundantly clear then that both James and John Douglas were important members of the medical fraternity, and the fact that young Smollett, with only his experience as a surgeon's mate at Carthagena plus possible further service at sea, in Jamaica, or on the Continent, moved into the residence of John Douglas demands more consideration than it has received. It indicates certainly that Smollett had larger ideas of a medical career than has been assumed hitherto. Since young William Hunter was assisting Dr. James Douglas in 1742, it is not fantastic to suggest that Smollett probably met Dr. James by means of Hunter, or better still, through the assistance of Robert Foulis, whom he knew at Glasgow. To be sure, Dr. James Douglas died in 1742, but Smollett, through similar connections, could certainly have met John Douglas before his death in 1743. We must remember that young Smollett was anything but shy or lacking in initiative, and that many leading spirits in the London medical world were Scotsmen to whom he would not have felt unduly inferior. Like Hunter, he may have assisted some prominent surgeon, possibly John Douglas. Only on such assumptions may we explain his setting up as surgeon in fashionable Downing Street early in 1744.

Why Smollett moved from Downing Street in the spring of 1745 is not clear. Seccombe suggested that he went to May Fair in "search of practice."[19] Possibly he managed a trip to Jamaica. Or his medical income may have been too small to justify his remaining among Scottish and Irish M.P.'s[20] and men of title and fortune.[21] Whatever the reasons were, Smollett was living on Chapel Street at the beginning of 1746. Though his lodgings were relatively inexpensive, there was plenty of fashionable life in adjoin-

[18] For information on William Hunter and Dr. James Douglas, see P. H. Aitken, *A Catalogue of the Manuscripts in the Library of the Hunterian Museum in the University of Glasgow* (Glasgow, 1908), p. 425 and *passim*.

[19] See Thomas Seccombe's account of Smollett in *DNB*.

[20] See George H. Cunningham, *London Being a Comprehensive Survey of the History, Tradition, and Historical Association of Buildings and Monuments Arranged under Streets in Alphabetical Order* (London and Toronto, 1927), p. 196.

[21] Among Smollett's neighbors in Downing Street were the Earl of Huntingdon, Sir Watkyn Wynne and "Delaval Esq.," probably Francis Blake Delaval, M.P.

ing Audley [Audsley] Street,[22] and in nearby Berkeley Square.
During his years in Chapel Street, 1746-1748, Smollett combined both medical and literary activity; the latter grew rapidly,
and, by 1748, began to be profitable. His medical work was maintained, nevertheless, for he secured in 1750 his M.D. from Marischal College, Aberdeen,[23] and published his medical essay in 1752.
However, as Smollett achieved fame not as a doctor but as a writer,
we must now consider at some length his literary apprenticeship.

The Regicide

Smollett's burning desire for literary recognition is best shown
by his amazing efforts over a period of eight years to find a pro-
ducer for his *Regicide*, that ill-starred tragedy, which cost him
vastly more pains than it merited.

Fortunately for his biographers, Smollett wrote two highly detailed expositions of the adventures of this tragedy: (1) the "Preface" to *The Regicide*, in 1749; and (2) the inset story of the poet
Melopoyn and his manuscript tragedy in *Roderick Random* (Chapters 62 and 63). These two accounts were admirably investigated
by Professor Buck,[24] who added to the identifications of the fictitious names in Melopoyn's story, and constructed a reliable chronology of Smollett's futile attempts to persuade Fleetwood, Lacy,
and Rich to produce his play. These efforts, which he began upon
his arrival in London at the end of 1739, he resumed after his return on the *Chichester* in the spring of 1742, and continued with
dogged persistence until 1747. Taken *in toto* they reveal a great
deal about Smollett's character and his rapidly widening circle of
social and literary acquaintances during his crucial years of struggle
for recognition as a writer. Professor Buck pointed out that the
"Preface" to *The Regicide*, probably written early in 1749, seems
to be a more exact and reliable statement, and that it can be understood completely only when read in conjunction with Melopoyn's
story, composed late in 1747, and which, though it has every appearance of being largely fictional, has always been accepted as

[22] Entered at this period on the Rate Books for "Audsley street" were Lord Hallifax,
Lord Ogle, Lord Petersham, and Lady Bobb Montagu.
[23] For a very informal account of some of the facts pertaining to this matter, see
W. D. Taylor, M.D., "Tobias Smollett, M.D., Aberdeen, 1750," in *Aberdeen University Review*, XXVI (1939), 125-35.
[24] Howard S. Buck, *A Study in Smollett, Chiefly "Peregrine Pickle"* (New Haven,
Yale University Press, 1925), Chap. 3.

preponderantly autobiographical.[25] At this point, careful outlines of the material in the "Preface" and in Melopoyn's story will be of interest.

I. THE PREFACE TO *The Regicide*, 1749

Smollett, having stated with pride that he finished his tragedy at the age of eighteen, proceeded to assert that "as early as the Year 1739, my Play was taken into the Protection of one of those little Fellows who are sometimes called great men; and like other orphans, neglected accordingly."[26] "Stung with Resentment" Smollett "discarded" his "Patron," and revised the play until "my Occasions called me out of the Kingdom." This refers of course to his entering the navy.[27] "Soon after my Return," the "Preface" continues, "I and my Production were introduced to a late Patentee, of courteous Memory, who (rest his Soul!) found Means to amuse me a whole Season, and then declared it impracticable to bring it on 'till next Year; advising me to make my Application more early in the Winter." The "whole Season" was the theatrical year 1742-1743, and judging from the advice of Fleetwood (the late Patentee), Smollett first approached him rather late in 1742. Thus disappointed, Smollett gave his play "to a Nobleman of great Weight" who kept it "four months" after which "it was retrieved by pure Accident," declared Smollett, "from the most dishonourable Apartment of his Lordship's House."[28] This nobleman remains unidentified, but the author regained possession of his manuscript in the fall of 1743. "Enraged at the behavior of this supercilious Peer," Smollett condemned his play to two years of oblivion (1743-1745), but at the end of 1745 was persuaded by a cultured young gentleman to "new model the Plan . . . and mould it into a regular Tragedy."[29] The manuscript was next presented by "a young Nobleman, since deceased"[30] to the "New Manager

---

[25] Robert Anderson's general statement may be cited: "In the story of *Melopoyn*, the severe reflections which are directed against the theatrical managers, Mr. Lacy and Mr. Garrick, who are designed under the characters of *Brayer* and *Marmoset*, confirm the opinion which prevailed at the time, that *Melopoyn's* tragedy and Smollett's were the same." From Anderson's 6th edition of *The Miscellaneous Works of Smollett* (Edinburgh, 1820), I, 26.

[26] "Preface" to *The Regicide*, 1749, p. [i].

[27] His naval warrant was dated March 10, 1740.

[28] "Preface," p. [ii].   [29] *Ibid.*

[30] This young nobleman was the Right Hon. Lord George Graham, son of the first Duke of Montrose. He was M.P. from Sterlingshire and captain of the *Nottingham*,

of Drury-Lane Theatre," James Lacy. About "the latter End of the Season" (i.e. *ca.* June 1745) "this candid Personage . . . received the Performance," assuring the nobleman that he would bring it on "the ensuing Winter" (i.e. the season of 1745-1746). But, alas, Lacy, "instead of fulfilling his own Promise and my Expectation, gratified the Town with the Production of a Player, the Fate of which every Body knows."[31] This player was Charles Macklin, whose first play, *King Henry VII, or the Popish Imposter*, was given at Drury Lane, January 18, 1746, and ran for three days only.[32] Returning to Smollett's "Preface," we learn that in the succeeding spring (i.e. 1746), *The Regicide* won "the Approbation of an eminent Wit [Chesterfield] who, after proposing amendments, recommended it to a Person, by whose Influence, I laid my Account with seeing it appear at last, with such Advantage as should make ample Amends for all my Disappointments."[33] The person thus referred to was Garrick, as will become clear when we examine Melopoyn's story. But these promoters availed nothing, for the "Master of Covent-Garden Theatre, bluntly rejected it, as a Piece altogether unfit for the Stage."[34] In other words, John Rich refused to accept it, apparently in the fall of 1746. At this juncture, Smollett had about given up hope when a humane Lady of Quality[35] succeeded in persuading Lacy to peruse the play again. Lacy characteristically postponed reading it "until the Season" (i.e. 1746-1747) "was almost consumed" and then, being reproached "by a Gentleman," condemned it "in the Mettle of his Wrath." Whereupon this gentleman showed Lacy a letter written two years before (1745) by Smollett's friendly young Nobleman, now dead, a letter which Smollett had carefully preserved:

---

60 guns. He died in January 1747. Smollett referred to him in a letter to Alexander Carlyle *ca.* March 1747, as follows: "I am vain of your approbation with regard to my Tragedy, which as you imagine suffered by the much lamented death of Lord George Graham." (See "New Smollett Letters" in *TLS*, July 24, 1943.) For Graham's obituary see *London Magazine*, XVI (1747), 53.

[31] "Preface," p. [iii].

[32] See Allardyce Nicoll, *A History of Early Eighteenth Century Drama 1700-1750* (Cambridge University Press, 1929), p. 342. According to the *DNB*, this play, given on the occasion of the Scottish Rebellion, was written in six weeks. Quin predicted that it would fail. For Mrs. Cibber's opinion, see *The Private Correspondence of David Garrick*, 2 vols. (London, 1831), I, 49.

[33] "Preface," p. [iii].   [34] *Ibid.*

[35] Perhaps Lady Vane, as Professor Buck suggested.

"Sir, I have received Mr. L——'s (i.e. Lacy's) Answer; who says
he thinks your Play has indubitable Merit, but has [his] prior Promises to
Mr. T——n, as an honest Man, cannot be evaded." —— And concluding thus; "As the Manager has promised me the choice of the Season
next year, if you'll be advised by me, rest it with me."[36]

Now the Mr. T——n, above, was surely James Thomson, whose
Tancred and Sigismunda was put on at Drury Lane, March 1745.
This letter impressed Lacy, who, pleading the usual excuse of the
advanced season of the year (i.e. the advanced theatrical season
of 1746-1747) agreed, on the proviso of further revisions, to produce the play "next Winter" (i.e. during the season of 1747-
1748). This agreement is precisely what Smollett reported in his
letter to Carlyle (about March 1747) as follows:

> Meanwhile I have just finished the alterations of my Play as they were
> agreed upon, by the manager of Drury Lane, who has given his word and
> honour to a person of Quality, that it shall be acted next Winter, at any
> time before Christmass [*sic*] that I desire.[37]

But to cap the unhappy climax, Lacy "renounced his Engagement
without the least Scruple, Apology, or Reason assigned."[38] Smollett's exposition of his woes is surprisingly exact and follows a
perfectly clear chronology, which may be summarized in the following outline:

1739	*The Regicide* was first shown to a patron.
1739	Smollett discarded his patron and revised the play.
1740	Smollett sailed on the *Chichester*.
1742	In the autumn(?) the play was submitted to Fleet-wood, who kept it a whole season and advised bringing it on in the winter.
1743	The play was in the hands of a nobleman of great weight who kept it four months.
1743-1745	The play remained two years in oblivion.
1745 March	Thomson's *Tancred and Sigismunda* was played.
1745	The play was shown to Lacy "about the latter end of the season," i.e. about June. Lacy promised to produce it the ensuing winter.
1746 January	Macklin's *Henry VII* was given, instead, and failed.
1746	The play won Chesterfield's "Approbation."
1746	The play was rejected by Rich in the fall.
1746	Lacy received the play again, and finally condemned it at the end of the 1746-1747 season.

[36] "Preface," p. [iv].   [37] "New Smollett Letters," *TLS*, July 24, 1943.
[38] "Preface," p. [iv].

1747   Lacy, under pressure, agreed to produce the play next
              winter.
1747   Lacy rejected the play again for no stated reason.

Such was the eight-year history of *The Regicide* as summed up by
Smollett in his "Preface."

II. THE VICISSITUDES OF *The Regicide* AS SET FORTH IN MELO-
      POYN's STORY IN *Roderick Random* (Chapters 62 and 63)

The account of *The Regicide* as told by Melopoyn presents more
detail (much of it purely fictional) than is found in the "Preface"
of the printed play. Managers, actors, and patrons are here presented under fictitious names, for which Professor Buck furnished
the following reliable key:

Melopoyn	= Smollett
Marmozet	= Garrick
Brayer	= Lacy
Earl Sheerwit	= Earl of Chesterfield
Supple	= Fleetwood
Vandal	= Rich
Bellower	= Quin
Lord Rattle	= a vague composite of all patrons except the lady of quality
Father O'Varnish	= unknown Catholic friend of Smollett

Melopoyn's account begins with the fortunes of the play under
the tender mercies of the gouty Supple (Fleetwood), with whose
son Father O'Varnish had interceded. According to the chronology
of the "Preface" this must have been in 1742. Supple kept the manuscript for weeks until Melopoyn finally called upon him, only to
learn that the sheets had been used for waste paper in singeing
fowls. Melopoyn then made from memory a new copy, which was
read by Supple (Fleetwood) too late for any possible production
that season (1742-1743). Melopoyn next tried his 'prentice hand
at miscellaneous Grub Street activities, such as secret histories,
conundrums, translations, ballads, and songs. Next fall (1743?)
Melopoyn again approached Supple (Fleetwood) who this time
introduced him to Lord Rattle (an unidentifiable patron) at whose
suggestion the tragedy was "new modelled . . . in less than a
month." Melopoyn then met an actor, "who had been a player

these twenty years" (probably Quin, later introduced as Bellower) and had the unhappy experience of hearing this actor read his play.[39] Shortly after this, Supple (Fleetwood) "disposed of his property and patent to one Mr. Brayer" (Lacy). Hence "fresh interest was to be made with the new manager." This sale occurred, as is known, about January 1745. We should observe that no mention is made by Melopoyn of the two years in which, according to the "Preface," the play lay buried in oblivion. The next step, according to Melopoyn, was Lord Rattle's success in getting Brayer (Lacy) to examine the play. A glance at the chronology of the "Preface" shows us that Lacy first saw the play about June 1745. Having read the play, Brayer (Lacy) "owned it had indubitable merit," offered the excuse that "he had long been preengaged to another author,"[40] and promised that if it were revised, he would take it next season, which would have been the season of 1745-1746. Being "thunderstruck at this disappointment," Melopoyn got a letter of recommendation from Lord Rattle to Mr. Bellower (Quin), "actor and prime minister to Mr. Vandal" (Rich). Both the letter and the play were duly presented to Quin, who did not even take the trouble to read the manuscript.[41] Enraged by Quin's insolence, Melopoyn again appealed to Lord Rattle, who advised him to keep the play "till the next season [1745-1746] for Mr. Brayer" (Lacy), who, as we have seen, had agreed to produce it. When the following season arrived, Melopoyn finally met Brayer (Lacy) and received from him a general theater-pass for this season, but no definite assurances as to the production of his play. To quote Melopoyn: "I became very uneasy about the season, that wasted apace, when I saw in the papers another new play advertised, which had been written, offered, accepted, and rehearsed, in the compass of three months. You may easily guess how much I was confounded at this event. I own to you, that in the first transports of my anger, I suspected Mr. Brayer of having acted toward me in the most pitiful perfidious manner; and was actually glad at his disappointment in the success of his favorite piece, which by the strength of art, lingered till

[39] *Roderick Random*, Chap. 63.

[40] This other author was evidently James Thomson.

[41] That this neglect was quite characteristic of Quin is shown by an actual episode in his life, described in the *Life of Quin* and cited by Professor Buck in his *A Study in Smollett*, p. 71.

the third night, and then died in a deplorable manner." The new play, mentioned above, was surely Macklin's *Henry VII*, produced, as we have seen, in January 1746 and alluded to in the "Preface." In fact, Melopoyn's description reads almost exactly like the account of this play given in the life of Macklin in the *Dictionary of National Biography*!

After this sharp disillusionment, Melopoyn, naturally enough, "withdrew the manuscript from the hands of Mr. Brayer" (Lacy) and through influential friends placed it in the hands of Earl Sheerwit (Chesterfield), who "read and approved it very much." We know from good evidence that Chesterfield first saw Smollett's play in 1746, before dispatching it to Garrick, who wrote to John Hoadley on September 14, 1746, as follows:

> I have a play now with me, sent to me by my Lord Chesterfield, and wrote by one Smollett. It is a Scotch story, but it won't do, and yet recommended by his Lordship and patronized by Ladies of Quality: what can I say or do? Must I belie my judgment or run the risk of being thought impertinent and disobliging ye great folks? Some advice upon that head, if you please.[42]

Melopoyn soon met Marmozet (Garrick) who, admitting that Earl Sheerwit (Chesterfield) had praised the opus, assured its author that he would appear in it "provided he should be engaged to play at all during the ensuing season" (1746-1747), and graciously took the manuscript to the country where he could suggest possible improvements. After a delay of six weeks, Marmozet (Garrick) became evasive, and Melopoyn learned indirectly that he had written Sheerwit (Chesterfield) that the drama was "altogether unfit for the stage." Nevertheless Melopoyn induced Marmozet to approach Mr. Vandal (Rich) about staging it, and in due course met the manager, who rejected it, apparently in the fall of 1746. The result was that Melopoyn, convinced that Marmozet (Garrick) had grossly deceived him, attacked him with much asperity. But Melopoyn did not give up, for thanks to "a lady of fashion" (perhaps the "humane lady of quality" of the "Preface"), Mr. Brayer (Lacy) condescended to have another look at it. After more delays, Brayer (Lacy) agreed to produce it the following winter (1747-1748), but when the time came, he was in

---

[42] George P. Baker, *Some Unpublished Correspondence of David Garrick* (Boston, 1907), p. 37.

partnership with Marmozet[43] (Garrick) and must have the latter's consent. Marmozet, however, "was pre-engaged to another author,"[44] and consequently the play was not accepted.

The chronology of Smollett's efforts to stage *The Regicide* is, according to Melopoyn's story, as follows:

ca. 1742	Supple (Fleetwood) received the play.
ca. 1742	The manuscript was burned.
ca. 1743	In the fall, the play was again presented to Supple (Fleetwood), revised at Lord Rattle's suggestion, and given a reading by Quin.
1745	Supple sold his patent to Brayer (Lacy).
ca. 1745	June, Lord Rattle induced Brayer (Lacy) to read the play. Lacy agreed to produce it 1745-1746.
1745	Quin had the play.
1746	January, Macklin's *Henry VII* appeared.
1746	Earl Sheerwit (Chesterfield) read the play.
1746	In the fall, Vandal (Rich) rejected it.
1747	Brayer (Lacy) failed to produce it because his partner, Garrick, was pre-engaged to another author.

A comparison of our two chronological outlines shows a remarkable similarity between them, granting, of course, that some of the dates in each are necessarily tentative. Despite the fact that Melopoyn's account is longer and contains what *appears* to be fictional material, it is much more specific in presenting personalities and more devastating in its satire. The "Preface," being more formal as a condensed statement of what the public should know about the unnecessary hardships of a young author in dealing with stupid and perfidious producers, is saturated with quite effective irony. Here, as so often later as an historian and critic, Smollett called attention to his "most impartial Manner."[45] He then stressed with pride the fact that his expectations of staging the play "were not derived from the partial Applause of my own Friends only, but inspired (as some of my greatest Enemies know) by the Approbation of Persons of the first Note in the Republic of Taste; whose Countenance, I vainly imagined, would have been an effectual Introduction to the Stage."[46] The last paragraphs of the "Preface"

---

[43] According to Melopoyn, "Mr. Marmozet, during the summer, became joint patentee with Mr. Brayer," but the agreement between Garrick and Lacy was reached **April 9, 1747.** See *Private Correspondence of David Garrick*, I, xix.

[44] The quoted passages are from *Roderick Random*, Chaps. 62 and 63.

[45] "Preface" to *The Regicide*, 1749, p. [iv]. [46] *Idem.*

attack in a general way the ignorance of playhouse managers (Fleetwood, Lacy and Rich, of course), their dissimulation, their breach of promise, "Abuse of Prerogative," inaccessibility, favoritism, avarice, pride, humour, and petulance—all of which evils, warned Smollett, the public should know.

Melopoyn's story and the "Preface" to *The Regicide,* when understood and closely considered, throw a brilliant light on Smollett's character and personal relationships for the years 1739 to 1748. They explain the genesis of his quarrels with Fleetwood, Lacy, Quin, and Garrick—quarrels reflected later in *Peregrine Pickle,* as Professor Buck has convincingly demonstrated in the third chapter of his *Study in Smollett Chiefly Peregrine Pickle.* From our analysis of this period it is abundantly evident that Smollett had an irrepressible ambition, like so many other novelists, to excel in drama. It is obvious, too, that in these early years he managed through effective social introductions, as well as by the appeal of his own personality, to meet influential patrons, and some of the leading theatrical personalities of the period. All this was accomplished under definite handicaps: he was a Scotsman; he had little money; and he was obliged to spend some part of his time in the practice of surgery.

But the years 1744 to 1747 were marked by much more constructive literary activity than was possible in the numerous revisions of *The Regicide.* In this critical period Smollett tried his hand at the occasional ode, and composed his first verse satires. It seems best to consider these early productions separately before summarizing their general import in his life and achievement.

The Tears of Scotland

In 1746, after the historic news of the defeat of the rebels at Culloden on April 16 had reached London, Smollett composed "The Tears of Scotland," perhaps his best verse, and certainly a poem widely read, sung, reprinted, and admired during his lifetime. Although Smollett was at no time a Jacobite, his indignation was naturally and rightfully aroused over the reported atrocities of the victorious troops of the Duke of Cumberland, known subsequently as "Butcher" Cumberland.[47] The following extract from the poem illustrates his attitude:

[47] Specific instances of the unnecessary cruelty of Cumberland's soldiers are listed in

Yet, when the rage of battle ceas'd
The victor's soul was not appeas'd:
The naked and forlorn must feel
Devouring flames, and murd'ring steel!

Something of the composition of Smollett's ode has long been known from the autobiography of his friend, Alexander ("Jupiter") Carlyle, who wrote (under the year 1746):

I was in the coffeehouse [located, as Carlyle stated, on Cockspur Street] with Smollett when the news of the battle of Culloden arrived, and when London all over was in a perfect uproar of joy. . . . About 9 o'clock I wished to go home to Lyon's, in New Bond Street . . . I asked Smollett if he was ready to go, as he lived at Mayfair; he said he was, and would conduct me. The mob were so riotous, and the squibs so numerous and incessant that we were glad to go into a narrow entry to put our wigs in our pockets, and to take our swords from our belts and walk with them in our hands, as everybody then wore swords; and, after cautioning me against speaking a word, lest the mob should discover my country and become insolent, "for John Bull," says he, "is as haughty and valiant to-night as he was abject and cowardly on the Black Wednesday when the Highlanders were at Derby." After we got to the head of the Haymarket through incessant fire, the Doctor led me by narrow lanes, where we met nobody but a few boys at a pitiful bonfire, who very civilly asked us for sixpence, which I gave them. I saw not Smollett again for some time after, when he showed Smith and me the manuscript of his *Tears of Scotland*, which was published not long after, and had such a run of approbation.[48]

This vivid and long-remembered experience of Carlyle suggests something of the circumstances under which Smollett wrote his poem. Light on the actual composition of the poem was furnished by Smollett's biographer, John Moore, in 1797: "The first copies of the Ode terminated with the sixth stanza. After the remonstrances to suppress it, he added the seventh."[49] A more dramatic account of the composition of this poem was contributed in 1803 by Anderson wherein he transcribed the following story, first set

---

Smollett's *A Complete History of England*, Book IX, Chap. IX of the quarto edition, Vol. 4 (1758), pp. 673-74. Smollett's vigorous denunciation of these cruelties brought him the bitter hatred of Andrew Henderson, M.A., a Scottish historian, who attacked Smollett in the preface of his *Life of William Augustus Duke of Cumberland* (London, 1766), and in other publications.

[48] *The Autobiography of Dr. Alexander Carlyle of Inveresk*, ed. John Hill Burton (London and Edinburgh, 1910), pp. 198-99.

[49] *The Works of Tobias Smollett, M.D.*, ed. Moore, I, cxvii.

forth by Professor William Richardson of Glasgow in 1801, as follows:

> Some gentlemen having met at a tavern, were amusing themselves before supper with a game at cards; while Smollet, not chusing to play, sat down to write. One of the company, who also was nominated by him afterwards to be one of his trustees, [Thomas Bontein] observing his earnestness, and supposing he was writing verses, asked him if it was not so. He accordingly read them the first sketch of his Tears of Scotland, consisting only of six stanzas: and on their remarking that the termination of the poem, being too strongly expressed, might give offense to persons whose political opinions were different, he sat down, without replying, and, with an air of great indignation, subjoined the concluding stanza.[50]

The final stanza vibrates with Smollett's personal independence and fervor for Scotland:

> While the warm blood bedews my veins,
> And unimpair'd remembrance reigns,
> Resentment of my country's fate,
> Within my filial breast shall beat;
> And, spite of her insulting foe,
> My sympathizing verse shall flow:
> "Mourn, hapless Caledonia, mourn
> Thy banish'd peace, thy laurels torn."

This poem soon came to the attention of Smollett's friends and the larger London public. Just when it first saw print is debatable: probably it preceded *Advice*. Smollett wrote Carlyle early in 1747: "If I had an opportunity, I would send you . . . a Ballad set to Musick under the name of the Tears of Scotland a Performance very well received at London as I hope it will be in your Country which gave rise to it—the truth is I have a Paternal concern for that and the Satires above mentioned."[51] That "The Tears of Scotland" was first published, as Thomas Seccombe and Professor Buck suggested, under the title, "The Groans of Scotland" is an assumption no longer tenable.[52]

[50] See William Richardson, A.M., *The Maid of Lochlin: A Lyrical Drama with Legendary Odes, and Other Poems* (London, 1801), pp. 122-23; also Anderson, *Life*, 4th ed. (Edinburgh, 1803), pp. 29ff.

[51] Quoted "New Smollett Letters," *TLS*, July 24, 1943.

[52] "The Groans of Scotland" was advertised in the *Gentleman's Magazine*, XVI (July 1746), 388. In *The General Advertiser* (July 16, 1746) appeared its expanded title: *The Groans of Scotland, or the Lamentations of the Ancient Genius of Caledonia for the Miseries of that Country . . . Printed for M. Cooper, at the Globe in Paternoster-Row. This day is Published. Price 6 d.* In the British Museum Catalogue (Vol.

"The Tears of Scotland" was soon married to music. John New-
bery in his *Art of Poetry on a New Plan* (London, 1762, I, 76)
recorded that it "was set to music by Mr. Oswald just after the
late rebellion." By 1746 James Oswald was a well-known musician in London. According to good authority[53] he left Edinburgh
for London in 1741, and was associated with John Simpson in a
music shop near St. Martin's Church. During the 1740's there
flourished the Society of the Temple of Apollo, attended probably
by Oswald, Charles Burney, Capt. John Reid, the Earl of Kelly,
Mallett, and Thomson. Smollett could not have missed knowing
this group, composed chiefly of Scots, who were so closely associated in that period. By 1747 Smollett was in touch with Oswald,
as is clear from his (Smollett's) correspondence with Carlyle.[54]
Oswald was patronized by Frederick, Prince of Wales, and in 1761
became Chamber Composer to his Majesty. He was an inventor,[55]
a pleasing musician, and a prolific composer, much of whose work,
marked by refinement and charming simplicity, survives in eighteenth-century English and Scottish magazines in the music collections of the British Museum and of the National Library of
Scotland. Among his works is a pleasing air[56] for Collins' imperish-
able "Ode Written in 1746," also occasioned by Culloden. Oswald
eventually set to music at least four of Smollett's lyrics.[57] Just
when "The Tears of Scotland" first appeared with music is not

---

88, p. 160), the same item is listed: "The Groans of Scotland; or, the lamentations of
the antient genius of Caledonia for the miseries of that country. pp. 24. For M.
Cooper: London, 1746. 8º." Surely this had no connection with Smollett's "Tears of
Scotland."

[53] See the article on James Oswald by Frank Kitson in Grove's *Dictionary of Music
and Musicians* (London, 1927), III, 778; and also an essay by Kitson in *The Musical
Antiquary*, II (1910-1911), 34-41.

[54] "New Smollett Letters," *TLS*, July 24, 1943.

[55] Musicians may be interested in this curious notice from *The General Advertiser*
(October 29, 1751): "By Authority This Day is Published Aeolus's Harp—A new-
invented musical instrument, which is played by the wind, as described by Mr. Thomson, in his *Castle of Indolence*. Sold only by the Inventor, J. Oswald, at his music-shop
in St. Martin's church-yard." Thomson described Oswald's harp in *The Castle of Indolence*, Canto I, stanza 40.

[56] This is found in *The Musical Magazine by Mr. Oswald and other celebrated
Masters* (London [1761-2?]), in Br. Mus., E. 1747 a, p. 60.

[57] See my article, "Smollett's Verses and their Musical Settings in the Eighteenth
Century," in *MLN*, XLVI (1931), 224ff. See also the recent and important article
by Mr. Otto Erich Deutsch, "Poetry Preserved in Music. Bibliographical Notes on
Smollett and Oswald, Handel and Haydn," in MLN, LXIII (February, 1948), pp.
73ff.

known, but the earliest reference is the following notice in the
General Advertiser (December 3, 1746):

> This Day is published Price 1 s. The Land of Cakes Book the First.
> Containing Six Songs set to Musick in the true Scots Taste. To which is
> added, The Tears of Scotland. Printed for R. Williams, and sold by
> Mr. Oswald in St. Martin's Church-Yard; J. Newberry in St. Paul's
> Churchyard; and W. Owen, next Door to the Devil-Tavern, Temple-
> Bar.

It seems very likely that this publication presented Oswald's music
for the first time. There are, indeed, two later appearances of Oswald's music,[58] and his composition in E Minor, with its simple but
effective themes, shifting occasionally into major strains, is not unworthy of the spirit of Smollett's poem.

Another musical setting for "The Tears of Scotland" was composed at an uncertain date during the eighteenth century by Allan
Masterton. The sheet bears the following title: "Mourn, Hapless
Caledonia, Mourn Written upon the Battle of Culloden by Tobias
Smollett Air—The Tears of Caledonia,—composed for this work
by Allan Masterton, Edinburgh."[59] This composition in D Minor
is inferior to Oswald's.

In 1746, Smollett was proud of the success of "The Tears of
Scotland." Its popular reception warmed his heart in the days of
his humble residence in Chapel Street, when he was getting no-
where with *The Regicide*, when he was perhaps disillusioned over
his medical practice, and when he was polishing the satirical couplets of *Advice*; it was good news to report to Anne Smollett. As
the years passed, he undoubtedly continued to cherish it. Hence we
can imagine his hot anger when his former friend Wilkes sneered
at its vogue among the Scots in 1762, in the *North Briton*, No. 6.

Advice and *Reproof*

Advice, the first example of Smollett's satirical writing, was
printed for M. Cooper, at The Globe in Pater-noster Row, and

---

[58] See Oswald's *The Caledonian Pocket Companion Containing a favourite Collection of Scotch Tunes with Variations for the German Flute or Violin.* Bk. IV. London.
Printed for the Author and sold at his Musick Shop in St. Martin's Church Yard in
the Strand. (Date conjectured in the Br. Mus. Cat. 1750-1760) Br. Mus., E. 1290
(Bk. IV, p. 14). See also *English Songs*, Br. Mus., I. 530, p. 100 [London, 1750].
[59] Br. Mus., G. 370, *Scotish Airs*—Pleyel (Set 4, No. 87), ed. G. Thomson, Edinburgh.

was available to the public in early September 1746.[60] The following January,[61] *Reproof* appeared as a sequel. These verse satires have more biographical significance than has been shown hitherto, although as poetry they do not possess outstanding literary merit. At the moment it is not our purpose to indulge in any criticism of them as literature, but rather to stress briefly their great indebtedness in purpose, content, and method, to the later satires of Pope. We refer to *The Epistle to Dr. Arbuthnot*, the *Satires, Epistles, and Odes of Horace Imitated*, *The Satires of Dr. John Donne . . . Versified*, and *The Epilogue to the Satires*. The last in this list, in particular, seems to have been Smollett's model for *Advice*, and for *Reproof*: these poems are remarkably similar to Pope's in their general satiric content; in their attack on specific persons; and in their device[62] of developing their points through a dialogue between the poet and his friend. In fact the general tone of Smollett's satires is very close to Pope's. What could be more natural than that young Smollett should have taken as his model the author of the *Dunciad*, who had died in 1744?

The general aims of Smollett, namely, to expound the hard lot of the poet, to attack vice and vicious or silly persons, and to distribute a few compliments, were precisely the purposes of Pope, whose note at the end of Dialogue II of *Epilogue to the Satires* (1738) is extremely revealing in helping us understand Smollett's own attitude. In his note, Pope declared: "This was the last poem of the kind printed by our author, with a resolution to publish no more; but to enter thus, in the most plain and solemn manner he could, a sort of PROTEST against that insuperable corruption and depravity of manners, which he had been so unhappy as to live to see. Could he have hoped to have amended any, he had continued these attacks; but bad men were grown so shameless and so powerful, that Ridicule was become as unsafe as it was ineffectual. The Poem raised him, as he knew it would, some enemies; but he had reason to be satisfied with the approbation of good men, and the testimony of his own conscience."[63] This realistic confession must

---

[60] It was announced in the *General Advertiser*, September 4, as "This day . . . published," Price 1 shilling.

[61] *Reproof* was announced in the *General Advertiser*, January 14, 1746-7, as printed for W. Owen, at Homer's Head near Temple-Bar in Fleet Street, and M. Cooper.

[62] There were, of course, satires other than Pope's which employed this convention.

[63] *The Complete Poetical Works of Alexander Pope* (Student's Cambridge Edition) [1903], pp. 660-61.

be kept in mind in any attempt to understand Smollett's motives in *Advice* and *Reproof*.

The "insuperable corruption and depravity of manners," as Pope expressed it, of the 1730's and 1740's is a fact abundantly proved by social historians of the period, and Smollett, as a sharp observer, and as a medical practitioner, was peculiarly aware of them. His violent indignation against all forms of evil, small or great, was not necessarily or primarily motivated by petty personal considerations. In reading *Advice*, one detects, along with a rather irritable and self-conscious personal indignation, and combined with a certain strain of melancholy (as in Johnson's *London*), a definite note of fearless moral fervor, and of the idealization of his personal conscience and honor. Certain lines toward the end of *Advice* prove this, where the Poet declared:

> Two things I dread, my conscience, and the law.

And when the Friend suggests that conscience is a meaningless myth, the Poet exclaims:

> Hail, sacred power: my glory and my guide!
> Fair source of mental peace, whate'er betide;
> Safe in thy shelter, let disaster roll
> Eternal hurricanes around my soul;
> My soul serene amidst the storms shall reign,
> And smile to see their fury burst in vain!

These lines (and the two satires in general) reveal Smollett's essential idealism and humanitarian desire to amend society. Amendment necessitated attack, and attack utilized the weapon of satire, which, in turn, involved libel, even personal libel. Such was Smollett's formula, one which was worked out on every hand.

Advice and *Reproof* contain a mixed group of figures, a representative rogues' gallery of the time, but along with the rascals, certain shining exceptions are introduced by way of contrast, or, shall we say, to prove the general rule of depravity and corruption. All together, Smollett pointed at some fifty individuals, a generous number, considering the brevity of the poems. Some of them are treated in a cursory, conventional way; others receive a more personal judgment. Some of them Smollett had heard of or read about; others he knew at first hand. To gaze briefly at them through Smollett's eyes is to sense much of his character and capacity for social criticism as he began his literary career. To start with, we will consider the extended list of characters whom he disliked or loathed.

Among the miscellaneous figures obscured by time is one H——[64] (*Advice*, l. 7)[65] who so scrupulously avoided his wife; and a "prostrate sycophant" who has risen a L-d,[66] (*Advice*, l. 88), whose identity is unknown: Smollett's note condemned him as this "child of dirt (to use a great author's[67] expression)" who "has arrived at the power of insulting his betters every day." Smollett also pointed at the perverted "Brush" Warren (*Advice*, l. 90) and at a homosexual named Chardin (*Advice*, l. 103). In the same group is Bubo (*Advice*, l. 117), a name which summoned up Bubb Dodington in the minds of Smollett's readers familiar with Pope. Dodington, as Fielding's patron by 1739, may have antagonized Smollett. Another rascal whose word "no mortal credits" is Curio (*Advice*, l. 119), surely William Pulteney, the Earl of Bath, satirized so frequently by Sir Charles Hanbury Williams, and also by Akenside in his *An Epistle to Curio*, 1744. In the first edition of *Advice*, Smollett grouped together three nasty creatures (F-nt-n, Sh-lly, and C-pe) but deleted the line later. Of these the last was Sir John Cope, whom he savagely attacked in both poems. Among this miscellaneous group is Williamson, Deputy Lieutenant-Governor of the Tower of London,[68] whom Smollett branded as "inhuman."

To add variety to his list of rascals, Smollett in *Reproof* (ll. 126-29), included "Rapacious Gideon"; "Insatiate Lascelles and the fiend Vanneck"; and "Griping Jasper."[69] Of these, Sampson Gideon,[70] a Jewish magnate, and friend and adviser of Robert Walpole, was a notorious figure satirized repeatedly by writers and cartoonists. The "fiend Vanneck" was Sir Joshua Vanneck,[71] promi-

---

[64] Printed "H - - me" in the first edition.

[65] My line-references follow the text of *Advice* and *Reproof* in *The Works of Tobias Smollett*, ed. W. E. Henley, 12 vols. (Westminster and New York, 1899-1901), XII, 3ff.

[66] Printed "L-yd" in the first edition.

[67] See Pope's *Epistle to Dr. Arbuthnot*, l. 310, where Pope called Lord Hervey a "painted child of dirt, that stinks and stings."

[68] Williamson died in November 1747. See *London Magazine*, XVI (1747), p. 532.

[69] Printed as "G--d--n, L--sc--s, V--n--k, and J--p--r" in the first edition.

[70] For Gideon, see Dr. H. R. S. Van Der Veen, *Jewish Characters in Eighteenth Century English Fiction and Drama* (Groningen, Batavia, 1935), pp. 134, 237.

[71] For Sir Joshua Vanneck, see L. B. Namier, *The Structure of Politics at the Accession of George III*, 2 vols. (London, 1929), *passim*.

nent London financier. Lascelles,[72] according to Smollett's note, was the third in a "triumvirate of contractors" who were fleecing England. "Griping" Jasper remains a forgotten usurer.[73] Better known, however, was another miser glanced at in *Reproof* (l. 143):

> At Peter's obsequies I sung no dirge.

In the first edition Smollett identified Peter as "Peter W-t-rs, Esq. whose character is too well-known to need description." The person attacked by Smollett, in spite of the final "s" in W-t-rs, was surely the well publicized Peter Walter of Stalbridge Park,[74] the Peter Pounce of Fielding's *Joseph Andrews*, land-stewart of the Duke of Newcastle, and the butt of Sir Charles Hanbury Williams' "Peter and My Lord Quidam." It was this notorious miser Walter, then, who died in 1745, to whom Smollett referred, rather than to Waters.[75]

In the gallery of rascals we next confront the medical quack, Dr. Thomas Thompson,[76] employed by Fielding and patronized by Dodington. Smollett was on very safe ground here in his irony:

> From Mead to Th--p--n shifts the palm at once,
> A medling, prating, blund'ring, busy dunce!
>
> (REPROOF, ll. 187-88)

And his implied praise of Mead, the very famous Dr. Richard Mead, was obviously a conventional gesture. Later, in his *Essay on the External Use of Water*,[77] Smollett cited Mead's views with approval.

In another corner of Smollett's exhibit are three military celebrities, dangerous game of course, but not out of the range of his fearless and rash satire. His chief onslaught was against Sir John Cope, attacked in both poems (*Advice*, ll. 8, 29 and *Reproof*, ll. 33ff.). In deriding Cope's cowardly flight at Prestonpans, and in

[72] I am unable to provide any information about Lascelles.

[73] In his footnote, Smollett declared that Jasper loaned money at 50 per cent. This Jasper was perhaps "Edw. Jasper of Tower-Hill Esq; and Agent," who died in August 1749. See *Gentleman's Magazine*, XIX (1749), 380.

[74] For an account of Peter Walter, see Fielding's *Joseph Andrews*, ed. J. Paul De Castro (London, 1929), p. 354.

[75] The footnote reads *Peter Waters* in *The Miscellaneous Works of Tobias Smollett, M.D.*, 6 vols. (Edinburgh, 1790), III, 507, and in later editions, including Anderson's and Henley's. This is obviously an error.

[76] See Lloyd Sanders, *Patron and Place-Hunter: A Study of George Bubb Dodington, Lord Melcombe* (London, 1919), pp. 174-76.

[77] See *An Essay on the External Use of Water*, ed. Claude E. Jones (Baltimore, 1935), p. 63.

the parody of his military trial, Smollett merely echoed wide-spread ridicule, but his sensational reference to Cope's homosexual practice was extreme, even in the libelous satire of that time. It may be explained as the product of Smollett's medical point of view, but its questionable taste cannot be wholly extenuated. Nevertheless Smollett in *Roderick Random* (Chapter 51), reprinted with courage, sincerity, and relevance lines on sexual perversion (*Advice*, ll. 91ff.), a move which frees him from the charge of being merely and cheaply sensational. Smollett's other allusions to army figures are brief but trenchant. The identity of the cowardly general "who sought the bosom of the wood" at Dettingen (*Advice*, ll. 242ff.), is uncertain. In *Reproof*, however, the exposé of "lewd" Tyrawley[78] (l. 185), was clear and doubtless acceptable. Here, Smollett had been anticipated by Pope.[79] Finally in the same poem (l. 186), two other generals were singled out—one for praise and one for blame, in an ironically twisted line:

> Gives Hawley praise, and Ingoldsby disgrace.

General Hawley had behaved badly in skirmishes preceding the battle of Culloden, according to Smollett's *History*,[80] whereas Brigadier General Ingoldsby won deserved honors at Fontenoy.

The beginnings of Smollett's long-continued and widening attacks on corrupt or inane politicians are exemplified in *Advice* and *Reproof*. His political satire is quite in the manner of Pope's later work and carries considerable ironical sting, as in the following:

> FRIEND
> Why sleeps the muse?—Is there no room for praise,
> When such bright names in constellation blaze?
> When sage Newcastle, abstinently great,
> Neglects his food to cater for the state;
> And Grafton, tow'ring Atlas of the throne,

---

[78] Printed T-r- - w-y in the first edition. The licentiousness of James O'Hara, Lord Kilmaine and second Lord Tyrawley, was notorious. In 1745 he commanded various troops of life-guards in London. See *DNB*.

[79] See Pope's "The Sixth Epistle of the First Book of Horace," ll. 120-21.

[80] Smollett furnished caustic comment on General Hawley in his *Complete History of England*, IV (1758), p. 670: "General Hawley, who had boasted that, with two regiments of dragoons, he would drive the rebel army from one end of the kingdom to the other, incurred abundance of censure for the disposition he made, as well as for his conduct before and after the action; but he found means to vindicate himself to the satisfaction of his sovereign. Nevertheless it was judged necessary that the army in Scotland should be commanded by a general in whom the soldiers might have some confidence; and the Duke of Cumberland was chosen for this purpose."

> So well rewards a genius like his own:
> Granville and Bath illustrious, need I name
> For sober dignity and spotless fame;
> Or Pitt th' unshaken Abdiel yet unsung:
> Thy candour, Chomdly! and thy truth, O Yonge!

> POET
> Th' advice is good; the question only, whether
> These names and virtues ever dwelt together?
> (ADVICE, ll. 13-24)

The Friend's lines, even without Smollett's footnotes, were pure irony to readers of 1746. Thomas Holles, Duke of Newcastle, rarely deviated into wisdom; and Charles Fitzroy, the second Duke of Grafton, as Lord Chamberlain, and Secretary of State, did not distinguish himself sufficiently to be entered in the *Dictionary of National Biography*, although as Smollett explained in his note, "he conferred the laureat" on Colley Cibber, Esq. "a delectable bard." John Carteret, Earl of Granville in 1744, a thoroughly unprincipled politician, was in 1744 the leader of The Drunken Administration,[81] and in February 1746, he and William Pulteney, Earl of Bath, tried in vain for four days to form an administration. In fact, both Bath and Granville were objects of public derision. Smollett's ironical characterization of Pitt as the "unshaken Abdiel" reflects Pitt's about-face in 1746,[82] resulting in sharp popular resentment, which seems also to have been directed against the dubious "candour" of George, third Earl of Cholmondeley, son-in-law of Robert Walpole, recently retired. And the biting words, "thy truth, O Yonge," were applied to Sir William Yonge, that most notorious liar of the day, dubbed "Stinking Yonge" by His Majesty the King. The retirement of Walpole, just mentioned, was, I believe, sneered at by Smollett in *Advice* (ll. 35ff.), for Atticus (l. 35) must have suggested at once to sophisticated readers "Pomponius Atticus," Walpole's pseudonym as a member of the Political Club,[83] the speeches of whose

---

[81] See the account of Granville in *DNB*.

[82] Pitt's change of policy is summed up as follows: "Pitt himself unblushingly advocated the measures he had before denounced. A ballad 'The unembarrassed Countenance' satirized the celerity of his conversion." Quoted from I. S. Leadam, *The History of England from the Accession of Ann to the Death of George II* (London, 1909), p. 412 in *The Political History of England*, eds. Hunt and Poole, Vol. IX.

[83] For a list of the "Characters assumed by the Gentlemen of the Political Club," see *The London Magazine*, 1743, verso of the title page.

members received wide publicity. Such were the "bright names" in the contemporaneous political constellation. In general, Smollett's political satire, which shows his keen dislike of Walpole and his supporters, was well aimed and shrewdly calculated for the applause of the anti-Walpole group.

Continuing our scrutiny of the lengthening rogues' gallery, we turn finally to a few satirical silhouettes of literary, musical, and theatrical persons. Of these some are well-known; others lie buried in obscurity. Smollett's slap at Colley Cibber, that "delectable bard," has been included above. In the concluding lines of *Reproof* there is a note of disdain for mere libelers and also for timid, vacillating, crop-eared critics, those "of smaller fry," as Smollett put it, illustrated by Clark, Banks, Barrowby and Chitty, sad creatures no longer recognizable. It is interesting, moreover, that in the first printing of *Reproof*, one M--k--n occupied the space in the line later filled by Clark and Banks. M--k--n must have signified Charles Macklin, the dramatist, whose *King Henry VII* was played in January 1746, to the annoyance of Smollett, whose *Regicide* was being postponed. Among contemporaneous minor poets Lockman[84] was pointed at, first as a failure (*Advice*, l. 62), and later (*Reproof*, l. 108), as a poet whose work resembled, in its "cloying mediocrity," a song by Hanbury—that is, one must assume, a song by Sir Charles Hanbury-Williams. A colorful, literary jack-of-all-trades of the 1740's was Guthrie[85] whose political snarling "for the public weal" irritated Smollett (*Advice*, ll. 201-2). His original footnote on Guthrie labeled him as a "political writer noted for gall," but this was deleted when *Advice* and *Reproof* were published together in 1748, a fact which suggests that Smollett came to like Guthrie better. The eccentric appearance and behavior of Guthrie, vividly described by Carlyle, who met him in 1746,[86] could not have escaped Smollett's sharp eye.

Climaxing the literary attacks in his first satires is an extremely

---

[84] Surely John Lockman, who wrote many ephemeral odes and occasional verses. He lived until 1771, but I know of no personal association between him and Smollett.

[85] William Guthrie (1708-1770). See *DNB*. Information about Guthrie in the 1740's is very slight. He seems to have championed the actors in the squabble between Fleetwood and the actors' league in 1743, according to a statement in the memoir of Garrick in *The Private Correspondence of David Garrick*, 2 vols. (London, 1831), I, xi-xii.

[86] *The Autobiography of Alexander Carlyle*, ed. J. H. Burton (London and Edinburgh, 1910), pp. 200-201.

angry and personal libel on John Rich, that great promoter of pantomime, who rejected Smollett's *Regicide* in the fall of 1746. Shortly after that, no doubt, Smollett wrote the following:

> Fraught with the spirit of a Gothic monk,
> Let Rich,[87] with dullness and devotion drunk,
> Enjoy the peal so barbarous and loud,
> While his brain spues new monsters to the crowd;
> I see with joy the vaticide[88] deplore
> An hell-denouncing priest and sov'reign whore.
>
> (REPROOF, ll. 167-72)

As the full import of this passage has never been expounded, its devastating meaning should be made clear. Rich, Smollett declares, is naturally a dullard, and, besides, drunk with devotion— that is to say, intoxicated by the Methodist doctrines of Mrs. Rich.[89] And, he continues, it is a source of joy to observe Rich distressed by two matters: (1) a Methodist priest (evangelist) denouncing hell, i.e. proclaiming hell-fire and (2) his sovereign whore, i.e. his tyrannical wife. This reading is confirmed only too well by Smollett's later account of "Mr. Vandal" [Rich], in *Roderick Random* (Chapter 63): "I have been since informed, that the poor man's head, which was not naturally very clear, had been disordered with superstition, and that he laboured under the tyranny of a wife, and the terrors of hell-fire, at the same time." In this passage from the novel there is an assumed air of pitying condescension, but only fury is reflected in the verse attack on "Lun" Rich and Mrs. Rich. This libel illustrates Smollett's amazing temper, a central characteristic in him, and a flaw which led him into repeated troubles as a man and an author.

Having inspected in *Advice* and *Reproof* the London figures whom Smollett hated, it is now proper to focus briefly on certain personalities whom he honored, admired, or championed. The only poet eulogized in the satires was Pope, whose "immortal strain" is celebrated in *Reproof* (l. 114). Pope's friend, Sir Richard Temple, Viscount Cobham, Walpole's opponent, is praised as "soaring Cobham" (*Reproof*, l. 122). Smollett's "tributary lay" to Chesterfield (*Reproof*, ll. 109ff.) was prompted, no doubt, by his as-

---

[87] "R---ch" in the first edition.
[88] This word vaticide was applied to James Lacy in the "Preface" to *The Regicide*. (First edition, p. [iii]). Here it indicates Rich.
[89] See the account of John Rich in *DNB*.

sistance with *The Regicide,* but impersonal considerations may have counted: there is much praise of Chesterfield's politics in Smollett's *History.* There is genuine warmth in the tribute to the humanitarian, Sir John Barnard,[90] another opponent of Walpole:

> Not ev'n the pleasing task is left, to raise
> A grateful monument to Barnard's praise;
> Else should the venerable patriot stand
> Th' unshaken pillar of a sinking land.
>
> (REPROOF, ll. 115-18)

Other recipients of Smollett's compliments were the opera singer, Giulia Frasi,[91] and Handel, although the former received only implied approval. The lines to Handel are more significant because of his connection with Smollett's *Alceste*:

> Again shall Handel raise his laurell'd brow,
> Again shall Harmony with rapture glow!
>
> (ADVICE, ll. 183-84)

And, for all we know, Smollett, who had a musical ear, may have truly admired Handel's music, apart from any personal like or dislike. In his satirical footnote (*Advice,* l. 187) on the ladies of quality who exploited the mimic Russell,[92] Smollett's attitude was clearly that of one who sympathized with Handel's sad struggle against the vogue of pantomime in the 1740's.

Smollett's warmest praise was given to Daniel MacKercher, Esq., the "melting Scot," who, according to Smollett's note, was a

[90] For Sir John Barnard (1685-1764), alderman, Mayor, and humanitarian, see *DNB.* In May 1747 the London citizens erected his statue on the Royal Exchange. Plans for this were in progress, presumably, when Smollett was composing *Reproof.* It is worth noting that Barnard had been a doughty opponent of Robert Walpole.

[91] Giulia Frasi arrived in London in 1743 with Signora Galli. Her first appearance in Handel's oratorios was in 1749. Charles Burney, who knew her in the 1740's, described her as "young and interesting in person, with a sweet and clear voice, and a smooth and chaste style of singing, which though unimpassioned, pleased natural ears, and escaped the censure of critics." See Charles Burney, *A General History of Music,* ed. Frank Mercer, 2 vols. (New York, Harcourt and Brace, n.d.), II, 841. For anecdotes of Burney, Frasi, and Handel, see Victor Schoelcher, *The Life of Handel* (London, ca. 1857), p. 374. See also Grove's *Dictionary of Music and Musicians.*

[92] Smollett's indignation over the tragic fate of the mimic Russell is highly characteristic of him. Judging from his notes on Russell in the first and later editions of *Advice,* this unfortunate person died in Bedlam between 1746 and 1748. I have found no obituary of Russell. He was the subject of a line or two in Horace Walpole's letter to Mann, written March 29, 1745:

> One Russel [*sic*], a mimic, has a puppet show to ridicule operas; I hear very dull, not to mention its being twenty years too late: it consists of three acts, with foolish Italian songs burlesqued in Italian.

See *Letters of Horace Walpole,* ed. Toynbee, 16 vols. (Oxford, 1904), II, 82.

"man of such primitive simplicity, that he may be said to have exceeded the scripture injunction, by not only parting with his cloak and coat, but with his shirt also, to relieve a brother in distress."[93] The tone of this compliment suggests that Smollett knew Mac-Kercher well by the time the poem was composed, presumably in late 1746, and in all probability he had met MacKercher some years before. MacKercher was, in fact, a much more important person than has hitherto been indicated.[94] By 1742 he was not only a philanthropic lawyer championing the unfortunate James Annesley, but he had been since its foundation in 1735 an active member of The Society for the Encouragement of Learning,[95] which included among its members such important figures as Dr. Mead; Duncan Forbes; Andrew Mitchell, Under-Secretary for Scotland and a distant relative of Smollett; the poet Thomson; Lord Elibank; and Dr. James Douglas. Smollett may well have met Mac-Kercher in 1739, or after 1742, through the offices of Mitchell or Dr. James Douglas. In praising him in *Reproof*, therefore, Smollett was not complimenting an obscure, publicity-seeking, Quixotic lawyer, but a very well-known London figure. Further suggestions as to Smollett's probable indebtedness to MacKercher will be advanced later in connection with an examination of the biographical account of him in *Peregrine Pickle*.

These complimentary portraits, where Smollett brought "fair Virtue's triumphs to the view"[96] are heavily outnumbered by the vice-ridden persons so angrily attacked. Composed in the tradition of Juvenal, the poems are charged with rankling anger and reckless spleen. In both of them, as Smollett's biographers, Moore and Anderson noted, he did his best to offend some of the most powerful personages in London, and no doubt created formidable enemies. In the spring of 1747 Smollett wrote to Carlyle: "If I had an opportunity, I would send you . . . Two Satires called Advice and Reproof, which made some noise here."[97] Just where the loud-

---

[93] Smollett's note to *Reproof*, l. 122.

[94] The most complete account of Daniel MacKercher is probably that by Andrew Lang in *The Annesley Case*, in the series of Notable English Trials (Edinburgh and London, [1912]), pp. 11-13. See also H. S. Buck's *A Study in Smollett, passim*, for MacKercher's connections with *Peregrine Pickle*.

[95] For MacKercher's activities in the Society, see British Museum Add., MSS 6184, 6185-6192. MacKercher was a charter member and attended annual meetings in 1736, 1739, 1740, 1741, 1742, 1744, and 1746, the final meeting of the Society.

[96] Quoted from *Reproof*, l. 120.

[97] "New Smollett Letters," *TLS*, July 24, 1943.

est explosions occurred is not known. Neither are there available records of how widely each poem was read when published. Smollett, at any rate, cherished them enough to make a few minor revisions before they again appeared in print (this time together) in March 1748.

Advice impressed Anderson as possessing "much poetical merit," but the modern reader finds it disappointing as literature. The same is true for *Reproof*. Yet these poems contribute not a little to our understanding of what young Smollett, aged twenty-five, really felt about himself and his prospects while in Chapel Street, struggling to build up income and reputation. His wife, who, before 1747, must have been in Jamaica, was presumably sending him an occasional sum to assist him. It is pretty certain that Smollett, like the "Poet" in his poems, was depressed by comparative poverty. It is also evident that his defiant spirit of personal independence, his pride, and his idealism, as well as his scorn of corrupt and venal society are all expressed in his satires. Having been exposed to the raw and naked brutalities of life in the navy, he was now outraged by the refined vices of London. Yet he was "too coy to flatter, and too proud to serve." And despite fits of spleen, depression, and misanthropy, he clung fast, like his "Poet" in *Advice*, to conscience.

Thus Smollett's uncompromising moral attitude makes his first poems more than mere literary exercises. In them burned a fiery pride and moral independence to which he gave the finest expression in his *Ode to Independence*, published after his death.

CHAPTER IV

Friendships and Ventures in Opera and Drama, 1747-1750

FOR Smollett the years 1747-1750 were exciting and memorable, marked by varied literary ventures, by the birth of his only child, by significant shifts in residence, by stimulating travel, and by an ever-increasing circle of acquaintances and friends.

In 1747 presumably, Anne Smollett sailed from Jamaica to London,[1] and in Chapel Street or in Beaufort Street the Smolletts' only child, Elizabeth,[2] was born in 1747 or 1748. In Chapel Street, May Fair, near Dean Street and Audley Street, Smollett lived during 1746, 1747, and a part of 1748, in a rental of £8 a year. Here resided the notorious Lord Tyrawley, satirized in *Reproof*. Here, too, dwelt in the latter half of 1747 one John Lewis, probably the same "John Lewis Bookbinder alias Strap" to whom Smollett referred years later when they were again neighbors in Chelsea.

Sometime in 1748,[3] the Smolletts left their small rental in May Fair to live in a more spacious place in Beaufort Street, St. Clement Danes, Savoy Ward, close to the site occupied today by the Savoy Hotel, near the Thames. Smollett's letter to Hayman, May 11, 1750, was written at Beaufort Buildings.[4] For this move two reasons may be suggested: first, the birth of Elizabeth; and second, the financial returns from *Roderick Random*, published in January 1748. In one of the most expensive rentals in Beaufort Street, off

---

[1] Oliphant Smeaton in his *Tobias Smollett* (p. 54), wrote that Anne arrived during "the publication of the second part of his Satires." This would have been in January 1747. Smeaton cited no source of his information.

[2] For Elizabeth Smollett, see my essay, "Elizabeth Smollett, Daughter of Tobias Smollett," in *RES*, VIII (1932), 312-15.

[3] The Rate Book for St. Clement Danes for 1748 shows that there was on Beaufort Street a £45 rental vacant all that year. It is possible that Smollett, having entered late in the year, was not assessed at the regular time, and if so, his name would have appeared in a supplementary list usually appended at the end of the Rate Book. No such list appears in the book for 1748.

[4] A part of Beaufort (or Beaufort's) Buildings was located in the Strand. See *London and its Environs Described*, 6 vols. (London, 1761), Vol. I.

the Strand, near Somerset House, Smollett paid his annual rent of
£45 in 1749 and 1750, as is recorded in the Rate Books.

This is the entry for 1749:

[£]   45 Smollett   15/15/15/15/[5]

The entry for 1750 appears as follows:

[£] 45 Tho Arne* - .. 15 ..- .. 15 ..- .. 18 .. 9 .. 18 .. 9[6]

It is surprising to find in this official record the nickname, Toby,
which Smollett detested and which his enemies exploited in print.
The Thomas Arne, listed above, who moved into the rental after
the Smolletts left, was presumably the well-known musician of
that name. The record also shows that Smollett paid his rate
through an uncertain portion of 1750. For about two years, then,
Smollett lived close by the great pulsing life in the Strand, with its
crowded coffeehouses and taverns. Not far away stood the Covent
Garden and the Drury Lane Theatres. Farther east in old Boswell
Court between Carey Street and Butcher Row, Henry Fielding
had lived in a rental ranging from £45 to £55 from 1744-1747.[7] To
these busy scenes and their society Smollett was certainly no
stranger, addicted, as he confessed himself in 1759 to have been, to
the pleasures of tavern society.[8] In the summer of 1750, Smollett
moved his family to the country air of Old Chelsea, probably just
before he (and perhaps Mrs. Smollett) visited Paris.[9] About this
time, moreover, he first hired his devoted servant, Alexander Tolloush, who was to remain with him for at least twelve years.[10]

Smollett's last London residences—Chapel Street, and Beaufort
Street—were in areas frequented in the mid-eighteenth century by
well-to-do, fashionable citizens. Both of these streets were very
accessible to sections where books and plays were produced and dis-
cussed, favorable centers in which to carry on medical practice, and
so located that Smollett, with his ambitions in literature as well as

* Written above "Toby Smollett" crossed out in original.

[5] Rate Book 160 (Poor Tax) for St. Clement Danes, Savoy Ward, Beaufort Street.
I am indebted to the courteous assistance of the custodian of the Rate Books in the
Record Department at the City Hall, Westminster.

[6] Rate Book 161.

[7] See J. Paul DeCastro in *Notes and Queries*, 12 Ser., 1 (1916), 264-65.

[8] See "An Important Smollett Letter" in *RES*, XII (1936), 77.

[9] Oliphant Smeaton asserted that "Smollett and his wife paid a visit to Paris" in
1750. (*Tobias Smollett*, p. 66.) Moore (*Works*, I, cxxiii) recorded how he traveled
in the environs of Paris with Smollett in 1750, but he did not mention Mrs. Smollett.

[10] See my article, "Rex versus Smollett: More Data on the Smollett-Knowles Libel
Case," *MP*, XLI (1944), 223.

in medicine and with his unusual interest in people, had excellent opportunities to cultivate old acquaintances and to meet new ones.

With some of the leading actors, managers, and their patrons, Smollett had been closely associated during his attempts to stage *The Regicide*. In this group were Quin, Lord Chesterfield, Lord Lyttelton, Charles Fleetwood, James Lacy, John Rich, and Garrick. Some of these persons felt the edge of Smollett's satire in *Advice* and *Reproof*, and others were slashed by it in *Roderick Random*, the preface to *The Regicide*, and *Peregrine Pickle*. Garrick impressed Smollett in 1747 as being a "little rascal" given to "pitifull intrigues."[11] By October 1, 1749, Rich's vacillation over the *Alceste* drove Smollett to describe him to Carlyle as "an infatuated miscreant," a "compound of indolence, Worthlessness and folly."[12]

Among Smollett's acquaintances before 1750 were certain Scottish clergymen, headed by Alexander Carlyle of Inveresk, whose vivid accounts of Smollett in his remarkable *Autobiography*[13] date from Carlyle's first visit to London in April 1745. There, through a mutual friend, Robert Smith, "Jupiter" Carlyle first met Smollett, whereupon a cordial and prolonged correspondence resulted. In *Humphry Clinker*, Bramble declared that Carlyle's "humour and conversation inflamed [him] with a desire of being better acquainted with his person."[14]

Young Carlyle's clerical Scottish friends appealed to Smollett. One of these, the Rev. Robert Paton,[15] Smollett knew in London at an early period, for about March 1747, he wrote Carlyle: "Pray let me know if Robt. Panton [*sic*] be settled near you, who was a very honest fellow when I knew him in London, and of whose welfare I am desirous to hear."[16] In this same letter Smollett complimented the Rev. Dr. Robert Dick,[17] who, he declared, like "others of my acquaintance . . . with a great share of Learning and Taste,

[11] "New Smollett Letters" in *TLS*, July 24, 1943.

[12] *Ibid.*, July 31, 1943.

[13] *The Autobiography of Dr. Alexander Carlyle*, ed. John Hill Burton (London and Edinburgh, 1910), *passim*.

[14] *Humphry Clinker*, Letter of Bramble, Edinburgh, July 18.

[15] In Carlyle's *Autobiography* there appear to be references to two ministers named Robert Paton.

[16] "New Smollett Letters" in *TLS*, July 24, 1943.

[17] Identified in Harold W. Thompson's *The Anecdotes and Egotisms of Henry Mackenzie* (Oxford University Press, 1927), as Robert Dick (1722-1782) minister of Grayfriars and later of Trinity College Church, Edinburgh.

have of late undertaken the Ministerial Function."[18] When Carlyle's good friend the Rev. George Logan died, Smollett recalled him as an amiable young fellow.[19] In letters to Carlyle written in 1747 and in 1748 Smollett expressed his aversion to John Blair, whom Carlyle always enjoyed, though he admitted that Blair possessed a "petulant and wrangling humor" which caused him to be disliked by many, particularly by Smollett. John Blair, LL.D.,[20] a Scottish clergyman, was educated in Edinburgh and because of the success of his *Chronology* in 1753, rose rapidly to high secular and clerical honors. His was a very humble status, however, in London in the 1740's, when he succeeded that minor historian, Andrew Henderson,[21] as usher of a school in Hedge Lane. Though Blair, who saw something of Smollett at this time, was associated with Henderson, the latter, according to his own words "never spoke with" Smollett.[22] As a rival historian, however, Henderson expressed more than once his rancorous dislike of him.

Another friend of Carlyle from his college days was the Rev. John Home, minister at Athelstaneford by 1747 and destined to achieve fame through his *Douglas*. In the fall of 1749, Home, like Smollett a decade earlier, started for London with the manuscript of a tragedy called *Agis* in his pocket. With him he also carried Carlyle's letter of introduction to Smollett, the first person whom he saw upon arriving, in November. Extracts from Home's letters[23] to Carlyle are notable for the light they shed on Smollett at the end of 1749, just after his trip to France, Flanders, and Holland. On November 6, Home wrote to Carlyle: "I have seen nobody yet but Smollett, whom I like very well . . . I am a good deal disap-

---

[18] "New Smollett Letters," in *TLS*, July 24, 1943.

[19] *Ibid.*, July 31, 1943.

[20] For Dr. John Blair, Vicar of Hinckley, see the account in *DNB* and also *Bibliotheca Topographica Britannica*, ed. John Nichols, Vol. 7 (1790), pp. 189ff. and p. 240. In 1754 there appeared Blair's extraordinary volume, made up of magnificently engraved sheets, entitled *The Chronology and History of the World. From the Creation to the Year of Christ, 1753* (London, 1754).

[21] For Andrew Henderson see *DNB*, and an interesting note by "A.G." in *Notes and Queries*, 3 Ser. III (1863) 216. Henderson's slander on Smollett is found in the preface to his *Life of William Augustus Duke of Cumberland* (London, 1766), and in his *Second Letter to Samuel Johnson* [1775]. More information on Henderson is needed.

[22] Henderson's *Life of William Augustus Duke of Cumberland* (London, 1766), pp. 260 ff.

[23] See Henry Mackenzie, *The Works of John Home, Esq.*, 3 vols. (Edinburgh, 1822), I, 134, 137.

pointed at the mien of the English, which I think but poor. I observed it to Smollett after having walked at High-Mall,[24] who agreed with me." In a later letter to Carlyle, after various persons (including Smollett, no doubt) had read the *Agis*, Home wrote to Carlyle early in 1750 as follows: "Your friend Smollett, who has a thousand good, nay, the best qualities, and whom I love much more than he thinks I do, has got on Sunday last three hundred pounds for his *Mask*." Allowing something for the usual sentimentality of Home,[25] it is undeniable that he found in Smollett a kind host and a sincere friend. It is evident that Home was in the group visited by Smollett in Scotland a few years later (1753), for in March 1754, the latter wrote to Carlyle: "Tell Jack Hume I think he might find leisure to write me."[26] As will become evident later, their friendship continued after Home became famous and politically influential in London.

With other prominent Scotsmen in London at this period Smollett had definite associations. For example, there was the aged Lieutenant-General Joshua Guest, through whose assistance Smollett had sent parcels to Edinburgh prior to the General's death in October 1747.[27] Shortly after this date, Smollett wrote Carlyle that he knew not "how to convey" to him copies of *Advice* and *Reproof*, "General Guest being dead."[28] From this it seems that Smollett and the General, whose lodgings were on Brook Street,[29] near Smollett's home on Chapel Street, were close acquaintances.

At one time in the 1740's Smollett was friendly with Alexander

[24] Home presumably meant The Mall by St. James's Palace, or Pall Mall.

[25] In his *Autobiography* (year 1749) Carlyle wrote apropos of Home and his failure to bring *Agis* on the stage: "Home was enraged, but not discouraged. I had given him a letter to Smollett, with whom he contracted a sincere friendship, and he consoled himself for the neglect he met with by the warm approbation of the Doctor, and of John Blair and his friend Barrow. . . . I had several letters from him [Home] at that time which displayed the character he always maintained, which was a thorough contempt of his non-approvers, and a blind admiration of those who approved of his works, and gave him a good reception, whom he attached still more to him by the most caressing manners, and the sincere and fervent flattery of a lover. In all the periods of his long life his opinions of men and things were merely prejudices."

[26] "New Smollett Letters" in *TLS*, July 31, 1943.

[27] For Lieutenant-General Guest see *DNB*, and Joseph L. Chester, *The Marriage, Baptismal, and Burial Registers of the Collegiate Church or Abbey of St. Peter, Westminster* (London, 1876), pp. 373 and 381. Guest died aged eighty-seven; he and his wife were both buried in Westminster Abbey.

[28] "New Smollett Letters," *TLS*, July 24, 1943.

[29] Of the several Brook Streets, the one near Grosvenor Square and Chapel Street was probably that on which General Guest lived.

Leslie, 6th Lord Lindores: in the course of a letter to Carlyle, October 1, 1749, Smollett declared: "If I have any opportunity of being acquainted with Lady Lindore [sic], you may be sure I shall lay hold on the occasion and cultivate it accordingly: I was formerly well with my Lord, but our correspondence has been dropt some years—Your Scotch Nobility I have more than once found whimsical and inconstant in their friendships." The Lord Lindores referred to married Jean, daughter of Colin Campbell, commissioner of the customs, and died advanced in years at his house in St. James's Place in 1765.[30] He was an army captain in 1745, and rose to the rank of Major-General. From Smollett's letter it appears that he may have been assisted by Lord Lindores in the early 1740's. Whether he courted the good graces of Lady Lindores is not known; Carlyle supped with her in London in 1769.

Another Scottish nobleman with whom Smollett is known to have been intimate was Lord George Graham, brother to the Duke of Montrose, who assisted Smollett in his attempts to stage *The Regicide.*

A few more intimate friends of Smollett in his early years in London remain to be considered. One of the most interesting of these was Robert Smith, whom Smollett admired as early as 1745. It was through Smith that Carlyle was introduced to Smollett in London in 1746, and years later in his *Autobiography* Carlyle recalled that Smith "had been abroad with the young Laird of McLeod[31] of that period, and was called home with his pupil when the Rebellion began. He had been ill rewarded, and was on his shifts in London. He was a man of superior understanding, and of a most gentlemanly address. With Smollett he was very intimate."[32] As Carlyle happily continued, Smith, along with John Blair and himself "frequently resorted to a small tavern in the corner of Cockspur Street at the Golden Ball, where we had a frugal

[30] See *Complete Peerage*, London, 1893. For his obituary see *London Chronicle*, August 31-September 3, 1765, p. 218. There is an account of him in Alexander Laing, *Lindores Abbey and its Burgh of Newburgh* (Edinburgh, 1876), p. 407.

[31] The Laird of the Macleods at the time of Culloden was Norman Macleod of Skye (1706-1772), nineteenth Chief. See Alexander Mackenzie's *History of the Macleods*, Inverness, 1889. Of his son John not much is known, according to Rev. R. C. Macleod's *The Macleods*, published by the Clan Macleod Society (Edinburgh, 1906), p. 31. John, presumably the young Laird, fought as a Commander of a company in Loudon's Highlanders. His father, Norman Macleod, was wealthy and influential and eventually became an M.P.

[32] Carlyle, *Autobiography*, p. 198.

supper and a little punch, as the finances of none of the company were in very good order. But we had rich enough conversation on literary subjects, which was enlivened by Smollett's agreeable stories, which he told with peculiar grace."[33] The friendship between Smith and Smollett flourished for many years, though their written correspondence has not survived. Through Smollett's generous letter to Dr. John Moore in 1754, Smith, then appointed tutor to Lord Garlies,[34] was recommended to Smollett's old Glasgow friends, and eventually became the tutor and companion of the distinguished bibliophile, John Ker, third Duke of Roxburgh.[35] It is clear that Smollett never lost interest in Robert Smith; it is also certain from Carlyle's characterization of him and from his career that he was a humanist and a well-bred gentleman, and greatly valued by Roxburgh.[36]

Smollett's strong instinct for fervid friendships led him to close association with Charles Bell, Governor at Cape Coast Castle, British West Africa, 1756-1757 and 1761-1763. With Bell Smollett (as he wrote a friend in 1759) had "lived these eighteen years in the most unreserved intimacy . . . I know him to be one of the best men that ever were born, and I love him with the warmest affection."[37] It must therefore have been in the West Indies, in 1741, that Smollett first came to know Bell. The letters which passed between them have all disappeared, and only a little is known about Smollett's friend. He was related to Andrew Lumisden,[38] that aristocratic Scottish Jacobite, exiled for years after the Forty-Five, and secretary to the Pretender; for Lumisden, in a letter of 1769 mentioned meeting at Marseilles, on May first, his cousin, Charles Bell of Craigfoodie, who having lost his health at Cape Coast had wintered at Montpellier.[39] Obscurity shrouds the later years of Charles

---

[33] *Idem.*

[34] Lord Garlies was John Steward, the seventh Earl of Galloway, born 1736.

[35] See William Jerdan's memoir of Roxburgh in *The National Gallery of Illustrious and Eminent Personages of the Nineteenth Century* (London, 1834), Vol. IV, opposite the portrait of Roxburgh.

[36] For more data on Robert Smith see my communication, "Smollett's Friend Smith" in *TLS* (London), October 9, 1943, p. 492.

[37] See my "An Important Smollett Letter" in *RES*, XII (1936), 77.

[38] See *DNB.*

[39] See James Dennistoun, *Memoirs of Sir Robert Strange, Knt., Engraver*, 2 vols. (London, 1855), II, 121.

Bell of Craigfoodie,[40] who died at Cupar, Fifeshire, in 1785.[41] There seems to be no record or legend of him in present-day Cupar.[42]

Bell's cousin, Andrew Lumisden, writing from Paris to Sir Alexander Dick, September 22, 1770, declared: "Your old friend and my cousin Dr. Armstrong is now with me. He is just returned from Italy, where he had gone on account of his health."[43] Lumisden did not add that Dr. John Armstrong had recently seen Smollett in Italy for the last time. Just when Smollett first met the author of *The Art of Preserving Health* cannot be ascertained. The two men had much in common: both of them were from the North of the Tweed, and both were interested in medicine and literature. Armstrong was practicing in London by 1735; in 1744 his *Art of Preserving Health* brought him into the literary limelight. In that small London world of writers and medical men of the 1740's Smollett could scarcely have missed meeting Armstrong between 1744 and 1746. Smollett's first reference to Armstrong is in a letter to Carlyle, dated October 1, 1749:

> MacGhie (next to Armstrong) is the most reserved Poet I ever met with, upon my soul, I cannot reconcile his shyness in that particular [i.e. *The Regicide*] with the Warmth of Friendship he manifests on every other occasion—it cannot be diffidence—I wish it may not be pride—the truth is I am piqued at the Superiority which the Wariness and Wisdom of such fellows gives them over the Weakness and Leakiness[44] of my own Disposition.—Yet notwithstanding, I admire their conduct and rejoice at their success—I am told that McGhie is in a very promising way.[45]

These remarks show that Smollett was irritated by McGhie's and Armstrong's unexpressed reservations about *The Regicide*. And yet Smollett seems to have maintained for some twenty-five years quite pleasant relations with the rather sensitive and splenetic

[40] Craigfoodie was the name of an estate in the parish of Dairsie, county of Fife, northeast of Cupar.

[41] For obituary notices see *Gentleman's Magazine*, LX (August 1785), 667, and *The Edinburgh Advertiser*, XLIV (No. 2259, Friday, August 19 to Tuesday, August 23, 1785), p. 125. The latter carried the following notice: "Died at Cupar, on Thursday last, Charles Bell, Esq.; late Governor of Cape Coast Castle, on the coast of Africa."

[42] My written inquiries have resulted in no new information about Charles Bell.

[43] See James Dennistoun, *op. cit.*, II, 137.

[44] "Leakiness" meant loquaciousness, lack of reticence, or condition of blabbing, according to the *NED*.

[45] "New Smollett Letters," *TLS*, July 31, 1943.

Armstrong,[46] even though not invariably an admirer of his verse.[47] The "reserved" poet, McGhie, alluded to by Smollett, was Dr. William McGhie (spelled sometimes Magie or Macgie) a Scottish physician, and, according to Sir John Hawkins, one of the members of a club organized by Dr. Johnson in the winter of 1748-1749 for weekly meetings at the King's Head in Ivy Lane.[48] McGhie's adventures in the Forty-Five were described by Carlyle,[49] who knew him well and valued him highly. After the Rebellion, McGhie, in the words of Hawkins, "took a doctor's degree, and came to London, where, trusting to the friendship of his countrymen he hoped to succeed in practice, but the town was overstocked with Scotch physicians, and he met with small encouragement, though, by the favour of Dr. Benjamin Avery, the treasurer of Guy's hospital . . . he got to be elected one of the physicians of that charity. He was a learned, ingenious, and modest man; and one of those few of his country whom Johnson could endure. To say the truth, he treated him with great civility and may almost be said to have loved him. He inherited a patrimony too small for his subsistence, and failing in his hope of getting forward in his profession, died of a broken heart, and was buried by a contribution of his friends."[50] It is surprising that, apart from Hawkins' account, nothing easily accessible has been written about McGhie, although all the other members of Johnson's Club in Ivy Lane have been commemorated in the *Dictionary of National Biography*. There are, however, a few records. McGhie received his B.A. and M.D. from Edinburgh —the former in 1739, and the latter in 1746.[51] He obtained his

---

[46] For Armstrong's character and his relations with Smollett, see my article, "Dr. John Armstrong, Littérateur, and Associate of Smollett, Thomson, Wilkes, and Other Celebrities," in *PMLA*, LIX (1944), 1019-58.

[47] In 1754, Smollett wrote Carlyle: ". . . have you seen a poem called Taste? I think there is stuff in it, and suspect that Armstrong has stole it upon the Public by which it is neglected." ("New Smollett Letters," *TLS*, July 31, 1943.) The poem thus decried was *Taste: An Epistle to A Young Critic*, published by Armstrong in 1753.

[48] See *The Works of Samuel Johnson, LL.D. Together with His Life*, edited by Sir John Hawkins, 11 vols. (London, 1787ff.), I, 220, 232-33, 360. Ivy Lane was near St. Paul's, between Paternoster Row and Newgate Street.

[49] *Autobiography*, pp. 121, 130ff., 144ff. McGhie is listed inaccurately as a minister in the index to Burton's edition.

[50] Hawkins' *Works of Samuel Johnson*, I, 232-33.

[51] In *A Catalogue of the Graduates in the Faculties of Arts, Divinity, and Law, of the University of Edinburgh since its Foundation* (Edinburgh, 1858), p. 207, there is the following entry: "26 Februarii 1739 Gulielmus McGhie." The record of his medical degree is in *Nomina Eorum, Qui Gradum Medicinae Doctoris in Academia Jacobi*

appointment to Guy's Hospital about January 1754[52] and died on June 7, 1756.[53] It appears, therefore, that he was about Smollett's age and liberally educated. According to Smollett he was a poet, and in Smollett's words, "a man according to my own heart."[54] With McGhie, Smollett planned to travel in June 1748 on a pleasure trip to Oxford, Blenheim, and Stowe; in a letter to Carlyle written March 1, 1754, Smollett, pleased about McGhie's appointment to Guy's Hospital (though it was not specifically mentioned), added in a postscript this sentence: "McGhie like truth has prevailed at last."[55] There were other happy meetings between the two friends, exemplified by the dinner at the Swan in Chelsea where Smollett, Armstrong, McGhie and L____ Kenmure once assembled.[56] But McGhie's life was too soon ended, the cause of his untimely death being, one suspects, more than a "broken heart," as Hawkins declared.

Johnson, Hawkins, and Smollett doubtless mourned McGhie's death, and they all may have contributed to the expenses of his funeral. Smollett's admiration for McGhie speaks well for his good taste in friendships, and it is significant that he and Johnson appreciated McGhie about the same time, namely in 1748. Then, and in the years following, Smollett, thanks to McGhie, surely heard much of Johnson, and probably met him.

Since most of Smollett's circle were Scotsmen, some sort of association between Smollett and the poet James Thomson, the best known Scottish writer in England up to his death in 1748, would have been natural and well-nigh inevitable. No intimate friendship between them can be demonstrated, but they had met by 1746 or earlier, probably through the offices of some mutual friend like Dr. Armstrong. Their acquaintance is confirmed in a recollection of the actress George Anne Bellamy, in whose *Apology* is found the following statement:

> The moment I was informed of Mr. Quin's return to town, I waited on him to apologize for the unpardonable neglect I had been guilty of in

Sexti Scotorum Regis, Quae Edinburgi est, Adepti Sunt (Edinburghi, 1846), p. 220: "Macghie, Gul., Scotus. De Frigore. 1746."

[52] In the *Gentleman's Magazine*, XXIV (January 1754), 48, is the record of his appointment: "Dr. Macgie—physician of Guy's hospital. (Clarke, resign'd.)"
[53] See the *Gentleman's Magazine*, XXVI (1756), 314.
[54] "New Smollett Letters," *TLS*, July 24, 1943.
[55] *Ibid.*, July 31, 1943.
[56] See my article, "Dr. John Armstrong," in *PMLA*, LIX (1944), 1028-29.

leaving England without paying my respects to him. I found at his apartments Sir George (since Lord) Lyttelton, Thomson, Mallet and Smollett. As I had been already introduced to these gentlemen, and was upon a footing of intimacy with them I was not sorry at their being present upon this occasion.[57]

The date of this meeting must have been after the end of the theatrical season of 1745-1746, and despite Mrs. Bellamy's occasional inaccuracies, there is no reason to doubt her recollection of the above situation and the characters present. Smollett's acquaintance with the famous author of *The Seasons* is reflected more than once in his letters and his writings. In a note to Carlyle at the end of 1747, Smollett alluded to some injustice that Thomson had recently received from Garrick,[58] which fact means that Smollett was no stranger to Thomson's affairs. Similarly, there is imbedded in Smollett's preface to *Count Fathom* what looks like rather private information about Thomson's personal attitude toward fulsome dedications to patrons, a theme on which the independent Smollett wrote with characteristic feeling and admirable style, as follows:

> Sometimes too, dazzled by the tinsel of a character which he [the poet] has no opportunity to investigate, he pours forth the homage of his admiration, upon some false Maecenas, whose future conduct gives the lie to his eulogium, and involves him in shame and confusion of face. Such was the fate of a late ingenious author,* [footnote: *The author of the "Seasons"] who was so often put to the blush for the undeserved incense he had offered, in the heat of an enthusiastic disposition, misled by popular applause, that he had resolved to retract in his last will, all the encomiums which he had thus prematurely bestowed, and stigmatize the unworthy by name: a laudable scheme of poetical justice, the execution of which was fatally prevented by untimely death.[59]

Finally, in a letter written by John Gray to Smollett in 1771 there is a sentence which suggests gossipy talk between the latter and Thomson: "The two other English were Capt. Wolesly & young Lyttelton,[60] whose character puts me entirely in mind of what you

---

[57] Quoted from *Apology for the Life of George Anne Bellamy*, 5 vols., third edition (London, 1785), II, 1 (Letter XXIX, dated May 16, 17—).

[58] "New Smollett Letters," *TLS*, July 24, 1943.

[59] Quoted from the Dedication to Doctor xxxxxx, in the first edition of *Count Fathom*.

[60] The young Lyttelton characterized by Gray was Thomas Lord Lyttelton. In Reginald Blunt's *Thomas Lord Lyttelton The Portrait of a Rake, with a brief Memoir of his Sister Lucy Lady Valentia* (London [1936]), the author, to whose kindness I owe much, quotes Gray's letter *as written by Smollett*, an unlucky slip of the pen.

told me of Thomson's opinion of his father.[61] His mind is ye most susceptible of delusive flattery of any that ever I met with."[62]

In view of these facts it is likely that Smollett cultivated a cordial friendship with Thomson. As Professor Buck pointed out, Smollett was familiar with *The Castle of Indolence*, published in 1748, and appears to have seen his posthumously produced *Coriolanus*.[63] What is more important, Smollett eulogized Thomson in his *Continuation of the Complete History of England*,[64] and probably inspired or wrote the review[65] of Thomson's *Works*, so handsomely published by Millar in 1762.

From Mrs. Bellamy's statement, cited above, it is also apparent that Smollett had met, by 1746 or earlier, David Mallet (Malloch) and Lord Lyttelton.

The circle of Smollett's friends here assembled was made up almost entirely of Scotsmen. It was a very varied group professionally and a very able group when considered individually. That it was so overwhelmingly Scottish may mean that Smollett felt exiled from English personalities of similar interests and achievements, but we cannot be wholly sure. Merely because Carlyle preserved Smollett's letters, it does not necessarily follow that Smollett's friends from 1745 to 1750 were limited to persons born in Scotland. But he probably moved chiefly in Caledonian circles. One thing is sure: he was socially gifted and not isolated, and he found time between medical calls and literary activities to enjoy his friends. He also found time to travel in 1748, 1749, and 1750.

Writing to Carlyle June 7, 1748, Smollett announced that in a few days he was going "in a Party of pleasure to Oxford, Blenheim and Stowe."[66] During the preceding months of 1748, *Roderick Random* had been published and *Advice and Reproof* had been issued. Previous to April 1748, Elizabeth Smollett had been born, and about this time the Smolletts had moved to Beaufort Street. Following, as it did, these busy months, this short excursion to Oxford and the show places of Blenheim and Stowe brought relax-

---

[61] George Lord Lyttelton, and not Thomson's father.

[62] This extract is printed from a photostat of the original manuscript of Gray's letter at the Massachusetts Historical Society.

[63] See Buck, *A Study in Smollett*, pp. 105-6.

[64] See the *Continuation of the Complete History of England*, Vol. IV (London, 1761), p. 129.

[65] See the *Critical Review*, XIV (1762), 122-30.

[66] "New Smollett Letters," *TLS*, July 24, 1943.

ation and pleasure. The party proceeded from London to Oxford, it is likely, either via Maidenhead and Dorchester, or via Acton, Gerard's Cross, Stoken Church and Wheatley Bridge. By either route it was a distance of some fifty-five miles. About eight miles northwest of Oxford, near Woodstock, were the palatial grounds and buildings of the Duke of Marlborough; a little farther, to the northeast of Oxford was Buckingham, some two miles beyond which were located the magnificent gardens and estates of Stowe, seat of Sir Richard Temple, Viscount Cobham. Of Smollett's impressions of Oxford, Blenheim, and Stowe there are no records.

On October 1 of the year following (1749), Smollett, toward the end of his letter to Carlyle, wrote in a rather casual tone: "I have no news wherewith to entertain you, notwithstanding I am but a Week returned from having made a tour thro' part of France, Flanders and Holland, which has only served to endear my own Country to me, the more."[67] Certain literary ventures had been launched between the summer of 1748 and that of 1749 which demand a glance before we deal briefly with the significance of this foreign excursion. "A thousand things occur to me, which I would fain communicate, but I must refer them to another occasion, when you shall receive a long letter," declared Smollett in his note to Carlyle, February 14, 1749.[68] This "long letter," if ever written, is not now available.[69] Among the thousand matters alluded to was a whole series of chessboard moves, now unknown, about *The Regicide*.

One project was the *Alceste*, an extraordinary combination of opera, tragedy, and masque, the precise nature of which has, for the most part, to be surmised. Smollett's own references to it are of primary importance. To Carlyle on February 14, 1749, he confided: "I have wrote a sort of Tragedy on the Story of Alceste, which will (without fail) be acted at Covent Garden next Season and appear with such magnificence of Scenery as was never exhibited in Britain before."[70] The play, as will be indicated later, was to be under the control of Rich, whom Smollett had flayed in

[67] *Ibid.*, July 31, 1943.   [68] *Ibid.*, July 24, 1943.
[69] In a *Catalogue of Autograph Letters and MSS of the Late F. Naylor*, sold 27 July ff., 1885 (in British Museum), there is evidence of a lost letter written in 1749: Item 900, "Smollett (Tobias) . . . A.L.S. 1749 1 p. 8ᵛᵒ rare." This manuscript was sold to one Harvey for £4/18/-.
[70] "New Smollett Letters," *TLS*, July 24, 1943.

Reproof and *Roderick Random*. Smollett's phrase "will (without fail) be acted" suggests that he had a stronger guarantee of production than Rich's spoken word. Elated because the *Alceste* was written, Smollett's sorrows over his failure to stage *The Regicide* were mitigated; following his confession about the *Alceste*, is this sentence: "Meanwhile despairing of seeing my old performance [i.e. *The Regicide*] represented, I have at last taken the advice of my Friends and opened a subscription for publishing it, which in all appearance will answer my warmest Expectations." With great expectations from several sources, then, and with a desire for the diversions and improvements of further foreign travel, Smollett set out, in the summer of 1749, for France, Flanders and Holland. He must have gone also to relax and to rest, after writing *Roderick Random* at amazing speed, after the laborious translation of *Gil Blas*, and work on his translation of *Don Quixote*, and following the death-throes of *The Regicide*, the creation of a comedy, and the completion of the *Alceste*. And who knows what else he may have done anonymously for the booksellers from 1747 to 1750, let alone devoting some energy to medical practice! Though equipped with the energy of three men, Smollett needed a complete change.

To travel through the Low Countries at this time was not unusual. The famous William Hunter, Smollett's friend, made such a trip in the summer of 1748.[71] It was a sort of preliminary step to the Grand Tour, in which all enlightened Englishmen of that period indulged. It is a loss to our knowledge of Smollett and to literature that his journal of this trip (if he kept one) has not survived. In his *Travels*, 1766, there is one definite echo of his experience in Ghent, where Smollett recalled: "in the year 1749, I had like to have had an affair with a Frenchman at Ghent, who affirmed, that all the battles gained by the great duke of Marlborough were purposely lost by the French generals, in order to bring the schemes of madame de Maintenon into disgrace."[72] Again in the *Travels* he wrote that he "drank excellent Burgundy at Brussels for a florin a bottle; that is, little more than twenty pence sterling."[73] Here, however, Smollett may have had in mind an earlier trip. The excursion in 1749 covered, in his own words, "part of France, Flanders

[71] See John Thomson, M.D., *An Account of the Life, Lectures, and Writings of William Cullen, M.D.*, 2 vols. (Edinburgh and London, 1859), I, 539.
[72] Smollett's *Travels*, ed. Seccombe, p. 38.   [73] *Ibid.*, p. 71.

and Holland." This meant, it may be guessed, that he passed through Boulogne and Amsterdam. He was on the verge of a duel in Ghent, and perhaps visited Bruges, Brussels, and Leyden, where so many British medical students were centered. Home in London in late September 1749, he wrote Carlyle, October 1, that the tour only increased his affection for his own country.[74]

Upon his return he dispatched to Rich the *Alceste*, the story of which may now be continued by citing Smollett's own comment on its status at that time.

> Two days ago I sent my masq[u]e to Rich that it may be put into Rehearsal immediately, but he is such a compound of indolence, Worthlessness and folly, that I cannot depend on any thing he undertakes—if he acted upon the maxims of common sense, tho' he were the greatest Scoundrel under the Sun, I should not have undergone the half of the trouble I have already suffered. but as his conceptions are not reducible within any Laws of reason that I know, his conduct is altogether unintelligible and his designs past finding out—Tho' he has no objection to the Peice [*sic*] which has been again and again approved of, by the very judges he himself appointed, tho' he has no other prospect of being saved from destruction, than that of exhibiting it immediately; And tho he is almost certain of uncommon success on its appearance; he is such an infatuated miscreant, that he has told some of his friends in confidence that the performance was crammed down his throat—I may with great justice say of the Managers, as my predecessor Michael Drayton the Water Poet says of Booksellers 'they are a pack of base knaves whom I both despise and kick at.'[75]

This tirade against Rich was, in view of all that is known of him, rather completely justified. Smollett's remark that he (Rich) "has no other prospect of being saved from destruction, than that of exhibiting it immediately," must mean that Rich had already sunk a good deal of money into the preliminary preparations for producing *Alceste*. And yet Smollett's worst suspicions were to be realized: the piece was never staged.

The *Alceste* raises certain interesting questions. When did Smollett write it? As we have noted, he confided to Carlyle, February 14, 1749: "I have wrote a sort of Tragedy on the Story of Alceste, which will (without fail) be acted at Covent Garden next Season," and the plain inference to be drawn is that Smollett had in mind a

---

[74] Compare Smollett's expression of his love of England at the beginning of his last "Letter" in his *Travels*.
[75] "New Smollett Letters," *TLS*, July 31, 1943.

recently completed project, not mentioned in his earlier letters to Carlyle. Yet it has been stated repeatedly that Smollett composed the *Alceste* about 1746 and that Rich's failure to stage it caused Smollett to satirize him in *Reproof*.[76] But this attack on Rich was sufficiently motivated by the latter's rejection of *The Regicide* in the fall of 1746, when, it seems, Smollett's *Alceste* had not yet been written. Another question is whether it was Smollett or Rich who first fathered the idea of producing an opera on the theme of Alceste. It originated as much with Rich as with Smollett, apparently, if we may trust Moore, who traveled with Smollett in 1750 and must have heard him grumble about it. Moore wrote that Smollett "was applied to by Mr. Rich."[77] It may seem odd that Rich, after *Reproof*, would ever apply to Smollett for anything, but Lun Rich was, after all, a most eccentric creature. In spite of *Reproof* and *Roderick Random*, he had planned by February 1749 a very elaborate stage show, for which Smollett was furnishing the libretto. Rich had decided, quite possibly, to placate Smollett so as to prevent being again the butt of personal satire. Or it may be that Smollett had made some sort of amends to Rich.

The fact remains, however, that grandiose plans were under way for producing the *Alceste*. According to Sir John Hawkins, Handel was under contract to produce the music, and Servandoni was engaged to furnish elaborate scenery.[78] The latter celebrity had designed the great fireworks, which, along with Handel's Firework Music, had created much excitement in London in April 1749, when the Peace of Aix-La-Chapelle was celebrated. Therefore it is small wonder that Smollett in February 1749 was elated: he might have written in relative seriousness Byron's laughing couplet:

> I've got new mythological machinery
> And very handsome supernatural scenery.

Just why or when Rich stopped all rehearsals of the *Alceste* is

[76] See John Moore's "Life" of Smollett in Moore's edition of the *Works*, I, cxviii. See also Howard S. Buck, *Smollett as Poet* (Yale University Press, 1927), pp. 34-35.

[77] See preceding note.

[78] Hawkins in his account of Handel's activities wrote as follows: "[Handel] removed to Covent Garden, and entered into some engagements with Rich, the particulars of which are not known, save that in discharge of a debt that he had contracted with him in consequence thereof, he some years after set to music an English opera entitled Alceste, written by Dr. Smollett, and for which Rich was at great expence in a set of scenes painted by Servandoni; but it was never performed." Sir John Hawkins, *A General History of the Science and Practice of Music*, 5 vols. (London, 1776), V, 324.

somewhat obscure. Moore wrote that "a dispute taking place between the author and the manager, the opera was never acted nor published."[79] Handel's editor, Chrysander, in his foreword to his edition of Handel's "Musikalische Scenen zu dem englischen Drama Alceste" suggested that the music was too grand for the drama.[80] The date of the collapse of all plans can only be conjectured from a document presented by W. S. Rockstro in his life of Handel. According to Handel's own record, therein printed, he finished the music for the fourth act of *Alceste* January 8, 1750.[81] It was after this, obviously, that the whole project broke down.

The results of the collapse are of interest. Handel embodied most of his music written for *Alceste* in his *The Choice of Hercules*, composed from June to July 1750. Servandoni may have found later use for his scenic designs when he staged in Poland in 1755 an opera on the same theme.[82] The best singers of the day[83] were presumably paid by Rich for their rehearsals. And Smollett, as is divulged in a letter written by Home to Carlyle, received "on Sunday last three hundred pounds for his *Mask*."[84] The "mask" here referred to was of course the *Alceste*.

In composing the *Alceste*, Smollett was creating an eighteenth-century version of a theme which had been treated repeatedly, since Euripides, in many literatures.[85] In operatic form the story of Alceste was presented in April and May 1744 at the King's Theatre, Haymarket, in a version written by the Italian, Lampugnani. In May 1744 the favorite songs from his *Alceste* were published.[86]

[79] *Works*, ed. Moore, I, cxviii.

[80] Handel's *Werke*, ed. Chrysander. Leipzig, 100 vols., Vol. 46B., Foreword.

[81] W. S. Rockstro, *The Life of George Frederick Handel* (London, 1883), p. 319. Rockstro's statement, unknown to me while I was investigating the *Alceste* at the British Museum, runs as follows: "The complete score of the work [i.e. Handel's music for Smollett's opera] no longer exists; but an autograph volume [Br. Mus. Add. MSS 30, 310] . . . contains nearly all that is known of the Fourth Act, dated, at the end of the last Chorus, *Fine | G. F. Handel | völlig geendiget den 8 January* 1750."

[82] See the account of Jean-Nicholas Servandoni in Dezallier D'Argenville, *Vies Des Fameux Architectes* and *Vies Des Fameux Sculpteurs*, 2 vols. (Paris, 1787), I, 459. As part of the success of Servandoni in Poland "le triomphe de l'amour conjugal tiré d'Alceste, qu'il donna cette année [1755] ne parut pas inférieur à ses productions précédentes."

[83] They were, according to papers examined by Rockstro, Miss Young, Mrs. Arne, Mr. Low, Mr. Waltz, and Mrs. Faulkner. See Rockstro, *op. cit.*, p. 319.

[84] See Henry Mackenzie, *op. cit.*, I, 137. From internal evidence Home's letter was written early in 1750.

[85] See Georg Ellinger, *Alceste in der modernen Litteratur* (Halle, 1885), and also Karl Dissel, *Der Mythos von Admetos und Alkestis* (Brandenburg, 1882).

[86] See *The Daily Advertiser*, May 10, 1744.

The Alceste story was later presented in operatic form by Christopher Gluck, 1769, and also by Gresnick in 1768. The central theme of the Alceste story was conjugal love: the Greek myth dealt with the winning of Alceste (or Alcestis) by Admetus; his being sentenced to death by Artemis owing to his failure to sacrifice to her on his wedding day; the self-sacrifice of Alceste in order to save her husband from death; and of how Alceste, through the aid of Hercules, was returned from Hades to the living world. In treating this theme Smollett might have received some inspiration from Buchanan's Latin version of Euripides' *Alcestis*,[87] because George Buchanan's works were read in Smollett's Dumbarton Grammar School, and, doubtless too, at Glasgow University.

Though Smollett's own manuscript for the *Alceste* has not been found, what appear to be copies of most of his lyrics for this work have been published very recently (*MLN*, February 1948) thanks to Mr. Otto E. Deutsch. Extremely conventional in style, these verses add nothing to Smollett's literary achievement. As to Servandoni's setting, one gets a vague impression of it by reading D'Argenville's account of his production in Poland, referred to above:

> Le public remarqua des beautés supérieures dans les décoration du temple de l'hymen . . . du monument élevé par les arts pour l'apothéose d'Alceste, du palais de Pluton & de celui d'Apollon.[88]

In London, however, no audience witnessed such glories or heard Smollett's lyrics sung to Handel's music, and no scholarly Hercules has yet brought to light the complete text of Smollett's libretto, which still rests in Plutonian night. Nor have we any record of how Smollett may have felt. Handel's reaction, perhaps invented by Oliphant Smeaton, is found in his *Tobias Smollett*: "Handel . . . is reported to have remarked, 'That Scotchman is ein tam fool; I vould have mate his vurk immortal.' "[89] But what Smollett himself thundered we are not privileged to know.

It can be said, in general, that Smollett's part in the *Alceste* brought him into close contact with Handel, Servandoni, Rich, and the musicians engaged to sing in the opera, not to mention the social group who for a time sponsored the undertaking. In this there was .

---

[87] See George Buchanan, *Opera Omnia*, 2 vols. (Lugduni Batavorum, 1735), tomus secundus, 575-601.
[88] See D'Argenville, *op. cit.*, I, 459.   [89] Smeaton, *op. cit.*, p. 56.

a kind of prestige. And after all there was the substantial sum of £300.

To Smollett's failure to get both *The Regicide* and the *Alceste* on the stage was added a third disappointment, that of never seeing his first comedy on the boards. In undertaking comedy, he may have been influenced by Lord Lyttelton, who, according to Horace Walpole,[90] advised him to try this genre during his unsuccessful efforts to stage *The Regicide*. At any rate he wrote Carlyle, June 7, 1748, that a comedy was "planned" and scheduled to be completed "by next Winter."[91] Something of the subsequent fortunes of this comedy we learn from the following forgotten letter of Smollett, written May 11, 1750, and addressed, it seems, to Francis Hayman, the eminent historical painter and illustrator:

Dear Sir,

After thanking you heartily for the Trouble you have taken in my Behalf, I must beg the additional favour of transmitting my Play to Mr Garrick, according to his Desire in the Letter which I send you back inclosed; tho I can forsee that I shall suffer the Mortification of a Second Refusal, which I assure you, I should save myself, but that I am resolved not to be wanting to my own Interest, in letting Slip any Opportunity (how small soever it may be) of promoting it, by just & honourable Means.

In revising & correcting the Performance, I have payed all the Regard to the Patentee's Remarks, which my own Reflection and the Advice of my friends would allow, & made several essential Alterations in the Plan, which he will plainly perceive in perusing it. it cannot be supposed that I would sit down to write a Comedy, before I had endeavoured to investigate the nature of the work; or that I am so ignorant of the Stage, so incorrigible, or unqualified as to produce a dramatic piece that should deserve no favour from an audience which never discountenanced any thing that had the least pretension to Encouragement—and yet, I have been frustrated in all my attempts to Succeed on the Stage,—not by the Publick which I have always found favourable & propitious; but by the Power of two or three Persons who (I cannot help saying) have accepted and patronized the works of others, with whom, in point of Merit, I think myself, at least, upon a par—this I speak not from Vanity, but Resentment for the hard usage I have met with[.] I own, I feel severely, when

[90] See Horace Walpole, *Memoirs of the Reign of King George the Second*, ed. Lord Holland, 3 vols. (London, 1846), III, 259, for the following: "Smollett was bred a sea-surgeon, and turned author. He wrote a tragedy, and sent it to Lord Lyttelton, with whom he was not acquainted. Lord Lyttelton, not caring to point out its defects, civilly advised him to try comedy."

[91] "New Smollett Letters," in *TLS*, July 24, 1943.

I reflect upon my (I was going to say) unjust Exclusion from the Theatre—but I begin to grow warm, & therefore, will conclude with assuring you that I am

Dr Sir,

Your obed^t & obliged Servt

T^s Smollett

Beaufort Buildings
May 11th 1750[92]

This letter reveals again Smollett's deep-seated ambition to succeed in drama, and his keen resentment over past failures. But the
comedy, as Smollett feared, was never accepted. A year or so later,
what was undoubtedly this same play turned up as Lot VII in a list
of "Books and Copies left unsold at Mr. John Osborn's 'Sale'"
(apparently in 1751) appended to a catalogue of the "entire Stock
of Mr. Tho. Woodward." There it was described as

> The Absent Man, a Comedy, wrote by Mr. T. Smollet, half the
> Copy-Right, and Profits in the Acting. The Copy is in the Possession of
> Mr. Smollet, and the Purchaser is to run all risks of its ever being acted,
> or printed.[93]

As Professor McKillop has well suggested, it looks as if Smollett,
by retaining half the copyright of "The Absent Man," still hoped
that it might eventually be produced or published.[94] But Smollett's
first comedy, to which he never referred later, was lost along with
his *Alceste*, and seven long years were to pass before Smollett
finally succeeded in staging his later comedy, *The Reprisal*.

[92] Printed in *The Athenaeum*, I (1880), 578. It is stated that this letter was placed
at the disposal of Mr. H. Barton Baker by a descendant of Fleetwood, manager of
Drury Lane. It is printed here from the original manuscript at the Harvard University
Library with the kind permission of Mr. William Jackson. The holograph consists of
one sheet, on the verso of which is written in an old hand: "Dr Smollett to Mr Hayman." Except for this letter and the fact that Hayman designed the frontispiece-plates
for the second edition of *Roderick Random* (1748), and for other books by Smollett,
nothing is known of the relations between the two men.

[93] Cited from Alan D. McKillop, "Smollett's First Comedy" in *MLN*, XLV (1930),
396.

[94] *Ibid.*, p. 397.

CHAPTER V

Success with *Gil Blas* and *Roderick Random;* Publication of *The Regicide,* 1747-1750

THE account of Smollett's friendships and diverse activities in his late twenties in Chapel Street and in Beaufort Street will now be enlarged by a survey of the central stream of his literary efforts during the years from 1747 to 1750. This period was notable for his first great success, *The Adventures of Roderick Random.* It also included much impressive work in translating LeSage and Cervantes. In 1749 *The Regicide* was printed. To these significant literary achievements this chapter is devoted.

Concerning the composition of *Roderick Random* the author himself furnished very specific information shortly before the novel was published, in a letter to Carlyle, about December 1747:

> Since I wrote my last Letter to you, I have finished a Romance in two small Volumes, called the Adventures of Roderick Random, which will be published in a Fortnight—it is intended as a satire upon mankind, and by the Reception it has met with in private from the best judges here, I have reason to beleive [*sic*] that it will succeed very well—As I have long ago disposed of the Copy, I know not what method the Booksell[er]s will follow in the sale of it, but I believe [*sic*] some Hundreds will be sent to Scotland—If you shall light on it, read it with candour, and report me and my cause aright.[1]

To this we subjoin an extract from Smollett's letter to Carlyle the following June, still on the subject of *Roderick Random*:

> As you have no doubt observed several inaccuracies in the stile I must do myself the justice to assure you that (one or two oversights excepted) they are all owing to the hurry in which it was printed, and here I am tempted to discover that the whole was begun and finished in the compass of Eight Months, during which time several Intervals happened of one two, three & four Weeks, wherein I did not set pen to paper, so that a little incorrectness may be excused.[2]

[1] "New Smollett Letters," *TLS*, July 24, 1943.   [2] *Ibid.*

There is no reason to assume any exaggeration in Smollett's statement, and his pride is justified. To complete *Roderick Random* within eight months was an amazing feat.

The speed with which *Roderick Random* was written seems to have been equaled by the expedition of its printing. Advertised in mid-December[3] as to be published the next month, it was available about January 21, 1748, in "two neat Pocket-Volumes (Price Bound 6*s*)," according to the *General Advertiser*.[4] These books were printed on the presses of William Strahan for John Osborn of Paternoster Row; they were issued anonymously, and on the title page of each appeared the Horatian adage, "Et genus & virtus, nisi cum re, vilior alga est."[5] The two volumes contained over 200,000 words, *Roderick Random* being considerably longer than Fielding's *Joseph Andrews*.[6]

What Smollett received for the copyright of his first novel is not known, but perhaps it approximated the sum which Fielding obtained from Andrew Millar for *Joseph Andrews*, namely £183.[7] It is likely that Smollett felt that he was not overpaid in view of the distinct success which his first novel achieved with the general public, a success which Smollett had hoped for because of the reception it had "met with in private from the best judges."

The success of *Roderick Random* was immediate, impressive, and prolonged. From the printing records of the publisher, William Strahan, it is evident that some 6,500 copies were put through his presses from January 1748 to November 1749.[8] Fielding's *Joseph Andrews*, it may be noted, sold better, as about 6,500 copies were called for in approximately a year (1742-1743),[9] but by 1742 Fielding was a well-known writer, whereas Smollett had published before 1748 only the "Tears of Scotland" and his verse-satires. As the years passed, *Roderick Random* continued to appear in edition

---

[8] The *Whitehall Evening Post* for December 15-17, 1747, announced *Roderick Random* for "next month."

[4] The *General Advertiser* for January 15 reported January 21 as the day of publication.

[5] See *Satirae* of Horace, 2, 5, 8.

[6] *Roderick Random* runs to about 220,000 words, whereas *Joseph Andrews* contains approximately 150,000.

[7] See H. K. Banerji, *Henry Fielding* (Oxford, Basil Blackwell, 1929), p. 133.

[8] See my article, "Smollett's Works as Printed by William Strahan" in *The Library* (Transactions of the Bibliographical Society), XIII (1932), 283ff.

[9] See Banerji, *op. cit.*, p. 130.

after edition[10] so that on the title pages of Smollett's novels (after *Peregrine Pickle*) there appeared the phrase, "By the author of Roderick Random." Not only by such statistics may the reception of Smollett's first novel be measured, but there are also records of how the book impressed certain sophisticated Londoners, who were looking for another *Joseph Andrews*, perhaps, or who were under the sway of Richardson's *Pamela* (1740), and his *Clarissa* (1748).

Typical of the last group was the refined and pious Mrs. Delany, friend of Lady Portland, and wife of the Dean of Down, who wrote her friend Mrs. Dewes about August 1750: "I have read (or rather heard read) The Man of Honour, Roderick Random and the Sieges of Drogheda and Derry."[11] That she did not object to the realism of *Roderick Random* is significant of the difference between the taste of 1750 and that of 1850. A devotee of Richardson and an admirer of *Joseph Andrews*, the accomplished Miss Catherine Talbot, in a letter to Mrs. Elizabeth Carter (February 15, 1748) inquired whether the latter had read "that strange book Roderic [*sic*] Random! It is a very strange and very low one, though not without some characters in it, and I believe some very just, though very wretched descriptions."[12] Then she added that the story of Melopoyn showed "in a striking manner" the cruelties of the rich and the great in dealing with struggling authors. Perhaps she was also impressed by Smollett's graphic account of the barbarities of naval life.

Another type of reader was the biographer, Thomas Birch, F.R.S., and later D.D., who was, in the opinion of Dr. Johnson, brisk as a bee in conversation. This influential figure, the kind friend of many celebrities,[13] read *Roderick Random* very promptly and in his letter to the Earl of Orrery, February 20, 1748, divulged that it was written by "Mr Smallet a Scotch surgeon" and that it contained "a variety of characters, especially in low life drawn up

---

[10] See the bibliography of the editions of *Roderick Random* compiled by Luella F. Norwood in *CBEL*.

[11] The *Autobiography and Correspondence of Mrs. Delany*, ed. Sarah C. Woolsey, 2 vols. (Boston, 1879), I, 375.

[12] *A Series of Letters between Mrs. Elizabeth Carter and Miss Catherine Talbot*, 4 vols. (London, 1809), I, 252.

[13] For Birch's friendship with Dr. John Armstrong see my essay, "Dr. John Armstrong, Littérateur, and Associate of Smollett, Thomson, Wilkes, and other Celebrities" in *PMLA*, LIX (1944), 1023.

with considerable vivacity and humour."[14] Probably as the result of Birch's recommendation, John Boyle, Earl of Orrery, and his circle enjoyed the novel, as the Earl wrote Thomas Carew, March 12, 1748: "*Clarissa* kept us up till two in the morning. *Rhodoric* will keep us up all night, and he, I am told, is to be succeeded again by *Clarissa*, whom I left, adorable girl, at St. Albans."[15]

Such comment would have pleased Smollett, who would also have particularly relished part of a letter sent to Admiral Boscawen, or Old Dreadnought (as the tars called him), by his wife, Fanny Boscawen. She began reading *Roderick Random* in January 1748 at her home on Audley Street in the very neighborhood where the novel was written. In her journal-letter to the Admiral (January 29, 1748) she revealed her latest reading:

> Last night I was well content with such entertainment as *Roderick Random* affords. He shall wait on you—and undressed[16]—for I foresee that all your officers will be desirous of a visit from him. I am already indebted to him for many a horse laugh, so that I am greatly prejudiced in his favour.

On February 5, 1748, after finishing the novel, she continued as follows:

> I am told 'tis not Fielding's, but the produce of a Scotch sea surgeon called Smollett, and that the ground of the story is his own, allowing for embellishments. I laughed at first, but I grew tired before I had done.[17]

This reaction of Mrs. Boscawen, one of the very attractive and cultivated women of her time, and the originator (with Elizabeth Montagu) of the Blue-Stocking Assemblies, is typical, no doubt, of that of many ladies of her circle. It is significant that, like Lady Mary Wortley Montagu, she assumed at first that Fielding wrote *Roderick Random*,[18] but from her remarks it is apparent that Smollett's authorship was no secret around London by February 1748.

[14] Quoted from Harvard MSS 281.2, Vol. 5, f. 121, at Harvard University. Birch's letter was omitted from the *Orrery Papers*.

[15] Harvard MSS 218.2, Vol. 5, f. 129. This passage is in the *Orrery Papers*.

[16] Mrs. Boscawen meant, obviously, that her copy of *Roderick Random* would be sent in its original publisher's boards, or in paper wrappers.

[17] Both quoted passages are from Cecil Aspinall-Oglander, *Admiral's Wife Being the life and letters of The Hon. Mrs. Edward Boscawen from 1719 to 1761* (London [1940]), pp. 77-79.

[18] When Lady Montagu first read *Roderick Random* abroad along with *Peregrine Pickle*, she wrote to the Countess of Bute: "There is something humorous in R. Random, that makes me believe that the author is H. Fielding." See *The Letters and Works of Lady Mary Wortley Montagu*, ed. Wharncliffe, 2 vols. (London, 1893), II, 222.

Of the probable laughter of Boscawen and his officers over *Roderick Random* no echo has been recorded, but the humane Admiral, knowing well the hard life of the tars on men-of-war, and destined to ameliorate such evils, was presumably a discerning reader of the material concerning Carthagena, where he had seen action on sea and on land.

In the periodical publications of 1748-1750, very little attention was paid to fiction. The *Gentleman's Magazine*, though partial to Richardson, largely ignored both Fielding and Smollett, except for printing a brief extract from *Roderick Random* (Miss Williams' account of her misfortunes) as an exemplification of the truth of Cobden's sermon, *A Persuasive to Chastity*.[19] The *London Magazine* for this period devoted almost no attention to literature. Only in the newly launched *Monthly Review* was there any real compliment to *Roderick Random*: imbedded in John Cleland's favorable review of *The Regicide*[20] is his praise of the "strokes of humour, and portraiture, peculiar to the author of *Roderick Random*."[21]

The immediate vogue of *Roderick Random* appears in the fact that its title was used to publicize a dramatic interlude at Bartholomew Fair in 1748. This piece was called *The Northern Heroes; . . . With a Comic Interlude, call'd The Volunteers; Or, the Adventures of Roderick Random, and his Friend Strap.* The newspaper announcement,[22] explaining that the interlude was never acted before, specified that the combined show was to be produced by Bridges, Cross, Burton, and Vaughan with a company from the Theatre Royal. This production must have had considerable suc-

---

[19] See *Gentlemen's Magazine*, XIX (1749), 126n. To the extract from Smollett the editor added: "Some strokes of this kind appear also in *Tom Jones* and in Mrs. *Philips's Apology*. [*sic*] . . . However the loose images in these pieces perhaps incite to vice more strongly than the contrast [*sic*] figures alarm us into virtue." Neither Smollett nor Fielding could have been pleased at being classified with Mrs. Teresa Constantia Philips.

[20] See Benjamin C. Nangle, *The Monthly Review First Series 1749-1789 Indexes of Contributors and Articles* (Oxford, Clarendon Press, 1934), p. 184.

[21] The *Monthly Review*, I [1749], 72.

[22] See an extra-illustrated edition of Henry Morley's *Memoirs of Bartholomew Fair*, Vol. 3, following p. 426. (Theatre Collection, Widener Library.) On the newspaper clipping is written in ink *1748*. The name of the newspaper is not recorded, but it is probably from the *Public Advertiser* because Isaac Reed in his manuscript-book, "Notitia Dramatica," (Br. Mus. Add. MSS 25, 391, f. 88) refers to the performance of *The Northern Heroes*. Reed recorded in his book that the notices of dramatic performances were taken chiefly from the *Public Advertiser*.

cess because its text was printed in 1748.[23] As a piece of writing it lacks any literary merit, and Smollett could not conceivably have had anything to do with it. As Professor Buck pointed out, it is in no sense a satire of episodes in *Roderick Random*,[24] but that it was acted and printed in 1748 shows the drawing power of the very names of the leading characters of this novel.

Of the great popularity of Smollett's first novel in England down through the eighteenth century there is abundant evidence in its long line of successive editions. In 1754 a secret spy assumed the name, Roderick Random;[25] in 1750 a remarkable racehorse bore the same title;[26] the book was honored by foreign translations; and when the news of Smollett's death in Italy reached London in the fall of 1771, readers of the newspapers were offered the following anonymous tribute, genuine, though informal:

> On the Report of the Death of Dr. Smollet.
> Death's *random* darts too certainly transfix,
> And souls unwilling Charon's sure to land 'em;
> Ah! take some gloomier soul to gloomy Styx,
> And give us back facetious *Roderick Random*.[27]

In the titles of jestbooks and of comic opera in the decades following Smollett's death the popularity of his first novel was reflected: in 1778 appeared *The jocular and agreeable Companion, or Roderick Random's Jests*;[28] in 1784 was printed *The Theatre of Fun, or Roderick Random in high glee, containing . . . jests*, London;[29] a little later S. W. Ryley's comic opera, *Roderick Ran-*

---

[23] *The Northern Heroes; or The Bloody Contest, between Charles the Twelfth— and Peter the Great—With a Comic Interlude, call'd The Volunteers; Or, the Adventures of Roderick Random; And his Friend Strap . . . As it is now acting . . . at the Great Booth in the George Yard, in West-Smithfield, London, Printed for M. Cooper —MDCCXLVIII (Price 6d)*.

[24] See Howard S. Buck, "A *Roderick Random* Play, 1748," in *MLN*, XLIII (1928), 111-12.

[25] Spies named Roderick Random and Pickle figure in The Newcastle Papers (Br. Mus. Add. MSS 32734, fol. 158ff.).

[26] See *Gentleman's Magazine*, XX (1750), 379, for the story of the racehorse, Roderick Random, who brought in a thousand guineas at Newmarket for the Earl of March and Lord Eglinton.

[27] *London Chronicle*, October 19-22, 1771, p. 392. The same stanza was printed in the *Whitehall Evening Post*, October 19, 1771, where it was followed by the initials E.E.E.

[28] For the complete title see Lowndes under *Companion*. I have not located a copy.

[29] The title of this item, which I have not seen, is from the British Museum Catalogue.

dom,[30] was performed at the Theatre Royal, Manchester, and printed for the public. Such facts prove beyond question that few novels of the eighteenth century pleased the British reader as much as Smollett's first venture in fiction.

In Scotland, *Roderick Random* was acclaimed by some and disliked by others. Extracts from Smollett's letter (recently published in full) to Carlyle, June 7, 1748, are revealing:

> I am so proud of your Panegyrick on Roderick, that I can no longer resist the inclination I feel to signify how much I am pleased with your approbation—I have had occasion to experience that Weakness of Vanity in an author which exults even in the applause of a fool. How much then must I triumph in that praise which (I flatter myself) is the result of Veracity and Taste.
>
> In the midst of my satisfaction (however) at the success of my Performance, I am not a little mortified to find the characters strangely misapplied to particular men whom I never had the least intention to ridicule—by which means I have suffered very much in my Moral Capacity; Some persons to whom I have been extremely obliged, being weak enough to take umbrage at many passages of the Work, on the supposition that I myself am the Hero of the Book, and they of consequence concerned in the History—
>
> I have heard of Love's indignation from many hands, and you may be sure treat it with the contempt it deserves; the more so as I am informed that he has by way of revenge, propagated many lies to my disadvantage.[31]

Carlyle's "Panegyrick" of *Roderick Random* would make good reading if it should turn up. The indignation of Love (John Love, headmaster at Dumbarton grammar school while Smollett was there) arose, it may be, over portraits and episodes in the fifth chapter of the novel, where Roderick, assisted by Bowling, Strap, and Gawky, chastised the schoolmaster. Whether or not Love was justified in his indignation is impossible to say, but Smollett was kind to Love's son in 1761.[32] The sentences just quoted also prove that Love was not alone among the "persons" to whom Smollett had been "extremely obliged," who felt, or at least fancied, that they saw themselves in characters in *Roderick Random*. Such per-

---

[30] *Roderick Random, a Comic Opera* was printed with *The Civilian, or Farmer turned Footman, a Musical Farce. As performed at the Theatre-Royal, Manchester.* Huddersfield, n.d. The manuscript of Ryley's *Roderick Random* is at the Huntington Library. See Dougald MacMillan, *Catalogue of Larpent Plays in the Huntington Library* (San Marino, California, 1939), Item 866.

[31] Quoted "New Smollett Letters," *TLS*, July 24, 1943.

[32] See *Letters*, p. 70.

sons, it would seem, were chiefly old Glasgow acquaintances. Consequently Smollett felt it necessary to write to Carlyle:

> I shall take this opportunity therefore of declaring to you, in all the sincerity of unreserved Friendship that no person living is aimed at in all the first part of the Book; that is while the scene lies in Scotland and that (the account of the Expedition to Carthagene excepted) the *Whole* is not so much a representation of my life as that of many other needy Scotch Surgeons whom I have known either personally or by Report— The character of Strap (who I find is a favourite among the Ladies everywhere) is partly taken from the life; but the circumstances of his attachment to Random entirely feigned.[33]

There is no reason for questioning the essential honesty of Smollett's assertion that in the first part of the novel (Scottish scenes, Chapters 1-10) no living person was "aimed at," though John Love was offended at resemblances real or fancied between the Scottish pedant and himself. Similarly Smollett's declaration that the entire book was not so much a picture of his own life as that of "many other needy Scotch Surgeons" is doubtless trustworthy; Smollett was careful to point out in his letter to Richard Smith of New Jersey in 1763 that the "low situations" in which he "exhibited Roderick," he "never experienced" in his "own Person."[34] But it must be noted that Smollett did not claim that there was no personal satire in *Roderick Random* in scenes after the characters leave Scotland.

To examine in detail all the suggested identifications between fictitious characters in *Roderick Random* and actual living persons is not within the scope of this work. That Smollett continued in his first novel the habit of personal satire begun in *Advice* and *Reproof* is not surprising: his novel, he wrote Carlyle, was "intended as a satire upon mankind," and to fulfill this purpose he felt free, like Swift, to satirize specific individuals as well as social types. Neither is it surprising that ever since 1748 many unfounded rumors have arisen concerning whom Smollett had in mind in this, that, or another character. Several examples will suffice. As a prototype for Captain Oakum, Lord Augustus Fitzroy was suggested by William Watson,[35] and an attempt has been made to show a connection between Smollett's Whiffle and Harry Paulet, the sixth

---

[33] Quoted "New Smollett Letters," *TLS*, July 24, 1943.
[34] *Letters*, p. 80.
[35] See William Watson, *Life of Henry Fielding* (Edinburgh, 1807), p. 157n.

Duke of Bolton.[36] Smollett's arrogant, ungrateful, and cowardly Jeremy Gawky has long been said to be a portrait of James Buchanan, who became Provost of Glasgow, and was known as Provost Cheeks;[37] the original of Crab is said to have been Dr. Crawford.[38] One can guess that Smollett's unpleasant Mr. Cringer, M.P., may have resembled the Scottish Member of Parliament from Glasgow in 1739, the year Smollett reached London, namely William Campbell of the Duke of Argyll's Regiment of the Horse.[39] Then again, Cringer may have been inspired by later M.P.'s from Glasgow[40] before the composition of *Roderick Random*. Another dubious identification was advanced by the historian of Chelsea and Kensington, Thomas Faulkner, who believed that James Elphinston, the author of *Education*, "was ludicrously portrayed in Smollett's *Roderick Random*, which in consequence became a forbidden book in his school."[41] Though Elphinston possessed mental and physical oddities akin to those of Smollett's schoolmaster (Chapter 14), there is nothing to prove that he was in London under Smollett's observation during the composition of the novel.[42]

[36] The theory that Smollett's Capt. Whiffle was modeled after Harry Paulet (or Powlett) the 6th Duke of Bolton seems to have originated in an article in *Notes and Queries*, 2 Ser., VIII (1859), 407. See also *Notes and Queries*, 3 Ser., II (1862), 198; Lewis Bettany, *Edward Jerningham and His Friends* (London, 1919), p. 188 n.1.; and A. M. W. Stirling, *The Letter-Bag of Lady Elizabeth Spencer-Stanhope*, 2 vols. (London and New York, 1913), I, 18. For an account of Harry Paulet, see *DNB*. In no memoir of him which I have read is there the slightest evidence that Smollett could have observed him. According to the article in *DNB*, Paulet was portrayed in Charles Johnston's *Chrysal, or the Adventures of a Guinea*.

[37] Buchanan's obituary in the *Annual Register*, XIV (1771), 146, played up the identification: "At Glasgow provost Buchanan; the person from whom Dr. Smollett took the character of Squire Gawky in *Roderic [sic] Random*." See *The Emmet; A Selection of Original Essays, Tales, Anecdotes, Bon Mots, Choice Sayings, &c.*, 2 vols. (Glasgow, 1824), II, 9-10. For a transcript, see Appendix, pp. 329-30. See also *Glasgow Past and Present*, 3 vols. (Glasgow, 1884), II, 38; and *Notes and Queries*, 9 Ser. (1903), XII, 205.

[38] See *The Emmet*, 2 vols. (Glasgow, 1824), I, 5.

[39] He is so described in *Return. Members of Parliament* ([London], 1878), p. 84.

[40] Cornet William Campbell was succeeded in 1741 by Neil Buchanan, who having died in 1744, was followed by John Campbell.

[41] Thomas Faulkner, *History and Antiquities of Kensington* (London, 1820), pp. 393-94.

[42] R. C. Dallas in his memoir of James Elphinston (*Gentleman's Magazine*, LXXIX [1809], 1063) referred to Elphinston's peculiar countenance, his addiction to old-fashioned attire, and his insistence on the purity of the English tongue. That Smollett incorporated all of these into his ludicrous schoolmaster does not prove that he had Elphinston in mind. Other Scottish pedants in London doubtless possessed the same

There is no doubt, however, that Smollett, to the keen enjoyment of his readers, occasionally painted portraits pretty exactly from the life. An undeniable instance of this is found in the character of the schoolmaster-landlord (Chapter 10) whom Roderick and Strap met en route to London in a small rural public house. The person here depicted was Richard Cooper of West Aukland, a village some thirty miles south of Newcastle on the main London highway. What is known of Cooper harmonizes completely with Smollett's delectable portrait.[43] Finally there is Strap, a most amusing creation, and the delight of all readers of Smollett, "partly taken from the life," as Smollett admitted to Carlyle in 1748. So well-known has Strap become to Smollett's readers that at least five persons have been championed as Smollett's model for him. These are Robert Foulis, the Glasgow printer;[44] Duncan Niven, bailiff of Glasgow;[45] Hutchinson, a barber of Dunbar;[46] John Lewis (*alias* Strap, according to Smollett);[47] and Hugh Hewson, hairdresser in London.[48] The last mentioned candidate left, as we learn from the writer of his obituary,[49] an interlined copy of *Roderick Random* revealing to what extent Strap was based on his life. As this touching relic from the year 1809 has disappeared, the validity of Hewson's claims will probably be challenged again.[50]

Such minor matters, together with the more important evidences of the reception of *Roderick Random* in England and Scotland in the period following its publication make it abundantly clear that Smollett's first novel was as complete a success as he could possibly have hoped for. This surely confirmed his self-confidence and pride, qualities which never deserted him. He seems to have been

---

peculiarities. The fact is, however, that Elphinston's students might have been struck by startling resemblances between their master and Smollett's vivid caricature.

[43] See William Lee, "Roderick Random in the North," in *The Monthly Chronicle of North-Country Lore and Legend*, Newcastle-on-Tyne, I (1887), 340-43.

[44] See David Murray, "Robert and Andrew Foulis and the Glasgow Press" in *Records of the Glasgow Bibliographical Society* (Glasgow, 1913), II, 6.

[45] See Chambers, *Smollett*, pp. 52-53.

[46] *Ibid.*, p. 53n.

[47] *Letters*, p. 45.

[48] See Chambers, *Smollett*, p. 52n.

[49] See *Gentleman's Magazine*, LXXIX (1809), 285-86, and *The Examiner, A Sunday Paper*, No. 65, March 26, 1809. For a recent roundup of many short references to Hewson, see in *The London Times* for September 16, 1936 (p. 8) a communication: "Pigtails and Pitch" by Mr. Alfred North.

[50] The list of other periodical entries concerning the originals for Strap is too long to cite here.

pleased over the revenge he took in *Roderick Random* on the theatrical managers, and arrogantly elated because Garrick, being "inexpressibly galled at the character of Marmozet"[51] made advances toward a reconciliation—advances which Smollett was not yet in the mood to encourage because he felt that Garrick needed more discipline. As we have seen, he planned for the winter of 1748-1749 another comedy which came to nothing. He was also working at his translation of LeSage's *Gil Blas*.

The story of Smollett's labors on the *Gil Blas* is still incompletely revealed. In his letter to Carlyle, February 14, 1749, Smollett referred to the translation as a "Bookseller's job, done in a hurry," a work to which he did not choose to put his name. He also informed Carlyle at the same time that only 400 copies remained out of 3000 issued. This number was printed, according to Strahan's ledger,[52] in September 1748. In the *General Advertiser* for October 14, 1748, the four pocket volumes were described as "elegantly printed on a new Elzevir Letter and Superfine paper," and as being "a new translation, from the best French edition," adorned with 33 cuts. These books were on sale at T. Osborne's in Paternoster Row in October 1748 as indicated by the *General Advertiser* and also by the *London Magazine*.[53] That is, the *Gil Blas* was first published, not in 1749,[54] as sometimes has been stated, but some nine months after *Roderick Random* appeared in print. But when did Smollett work, "in a hurry" (to repeat his phrase), on the laborious job of translation? The first point to raise is whether or not he translated from the edition of *Gil Blas* issued at Paris in 1747[55] with LeSage's final corrections. This seems likely, judging

---

[51] Smollett's letter to Carlyle, June 7, 1748, in "New Smollett Letters" (*TLS*, July 24, 1943).

[52] See my article, "Smollett's Works as Printed by William Strahan," in *The Library*, XIII (1932), 285.

[53] The *London Magazine*, XVII (1748), 480. See also *General Advertiser*, October 14, 1748.

[54] The first edition of Smollett's *Gil Blas* has been usually assigned to the year 1749. See Eugène Joliat, *Smollett Et La France* (Paris, 1935), p. [59]. I have never seen an edition dated 1748, but Léo Claretie in his *Lesage Romancier D'Après de Nouveaux Documents* (Paris, 1890), p. 434 (under English translations) recorded the following: "The Adventures of Gil Blas of Santillano translated by M. Roderick Random (T. Smollet [*sic*]) London, Osborn, 1748."

[55] This edition, which I have not seen, was listed in a "Catalogue of Armorial Bindings; Books etc." issued by T. Pearson & Co., Ltd., 1930-1931, item 130: *Histoire De Gil Blas De Santillane Par M. LeSage. Dernière Édition revue, & corrigée. A Paris.* 4 vols. 1747. There is a copy of this edition in the J. Pierpont Morgan Library.

from the phrase, "the best French edition," used in advertising the translation. As this French edition appeared late in 1747,[56] it would scarcely have been available for the use of Smollett until the end of that year, by which time *Roderick Random* was being printed. This is not to imply that Smollett had not become familiar with an earlier French edition of *Gil Blas*, but it is a good guess that in translating it, he used a copy of the 1747 edition, furnished him by the booksellers. The latter, sensing soon after LeSage's death an English demand for his masterpiece, approached Smollett to do a translation. Or perhaps Smollett approached them. At any rate an elegant edition with 33 cuts appeared (the Paris edition of 1747 had 32 cuts)[57] and sold rapidly. And this translation, on which Smollett did not allow his name to appear, is probably the best and certainly the most popular one which has ever been made.[58]

Because the bookseller, T. Osborne, made money on Smollett's translation of *Gil Blas*, he had Strahan, in or before February 1750, print 2000 copies of *The Devil upon Crutches*, a translation of Le-Sage's *Le Diable Boiteux*. The *General Advertiser* for February 1, 1749-50 announced this work as forthcoming "elegantly printed on a new Elzevir letter and superfine Dutch paper, adorned with a new set of Cuts."[59] That Smollett prepared this translation is all but certain, though he never referred to it in any known correspondence. For this assertion there are valid reasons. The first is a statement in the *Biographical Magazine*, London, 1794, in a memoir of Smollett: "It would be difficult to enumerate all his literary labours. He translated Gil Blas, the Devil on Two Sticks, and Telemachus." This statement alone is not very impressive, but there is documentary proof that in 1759 Smollett corrected what appears to be his own translation of *The Devil upon Crutches* in the following receipt in Smollett's own hand:

[56] According to Auguste Dupouy's introduction to his edition of *Gil Blas* (Paris, 1935), LeSage lived just long enough to see his revised 1747 edition of *Gil Blas*; LeSage died at Boulogne-sur-Mer, November 17, 1747.

[57] See Catalogue of the J. Pierpont Morgan LeSage Collection in Harvard University Library.

[58] See Joliat, *op. cit.*, p. 66.

[59] For the complete announcement, see my article, "Smollett and LeSage's *The Devil upon Crutches*" in *MLN*, XLVII (1932), 91-93. My suggestion in this article that *The Devil upon Crutches* might have appeared in 1748 is erroneous.

London Jan. 5, 1759
Received of Mr. A. Millar Seven Guineas and a half,
on Account of Correcting the Devil on Crutches by me
Ts Smollett

On the verso of the manuscript, possibly in Millar's hand, is the following endorsement:

D Smollets rect for
correcting
Devil on Crutches
5 Janry 1759   7.17.6[60]

This edition of *The Devil upon Crutches* corrected by Smollett was certainly the one published in 1759 for T. Osborne, A. Millar and others. When the latter text is compared with that of 1750, Smollett's improvements are readily observed. Like his manuscript corrections of his *Travels*, the emendations illustrate his fondness for precise diction and his scrupulous care in syntax.

In 1748 and 1749, then, Smollett was translating LeSage. He was also, by June 1748, hard at work on his translation of Cervantes' *Don Quixote*, though it was not to be published until 1755. On June 7, 1748, he confided in Carlyle:

I have contracted with two Booksellers to translate Don Quixote from the Spanish language which I have studied some time—this perhaps you will look upon as a very desperate undertaking there being no fewer than four translations of the same Book, already extant, but I am fairly engaged and cannot recede.[61]

By November 1748 the translation was announced in the press.[62] It is not surprising that this time-consuming and exacting project had eventually to be deferred in favor of other undertakings, but the astonishing fact is that by about 1749 Smollett had completed enough of the translation to receive his pay for the entire project. This is evident from what he wrote to Dr. Macaulay December 11, 1754:

[60] Printed here from Bodleian MSS 25444, f. 57, at Oxford. This document was printed in a Sale Catalogue of Peter Cunningham, 1855. See Br. Mus. Sale Catalogues S. and W., 394.

[61] Letter to Carlyle in "New Smollett Letters," *TLS*, July 24, 1943.

[62] The *General Advertiser*, November 21, 1748, ran the following: "Preparing for the Press, a new Translation of 'The Life and Achievements of the Ingenious Knight Don Quixote De La Mancha' from the original Spanish of Miguel Cervantes de Saavedra. By the author of Roderick Random. With a new set of cuts design'd by Hayman, and engrav'd by the best masters. Printed for J. Osborn, at the Golden-Ball in Paternoster-Row." This identical notice appeared again on September 7, 1749.

Nay I am put to very great straits for present subsistence, as I have done nothing all the last summer but worked upon Don Quixotte, [*sic*] for which I was paid five years ago.[63]

In 1749, as we have noted in the preceding chapter, Smollett wrote the *Alceste*. In February of the same year he "opened a subscription," as he expressed it, or, in other words, advertised his proposals for printing *The Regicide*, all thoughts of staging which he now abandoned after his indomitable ten-year struggle with the theatrical managers. Readers of the *General Advertiser* for February 11, 1749, were struck by this comprehensive and arresting notice:

This Day is Publish'd Proposals for Printing by Subscription on a superfine royal paper, for the benefit of the Author, 'The Regicide, or James the First of Scotland, a Tragedy' By the author of Roderick Random. The singular way in which this performance has been excluded from both theatres (as will appear in the Preface) obliges the Author to publish it in a way otherwise not agreeable to his inclination. The Price to Subscribers will be five shillings. Subscriptions are taken and Receipts signed by the Author, deliver'd by J. Osborn in Paternoster-Row; A. Millar in the Strand; J. Brackstone at the Royal Exchange; J. Jolliffe in St. James's Street; and H. Chapelle in Grosvenor Street. N.B. Those who are willing to encourage the above subscription are desired to subscribe as soon as possible, that the Number to be printed may be ascertained.[64]

In February Strahan printed 2000 proposals, none of which seems to have been preserved. Perhaps they contained little more than what appeared in the newspaper notice. On the first of May came the preliminary announcement[65] of the subscription edition of *The Regicide*, which duly appeared about May 12 on royal paper. The title page carried the phrase, "By the Author of Roderick Random" and quotations from Euripides and Juvenal.[66] Preceding the text Smollett featured his account of his struggles with the managers, the content of which has already been analyzed. No list of subscribers has turned up. Although Smollett, sanguine to the end

[63] *Letters*, p. 32.

[64] This notice was repeated on February 13, 14, 15, and on March 9, 10, 11.

[65] See the *General Advertiser* for May 1, 1749.

[66] The brief quotation from Euripides' *The Suppliants* (ll. 180-84) may be translated as follows: A real poet rejoices in bringing forth song, for a man who struggles greatly cannot delight others. In the quotation from Juvenal (Satire VII, 53ff.) the central idea is similar: the great poet must be free of care and bitterness. By these quotations Smollett is suggesting to the public that *The Regicide* would have been a finer dramatic poem had he composed it without the worry and bitterness caused by theatrical producers.

about *The Regicide,* foresaw in February 1749 that the subscription would fulfill his "warmest Expectations,"[67] the final list of names may have been such that it seemed wise to all concerned not to publish it. At the end of his preface Smollett thanked the public for the "uncommon Encouragement . . . received in the Publication"[68] of his play. As to the printing of the subscription edition, no certain information is available, though Professor McKillop has advanced the plausible suggestion that Samuel Richardson may have had a hand in it.[69]

The Regicide was offered to the general public in June 1749[70] in a trade edition prepared for J. Osborn and A. Millar, and it also appeared in Dublin the same year.

In general, little seems to be on record as to the immediate reception of Smollett's tragedy, though in later years his enemies were forever jeering at it. There was, however, one exceedingly prompt and flattering review in the very first issue of the *Monthly Review,* just launched by "Several Hands" under the direction of Ralph Griffiths. The writer of this review, apparently John Cleland,[71] declared:

As to the merit of the play itself, we shall not affront the author so much as to compare it with any of those wretched pieces which the judicious managers preferred to it. The diction is everywhere animated, nervous, and pathetic. The character of the virtuous, brave, and gentle *Dunbar,* is finely contrasted to that of the headstrong, fierce, ambitious *Stuart. Eleanora,* esteeming most the first, but loving the latter, and distracted between her passion and her duty, is a character both natural and well touched. We shall say no more here of it, than that we think it no hazarded judgment to pronounce it one of the best theatrical pieces that has appeared these many years.[72]

[67] See Smollett's letter to Carlyle, February 14, 1748/9, in "New Smollett Letters," *TLS,* July 24, 1943.
[68] "Preface" to *The Regicide,* subscription edition, p. [v].
[69] See Alan D. McKillop, *Samuel Richardson Printer and Novelist* (University of North Carolina Press, 1936), p. 180 and 180 n.
[70] The advertisement in the *General Advertiser* for June 22, 1749, follows:
This day is published, Price 1s 6d "The Regicide, or James the First of Scotland, a tragedy." By the author of Roderick Random. Printed for John Osborn in Pater-Noster-Row and A. Millar in the Strand. Where may be had the same on Royal paper, Printed by Subscription for the author. Price 5s. Where also may be had "The Adventures of Roderick Random" The Second Edition, in Two Volumes. Price 6s.
[71] See Benjamin Christie Nangle, the *Monthly Review . . . Indexes of Contributors and Articles* (Oxford, 1934), p. 184.
[72] Quoted in the *Monthly Review,* I [1749], 72.

Following this was added *in toto* Smollett's preface, which, Cleland said, ought to be presented as a warning to ambitious dramatists. The preface, it seems certain, was more widely read than *The Regicide* itself, which, in spite of (perhaps because of) a decade of revisions had little life in it, and remains for the modern reader far and away the dullest thing Smollett ever wrote. Its fatal weakness as a stage play had been obvious all along: Alexander Carlyle in his *Autobiography* summed up the whole matter rather well:

> Soon after our acquaintance, Smollett showed me his tragedy of *James I. of Scotland*, which he never could bring on the stage. For this the managers could not be blamed, though it soured him against them, and he appealed to the public by printing it; but the public seemed to take part with the managers.[73]

In this kind understatement, Carlyle embodied, no doubt, both Scottish and English opinions in 1749 and later. To Smollett, however, the mere publication of *The Regicide* was a compelling necessity. At last his tragedy had a kind of triumph, at least in beautiful paper and print. And the preface was a necessary release for Smollett's inner psychological tensions, of which he himself was aware, as is remarkably clear in a bit of self-analysis he included in a letter to Carlyle, October 1, 1749. Therein after complaining because Drs. Mc Ghie and Armstrong, unlike Carlyle, were very reticent over *The Regicide*, Smollett added, "The truth is I am piqued at the Superiority which the Wariness and Wisdom of such fellows gives them over the Weakness and Leakiness of my own Disposition."[74] The dynamic energy which produced this Leakiness (loquaciousness) in speech and in print spurred Smollett on to excessive personal satire; it led to angry controversies; it was an urge which produced in later years very revealing self-analysis; it motivated the comic power (the *vis comica*) of portions of *Roderick Random*. It was to vibrate again in the pages of *Peregrine Pickle*, which work and other related matters we shall examine in the next chapter.

[73] Dr. Alexander Carlyle, *Autobiography*, ed. Burton (London and Edinburgh, 1910), p. 198.
[74] See "New Smollett Letters," *TLS*, July 31, 1943.

CHAPTER VI

Chelsea and Paris; *Peregrine Pickle*, 1750-1752

IN 1750 Smollett changed his residence from Beaufort Buildings, Beaufort Street, near the Strand and Somerset House, to Old Chelsea. In the Parish Book[1] he was rated twice that year as follows:

24 Tobias Smollet Esqr 3 m^os to Mich^s   o   9   o
24 Tobias Smollet Esqr   o   18   o[2]

From the first entry we conclude that Smollett settled at Chelsea about the end of June; in that charming spot he maintained his residence until 1763,[3] when he went abroad for his health. For those thirteen years his rent continued to be £24 per year.

Smollett's reasons for moving to Chelsea are not known. Possibly he and Mrs. Smollett wished a quieter and more healthful spot for their daughter Elizabeth, now about three years old. Possibly Smollett's mother-in-law arrived from Jamaica at this time so that a larger establishment was required. The most compelling reason, we believe, was that Smollett saw in Chelsea an ideal place in which to combine his writing and his medical practice.

As Smollett lived for thirteen strenuous and memorable years in the Village of Palaces, as Chelsea was called, a reconstruction of his new surroundings will be useful. Peter Kalm, the Swedish horticulturalist who visited Chelsea in 1748, was impressed by its charm. "The place," he wrote, "resembles a town, has a church, beautiful streets, well built and handsome houses, all of brick, three or four stories high."[4] He also noted that it thrived in business because the Londoners came out in throngs in fine weather on

[1] I am indebted to the kind assistance of the Keeper of the Rate Books at the Town Hall, Chelsea, in examining the records of Smollett's residence.

[2] Chelsea Rate Book for 1750, First Assessment, f. 27; Second Assessment, f. 25.

[3] Smollett's name is in all the Chelsea Rate Books from 1750 to 1763 except those of 1752 and 1753, which were missing in 1930, when I searched the records.

[4] Kalm's *Account of his Visit to England on his Way to America in 1748*, translated by Joseph Lucas (London and New York, 1892), pp. 96ff.

weekends to enjoy its fresh air and to patronize its shops. That Smollett liked the Chelsea scene is apparent from his calling it in 1763 his "Second native Place."[5] His feeling for it, however, was not expressed in any ode to the Thames to match his "Ode to Leven-Water." Yet Chelsea must have pleased Smollett, much as it later attracted Thomas Carlyle, whose description of it in 1834 conveyed its rural charm:

> We lie safe at a bend of the river, away from all the great roads, have air and quiet hardly inferior to Craigenputtock, an outlook from the back windows into mere leafy regions with here and there a red high-peaked old roof looking through; and see nothing of London except by day the summits of St. Paul's Cathedral and Westminster Abbey, and by night the great Babylon affronting the peaceful skies. . . . We . . . could shoot a gun into Smollett's old house (at this very time getting pulled down), where he wrote "Count Fathom," and was wont every Saturday to dine a company of hungry authors and then set them fighting together. Don Saltero's coffee-house still looks as brisk as in Steele's time; Nell Gwynne's boudoir, still bearing her name, has become a gin-temple (not inappropriately); in fine Erasmus lodged with More (they say) in a spot not five hundred yards from this.[6]

Smollett's house occupied the area where Nos. 23 and 24 Lawrence Street were located when the *Survey of London* was issued, about 1913. On their site in 1750 stood a group of four early eighteenth-century houses forming a single architectural unit, then called Monmouth House because the Duchess of Monmouth had occupied two of them from 1718 to 1732. Into one of the western sections of this cluster of buildings[7] the Smolletts moved. In the rear lay an extensive garden with "a small remote filbert walk," happily alluded to by Smollett in his account of his Sunday dinners for "unfortunate brothers of the quill" in *Humphry Clinker*.[8] Some idea of the house itself and of its interior can be gained by examining the water-color drawings of it preserved at the Chelsea Public Library.[9] From them one gets a general impression of dignity, space, and charm.

[5] *Letters*, p. 84.
[6] Quoted from Reginald Blunt, *The Carlyles' Chelsea Home* (London, 1895), pp. [14]-15.
[7] See *Survey of London*, Vol. IV (The Parish of Chelsea, Part II) (London, 1913), pp. 58-59. See Plate 57 for a picture of Monmouth House.
[8] See *Humphry Clinker*, Letter from Jerry, London, June 10.
[9] See *Chelsea a Hundred Years Ago. Catalogue of an Exhibition of Water-Colour Drawings 1800-1820*, published by The Chelsea Society [ca. 1929], pp. 10, 20, 22 for a description of the original drawings.

That Smollett was no recluse in Chelsea is clear from his correspondence with, and relating to, his friends there. One of these, Dr. Alexander Reid, lived for a time on Cheyne Row very near Lawrence Street and later on Paradise Row, off Cheyne Walk, no great distance east of Smollett's house. Reid, a versatile figure, interested not only in medicine, but in music and literature, was a member of the Sublime Society of Beef Steaks.[10] This gentleman was also a leading spirit in the Chelsea Bowling Green Society,[11] and a member of what Smollett described as "our Brotherhood at the Swan,"[12] presumably a Masonic group, as there is a record of Masonic meetings at the White Swan, Chelsea, and in other places in Chelsea in the 1750's.[13] The White Swan tavern,[14] which Smollett patronized, stood on the bank of the Thames east of the Pharmaceutical (or Botanical) Gardens, a short walking distance from Lawrence Street. Near the Swan, in the vicinity of the Botanical Gardens and in charge of them lived the very distinguished botanist, Philip Miller, who assisted Smollett occasionally in the *Critical Review*.[15]

To the east on Cheyne Walk, a short stroll from Smollett's home, stood the famous Don Saltero's Coffee House with its museum of curiosities to which Smollett contributed,[16] and where he is known to have passed convivial hours in 1761.[17] That in spite of failing health he frequented Don Saltero's as late as 1763 is

[10] Dr. Alexander Reid became a member, April 28, 1759. For a good account of this Club see Walter Arnold, *The Life and Death of the Sublime Society of Beef Steaks* (London, 1871), *passim*.

[11] See Thomas Faulkner, *Historical and Topographical Description of Chelsea and its Environs*, 2 vols. (Chelsea, 1829), II, 280ff.

[12] *Letters*, p. 86.

[13] According to John Lane's *Masonic Records 1717-1886* (London, 1886), Medina Lodge 35 met at the Old Cheshire Cheese at Chelsea in 1750, at Queen's Head, Chelsea, 1753, and at the White Swan, Chelsea, 1759.

[14] For the White Swan tavern, see Faulkner's *Chelsea* (Chelsea, 1829), II, 187ff., and Alfred Beaver, *Memorials of Old Chelsea* (London, 1892), pp. 249ff. See Beaver's reproduction of an old print of the White Swan, which dated from the seventeenth century. Pepys visited it in 1666. In the eighteenth century it was the goal of Doggett's Coat and Badge Race.

[15] See my communication, "Smollett's Letter to Philip Miller" in *TLS* (June 24, 1944), p. 312.

[16] See John Timbs' *Curiosities of London* (London, 1855), p. 75; Faulkner's *Chelsea* (1829), I, 378; and *Survey of London*, II (Chelsea, Part I), 61-63. In the latter is printed the "Complete List of Benefactors." Among the names is that of Smollett.

[17] For Smollett's dinner at Don Saltero's in May 1761, see John Forster, *The Life and Times of Oliver Goldsmith*, 2 vols. (London, 1871), I, 149n.

indicated by George Canning's satirical lines, entitled "On the Tragedy of Elvira":

> Toby Smollett last night, sipping punch at Saltero's,
> Cast his eye o'er a list of our Tragedy Heroes;
> At this one he wink'd, at another he nodded—
> In short, some he censur'd, and some he applauded:
> When he came to his Countryman, David Malloch,
> The Doctor tremendously see-saw'd his block;
> Half-grinning he cried, "What a pitiful story!
> "Davy Malloch the Whig in his old age turn'd *Tory*!
> "How convenient to *some* their political Creed!—
> "Troth, David, we're baith frae the Noarth o' the Tweed."[18]

At Don Saltero's Smollett could not have failed to observe a great variety of foreign tourists as well as celebrities from all over the British Isles.

Another remarkable social center in Chelsea was Ranelagh Gardens,[19] with its famous Rotunda, first opened in 1742. There is no record that Smollett patronized this resort, but surely it may be assumed that he and his family were familiar with it.[20]

Adjoining Monmouth House was the remarkable Chelsea China Manufactory, operated from 1747-1769 by Nicholas Sprimont,[21] who produced the most beautiful porcelain of that era. There is a pleasing tradition that Dr. Johnson at an uncertain period visited the Chelsea China Factory about twice a week and was allowed to bake in their ovens his own mixtures, which never turned out to be satisfactory.[22] The great Cham of Literature, as Smollett dubbed Johnson in 1759,[23] could hardly have missed calling on Smollett and sauntering in his garden, though the lexicographer and Smollett, in the latter's words in 1759, "were never catercousins."[24] Nothing specific is known of their association, but it is significant that Johnson presented to Mary Palmer, niece of Sir Joshua Reynolds, the third edition of Smollett's translation of *Gil Blas*, printed in 1751.[25]

[18] See George Canning, *Poems* (London, 1767), p. 89.
[19] For views of Ranelagh see Warwick Wroth, *The London Pleasure Gardens of the Eighteenth Century*, London, 1896.
[20] For Smollett's varied comments on Ranelagh, see *Humphry Clinker*, Letter of Bramble, London, May 29; and Letter of Lydia, London, May 31.
[21] See Dr. Bellamy Gardner, "The Site of the Chelsea Porcelain Factory," in the *Connoisseur*, XCI (1933), 170-73. Bellamy reproduced here a painting of Smollett's house done about 1810 and now in the Chelsea Public Library.
[22] Faulkner's *Chelsea* (1829), I, 273-74.   [23] *Letters*, p. 56.   [24] *Ibid*.
[25] See Catalogue No. 23 (February 1929) of Elkin Mathews Ltd., item 50.

From the china factory and Monmouth House it was only a short walk to Chelsea Old Church. There are some indications that Smollett and his family were members there in good standing. In the first place, the records of this church disclose that both Mrs. Leaver, Smollett's mother-in-law, and his own daughter Elizabeth, were buried there beneath a stone in the middle aisle, the former in 1762, and the latter in 1763.[26] Secondly, Smollett's participation in the affairs of this church is proved by the following record salvaged by the historian Faulkner from the vestry minutes:

> 1759. *March*. At a Vestry, the Parishioners proceeded to the choice of a Lecturer, in the room of the Rev. Mr. Rothery, lately deceased; and the Rev. Mr. T. Martyn was nominated by Dr. Martyn; and in opposition, Dr. Smollett nominated the Rev. Mr. William Gardner; and, upon a poll being demanded, the numbers appeared as follow:—
>
> For the Rev. Mr. Gardner 185
> For the Rev. Mr. Martyn .... 167[27]

A preliminary announcement of this election in the *Public Advertiser* of February 27, 1759, identified the winner of the election as "the Rev. William Gardiner, M.A., Curate of the Parish," and the defeated candidate as "the Rev. Thomas Martyn, B.A., Fellow of Sidney-Sussex College in Cambridge."[28] Though the relative merits of the candidates and the significance of the contest are not wholly clear,[29] Smollett's support of the Rev. William Gardner [Gardiner], curate of Chelsea from 1755 to 1764, must be remembered as a significant fact in the story of his social connections in Chelsea.

There were other Chelsea figures with whom Smollett was on very friendly terms. In 1750 there lived on Beaufort Street, Chel-

---

[26] For further notes on their burial in Chelsea Church, see my article, "Elizabeth Smollett, Daughter of Tobias Smollett," in *RES*, VIII (1932), 312-15.

[27] Faulkner, *op. cit.*, II, 90.

[28] For information on Thomas Martin and his father, John Martin, who practiced medicine in Chelsea 1730-1752, see *DNB*. See also George Cornelius Gorham, *Memoirs of John Martyn, F.R.S., and of Thomas Martyn, B.D., F.R.S., F.L.S.* (London, 1830), p. 94.

[29] It is possible that Smollett in his medical practice in Chelsea had come to dislike John Martin, his professional rival, and for that reason opposed his son. Thomas Martin, the defeated candidate, believed he lost because the Rev. Gardner, "having married the daughter of a carpenter, had all the tradesmen with him," who outvoted his supporters, "the nobility and gentry, and the lower orders." See Faulkner, *op. cit.*, II, 90, and Gorham, *op. cit.*, p. 94, where it is stated that Martin was much beloved by the poorer classes in Chelsea.

sea,[30] John Lewis, who, in 1757, Smollett characterized as my "neighbor John Lewis Bookbinder, alias Strap" in his letter to Rivington.[31] Faulkner, the historian of Chelsea, declared that a bookbinder, "Mr. W. Lewis," resided for many years in Lombard Street[32] until his death about 1785, that he was the intimate friend of Smollett and his traveling companion on their journey from Edinburgh, and that he was portrayed as Strap in *Roderick Random*. Faulkner, who lived for seven years in the house occupied by Lewis' widow, stated that she confirmed the truth of this relationship, and went on to credit the tradition that Smollett induced Lewis to carry on bookbinding in Chelsea and recommended him to the nobility and gentry there.[33] It may be assumed, then, that Lewis owed much to Smollett's kindness and that he occasionally bound the novelist's books. Another friend of Smollett in Chelsea may have been Oakley Halford, who resided after 1748 on Cheyne Walk,[34] and was presumably the Halford twice referred to in Smollett's letters.[35] Halford's neighbor, one Major Macdonald,[36] was also a Chelsea acquaintance of Smollett, who referred to him while they both were in Bath in 1768. Other friends were the elderly and eminent gardener, Philip Miller, whose appraisal of botanical works Smollett solicited for the *Critical Review*; and two individuals named Wilton and Russell, who remain obscure.[37] The

[30] John Lewis was taxed from 6/0 to 9/0 in the Chelsea Rate Book, under Beaufort Street from 1748-1750.

[31] *Letters*, p. 45.

[32] The Beaufort Street on which Lewis was rated in 1750 seems to have been in the area called Beaufort Place. The latter was just west of Lombard Street. See C. & J. Greenwood's Map of London published by Greenwood & Co., Regent St., Pall Mall, 1830.

[33] Faulkner, *op. cit.*, I, 171. In spite of the fact that Faulkner referred to Smollett's John Lewis as W. Lewis, there is no reason to doubt the general veracity of his account.

[34] See Walter H. Godfrey, *Survey of London*, Vol. II (Chelsea, Part I), London, *ca.* 1909, p. 36.

[35] *Letters*, p. 86, and my article, "More Smollett Letters," *MLN* (1933), 248.

[36] This Major was perhaps the "Major M'Donald" on the list of the benefactors of Don Saltero's.

[37] In 1763 Smollett in his letter to Alexander Reid wished to be remembered to his "good Friends, Messr⁸ Wilton & Russel, & to all our Brotherhood at the Swan." See *Letters*, p. 86. The *Russel* in the preceding was printed *Russell* in Faulkner's *Historical and Topographical Description of Chelsea*, I, 272. Faulkner printed Smollett's letter from the original manuscript then owned by C. W. Reid of Durham Place, to whose grandfather Smollett sent it. As to the identity of Wilton, Professor Noyes suggested that possibly he was the sculptor Joseph Wilton, but Wilton lived in Rome and Florence until 1755 and after that year he settled in Charing Cross. (See *DNB*.) It is more likely that Smollett's friend was John Wilton, Deputy Treasurer of Chelsea in

last personality in this group of Chelsea friends was a naval figure, Captain Robert Mann. "If you want to know how I spend my Time in this retreat," Smollett wrote to Dr. Moore in 1757, "he [Capt. Mann] can satisfy you in that particular, for he has been my Club companion these seven long years."[38] But Moore recorded nothing of Mann's revelations of Smollett's life in Chelsea; and the gallant captain, whom Smollett recommended as "a brave, experienced officer, and an honest Tar in whom there is no guile"[39] was killed in action in March 1762, though his ship, the *Milford*, emerged victorious.[40]

Such were some of the Chelsea worthies whom Smollett found congenial, but many Englishmen whom he met in Chelsea he found inferior to his friends in old Scotland, as we see from the following confession to Carlyle written after his trip to Scotland in 1753:

> I do not think I could enjoy life with greater relish in any part of the World than in Scotland among you and your friends . . . I am heartily tired of this land of indifference and phligm [*sic*] where the finer sensations of the soul are not felt, and felicity is held to consist in stupifying Port and overgrown buttocks of Beef—Where Genius is lost, learning undervalued, Taste altogether extinguished, and Ignorance prevail, to such a degree that one of our Chelsea club asked me if the Weather was good when I crossed the sea from Scotland, and another desired to know if there were not more Popes than One, in as much as he had heard people mention the Pope of Rome, an expression which seemed to imply that there was a Pope of some other place. I answered there was a Pope of Troy and another of Tartary, and he seemed perfectly well satisfied with the Information, which no person present pretended to contradict. The same Stolidity prevails among the audience at our Theatres.[41]

How revealing this is of Smollett's nostalgia for Scotland, and of

---

1755. Russell may have been the poet, Dr. Thomas Russell, as Professor Noyes has suggested, but I am not satisfied that he frequented Chelsea during Smollett's residence there.

[38] *Letters*, p. 46.   [39] *Ibid.*

[40] For details of Robert Mann's naval career, see John Charnock, *Biographia Navalis*, VI, 262ff. Mann's appointment as commander of the *Porcupine*, to which Smollett referred in his letter to Moore, was dated November 10, 1756. In 1762 he was made commander of H.M.S. *Milford*. The fight between the *Milford* and the French letter of marque, the *Gloire*, was unusual because the *Milford* lost only four killed and thirteen wounded, but among the casualties were Capt. Mann and his First Lieut. Day. See William Laird Clowes, *The Royal Navy*, 5 vols. (Boston and London), III, 308, 308n. For a detailed contemporaneous account of the battle, see *London Chronicle*, April 6-8, 1762.

[41] From Smollett's letter to Carlyle, Chelsea, March 1, 1754, in "New Smollett Letters," *TLS*, July 31, 1943.

his idealization of genius, taste, learning, and the "finer sensations of the soul." And yet he became very devoted to Chelsea by 1763. In its pleasant streets by the Thames, in his own garden, at Don Saltero's and the Swan, and among its varied human types he could escape from the tremendous labors, and from the ill health and misfortune which the years after 1750 brought him.

Soon after moving to Monmouth House about June 1750, Smollett visited Paris. Dr. John Moore's statement is the basis for all that is known of this trip:

> In the summer of 1750, Dr. Smollett went to Paris. The author of this Essay, who had been introduced to him in England, renewed his acquaintance, and accompanied him in some excursions to St. Cloud, Versailles, and other places in the environs of Paris.[42]

Very little is certain about Smollett's experiences in Paris except that, as Moore stated, he met a painter (the Pallet of *Peregrine Pickle*), and some Scottish exiles, among them Mr. Hunter of Burnside. How much Smollett moved in Moore's Parisian circles[43] is not known. Moore recollected Smollett's anti-French prejudices and his lack of facility in speaking French—both barriers to much understanding of the Parisians. In the long line of Smollett biographers Smeaton was the first to assert that Mrs. Smollett accompanied her husband and to cite quotations from Smollett's correspondence not located or printed in full.[44] The length of this visit in Paris can be estimated only roughly by the fact that Smollett was corresponding with Moore from Chelsea, September 28, 1750.[45] By this time Smollett was in the midst of writing *Peregrine Pickle*.

Professor Buck's conjecture that Smollett had written most of the first volume of *Peregrine Pickle* before his trip to Paris[46] must be accepted because it is inconceivable that Smollett could have

---

[42] Quoted from Dr. Moore's "Life" in his edition of *The Works of Tobias Smollett, M.D.*, 8 vols. (London, 1797), I, cxxiii.

[43] The brilliant and industrious John Moore (1729-1802), lived in Paris about two years before he was twenty-one. He was a fellow student in Paris with William Fordyce and surgeon to the household of William Anne Keppel, Earl of Albemarle, the British Ambassador.

[44] " 'To live in Paris,' he says in one of his letters of the period, 'is to live in heaven,' " wrote Smeaton in his *Tobias Smollett* (Edinburgh [1897]), p. 66.

[45] Smollett's letter (*Letters*, p. 10) was written after an implied delay in answering a letter from Moore. As the place where Moore wrote to Smollett is not known, the time element in the correspondence cannot be computed.

[46] Buck, *op. cit.*, p. 2.

written some 330,000 words[47] between September 1750 and January 1751, when advance notices of the publication of *Peregrine Pickle*[48] began to appear. Even the tireless hand of Smollett, which penned *Roderick Random* (about 220,000 words) in less than six months, could not have achieved the impossible. It is probable, since *Peregrine Pickle* (exclusive of "The Memoirs of a Lady of Quality," the account of Lady Vane's amours) is fifty per cent longer than *Roderick Random*, that Smollett was working on the second volume of *Peregrine Pickle* before September 1750. As for the "Memoirs," it is likely, as Professor Putney suggests, that Lady Vane furnished the materials but that Smollett made some revisions in them.[49] At any rate, he had to finish the third and fourth volumes at top speed.

The circumstances of the printing of *Peregrine Pickle* remain obscure. The printer may have been Strahan;[50] perhaps Richardson assumed the contract;[51] at least he knew who was printing Lady Vane's "Memoirs" (in volume 3) in December 1750, as appears in his letter to Mrs. Sarah Chapone, December 6 of that year:

> I mentioned to Mr. Chapone my Wishes, that the Lady who so admirably wrote to correct and instruct a very profligate Woman,[52] would, from the same right Principles and Motives, undertake a Woman of Quality, whom I think, if possible, a worse Woman. If I can procure a Specimen Sheet of the Work, for it is not yet printed quite off, I will cause it, in Confidence, to be sent to that Lady.[53]

From Richardson's statement it can be surmised that *Peregrine Pickle* was about half printed early in December 1750. Advance rumors of the presence of Lady Vane's "Memoirs" in the novel led

[47] The four volumes of *Peregrine Pickle*, 1751, contain approximately 380,000 words, of which "The Memoirs of a Lady of Quality" provide about 50,000 words.

[48] The *General Advertiser*, January 23, 1751, announced *Peregrine Pickle* as speedily to be published.

[49] See Rufus D. S. Putney, "Smollett and Lady Vane's Memoirs" in *PQ*, xxv (April 1946), 120-26.

[50] There is no record of the printing bill in Strahan's ledgers, but *Peregrine Pickle* was printed for the author, not for a bookseller, which fact may explain the absence of a record in Strahan's ledgers, which, on the whole, recorded accounts with booksellers.

[51] This has been suggested as a possibility by Professor Alan D. McKillop in his *Samuel Richardson, Printer and Novelist* (The University of North Carolina Press, 1936), p. 318.

[52] Richardson referred to Teresa Constantia Phillips Muilman, author of *An Apology* and *A Letter . . . to the Right Honourable the Earl of Chesterfield*. To the latter Mrs. Chapone published a reply.

[53] Printed from McKillop, *op. cit.*, p. 180.

the journalist, Dr. John Hill, to prepare his *Lady Frail*.[54] Alarmed upon hearing of this move, Smollett, it seems, added February 7, 1751, to the usual newspaper advertisement of *Peregrine Pickle* the following warning:

> That the publick may not be imposed on, we are authorized to assure them, that no Memoirs of the above Lady, that may be obtruded on the World, under any Disguise whatever, are genuine, encept [*sic*] what is comprised in this Performance.[55]

The very next day, according to the *General Advertiser*, *The History . . . of Lady Frail* appeared. On February 22, 1751, Smollett secured for himself the exclusive copyright of *Peregrine Pickle*. The Register at Stationers' Hall contains the following entry:

Dr. Tobias } The Whole   February 22 1750 [1751]
Smallet   }   Then entered for his copy The
                           Adventures of Peregrine Pickle.
                           In which are included Memoirs
                           of a Lady of Quality. In four
                           Volumes Reced [*sic*] nine books.[56]

Three days later *Peregrine Pickle* was officially published,[57] the price of the four volumes being 12/0 bound, and 10/6 in boards.

Smollett's second novel must have created considerable commotion, though few relevant facts have been preserved. As Professor Buck pointed out,[58] its immediate success in terms of copies sold has been overstated. Although it was printed in Dublin in 1751, and although French and German translations were issued in 1753, a glance at Professor Norwood's list of editions in the *Cambridge Bibliography* will convince one that the novel was not repeatedly reprinted in 1751. Smollett blamed its poor sale partly upon certain booksellers, who, he declared in his Advertisement to the revised edition of 1758, used art and industry "to stifle him [the novel] in the birth" and "were at uncommon pains to misrepresent the work and calumniate the author. . . . The performance," Smollett continued, "was decried as an immoral piece, and a scurrilous libel; the author was charged with having defamed the characters

[54] *The History of a Woman of Quality: or, The Adventures of Lady Frail.* By an Impartial Hand. This was published February 8, 1751, according to the *General Advertiser* of that date.
[55] From the *General Advertiser*, February 7, 1751.
[56] From the Register of 1746-1773, folio 94, at Stationers' Hall. I am indebted to Mr. R. T. Rivington for this entry.
[57] See *General Advertiser*, February 25, 1751.   [58] Buck, *op. cit.*, p. 3.

of particular persons, to whom he lay under considerable obligations: and some formidable criticks declared that the book was void of humour, character and sentiment." Just why the booksellers tried to stifle the sale of *Peregrine Pickle* is not wholly clear, but it may well be that they disapproved of Smollett's independent reservation of the whole copyright. Probably other matters were involved. At any rate there developed a serious feud, the general nature of which is shown by the following extract from a letter written October 14, 1752, by Thomas Birch to his patron, Philip Yorke, Earl of Hardwicke:

> Smollet, who now appears under the character of a Doctor of Physic, is not so far engaged by his profession but that he is trying his fortune again as writer of romance, notwithstanding the ill success of his *Peregrine Pickle* which ruined his reputation among the booksellers in general, against whom he breathes immortal revenge; one of them, Millar, who has particularly offended him by refusing to have any more concern with him, is to have a large share of invective in the new romance, in which Sir George Lyttelton also is to be again introduced.[59]

Birch's statement is distressingly general, but it is obvious that Smollett lost caste with the booksellers because of *Peregrine Pickle*.

In spite of opposition, however, *Peregrine Pickle* was widely read because of its magnificent naval characters;[60] its unfortunately bitter attacks on Fielding, Lyttelton, Akenside, Quin, and Garrick; its depiction of Daniel MacKercher and the famous Annesley Case; and Lady Vane's "Memoirs." To give an exhaustive summary of the contemporaneous reception of the novel would not be appropriate for a biography, but a few opinions may be cited. Elizabeth Montagu, the Queen of the Blue-Stockings, wrote on January 1, 1752, to her sister: "I recommend to your perusal 'The Adventures of Peregrine Pickle.' Lady Vane's story is well told."[61] Lady Luxborough, Lord Bolingbroke's sister, passed on to the poet, William Shenstone, two comments, the first on May 27, 1751:

> Peregrine Pickle I do not admire: it is by the author of Roderick Random, who is a lawyer: but the thing which makes the book sell, is the History

---

[59] Printed from a copy sent me by the late J. Paul De Castro, who transcribed it from literary manuscripts of W. T. Whitley, who took it down from Br. Mus. Ad. MSS, 35393. I have been unable to check this.

[60] See George M. Kahrl, *Tobias Smollett, Traveler-Novelist* (University of Chicago Press [1945]), Chap. 3.

[61] Elizabeth Montagu's *Correspondence from 1720 to 1761*, ed. Emily J. Climenson, 2 vols. (London, 1906), II, 2.

of Lady V-, which is introduced (in the last volume, I think) much to her Ladyship's dishonour; but published by her *own* order, from her *own* Memoirs, given to the author for that purpose; and by the approbation of her *own* Lord. What was ever equal to this fact, and how can one account for it?[62]

Later, on August 25, 1751, she reverted to the same subject:

As to Peregrine Pickle, I hired it, and that merely for the sake of reading one of the volumes, wherein are inserted the Memoirs of Lady V-; which, as I was well acquainted with her, gave me curiosity. The rest of the book is, I think, ill wrote, and not interesting.[63]

Horace Walpole received on March 3, 1751, the opinion of the poet Gray: "Has that miracle of *tenderness and sensibility* (as she calls it) lady Vane given you any amusement? Peregrine, whom she uses as a vehicle, is very poor indeed with a few exceptions."[64] On the 13th of March, Walpole expressed himself to Sir Horace Mann as follows:

My Lady Vane has literally published the Memoirs of her own life, only suppressing part of her lovers, no part of the success of the others with her: a degree of profligacy not to be accounted for; she does not want money, none of her stallions will raise her credit; and the number, all she has to brag of, concealed![65]

In all these comments the emphasis on Lady Vane is significant. In Paris, where she was well-known in fashionable circles, her "Memoirs" received extravagant praise from Pierre Clement, a friend of hers, and author of *Les Cinq Années Littéraires*.[66] In the *Monthly Review* for March 1751, a word on the "Memoirs" was introduced discreetly by John Cleland, the supposed reviewer:[67]

[62] *Letters written by the Late Right Honourable Lady Luxborough to William Shenstone, Esq.* (London, 1775), pp. 265-66.

[63] *Ibid.*, pp. 290-91.

[64] *Correspondence of Thomas Gray*, eds. Paget Toynbee and Leonard Whibley, 3 vols. (Oxford, Clarendon Press, 1935), I, 344.

[65] *The Letters of Horace Walpole*, ed. Mrs. Paget Toynbee, 16 vols. (Oxford, 1903-1905), III, 37.

[66] For Clement's praise of the "Memoirs" see *Les Cinq Années Littéraires*, 2 vols. (Berlin, 1755), II, 28, and II, 51-54. Clement's enthusiasm no doubt pleased Lady Vane, who was a subscriber to *Les Cinq Années*, along with Chesterfield, Lyttelton, Pitt, the Duke of Dorset, the Duke of Waldegrave, Lord Temple, and others.

[67] See Nangle, *op. cit.*, p. 49. It is a good guess that Cleland wrote the unfavorable review of *The History . . . of Lady Frail*, in the *Monthly Review*, IV (Feb. 1751), 307-8. Therein the reviewer announced the publication of *Peregrine Pickle* by the "author of a famous novel," *Roderick Random*. The former work would contain, he declared, the genuine memoirs "of a lady, who is credibly reported to have given real memoirs of herself" to the author.

As these memoirs are not only taken from a character in real life but seem to be voluntarily furnished by the lady V- herself, who is the subject of them, they cannot but be interesting, both from the rarity, as well as the ingenuity of her confessions.[68]

The concluding sentence of Cleland's urbane and friendly review ran as follows:

It [*Peregrine Pickle*] also contains the personal history of Mr. M-r, the manager in the extraordinary cause between the claimant Mr. A-, and the Earl of A-, defendant; in which the author seems to be much delighted with an occasion of paying respect to worth, or what he looks upon as such, tho' unseconded by success.

Herein Cleland glanced at Smollett's account of Daniel MacKercher and the Annesley Case in *Peregrine Pickle*, volume 4. That Smollett was friendly with MacKercher in 1753 is proved by the former's correspondence,[69] and that they had met much earlier is suggested by Smollett's tribute to him as "the melting Scot" in *Reproof*, 1747. Beyond this, all is guesswork. It may be, as Professor Noyes conjectured, that in *Peregrine Pickle* Smollett's compliment to him was a means of showing gratitude for obligations received.[70] It may be that Smollett first met Lady Vane through MacKercher, at one time her lover, if the gossipy John Taylor is to be trusted.[71] In any event, Smollett's account of MacKercher in *Peregrine Pickle* may be accepted as generally accurate, though not complete, for his career down to 1750.[72] The fact is, however, that

[68] *Monthly Review*, IV (March 1751), 362.
[69] *Letters*, pp. 14, 127-30.   [70] *Ibid.*
[71] See John Taylor, *Records of My Life*, 2 vols. (London, 1832), II, 409.
[72] For a print of MacKercher and scattered references to him see Andrew Lang, *The Annesley Case*, in English Notable Trials Series (Edinburgh and London [1912]), p. 116, and "Introduction." MacKercher's life, could it be resurrected, would make an amazingly romantic tale. Smollett says in *Peregrine Pickle* that he entered military service in the Scottish rebellion of 1715 when he was thirteen. He was born, then, about 1702. Smollett's account of his learning and literary activity is supported by the fact that he was a charter member of the Society for the Encouragement of Learning in London in 1736, a member of its committee of 24 managers, and a steady attendant of its meetings down to its final session in 1746. (See Br. Mus. Add. MSS, 6184, 6185-6192.) In this group MacKercher was intimate with such figures as Sir Andrew Mitchell, Lord Elibank, and Dr. James Douglas, all of whom Smollett knew as a young surgeon in Downing Street in 1744. Hence Smollett met MacKercher, it would seem, about that time. In 1737 he was the head of a group of tobacco merchants, probably Scottish, to form a monopoly to compete with the French. (See William and Mary College, *Quarterly Historical Magazine*, Series II, VIII [1928], 9.) This activity was written up by Smollett. By 1740, MacKercher was a well-to-do humanitarian, who championed the cause of James Annesley for many years. In *Peregrine Pickle* Smollett portrayed him as a prisoner in jail, but even there he had money to give to

MacKercher was not wholly pleased when he read *Peregrine Pickle* because he sent to a newspaper for March 8, 1751, this curious communication:

> It being industriously insinuated that the narrative of Mr. M-e in the 4th Volume of the Adventures of Peregrine Pickle are the genuine memoirs of my Life; I cannot help taking this method of undeceiving such as may have been impressed with so groundless a notion by declaring that I never had the vanity or presumption to believe any particulars of my life of that consequence as to merit the attention of the Publick; and that I no sooner had intelligence of the intended Publication of that Narrative than I used my utmost endeavours with the ingenious Author to suppress it but happened to be too late in my application for that purpose.
>
> DANIEL MACKERCHER[73]

This statement, if taken literally, means, surprisingly enough, that Smollett, in his rush for copy to complete his novel, prepared the material on MacKercher without consulting him at all. Yet the latter appears not to have been permanently offended at being thrust in the limelight because he was on friendly terms with Smollett in 1753.

In appraising this unusual situation another matter must be faced. The latter half of Smollett's chapter on MacKercher and the Annesley Case looks like a condensation of a longer version (presumably existing in manuscript in 1750) and published sometime in 1751 with the following title: *An Abstract of the Case of James Annesley, Esq.; Veritas praevalebit Printed in the Year 1751*, no place or publisher being given. In the preface to this tract of approximately 200 pages it is stated that "the following account, was some years ago drawn up, by a person well acquainted with the proceedings of all the parties engaged in the extraordinary contest to which it relates."[74] Now Smollett could have been familiar only in a very general way with the *cause célèbre* of Annesley;

---

his associates. (See the final paragraph of *Peregrine Pickle*, Chap. 98.) Almost complete obscurity covers MacKercher's later years. In 1761 he was taking legal possession of estates in Buckinghamshire and other counties for young Lord Anglesea, son of James Annesley recently deceased. (See the *Public Advertiser*, March 9, 1761.) MacKercher died March 2, 1772, on Margaret Street, Cavendish Square. (See *London Chronicle*, March 5-7, 1772.)

[73] *Notes and Queries*, CXC (May 18, 1946), 213. According to "C.E.J." [Claude E. Jones], the contributor of this item, MacKercher's statement "appeared in the *General Advertiser* for 8 March, 1750/1."

[74] Preface to *An Abstract*, p. iii, in the copy in the British Museum.

and yet the prose of *An Abstract* is extraordinarily Smollettian in diction, and the similarities between it and the account of the Annesley case in *Peregrine Pickle* are very remarkable.[75] Smollett may have prepared the manuscript of *An Abstract* with MacKercher's assistance, and having done so, felt free to embody a précis of it in *Peregrine Pickle*. MacKercher's uneasiness upon reading the novel resulted, conceivably, not from the story of legal activities as much as from the pages dealing with his life before 1740. Hence he probably did not object when *An Abstract* was printed.

The facts of Smollett's acquaintance with the notorious Lady Vane are even more obscure.[76] The only reference to her in Smollett's correspondence is found in a letter written very soon after his return from Paris, in September 1750: "I have been favoured with two letters from Mr. Hunter of Burnsyde,[77] the first of which was shown to the Duke of Dorset by Lady Vane, who spoke of the author as a gentleman worthy of the Government's clemency."[78] This simple gesture by Lady Vane appears to have been the sequel to an interview with Smollett wherein she "spoke" favorably of

---

[75] See my communication, "Smollett and the Case of James Annesley," in *TLS*, December 28, 1935. This note was too short to do justice to the similarities. I have not been able to find another copy of *An Abstract*.

[76] The Viscountess Vane (née Frances Anne Hawes) was born in 1713. She married in 1732 William Hamilton (second son of the fourth Duke of Hamilton) who became M.P. for Lanarkshire in 1734, and died that year. In 1735 she married the very wealthy and highly eccentric William Holles, Viscount Vane, cousin of the Duke of Newcastle. A print of Vane and a story of his amours is in the *Town and Country Magazine*, III (1771), 233ff. Lady Vane, after marital quarrels and publicized gallantries (see her own "Memoirs" for her adventures down to 1750) for several decades, lived in comparative retirement in Hill Street, Berkeley Square, where she died March 31, 1788. (See *London Chronicle*, April 5-8, 1788, p. 339.) Lord Vane died in Downing Street April 7, 1789. (See *London Chronicle*, April 9-11, 1789, p. 346.) Lord and Lady Vane were both buried in Shipborne Church, on Vane's estate, Fairlawn, Kent, four miles from Tunbridge Wells.

[77] This person may be identified as David Hunter of Grange House, parish of Monifieth, Forforshire, and known as Hunter of Burnside. He was a captain in the Pretender's Life Guards and a companion of the prominent Lord Elcho in Europe after Culloden. This David Hunter appears to be referred to, inaccurately, as Robert Hunter in *The Origins of the 'Forty-Five*, ed. Walter B. Blaikie (Edinburgh, 1916), p. 155n. For David Hunter, see *A Short Account of the Affairs of Scotland in the Years 1744, 1745, 1746*, by David, Lord Elcho, ed. The Hon. Evan Charteris (Edinburgh, 1907), indexed references, and p. 458. See also J. Malcolm, *The Parish of Monifieth* (Edinburgh and London, 1910), *passim*. In the latter there is a reference (p. 71) to Hunter's return to Scotland in 1747, but his visit must have been temporary because Smollett and Dr. John Moore met him among the Scottish exiles at Boulogne in 1750. (See *Peregrine Pickle*, Chap. 36, and Moore's "Life," p. 125.) I can find no record of his later life.

[78] *Letters*, p. 10.

Hunter. Such a meeting took place, it would seem, after Smollett's return from France. As to earlier correspondence or interviews nothing is known. Neither are there any available documents which show whether Smollett asked Lady Vane for her memoirs or whether she suggested that they be embodied in *Peregrine Pickle.* Nor is there any documentary foundation for the tradition, originating in an obituary notice of Lady Vane, that Smollett received a handsome reward[79] for putting them into his novel. Had Smollett been liberally rewarded, and had either he or Lady Vane divulged it, Smollett's many enemies would surely have publicized it in print.[80]

It has been suggested that Smollett might have been personally attracted to Lady Vane, and that he expressed his admiration of her through Peregrine's verses in chapter CIV of the first edition (1751), wherein the lady's "transcendent charms" and "blooming form divine" are portrayed as accompanied by what is completely irresistible, her "enlightened soul" and "wit sublime."[81] If there is much of Smollett's own feeling in the verses, then he was, like his Peregrine, in a mad mood and given over to blind adulation because by 1750 Lady Vane's former physical charms, at least, were greatly diminished, judging from a revealing portrait of her written by Lady Jane Coke[82] just returned to London from Tunbridge Wells, August 21, 1750:

> Lady Vane was there with her lord, and began several balls. She seems quite easy, though no woman of any rank took the least notice of her. In my whole life I never saw anybody altered to the degree she is. I have not seen her near since her days of innocence and beauty, and really should

[79] See *Gentlemen's Magazine*, LVIII (1788), 368, where the anonymous writer declared that Smollett received "a very handsome reward." This phrase was appropriated by Anderson in his "Life," 1796, p. 10, was accepted by the heavily moral Alexander Chalmers, and later found its place in memoirs of Smollett by Scott, Chambers, Seccombe, and Henley. An "original" note was introduced by Smeaton, who asserted that "though Smollett received a handsome sum (£150 one account mentions, £300 another) for granting the favour of their insertion in the novel, he lived to regret most deeply the indiscretion." (*Tobias Smollett*, p. 75.)

[80] No charges that Smollett was paid by Lady Vane was ever noted in the many attacks on him during his life.

[81] See Buck, *op. cit.*, pp. 28 ff.

[82] Lady Jane Coke was the daughter of the Marquis of Wharton and was the last representative of the Wharton family. Her second husband, Robert Coke, brother to the Earl of Leicester, died in March 1750. Her letters on society and life at Tunbridge Wells display her as an agreeable and sophisticated lady.

not have known her if I had not been told her name, as there is not the least remains of what she was.[83]

In the light of this, we may raise two questions, which must go unanswered: did Smollett, like Peregrine, in a mood of lover, lunatic, and poet, see Helen's beauty in the brow of Lady Vane? or did he, disillusioned by correspondence or meetings with her occasioned by the publication of her memoirs,[84] indulge in some superlative irony? Whatever Smollett's attitude toward Lady Vane may have been, her "Memoirs" and the cluster of related publications,[85] most of which followed them, distracted the attention of the public from the permanent merits of *Peregrine Pickle*.

Any account of the light thrown by *Peregrine Pickle* on Smollett's personal relationships must take stock of his attacks on Quin, Chesterfield, Akenside, Garrick, Lyttelton, and Fielding in the first edition of that novel. No detailed exposition of Smollett's rash satire of these individuals is needed here, in view of Professor Buck's accurate and thorough investigation of it in chapter 3 of his *Study in Smollett*. Quin, it must be confessed, was unfairly satirized in *Peregrine Pickle* because he had offended Smollett in the matter of *The Regicide*. The attack on Dr. Mark Akenside, however, was apparently an impersonal caricature motivated by Akenside's reflections against Scotland.[86] The satire of Chesterfield,

[83] *Letters from Lady Jane Coke to her friend Mrs. Eyre at Derby, 1747-1758*, ed. Mrs. Ambrose Rathborne (London, 1899), p. 54.

[84] If Lady Vane superintended the press while her "Memoirs" were printing (see her obituary in *Gentleman's Magazine*, LVIII, 368), she may have been a nuisance to the printer and indirectly to Smollett. She may have inserted in the *Royal Magazine*, or *Quarterly Bee* the advertisement for *Peregrine Pickle* in which it was stated that the "Memoirs" are "most elegantly wrote, and greatly outshine the rest of the work." (See Buck, p. 36.) This must have offended Smollett.

[85] Preceding *Peregrine Pickle* was Mrs. Teresa Constantia Phillips' *Apology* [1748-1749], and *The History of a Woman of Quality: or, The Adventures of Lady Frail*, supposedly by Dr. John Hill, published about February 8, 1751. Following *Peregrine Pickle* appeared these items:

(1) *A Letter to the Right Honourable the Lady V——ss V—— Occasioned by the Publication of her Memoirs in the Adventures of Peregrine Pickle*, published about March 6, 1751. On page 33 the writer asserted: "With all your Art, you can scarce show the faint Traces of that Beauty, which laid so many Lovers at Your Feet," and went on to relate how Lady Vane invited more than forty ladies to a public breakfast at Tunbridge, of whom not one appeared.

(2) *A Parallel between the Character of Lady Frail and the Lady of Quality in Peregrine Pickle*, published about March 11, 1751.

(3) *An Apology for the Conduct of a Lady of Quality, Lately traduced under the Name of Lady Frail . . . in a Letter from a Person of Honour to a Nobleman of Distinction*, published about July 9, 1751.

[86] See Howard Buck, "Smollett and Akenside," in *JEGP*, XXXI (1932), 10-26.

like that of Quin, was also related to *The Regicide*. Smollett's ridiculing of Garrick as Marmozet in *Roderick Random* has already been referred to. In *Peregrine Pickle* the satire was continued—here, not against Garrick's alleged duplicity, but against his acting. This unduly abusive assault was eventually to be expunged from the revised *Peregrine Pickle* published in 1758. However, despite what appears on the surface to have been a cordial reconciliation between Smollett and Garrick, the angry tirade against the personal unreliability of the famous actor was never deleted.

In *Peregrine Pickle*, Smollett exhibited in typical fashion the climax of his violent dislike of Lord Lyttelton and of the latter's friend and beneficiary, Henry Fielding. As Smollett has been severely censured for his satire of these men (of Fielding especially) the complicated history of his satire must be re-examined carefully and impartially. In the first edition of *Peregrine Pickle*, published in February 1751, Smollett introduced his attack on Lyttelton by the following parody, which Henley in his edition of Smollett has called the "Burlesque Ode":[87]

Where wast thou, wittol Ward, when hapless fate
From these weak arms mine aged grannam tore:
These pious arms essay'd too late,
To drive the dismal phantom from the door.
Could not thy healing drop, illustrious quack,
Could not thy salutary pill prolong her days,
For whom, so oft, to Marybone, alack!
Thy sorrels dragg'd thee thro' the worst of ways?

Oil-dropping Twick'nham did not then detain
Thy steps, tho' tended by the Cambrian maids;
Nor the sweet *environs* of Drury-lane;
Nor dusty Pimlico's embow'ring shades;
. . . .
Her lib'ral hand and sympathising breast,
The brute creation kindly bless'd:
Where'er she trod grimalkin purr'd around,
The squeaking pigs her bounty own'd;
. . . .
While redbreast hopp'd before her in the hall,
As if she common mother were of all.

[87] See *Works of Tobias Smollett*, ed. W. E. Henley, 12 vols. (Westminster and New York, 1899-1901), XII, 26-27.

For my distracted mind,
What comfort can I find?
O best of grannams! thou art dead and gone,
And I am left behind to weep and moan,
To sing thy dirge in sad funereal lay
Ah! woe is me! alack! and well-a-day![88]

At first blush this does not strike one as a parody of Lyttleton's elegy to his wife Lucy, entitled *To The Memory of Lady Lately Deceased. A Monody*, a poem in nineteen stanzas published in folio in October 1747. On the surface Smollett's lines seem to be a parody of a poem to someone's grandmother, although they begin with an extended satire of the famous quack, Dr. Joshua Ward. But in a very limited but effective way Smollett's lines do mimic Lyttelton's spirit and diction in stanzas 7, 16, and 17 of his monody, and his classical topography in stanza 8.

Following Smollett's parody in the text of the first edition of *Peregrine Pickle* is a passage wherein Lyttelton is severely mauled, not only for his questionable taste in making literary "copy" out of his bereavement, but for his silly pretensions as a wit and as a literary critic. Speaking through the chairman of the critics assembled, Smollett asserted of Sir Gosling Scrag [Lyttelton]:

I should be glad to know, upon what pretensions to genius this preheminence [*sic*] is founded. Do a few flimsy odes, barren epistles, pointless epigrams, and the superstitious suggestions of an half-witted enthusiast, intitle [*sic*] him to that eminent rank he maintains in the world of letters? or did he acquire the reputation of a wit, by a repetition of trite invectives against a minister, conveyed in a theatrical cadence, accompanied with the most ridiculous gestures, before he believed it was his interest to desert his master, and renounce his party?[89]

In the last sentence Smollett alluded to Lyttelton's desertion of Prince Frederick and his party, rather than to his later break with Pitt.[90] Following this tirade, Smollett vigorously assailed Lyttelton's characteristics as a patron, glancing incidentally at his relations with Thomson:

Never did he befriend a man of poetical merit, who did not court and retain his favour by . . . slavish prostitution, except one author, lately deceased; and even he extended his complaisance too far, in complimen-

---

[88] *Peregrine Pickle* (London, 1751), IV, 117-18.
[89] *Ibid.*, IV, 120-21.
[90] See Rose Mary Davis, *The Good Lord Lyttelton* (Bethlehem, Pennsylvania, 1939), p. 221n.

tal lines, which the warmth of his gratitude inspired, though he would never submit to the tame criticisms of his patron, or offer such an outrage to his own judgment, as to adopt the alterations which he proposed.[91]

And yet Smollett insisted that Lyttelton, if fed "with the soft pap of dedication," was the "best milch-cow an author ever stroked," and to conclude his attack he had his chairman speak the following, which culminates with an explosive outburst against Fielding:

> Yes, I insist upon it, these are arts which will never fail to engage the friendship of Mr. Scrag, which will be sooner or later manifested in some warm sine-cure, ample subscription, post or reversion; and I advise Mr. Spondy [Fielding] to give him the refusal of this same pastoral: who knows but he may have the good fortune of being listed in the number of his beef-eaters; in which case he may, in process of time, be provided for in the customs or church; when he is inclined to marry his own cook-wench, his gracious patron may condescend to give the bride away; and finally settle him in his old age, as a trading Westminster justice.[92]

Herein, obviously, Smollett was alluding to Fielding's second marriage in November 1747 and to his appointment as Bow-Street Justice in 1748.

We may now look into the reasons for these ill-tempered attacks on Lyttelton, remembering that Smollett deleted these passages from his revised *Peregrine Pickle* in 1758. Just what was the basis in 1750 for Smollett's violent dislike of Lord Lyttelton? It was not, as Professor Buck was the first to show, because Lyttelton had had any part in the early fortunes of *The Regicide*.[93] Rather it arose from something Lyttelton said or did concerning Smollett's first comedy, the adventures of which we have already noted. It appears that he was encouraged to write this piece by Lyttelton, whose relations with Smollett were recalled by Horace Walpole as follows:

> Smollett was bred a sea-surgeon, and turned author. He wrote a tragedy, and sent it to Lord Lyttelton, with whom he was not acquainted. Lord Lyttelton, not caring to point out its defects, civilly advised him to try comedy. He wrote one, and solicited the same Lord to recommend it to the stage. The latter excused himself, but promised, if it should be acted, to do all the service in his power for the author.[94]

It was Lyttelton's failure to recommend this play, then, which was

[91] *Peregrine Pickle*, London, 1751, IV, 121-22.
[92] *Ibid.*, 123.
[93] Buck, *op. cit.*, pp. 100ff.
[94] See Horace Walpole, *Memoirs of the Reign of King George the Second*, ed. Lord Holland, vols. (London, 1846), III, 259.

probably at the root of Smollett's animosity, stimulated no doubt by other provocations.

Judged by ideal standards, the satire against Lyttelton in the first edition of *Peregrine Pickle* was far too personal and violent. Many readers of that novel, however, were mildly amused over Smollett's pretty accurate picture of the well-known eccentricities of the appearance and character of Lyttelton. What their attitude was toward the "Burlesque Ode" may be estimated by the poet Shenstone's comment in September 1751 in his letter to his friend the Rev. Richard Graves:

> There was something accountable enough to me in their burlesquing Mr. L[yttelton]'s monody. He is, you know, engaged in a party; and his poem (though an extraordinary fine composition) was too tender for the public ear. It should have been printed privately, and a number of copies dispersed only among their friends. . . . I wish the burlesquers of such *ingenuous* profusions could be punished, consistently with English liberty. . . . I heard, once before, it was burlesqued under the title of "An Elegy on the Death of a Favorite Cat," but the burlesque will die, and the poem will survive.[95]

The poem alluded to by Shenstone was entitled *A Sorrowful Ditty; or, the Lady's Lamentation for the Death of her Favourite Cat, A Parody*. It was printed in folio and published about May 12, 1748,[96] for J. Tomlinson, and has been attributed to Smollett without any real evidence.[97] As a piece of ridicule, *A Sorrowful Ditty* is more thorough and ruthless than Smollett's "Burlesque Ode" because it contains nineteen stanzas, each of which parodies its corresponding stanza in Lyttelton's *Monody*. The author derided both Lyttelton and Fielding in the following characteristic stanza, No. 8:

> But if coining Names for Pelagius's Work,
> Or spinning an Ode from bright J---n--gs to Y--k;
> If teaching lank L--tt--lt--n graceful to weep,
> Or rocking poor supperless F--ld--ng to sleep;

[95] See *Letters of William Shenstone*, ed. Marjorie Williams (Oxford Press, 1939), p. 319.
[96] See the *General Advertiser* for this date.
[97] See *Anonyma and Pseudonyma* by Charles A. Stonehill, Andrew Block, and H. W. Stonehill, 4 vols. (London, 1926), III, 2366. Strongly against attributing *A Sorrowful Ditty* to Smollett is the fact that it was published just when Smollett, presumably at Lyttelton's suggestion, was planning his lost comedy.

These I own,
Might atone,
For what's done;
Nor could less essential Reasons excuse
This shameless Desertion of every Muse.

The satirical couplet linking the names of Lyttelton and Fielding in *A Sorrowful Ditty* resulted from the close association of the two in 1748. Similarly, as we have seen, Smollett made Fielding a mere sycophant of Lyttelton in *Peregrine Pickle*. But why, in the fourth volume of that novel, written late in 1750, did Smollett wish to belittle the author of *Tom Jones?* One reason was that though Fielding advertised *Roderick Random* repeatedly in his *Jacobite's Journal*, wherein he often commended books, he never made a gesture of recognizing or approving Smollett's first novel (which, according to Professor Cross, he read) merely because it was written by a Scotsman.[98] This neglect was surely galling to Smollett. There is nothing to indicate that the two men ever met; except for Dr. William Hunter, they had no known friends in common, and Fielding was so ill by 1748 and so engrossed in completing *Tom Jones* that it is not surprising that he never bothered to cultivate Smollett's acquaintance. Smollett may have disliked Fielding as a rival writer, whose successful *Tom Jones*, dedicated to Lyttelton, was published in February 1749, just when Smollett was soliciting subscribers for his *Regicide*. But in Smollett's own comment on *Tom Jones* no angry jealousy is shown. Here follows what he wrote to Carlyle October 1, 1749:

> If I should pretend to set up in defence of Tom Jones, in these particulars where he is affected by your Censure, you would easily discover my affectation and be justly offended at my feigned Candour: I will therefore own that the same observations occurred to me which you have communicated and are indeed obvious to every reader of discernment, even the Authors most sanguine adherents confess that there is an evident difference between that part of his Book which he wrote for the Town and that which was composed for the benifit [*sic*] of his Bookseller.[99]

In the absence of Carlyle's adverse criticism of *Tom Jones*, Smollett's remarks are cryptic: does he mean that there is a discrepancy between Fielding's realistic and picaresque material (written to

[98] See Wilbur L. Cross, *The History of Henry Fielding*, 3 vols. (Yale University Press, 1918), II, 91. Professor Cross asserted that Fielding read *Roderick Random*, but where is the evidence?
[99] See "New Smollett Letters," *TLS*, July 31, 1943.

insure the popular sale of *Tom Jones*) and his philosophical intro-
ductory chapters invented for the intelligensia? Whatever Smollett
meant, it must be noted that he did not here reveal to Carlyle, to
whom he had previously confessed many of his authorial secrets,
one bit of personal dislike of Fielding. In fact, Smollett's remarks
were so general that it is impossible to say whether or not he had, by
October 1749, read *Tom Jones* with care. This may explain why
there is no attack in *Peregrine Pickle* on Fielding's recent novel, or
upon Fielding as a plagiarist,[100] the latter charge appearing in an
anonymous pamphlet, *Habbakkuk Hilding*,[101] published January
15, 1752.

That Smollett wrote *Habbakkuk Hilding* is not absolutely certain
despite the fact that Professors Jensen, Cross, and Buck, and certain
modern booksellers have accepted it as his. It has been attributed to
Smollett solely because a contributor to the *Gentleman's Magazine*
for January 1752 declared that it was "supposed to be written by
the author of *Peregrine Pickle*." Whoever wrote this abusive attack
on Fielding and Lyttelton cordially hated them both, had read both
Roderick Random and *Peregrine Pickle*, and accused Fielding of
stealing the concept of Partridge from Strap and that of Miss Mat-
thews in *Amelia* from Miss Williams in *Roderick Random*. It must
be admitted that Smollett may have written *Habbakkuk Hilding*,
but among Fielding's many political enemies, who had been abus-
ing him, his second wife, and Lyttelton, in *Old England* and elsewhere[102] were persons, such as Dr. John Hill or William Kenrick,
also quite capable of composing it. Those who feel sure that Smollett was guilty of the extravagant abuse of Fielding and Lyttelton
in *Habbakkuk Hilding* suggest that he was taking therein an extreme and swift revenge for good-natured raillery leveled at him
by Fielding in *Amelia* (published December 1751) and in his
Covent-Garden Journal, January 7, 1752. In the former, he may
have glanced at Lady Vane, and Smollett's propensity for personal
satire;[103] in the latter, in describing the Grub-Street battle Fielding
ridiculed Smollett as follows:

[100] See Buck, *op. cit.*, pp. 116ff.
[101] For the complete title of *Habbakkuk Hilding* see Cross, *op. cit.*, III, 346. For a
synopsis see *The Covent-Garden Journal*, ed. Gerard E. Jensen, 2 vols. (Yale University Press, 1915), I, 52ff.
[102] For these attacks in *Old England* see Cross, *op. cit.*, II, 61, 83-84, 93, 114.
[103] See Buck, *op. cit.*, pp. 50-51, 113.

A small Body, indeed, under the Command of one Peeragrin Puckle, made a slight Show of Resistance; but his Hopes were soon found to be in Vain; and, at the first Report of the Approach of a younger Brother of General Thomas Jones, his whole Body immediately disappeared, and totally overthrew some of their own Friends, who were marching to their Assistance, under the Command of one Rodorick Random. This Rodorick, in a former Skirmish with the People called Critics, had owed some slight Success more to the Weakness of the Critics, than to any Merit of his own.[104]

About one week after Fielding's depreciation of Smollett's novels, *Habbakkuk Hilding* was for sale.[105] Smollett, if he wrote it, effected a very swift as well as ruthless retaliation. On January 20, 1752, in the *Covent-Garden Journal Extraordinary*, appeared a mock advertisement relating to *Habbakkuk Hilding*. In the same pamphlet someone (perhaps Bonnell Thornton, perhaps Fielding) made an ingratiating allusion to Smollett as "a *small Hutt*, built of mud and covered with thistles."[106] Such were the amenities of 1752.

There was one other publication which may have been related to the paper war between Smollett and Fielding. There appeared in the *General Advertiser* for April 30, 1751, and in several subsequent issues the following advertisement:

> This day is publish'd, Price 1 s. A Vindication of the Name and Random Peregrinations of the Family of the Smallwits. In a letter to a Friend. Printed for R. Griffiths at the Dunciad in St. Paul's Church-Yard; and G. Woodfall, the corner of Craig's Court, Charing Cross.

Although no copy of this shilling pamphlet has turned up, one can imagine the mounting anger of Smollett when he read it. He may have known whether or not it was inspired or written by Fielding.

It is regrettable that Smollett and Fielding did not become brothers in a guild of novelists. After two centuries, much of the genesis and evolution of their quarrel is necessarily incomplete and obscure. Remembering Smollett's earlier libels on Rich and Garrick, biographers have been inclined (especially the champions of Fielding) to assume the worst about Smollett—even to the point of accepting without reservations his authorship of *Habbakkuk Hil-*

[104] *The Covent-Garden Journal*, ed. Jensen, I, 145. See also [William Kenrick], *Fun: A Parodi-tragi-comical Satire*, London, 1752.
[105] *Ibid.*, 51. Jensen quotes the advertisement of *Habbakkuk Hilding* in the *London Daily Advertiser*, January 15, 1752, for "This Day at Noon." I have seen only an advertisement as "This day—publish'd" in the *General Advertiser* for January 20, 1752.
[106] See Cross, *op. cit.*, II, 404.

ding. Smollett was often, but not always, guilty of personal libel. He was destined to be tossed about for two decades in the swirling waters of personal and political controversy. Yet he recognized some six years after Fielding's death (perhaps he had always seen it) the genius of the author of *Joseph Andrews* and *Tom Jones*. In his *Continuation of the Complete History of England*, Smollett averred that the "genius of Cervantes was transfused into the novels of Fielding, who painted the characters, and ridiculed the follies of life with equal strength, humour and propriety."[107]

[107] Smollett's *Continuation of the Complete History of England*, Vol. 4 (London, 1761), p. 127.

CHAPTER VII

Book Reviewing and Medical
Interests, 1750-1752

SHORTLY after the publication of *Peregrine Pickle*, Smollett had three book reviews accepted by the editors of the *Monthly Review*,[1] a new periodical launched by Ralph Griffiths, with the assistance of William Rose and others, in May 1749. In the early numbers of this periodical, Griffiths and his staff were usually content to furnish brief résumés and extracts of the books which they noticed. As Griffiths expressed it, their purpose was "to enter no farther into the province of criticism, than just so far as may be indispensibly necessary to give some idea of such books as come under our consideration."[2] In the first volumes of the *Monthly* (1749-1752) the field of literature was covered principally by Griffiths himself and by John Cleland. The latter, for example, during those years, reviewed Coventry's *The History of Pompey . . . a Lap-Dog*, Fielding's *Amelia*, and Smollett's *Regicide* and *Peregrine Pickle*. Other early reviewers of the belles-lettres were Dr. John Hill and William Rose.

Just how Smollett became associated with the *Monthly* is not clear, but Cleland's enthusiasm over *The Regicide* surely led Smollett to know him by 1749. Two years later, in the issue for October 1751 was printed Smollett's first known review, his appraisal of Cleland's *Memoirs of a Coxcomb*. In view of Smollett's later prowess and prominence as a reviewer in his own *Critical Review*, his final paragraph on Cleland is significant for its method; its clear, incisive, and vigorous style; and its criteria, expressed or implied:

> The story is well connected, and rises in importance from the beginning to the end; the incidents are entertaining and instructing; the re-

---

[1] See Benjamin C. Nangle, *Monthly Review First Series 1749-1789 Indexes of Contributors and Articles* (Oxford, 1934), p. 42. Griffiths' attribution of three reviews to Smollett is probably accurate.

[2] Cited from Griffiths' review of Kirkpatrick's *Sea-Piece*, in the *Monthly Review*, II (1750), 260.

flexions judicious and uncommon; the satire nervous, just, and fraught with laudable indignation; the characters well contrasted and sustained, and the stile spirited and correct. On the other hand, the plan is too thin for the intriguing taste of our modern cricticks; there is a total want of episodes: the adventures are not enough diversified; certain *French* idioms have crept into the language; a trespass for which the author is the less excusable, because he seems to be master of the *English* tongue; which is as well adapted as any other, for all the purposes of writing; nor is the performance free from stiff, compounded epithets, quaint terms of expression, that debase the stile, and new words affectedly coined. Nevertheless, we will, upon the whole, venture to pronounce the work one of those few productions, which, though hastily, nay and carelessly composed, a discerning reader may peruse to an end, without yawning, and even rise from it, with a wish, that the entertainment had been prolonged.[8]

Smollett wrote two more reviews for the *Monthly Review*: one dealt with Dr. William Smellie's *Treatise on the Theory and Practice of Midwifery*,[4] printed in the number for December 1751;[5] and the other appraised Dr. John Pringle's *Observations on the Diseases of the Army*, in the July issue, 1752.[6] In his review of the former, Smollett praised a great pioneer work in obstetrics, on the bases, as we shall see, of some personal practice in that science and of some acquaintance with the author. Smollett's recommendation of the *Observations* was well deserved, as Sir John Pringle was a recognized reformer of military medicine and sanitation. With him, however, Smollett had no discoverable personal association.

The fact that three of Smollett's reviews were accepted for publication in the *Monthly Review* does not necessarily mean that he had much personal contact with Ralph Griffiths, the bookseller, whose headquarters were at the Dunciad in St. Paul's Churchyard, a considerable distance from Chelsea. Yet it is very likely that he met Griffiths from 1751 to 1752 and perused his *Monthly Review* with interest. The two men had little in common: Griffiths, in 1750, appears to have been an uncouth, unscrupulous, and even notorious bookseller and pamphleteer of dubious capacities;[7] Smol-

---

[8] *Monthly Review*, v (1751), 386-87.
[4] This was the first of a series of three important volumes by Smellie on obstetrics, published in 1751, 1754, and 1764. See John Glaister, *Dr. William Smellie and his Contemporaries* (Glasgow, 1894), pp. 165ff.
[5] *Monthly Review*, v (1751), 465-66.
[6] *Ibid.*, vii (1753), 52-56.
[7] See my article, "Ralph Griffiths, Author and Publisher, 1746-1750" in *The Library* (Transactions of the Bibliographical Society, 1939), pp. [197]-213.

lett, despite his violent temper, was, in contrast to Griffiths, an urbane, sophisticated and successful writer of approved abilities. Smollett was much too proud and independent, it would seem, to become a regular contributor to Griffiths' magazine, though the precise reason for his abandoning the *Monthly Review* is not known. The report that he left because of displeasure over a review by Elizabeth Carter in the *Monthly* of his translation of *Don Quixote* is without foundation.[8] The chances are that Smollett deserted the *Monthly* because of his cordial dislike of Ralph Griffiths, a feeling to be expressed repeatedly in the pages of the *Critical Review* a few years later.

Smollett's two medical reviews in the *Monthly* are inadequate for demonstrating what may be called his medical background by 1752. This central aspect of Smollett must now be expounded from what is clearly suggested by his associations with medical men, by his medical theories and practice, by his degree, and by his *Essay on the External Use of Water*, published in 1752.

As we have noted previously, Smollett was associated in his early years in London with prominent members of the medical faculty, such as the distinguished surgeon, John Douglas, in whose house Smollett began practicing about 1744. Other friends were Dr. John Armstrong and Dr. William McGhie. With Dr. John Moore, his biographer, he was a tourist in Paris in 1750. The greatest of the doctors whom Smollett knew, however, were the brothers William and John Hunter, and William Smellie.

With Dr. William Hunter, Smollett was intimate. It has been stated by Sir D'Arcy Power that "William Hunter lodged with Tobias Smollett, the novelist, in Downing Street."[9] This assertion may be true, but evidence is not complete.[10] Nevertheless, Smollett must have been aware of Hunter's famous course of anatomical lectures, launched in 1743, which, as Sir D'Arcy Power observes,

[8] See Thomas Faulkner, *The History and Antiquities of Brentford, Ealing, & Chiswick* (London, 1845), p. 352; and Nangle, *op. cit.*, p. 42. I can find no record that Elizabeth Carter ever made any criticism of any translation by Smollett.

[9] Cited from Sir D'Arcy Power's article on medicine in *Johnson's England*, ed. A. S. Turberville, 2 vols. (Clarendon Press, Oxford, 1933), II, 269.

[10] William Hunter, who lodged with the son of Dr. James Douglas in 1742, accepted in 1743 an offer from Dr. Robert Owen to become his partner. They were to move the following spring into the late John Douglas' house on Downing Street, but there is no proof that they did so. If they did, then Hunter and Smollett lodged together. See George C. Peachey, *A Memoir of William & John Hunter* (Plymouth, 1924), pp. 74, 76-77, 79.

meant the beginning of scientific surgery. All traces of the relation-ship between Smollett and Hunter before 1750 have vanished, but a letter written that year by Smollett "To Mr Wm Hunter Sur-geon in Covent Garden" ran as follows:

> Dr Prof.
>
> I called at your house in hopes of getting a Dinner bu[t] my principal Design was to desire you will appoint a meeting with Drs Smellie & Pit-cairn,[11] & I shall take care to attend you—Peter Gordon[12] shall wait on you tomorrow to receive your directions on that Subject, & I am Yrs &c
>
> T^s Smollett
>
> Ra[i]nbow Coffeehouse[13]
> Monday   Octr 15   1750[14]

Although the purpose of this projected meeting and the activities of Peter Gordon are not stated, the tone of this letter shows that Smollett was on very friendly terms with William Hunter in 1750. About that year, another note from Smollett is addressed "To Mr Hunter Surgeon[15] at his House in Covent Garden":

> Mr Professor,
>
> Louttit[16] was with me on Saturday last, earnestly solliciting my Interest with Dr Pitcairn, in behalf of his Boy who is (it seems) a miserable object, afflicted with scorbutic, lep'rous, or scrophulous ulcers, for which he desires the child should be admitted into Bartholomew's Hospital. Such Admission would be an act of Charity (I'm afraid) on more accounts than One; & I doubt not but the Doctor out of his own humanity, will be ready to befriend him, especially when recommended by you.

[11] William Pitcairn, M.D. (1711-1791), was another Scot successful as a doctor in London. He was appointed a physician at St. Bartholomew's in February 1750. See *Gentleman's Magazine*, xx (1750), 92. For his character, see Dr. Alexander Carlyle, *Autobiography* (1910), pp. 349ff.

[12] Presumably the Peter Gordon to whom Smollett lent money and whom he chastised in 1752. See H. P. Vincent, "Tobias Smollett's Assault on Gordon and Groom," *RES*, XVI (1940), 183-88.

[13] Smollett asked Carlyle, October 1, 1749, to address him at the "Rain-bow Coffee House in Lancaster Court by St. Martin's Church." See "New Smollett Letters," *TLS*, July 31, 1943.

[14] Printed from the original manuscript at the University of Glasgow. The main part of this letter appears in Thomas H. Bryce's pamphlet, "William Hunter and His Museum" (Glasgow, MacLehose, Jackson and Co., 1922), p. 13.

[15] It is clear from Smollett's postscript in the following letter that he was writing to William Hunter. The fact that the latter received his M.D. from Glasgow in October 1750 does not mean that Smollett would have necessarily addressed him as Doctor after that time, because William Hunter was styled "Mr. Hunter" until 1755. (See Peachey, *op. cit.*, p. 94.)

[16] This was an apothecary named Louttit referred to in "A Letter from Andrew Reid, Esq. to Dr. Wilmot, concerning The Effects of Tonquinese Medicine," dated London, 1745, printed in *The Philosophical Transactions of the Royal Society of London . . . Abridged*, Vol. IX (London, 1809), pp. 89-93.

Louttit has been advised to have Recourse to the Doctor, by a Gentleman belonging to the Hospital, who assures him that the Boy will be admitted, should our Friend make a Point of it, tho' otherwise, objections might be made to his Reception on account of the Circumstances of the Disease—in the Name of God, use your Influence with the Doctor; for Louttit is very clamorous & importunate, & will consider the favour as an indelible obligation—as you will probably see him soon, take some method of letting me know whether or not the Boy can be admitted Wednesday which, I hear is the Doctors taking in day—

Yours

T^s Smollett

Whence all those petulant queries upon the Margins of Smellie's Manuscript? have we not Hiren here? [17]

About 1750, the approximate date of this letter, Hunter, it appears, had been looking over Dr. William Smellie's manuscript of his forthcoming book, *A Treatise on the Theory and Practice of Midwifery*, 1751, the first of a series of three volumes, all of which Smollett prepared for the press. [18] In 1750, then, judging from these letters, Smollett and William Hunter were on pleasant terms. Within a year or so Smollett wrote asking Hunter for a loan of eight or ten pieces (guineas) to meet family expenses, in an undated letter, with a postscript here first published:

I yesterday sent Gordon to David Wilson, for a small supply, & find the Creature has been in Holland these ten days; so that I am compelled in this manner, to add a Load to your Difficulties: for, if you was a man of Fortune, I could apply to you without reluctance or apprehension. [19]

Sometime before 1757 there developed between Smollett and William Hunter what the latter called in 1758 "a great shyness," in his most revealing appraisal of Smollett sent in a letter to his good friend, Dr. William Cullen:

I am persuaded you will find me as constant in my friendship, as some others will find me implacable in resentment and determined in contempt.

[17] This jocular expression, used by Pistol in Shakespeare's *Henry IV, Part Two*, Yale Shakespeare, ed. Samuel Hemingway (II, 4, 172 and 188), seems to signify: have we not a desirable asset here?

[18] Smellie's second volume was called *A Collection of Cases and Observations in Midwifery. To Illustrate His Former Treatise, or First Volume, on that Subject* and appeared in 1754. The final volume, *A Collection of Preternatural Cases and Observations in Midwifery . . . Compleating the design of illustrating his First Volume, on that Subject*, was published in 1764, the year after his death.

[19] Printed from the original manuscript at the Royal College of Surgeons, London. This postscript belongs to Letter 56 in *Letters*, p. 74. It must have been written before Smollett's assault on Peter Gordon, November 1752.

I am always the same, yet just what the object makes me; good or bad as I am treated, and so I think every man should be . . . . Pitcairn desires me to remember his best respects to you . . . Armstrong, too, remembers you always kindly, and I am sure he esteems you . . . . Smollett I know not what to say of. He has great virtues, and has a turn for the warmest friendships. I have seen him very little for some years. He is easily hurt, and is very ready to take prejudices. There had been a great shyness[20] between him and me, which his very kind behaviour to me when I was attacked by Douglass, Pott, and Monro,[21] has as yet scarcely conquered, so that I cannot well say how you stand with him; but if I can make you friends I will most certainly.[22]

Hunter's most valuable analysis of Smollett stressed what was essentially true of him—his often demonstrated readiness to embrace personal prejudice, coupled with his great virtues (especially that of generosity, as we shall see) and his capacity to be not only a violent hater, but an ardent friend. Hunter, indeed, became devoted to Smollett in later years and preserved his letters, as did his brother, John Hunter.

Next to William Hunter, Smollett's most distinguished medical friend was the great obstetrician, Dr. William Smellie (1697-1763). Having arrived in London by 1739 at the age of 42, Smellie, a close friend of Dr. John Gordon, Smollett's teacher, might very well have known young Smollett before he entered naval service.[23] If not, the two men surely met by 1744, when Smellie, friend of William Hunter and teacher of John Moore, was lecturing on midwifery at his house in the vicinity of Pall Mall. By this time Smellie was well-known and successful. In 1748, Smollett sent him data on an unusual obstetrical case, and by 1750 he was preparing Smellie's first publication for the press.[24] As Smellie was in all likelihood Lady Vane's physician (the "Dr S——" of her "Memoirs"),[25] it may have been he rather than MacKercher who

[20] By "shyness," Hunter seems to have meant standoffishness or distrust.
[21] For this medical controversy see *Letters*, pp. 189-90, and William Hunter's letter to Smollett August 23, 1757, in Smollett's *Works*, ed. Anderson (1820), I, 181.
[22] Quoted from John Thomson, *An Account of the Life, Lectures, and Writings of William Cullen, M.D.*, 2 vols. (Edinburgh and London, 1859), I, 548-49.
[23] See Glaister, *op. cit.*, pp. 111-12.
[24] It is known from his letter to Dr. John Moore (*Letters*, p. 28) that Smollett prepared Smellie's second volume of 1754, and in the prefatory Advertisement to his third volume, doubtless written by Smollett, we read that the "manuscript was transmitted to the person who prepared the two other volumes for the press." See *A Collection of Preternatural Cases*, 1764.
[25] Both Buck (*op. cit.*, p. 44), and Professor James R. Foster ("Smollett's Pamphleteering Foe Shebbeare," *PMLA*, LVII [1942], 1058) have accepted Dr. John

brought about a meeting between her and Smollett. Be that as it may, there seems to have developed a lifelong friendship between Smollett and Dr. and Mrs. William Smellie.[26]

From such leading exponents of medical research as William Smellie and William Hunter, Smollett could have received liberal ideas in obstetrics and anatomy. How much he was influenced by them is impossible to ascertain because, with the exception of his *Essay on the External Use of Water*, he did not publish his views directly. From the numerous articles on medical books in the *Critical Review*, 1756-1763, Smollett's views cannot be abstracted as there is no way of knowing with absolute certainty which reviews he wrote. In general, the conclusion of Dr. E. Ashworth Underwood that Smollett's *Essay on . . . Water* "shows no evidence that the author was possessed of a scientific mind,"[27] is not wholly con-

---

Shebbeare as the "Dr S——" of Lady Vane's "Memoirs." On the other hand David Herbert, in his edition of Smollett's *Works* (Edinburgh, 1903), p. 361, and Dr. Glaister, in his *Dr. William Smellie*, pp. 12-13, adduced reasons for believing that Lady Vane's "Dr S——" and his lady were Dr. and Mrs. Smellie. The assumption of Buck and Foster rests solely on a statement in the *Gentleman's Magazine*, LIX (1789), 403, that Shebbeare aided Lady Vane in her "Memoirs." In Shebbeare's obituary, however, in the *Gentleman's Magazine*, LVIII (1788), 753, and in a later account of him in the *Universal Magazine*, LXXXV (1789), 319, nothing is noted of his having had any connection with Lady Vane. Moreover, Norgate, his biographer in the *DNB*, asserted that her memoirs had "been erroneously assigned to him." After a careful study of the chronology of the "Memoirs," it is clear to me that "Dr S——" first visited Lady Vane in London about 1739, which was years before Shebbeare ever resided there. Lady Vane's subsequent references to "Dr S——" were all for services rendered before the death of her lover, Henry Berkeley, at the battle of Dettingen, in 1743—again, years before Shebbeare's arrival in London. That Shebbeare was "Dr S——" is therefore quite incredible. On the other hand, it is pretty certain that Smellie was "Dr S——," as he was in London by 1739, and an eminent figure in medical circles. Moreover, he had been the leading medical man around Lanark and the parish of Hamilton when Lady Vane lived at the country seat of the Hamiltons in Lanarkshire, from which her first husband, Lord William Hamilton, was M.P. in 1734.

[26] See Glaister, *op. cit.*, pp. 111, 113, 116, where it was suggested that Smollett visited Mrs. Smellie in Lanark in 1766. (See *Humphry Clinker*, Letter of Jerry, Carlisle, September 12.) Glaister also noted that some of Smollett's books were at Lanark. In response to a letter of inquiry, Mr. A. D. Robertson of the County Council of the County of Lanark has kindly informed me that there were, in 1944, in the Public Library of Lanark the following:

Peregrine Pickle, Vols. II and III, 1751.
Ferdinand Count Fathom, Vol. I, 1753.
Three volumes of the *Critical Review*, one "dated January 1758."

According to Mr. Robertson, "there are no inscriptions or annotations on any of these volumes. Flyleaves may have been removed while the books were being rebound."

[27] See E. Ashworth Underwood, M.A., B.Sc., M.D., D.P.H., "Medicine and Science in the Writings of Smollett," reprinted from the *Proceedings of the Royal Society of Medicine*, XXX, 25-38 (London, 1937), p. 5.

vincing because it is a diagnosis derived necessarily from too limited data. It is obvious that the scientific mind, a mind exercising scientific research, was extremely rare in the medical guild of Smollett's day. After an extended survey of Smollett's numerous allusions (in his novels) to medical matters, Dr. Underwood was of the opinion that anatomy and pathology were poorly represented, as was general surgery; that in phlebotomy, physiology, and medicine, Smollett took no original stand; that he merely reflected his own times in his presentation of dropsy, apoplexy, epilepsy, and delirium; that he was not ahead of his day in his observations on infectious diseases; and that his views on tuberculosis, which contributed to his own tragically premature death, were relatively conventional and dogmatic. It should be borne in mind, however, that owing to Smollett's method of farcical exaggeration, it is not easy to deduce from his fiction precisely what his medical theories were. Writing about 1760, Smollett, in summing up his views on the progress of medicine during the reign of George II, seemed quite aware of the value of medical research and was curiously complacent, for one of his critical temper, over its accomplishments:

Many ingenious treatises on metaphysics and morality appeared . . . and a philosophical spirit of inquiry diffused itself to the farthest extremities of the united kingdom. Tho' few discoveries of importance were made in medicine, yet that art was well understood in all its different branches; and many of its professors distinguished themselves in other provinces of literature. Besides the medical essays of London and Edinburgh, the physician's library was enriched with many useful modern productions; with the works of the classical Friend, the elegant Mead, the accurate Huxham, and the philosophical Pringle. The art of midwifery was elucidated by science, reduced to fixed principles, and almost wholly consigned into the hands of male practitioners. The researches of anatomy were prosecuted to some curious discoveries by the ingenuity and dexterity of a Hunter and a Monro. The numerous hospitals in London contributed to the improvement of surgery, which was brought to perfection under the auspices of a Cheselden and a Sharpe.[28]

The note of praise which permeates this passage, however, was not characteristic of Smollett's opinion of the rank and file of apothecaries, surgeons, and physicians whom he so vividly delineated in *Roderick Random, Peregrine Pickle, Count Fathom,* and *Humphry Clinker.* In those novels he was forever burlesquing

[28] From *Continuation of the Complete History of England,* IV (1761), 124.

quacks, berating charlatans, and blasting medical hypocrites and nincompoops. He inveighed against them individually and collectively. He saw the sons of Paean functioning as a corrupt crowd, organized against the public welfare, as in the following passage from *Count Fathom*:

> In his researches, he found that the great world was wholly engrossed by a few practitioners who had arrived at the summit of their reputation, consequently were no longer obliged to cultivate those arts by which they rose; and that the rest of the business was parcelled out into small inclosures, occupied by different groupes [*sic*] of personages, male and female, who stood in rings, and tossed the ball from one to another, there being in each department two sets, the individuals of which relieved one another occasionally. Every knot was composed of a waiting-woman, nurse, apothecary, surgeon and physician, and, sometimes, a midwife was admitted into the partie; and in this manner the farce was commonly performed.[29]

This exposé is followed by devastating satirical detail on the London medical scene.

Concerning Smollett's own medical practice the available information is extremely meager. It would seem that he did not practice much after 1753, the year *Count Fathom* was published, and yet in the magnificent painting, done presumably in 1756 by Verelst, Smollett posed in the costume of a physician, wearing a stone-colored coat, with ruffles at the cuffs; a gold-laced, green satin waistcoat; a tie-wig; and sword.[30] Consequently he may have continued practice on a reduced scale in 1756 and even later. It is most unlikely that Smollett ever enjoyed the luxury of a chariot[31] as did Dr. Armstrong. In *Count Fathom*, Fathom bought one and hired a footman, having seen that "a walking physician was considered as an obscure pedlar, trudging from street to street, with his pack of knowledge on his shoulders, and selling his remnants of advice by retail."[32] Though Smollett must have attended hundreds of patients, the records of only two of them have been preserved. The first was an abnormal obstetrical case which Smollett reported to Dr. Smellie and which the latter printed in his *Collection of Cases and Observations in Midwifery*, 1754. Smollett's report began as

[29] From *Count Fathom*, London, 1753, II, 144-45 (Chap. 52).
[30] The original painting is at Cameron House in the possession of Major General Telfer-Smollett.
[31] A light, four-wheeled carriage with only back seats and having a coach-box.
[32] From *Count Fathom*, Chap. 52.

follows: "In the year 1748, a gentlewoman about the age of twenty-seven, of a very slender make, thin habit, and lax fibre, was in the eighth month of her first pregnancy, incommoded by a pain and crackling," due to a separation of the pelvic bones. "Although I myself have never perceived such separation in the bones of a living subject," Smollett added, "Dr. Lawrence once showed me the *Pelvis* of a woman, who died soon after delivery. . . . I likewise saw the same phenomenon in a *Pelvis* belonging to Dr. Hunter. . . . Mr. Monro owns he had never met with this kind of separation."[33] This report, together with Smollett's contact with Dr. Lawrence (presumably Dr. Thomas Lawrence, an anatomist), and Mr. Monro (perhaps Alexander Monro, Jr.) indicates a desire to learn, as well as to share unusual medical experience.

The second notice of Smollett's practice is found in a column called "Stephensiana No. 1" in the *Monthly Magazine* for 1821. This entry from the notes of Alexander Stephens, biographer, and a resident of Chelsea,[34] runs as follows:

Dr. Smollett lived in two different houses[35] in Chelsea and practised his profession there. A very respectable apothecary, Mr. North,[36] when he was learning his business with Mr. Reid of that place, recollects that Dr. S. attended a young gentleman at the great school towards the end of Church lane. On his death he recollects to have seen Smollett's corpse, [i.e. the body of the patient] to discover the nature of his disease; and on that occasion remembers to have lost all appetite for his dinner.[37]

The great school in Church Lane, Chelsea, here mentioned, was in Smollett's time a charity school, called then, or later, Petyt's Char-

[33] Quoted from *A Collection of Cases and Observations in Midwifery* (London, 1779), pp. 3-5. See also Claude Jones, "Tobias Smollett on the 'Separation of the Pubic Joint in Pregnancy,' " in *Medical Life*, XLI (New York, 1934), 302-5.

[34] For Alexander Stephens see *DNB*. For his antiquarian interest in Chelsea, see Faulkner's *Chelsea*, 2 vols. (Chelsea, 1829), I, 151-53. Stephens, in his *Memoirs of John Horne Tooke*, 2 vols. (London, 1813), I, 355-56, wrote an appraisal of Smollett, in part, as follows: "he was a man, who, to a high sense of honour, is said to have added considerable talents, and only wanted that leisure and opportunity, which wealth alone affords, to excel in every branch of science."

[35] There is no documentary record that Smollett was taxed in Chelsea anywhere except at Monmouth House. It is possible that he had a medical office away from his home.

[36] Perhaps William North. Faulkner listed him as Deputy Surgeon of Chelsea Hospital for many years. (See his *Chelsea*, II, 37.) He also listed a W. North, Apothecary (*Chelsea*, II, 261). William North died in 1816, aged 72, and hence as apprentice he could have known Smollett in Chelsea about 1758.

[37] The *Monthly Magazine*, LII (1821), 236.

ity School,[38] and stood close by Chelsea Church. The case indicates Smollett's post-mortem examination of the cadaver of a charity-school patient, in the presence of one, and probably more, apothecaries, or other medical men.

The fact that Smollett appears gradually to have given up medical practice has led to the assumption that he failed in the profession, not from any lack of scientific ability or correct method but because of temperamental limitations. The writer of his memoirs in 1777 declared that he "could not render himself agreeable to the women,"[39] and Moore asserted that he "could neither stoop to impose on credulity, nor humour caprice."[40] In these statements there is probably much truth. Furthermore, his satire of the medical profession was bound to create enemies who worked against him. Another handicap in his career before 1750 was his lack of a medical degree. This he secured before his visit to Paris that year.

Glasgow, Smollett's own university, would have been a natural place for him to apply for the M.D., just as William Hunter did with success in October 1750. But instead, Smollett approached the faculty of Marischal College, Aberdeen, prior to June 1750, following the procedure of that period by offering recommendations from other doctors, and paying a fee of £28 Scots.[41] In the records at Aberdeen the names of Smollett's sponsors are not extant,[42] nor can one gather from the entry whether or not Smollett was present when the authorities at Aberdeen granted him his M.D. in June 1750.[43] It seems fairly certain that he received the degree *in absentia*: he was too busy in the spring of 1750 to travel from London to Aberdeen, a trip of some five hundred miles. This medical diploma, signed presumably by Dr. James Gordon,[44] was

[38] See Faulkner's *Chelsea*, I, 75, for a print of Petyt's Charity School.

[39] Smollett's *Plays and Poems* (London, 1784), XI.

[40] Smollett's *Works*, ed. John Moore, I, cxcvi.

[41] See W. D. Taylor, "Tobias Smollett, M.D. Aberdeen, 1750" in *Aberdeen University Review*, XXVI (1939), 125-35.

[42] Taylor (*op. cit.*, p. 129), states that Smollett "sent a fee of £28 Scots and certificates from two sponsors," and adds that their names are not in the records.

[43] The entry, printed in *Fasti Academiae Mariscallanae Aberdonensis*, ed. Peter John Anderson, 2 vols. (Aberdeen, 1889-1898), II, 116, under Doctors of Medicine for 1750, runs as follows: "June [,] Tobias Smollett [The novelist and historian]." This entry, according to the editor, was transcribed from the Register kept from 1736-1755 by Dr. James Gordon, professor of medicine. The bracketed identification was presumably added later.

[44] For the wording of such diplomas see *Fasti Academiae Mariscallanae Aberdonensis*, II, 111.

preserved with Smollett's papers in Italy. As is known from the following account, it was ignorantly destroyed years after his death:

> While speaking of physicians, I may inform you, that a gentleman, on visiting a lady here [in Leghorn] the other day, saw, among some papers on her table, the diploma granted by Dr. Smollet by the University of Aberdeen. Wishing to obtain the curious document, he waited on the lady a second time, but, upon inquiry, he discovered that she had cut it down for thread paper.[45]

How much his medical degree meant to Smollett and how much it helped him professionally are difficult questions. No doubt he took a certain pleasure in his new title, which ought to have given him added prestige among prospective patients. Perhaps Mrs. Smollett was pleased. But there is convincing evidence that a medical degree from Aberdeen or from St. Andrews was vigorously depreciated in London in Smollett's time. For example, Sir John Hawkins sneered, with some justice, over the scandal that Dr. John Hill, who had received "no academical education . . . obtained, from one of those universities which would scarce refuse a degree to an apothecary's horse"[46] his honorary label. Hawkins referred to St. Andrews. More important was the attitude of Dr. William Hunter in 1754. Hunter, an M.D. from Glasgow, wrote Dr. Cullen of that place complimenting him on his scrupulousness in conferring degrees, and adding:

> You no doubt know how contemptuously the College of Physicians here have treated all Scotch degrees indiscriminately. You must have heard what efforts have been made, and are now making, by our countrymen in this place to support the honour of our Universities; and you can hardly be ignorant that, notwithstanding this, the professors of one Scotch University at least, shamefully prostitute their degrees still to any one who can pay them a small sum of money, and procure, perhaps purchase, a recommendation from some necessitous doctor. . . . But, after all, we are very inclinable to think that the prostitution of degrees, which we have so much reason to complain of, and which is indeed sometimes with justice, but often insidiously, thrown out against all Scotch graduates here, does not appear in that light to the authors of this evil (I mean, to say it frankly, the gentlemen of Aberdeen and St[.] Andrew's), who may be

[45] Cited from Hugh W. Williams, *Travels in Italy, Greece, and the Ionian Islands.* 2 vols. (Edinburgh, 1820), I, 198.

[46] Quoted from Sir John Hawkins, *The Life of Samuel Johnson, LL.D.*, second edition (London, 1787), p. 211.

influenced by good nature, and abused by some people here, who pass by the name of Brokers of Scotch Degrees.[47]

Of this English superciliousness toward Scottish degrees both good and bad, and of how little the degree from Aberdeen or from St. Andrews often represented, Smollett must have been quite aware in 1750. One has the suspicion that the temporary misunderstanding between him and Dr. William Hunter originated in some remarks which passed between the two on the subject of the Aberdeen degree.

Or was Hunter insufficiently enthusiastic over Smollett's medical paper, called *An Essay on the External Use of Water*,[48] published about March 6, 1752?[49] This essay, according to its original title page, was set forth "in a Letter to Dr. **** with Particular Remarks upon the present Method of using the Mineral Waters at Bath in Somersetshire, and a Plan for rendering them more safe, agreeable, and efficacious." The pamphlet was printed for M. Cooper, in Paternoster Row, and sold by D. Wilson in the Strand and by the booksellers Leake and Frederick in Bath. It ran to 48 pages in quarto format.

The *Essay* consists of two main divisions. In the first, Smollett, in a very conciliating mood, expounded his opinions (which he admitted to be "singular") on the efficacy of simple, non-mineral water in various kinds of cold and hot baths. In general, his conclusion was that plain water, as far as its external use was concerned, was superior, with a few exceptions, to mineral water.[50] In the latter portion of the *Essay* he exposed the unhygienic conditions which endangered those who sought health at Bath. In so doing, he attacked the Bath Corporation, together with the managers and directors of the Bath Hospital, who not only had stupidly refused to effect a plan of improvement submitted by Mr. Cleland, surgeon, but had maliciously injured his reputation. The evils of Bath—promiscuous bathing of "diseased persons of all ages, sexes, and conditions," inadequately sheltered from "wind, rain, hail, and

[47] Quoted from a letter of William Hunter to Dr. Cullen, written at London, October 1, 1754 and printed in John Thomson's *Account of . . . William Cullen, M.D.*, 2 vols. (Edinburgh and London, 1859), I, 660-61.

[48] See the imprint of this essay edited by Claude E. Jones (Baltimore, The Johns Hopkins Press), 1935.

[49] See *General Advertiser* for March 6, 1752, which newspaper announced its price as one shilling and sixpence.

[50] See *An Essay on the External Use of Water*, ed. Claude E. Jones, p. 70.

snow,"[51] under surroundings of nauseating filth—Smollett exposed with admirable vigor. The full blaze of his anger, however, flashed out in his defense of Mr. Archibald Cleland, surgeon, with the printing of whose "Proposals" the *Essay* was concluded. Smollett, in championing Cleland in 1752, renewed the violent battle of pamphleteers[52] at Bath, 1743-1744, after Cleland was summarily dismissed from the General Hospital there by the Governors on what were, apparently, crudely trumped-up charges of immorality in the performance of his duties as obstetrician and surgeon. The controversy over Cleland[53] was lively and bitter and involved indirectly some of the leading citizens of Bath, including Ralph Allen. Among Cleland's vindicators were two clergymen; the Countess of Inchiquin;[54] a brilliant commentator on Cleland's trial, one John Trevanion of Cheltenham; "Britannicus," in 1748; and Smollett, in 1752. Among those attacking Cleland was, we believe, William Warburton, the Bishop of Gloucester, the pro-

---

[51] *Ibid.*, p. 73.

[52] The chief pamphlets were as follows:

1. Archibald Cleland, *An Appeal to the Public*, 1743.
2. *A Short Vindication of the Proceedings of the Governors of the General Hospital at Bath, In Relation to Mr. Archibald Cleland . . . By the Governors,* Bath and London, 1744.
3. John Trevanion, *A Review of Two Pamphlets lately publish'd,* Bath and London, 1744.
4. Archibald Cleland, *A Full Vindication of Mr. Cleland's Appeal to the Publick . . . Address'd to the Thirteen Governors,* Bath and London, 1744. This contains a letter from the Countess of Inchiquin in Cleland's behalf.
5. [William Warburton], *A Letter to Mr. Archibald Cleland, occasioned by his full Vindication.* London, 1744. 15 pp. Second edition, 1745.
6. Britannicus, *Remarks on An Appeal to the Publick . . . And on A Letter to him (from a Reverend Advocate for the Thirteen Governors) occasioned by his Full Vindication of the said Appeal.* Dedicated to Philip, Earl of Chesterfield. London and Bath, 1748. For supplementary items and complete titles, see Emanuel Green, *Bibliotheca Somersetensis,* 3 vols. (Taunton, 1902), I, 115-16. I consulted at the Bath Reference Library and the Bristol Central Library items 1-5. Item 6 I read at the British Museum.

[53] Archibald Cleland, a Scot, arrived in Bath about 1740, after some twenty years of medical experience. (See his *An Appeal to the Public,* p. 3.) In June 1740, his son William was christened in the Abbey Church. See *The Registers of the Abbey Church of . . . Bath,* 2 vols. (London, 1900-1901), I, 116. In 1742 he was appointed surgeon to the General Hospital, from which he was ousted *ca.* 1743. Smollett had probably followed the resulting controversy. In 1752 Cleland was still in Bath and still the object of persecution according to Smollett, who insisted that he was a "man of good morals, and uncommon ability." (See Smollett's *Essay,* ed. Jones, p. 77.)

[54] Lady Inchiquin, after 1737, *suo jure,* the Countess of Orkney, was the daughter of the 1st Earl of Orkney, a representative peer of Scotland. She married in 1720 William O'Brien, the 4th Earl of Inchiquin, an Irish peer. She died in 1756.

tégé of Ralph Allen, and later the husband of Allen's niece. From statements made in a pamphlet by "Britannicus" in 1748,[55] it is quite clear that Warburton wrote *A Letter to Mr. Archibald Cleland* (1744) though it has not hitherto been attributed to him.

Aided by this background of controversy, we can feel the indignation of Smollett in the following invective and irony leveled against Warburton, that truculent and vociferous Goliath in polemics:

The cruel treatment he [Cleland] underwent upon that occasion, compelled him to appeal to the public, and the whole contest betwixt him and his adversaries appeared in print; when he was allowed, by every unprejudiced person, to have greatly the advantage in the dispute. At last, his enemies had recourse to the pen of an author as notorious for the servile homage he yields to his patrons, as for the insolence and scurrility with which he treats all the world besides. True to these principles, this champion published an anonymous letter to Mr. *Cleland*, wherein, after a chain of false reasoning, twanged off in all the arrogance of expression, some aukward attempts to ironical humour, and the most abusive low sarcasms, levelled at a lady of distinction, and, indeed, at a whole nation, on her account,[56] he takes it for granted, that he has fully proved the truth of his unjust allegations. This author must have entertained a very contemptible idea of the understanding and judgment of the public, if he hoped to impose upon them by such an effusion of idle sophistry, in the course of which, he is even driven to the subterfuge of making false quotations:[57] but his talents, as a commentator, are so well understood, and so justly celebrated, that he had nothing further to fear for his reputation on that score.[58]

Smollett's wrath over the injustice done to Archibald Cleland seems not to have been motivated by an intimate acquaintance with him, but arose, rather, because the wrong done to the surgeon was an example of moral corruption in the corporate government of the Bath Hospital, which evil was fully as scandalous as were the

[55] "Britannicus" stated that the anonymous *Letter to . . . Cleland* was by "a certain Reverend Sir," and hoped that Mr. Allen would "correct his Wildgoose K——n" [kinsman], the author. Elsewhere, "Britannicus" implied that Allen was the Un——e [?uncle] of the writer of the *Letter*. As Ralph Allen's nephews were not clergymen (see R. E. M. Peach, *The Life and Times of Ralph Allen*, London, 1895, pp. 231ff.), "Britannicus" was obviously alluding to Warburton, who married Allen's niece in 1746 and was therefore a kinsman, and in a sense a nephew of Allen.

[56] Smollett referred to Scotland, Lady Inchiquin's native country.

[57] This charge is true: the author [Warburton] of *A Letter to Mr. Archibald Cleland*, 1744, p. 2, is guilty of incomplete quoting and of misquoting. On this point see *A Familiar Epistle to the Most Impudent Man Living*, London, 1749.

[58] Quoted from Smollett's *Essay*, ed. Jones, p. 72.

unhygienic conditions in the public baths. Smollett, in very characteristic fashion, persisted in renewing later his attack on both evils. In 1758 he sanctioned, and in all likelihood wrote, a review of Dr. William Baylies' *An Historical Account of the Rise Progress and Management of the General Hospital . . . of Bath*. The reviewer asserted:

> We could have wished, that for the sake of truth, and in justice to injured innocence, Dr. Baylies, in mentioning Mr. Cleland, surgeon, had, in some measure, explained the very singular case of that gentleman. As his name now stands, the reader is left in the dark, to put the most unfavourable constructions on his being suspended, and dismissed from the hospital: whereas that suspension, and that dismission, as Dr. Baylies[59] well knows, were instances of the most illegal despotism, of the most flagrant iniquity, and cruel oppression.[60]

The immediate effect of Smollett's medical essay on his general reputation is impossible to fathom. Its publication caused no violent reverberations. In London, its anonymous reviewer in the *Monthly Review*[61] noted Smollett's attempt to vindicate Cleland but asserted that this effort was not at all connected with the main purpose of his essay. On Smollett's medical ideas he ventured no opinion. In Bath circles, the *Essay* must have caused talk in Ralph Allen's circle and in medical groups in the March days after its appearance. Warburton seems not to have replied in print, but his anger may be recognized in his letter to Hurd, January 30, 1759, wherein he calls Smollett "a vagabond Scot."[62]

Smollett's *Essay*, though reprinted during his lifetime,[63] and the subject of comment by able modern doctors,[64] is not available

---

[59] For Dr. William Baylies see my article, "Rex Versus Smollett: More Data on the Smollett-Knowles Libel Case," in *Modern Philology*, XLI (1944), 225. Dr. Baylies seems to have sympathized with Cleland. See William Baylies, *A Full Reply to a Pamphlet entitled, A Short Answer to a Set of Queries Directed to The Principal Conductors of the General Hospital, or Infirmary, in the City of Bath* (London, 1759), Preface, p. viii.

[60] Quoted from the *Critical Review*, VI (1758), 517.

[61] *Monthly Review*, VI (1752), 400.

[62] In *Letters from a Late Eminent Prelate to one of his Friends* (London, 1809), p. 278, is found the following: "It was well observed, that nobody in the Augustan age could conceive that so soon after, a Horse should be made Consul: and yet matters were so well prepared by the time of Caligula, that nobody was surprised at the matter. So when Clarendon and Temple wrote History, they little thought the time was so near when a vagabond Scot should write nonsense ten thousand strong." Warburton was here alluding to the sale of Smollett's *History*.

[63] Editions of 1767 and of 1770 were listed by Emanuel Green, *op. cit.*, I, 482.

[64] For example, see Dr. Cecil K. Drinker's stimulating article, "Doctor Smollett,"

in his collected works. Professor Jones' edition, printed by the Johns Hopkins Press in 1935, is therefore very welcome to students of Smollett and of Bath. The *Essay*, in general, shows Smollett's independent medical views. More important, it reveals his indignation over conditions physical and moral at Bath, then "the great hospital of the nation," as he called it. Again, it shows his absolute fearlessness in speaking the truth as he saw it. Nothing in it suggests that it was written to fatten his medical fees, nor in vindicating Cleland was he feathering in any way his own nest. The whole *Essay* appears to have been prompted by a generous desire to help a badly treated surgeon,[65] and to improve the hygienic and moral conditions of England. In his *Essay*, then, he played the roles of a medical investigator, satirist, and humanitarian. These activities he was to repeat in the later years of his career in fiction and in political satire. He was destined, also, to be active as dramatist, translator, book reviewer, and commentator, in his role of a sophisticated traveler in England, Scotland, France, and Italy.

---

reprinted from *Annals of Medical History* (Vol. VII, No. 1, pp. 31-47) by Paul B. Hoeber, Inc. (New York, 1925), p. 45.

[65] Smollett may have helped Archibald Cleland obtain an M.D. from Aberdeen, which on June 30, 1752, granted one to "Archibaldus Cleland" (see *Fasti . . . Mariscallanae Aberdonensis*, II, 116), unless the preceding entry refers to another Archibald Cleland. In 1754, an Archibald Cleland, M.D., of Bath was listed among those subscribing for the Rev. John Blair's *Chronology*. Apparently, then, Cleland remained for some years at Bath. I have been unable to find his obituary.

CHAPTER VIII

Lawsuits; *Count Fathom* and *Don Quixote,* 1752-1755

SMOLLETT suffered from 1752 to 1757, when his *Complete History* brought him financial success, many of the petty vexations resulting from a Grub Street income. *The Essay on the External Use of Water* brought him little money. In October 1752, there was a rumor, which we have noted, that he was on bad terms with the booksellers and planning to satirize Millar, and Lyttelton as well, in his next novel, a purpose never effected. About this time, however, he translated, according to Ralph Griffiths,[1] Voltaire's short comic romance, *Micromegas*, published in November 1752[2] for D. Wilson, and T. Durham, in the Strand. This type of job for the trade could have yielded only a small sum in a lean year.

What made his financial status even more acute was that in 1752 he had, with characteristic generosity, lent money to Peter Gordon, who retreated into the verge of the King's Bench[3] to avoid paying his debt. Angered by Gordon's tactics, Smollett forced himself upon him and came to blows with him and his landlord, Edward Groom. Consequently, as Professor Parker has shown, Smollett was sued by Gordon for £1000, and by Groom for £500 on the plea of trespass and assault.[4] Other details of this case and its aftermath have been published by Professor Vincent.[5] The scene of the encounter was in Westminster, and it took place on November 2, 1752. Peter Gordon was an obscure compiler, who, because of Smollett's recommendation was employed in writing part of the *Universal History*,[6] and he may perhaps be identified with the

---

[1] See Nangle, *The Monthly Review . . . Indexes*, p. 55.

[2] See Louis L. Martz, *The Later Career of Tobias Smollett* (Yale University Press, 1942), p. 92, n.11.

[3] This area lay within the precincts of Whitehall.

[4] See Alice Parker, "Tobias Smollett and the Law," in *SP*, XXXIX (1942), 547.

[5] H. P. Vincent, "Tobias Smollett's Assault on Gordon and Groom" in *RES*, XVI (1940), 183-88.

[6] *Ibid.*, p. 184 and n.1.

schoolmaster, Peter Gordon, imprisoned for debt in 1748.[7] There is no doubt that Gordon owed much to Smollett besides the loan which he refused to pay: according to Smollett's letter, dated February 23, 1753, he had rescued Gordon from jail and clothed and fed him.[8]

Against the charges of the plaintiffs, Gordon and Groom, that Smollett "with force and arms, that is to say with Swords Staves Stones Knives Clubbs fists Sticks and whipps ... beat wounded and ill treated" each of them "so that his life was greatly despaired of,"[9] Smollett pleaded not guilty and asserted that any damage which he had inflicted was the result of self-defense. Whatever had happened, it was a violent fracas, in which Smollett laid on his cane or cudgel with a right good will, putting to rout without much difficulty both of his opponents. Later he referred to his exploit as "a simple blow given to a rascal after repeated provocation, and that of the most flagrant kind," and insisted that "no advantage was taken in point of weapons."[10] But the above charges in a King's-Bench case might have been very serious for Smollett, who had so rashly taken the law into his own hands. Fortunately, however, as the court[11] instructed the jury that Smollett could not be held guilty of an intended homicide, he got off by paying damages of twenty pounds and ten shillings to Gordon, and forty shillings to Groom plus the costs of both cases. The costs included the fees of Smollett's lawyer, Richard Balshaw,[12] and those of Nicholas Coulston, attorney for Gordon and Groom.[13] There was also a sum

[7] Alice Parker, *op. cit.*, p. 546. If Peter Gordon was a schoolmaster, then it is quite likely that Andrew Henderson, another schoolmaster, knew him personally. (See Andrew Henderson, *The Life of William Augustus Duke of Cumberland* [London, 1766], Preface.) Henderson, a violent detractor of Smollett, left his version of the fracas: "In 1753 he [Smollett] was found guilty of a cowardly assault upon an innocent man, Mr. Patrick Gordon, the real compiler of Rhoderic Random, and striking the man after he was down." See Andrew Henderson, *A Second Letter to Dr. Samuel Johnson . . . with an impartial Character of Doctor Smollett* (London, ca. 1775), pp. 12ff. That Gordon compiled *Roderick Random* is obviously absurd.

[8] *Letters*, p. 18.

[9] See Parker, *op. cit.*, p. 547.

[10] *Letters*, p. 19.

[11] Perhaps Sir William Lee, then Chief Justice of the King's Bench.

[12] I can find nothing to indicate the professional status of Balshaw. He was called in to witness the will of Mrs. Elizabeth Leaver, Smollett's mother-in-law, July 25, 1753, while Smollett was presumably in Scotland.

[13] Probably the Mr. Coulston who lived in the Inner Temple. See *A Calendar of the Inner Temple Records*, 5 vols. (London, 1896-1936), IV, 521. See also Vincent, *op. cit.*, p. 185, n.6.

due to Alexander Hume Campbell, who, according to Smollett, "opened the cause"[14] for Gordon. It was all very expensive. However, according to a traditional report, the citizens of Chelsea celebrated Smollett's acquittal by a "general illumination,"[15] a demonstration of loyalty which must have caused him to forget for a time the strain of the trial and the lawyers' bills.

Why Alexander Hume Campbell, a very prominent lawyer,[16] was prevailed on by the impecunious Gordon to act as his attorney is not easy to explain. Nor is it wholly clear why Campbell insulted Smollett in court when he "opened the trial with such hyperbolical impetuosity, and conducted it with such particular bitterness and rancour, that everybody perceived [he] was more than ordinarily interested."[17] At any rate Smollett was so outraged by Campbell's courtroom tactics that he wrote him on February 23, 1753, some days after the trial,[18] a letter probably never delivered to him. This long and bitter epistle[19] still communicates the living excitement of personal rage, and had Campbell ever received it, he would have been forced either to apologize or to fight a duel.[20]

Close on the heels of Smollett's trial in the King's Bench came the publication of his *Adventures of Ferdinand Count Fathom*, about February 15, 1753.[21] This novel of approximately 155,000 words is considerably shorter than *Roderick Random*, which runs to about 220,000 words, and less than half as long as *Peregrine Pickle*. There are two reasons for assuming that *Count Fathom* was written in 1752: first, after his *Essay* was published in March

---

[14] *Letters*, p. 15.

[15] Cited from the "Life of Dr. Smollett" [by ? William Watson], in *Peregrine Pickle*, 4 vols. (London, 1811), I, xi.

[16] For Alexander Hume Campbell, twin brother of the third Earl of Marchmont, see [Julian Margaret Warrender], *Marchmont and the Humes of Polwarth* (Edinburgh and London, 1894), pp. 88, 91, 179-80. See also *A Selection from the Papers of the Earls of Marchmont*, ed. Sir George Henry Rose, 3 vols. (London, 1831), I, 165, and Preface, xliv-xlv, xlvii. By 1742 Campbell was Solicitor General to the Prince of Wales. He was prominent in the Inner Temple. See *A Calendar of the Inner Temple Records*, IV, *passim*.

[17] *Letters*, p. 20.

[18] The trial took place in the Hilary Term (see Alice Parker, *op. cit.*, p. 547, n.10), and therefore must have ended not later than February 12, 1753.

[19] *Letters*, pp. 15-23.

[20] Smollett concluded his letter by demanding reparations; otherwise, he maintained, "I will in four days put this letter in the press, and you shall hear in another manner—not from a ruffian and an assassin—but from an injured gentleman."

[21] The *Public Advertiser* ran the notice on February 15, 1753. In the same newspaper the novel was announced January 8, 1753, as speedily to be published.

of that year, Smollett was not engaged on any other time-consuming literary project; and second, it looks as if Smollett, in drawing his benevolent Jew, Joshua Manasseh, was influenced by a similar character in Christian Gellert's *Das Leben des swedischen Grafin G.xxx*, which appeared in an English translation as early as March 1752.[22]

As to the printer of *Count Fathom* and the number of copies issued there appears to be no satisfactory information.[23] There is nothing, moreover, to prove that it had much of a sale. Its brilliant dedication, containing Smollett's self-portrait as well as his often quoted definition of a novel, conveyed in its final paragraph a note of relative uncertainty, felt while the shadow of the coming King's-Bench trial hung over him. From that concluding paragraph one senses that Smollett was not wholly confident that the public would like *Count Fathom*:

> If I have not succeeded in my endeavours to unfold the mysteries of fraud, to instruct the ignorant, and entertain the vacant; if I have failed in my attempts to subject folly to ridicule, and vice to indignation; to rouse the spirit of mirth, wake the soul of compassion, and touch the secret springs that move the heart; I have at least, adorned virtue with honour and applause; branded iniquity with reproach and shame, and carefully avoided every hint or expression which could give umbrage to the most delicate reader: circumstances which (whatever may be my fate with the public) will with you [Doctor xxxxxx] always operate in favour of,
>
> Dear Sir,
Your very affectionate
friend and servant,
THE AUTHOR.

A further suggestion that Smollett was in a depressed and romantically introspective mood when he wrote the dedication of *Count Fathom* must now be advanced. That Smollett actually dedicated this novel to himself, rather than to some medical friend (Dr. John Armstrong, for instance)[24] was the belief of the person who composed Smollett's memoir for the 1777 edition of his *Plays and Poems*, and who declared: "In the Dedication of Count

---

[22] Gellert's novel received a short but favorable notice in the *Monthly Review* for March 1752 (*Monthly Review*, VI, 231-32). For good evidence that Smollett was influenced by this work, see Dr. H. R. S. Van Der Veen, *Jewish Characters in Eighteenth Century English Fiction and Drama* (Batavia, 1935), pp. 41ff.

[23] See my article, "Smollett's Works as Printed by William Strahan," *loc. cit.*, p. 288.

[24] See my article, "Dr. John Armstrong," *loc. cit.*, p. 1058, n.168.

Fathom to Dr. ———, by which he meant himself, he has drawn his own character."[25] Granting that this is true (and there is no reason to doubt it), the passage portraying the recipient of the dedication takes on extraordinary interest. It runs as follows:

> Know, then, I can despise your pride, while I honour your integrity; and applaud your taste, while I am shocked at your ostentation. I have known you trifling, superficial and obstinate in dispute; meanly jealous, and awkwardly reserved: rash and haughty in your resentments: and coarse and lowly in your connections. I have blushed at the weakness of your conversation, and trembled at the errors of your conduct. Yet as I own you possess certain good qualities, which overbalance these defects, and distinguish you on this occasion as a person for whom I have the most perfect attachment and esteem, you have no cause to complain of the indelicacy with which your faults are reprehended: and as they are chiefly the excesses of a sanguine disposition and looseness of thought, impatient of caution or controul, you may, thus stimulated, watch over your own intemperance and infirmity with redoubled vigilance and consideration, and for the future profit by the severity of my reproof.[26]

Now it is undeniable that most of the temperamental weaknesses so clearly expounded here—pride, obstinacy, jealousy, impetuosity in taking offense, lack of emotional control—are the very ones which Smollett, to his sorrow, occasionally displayed. They are also those which he was to confess repeatedly in his confidential correspondence. Here in 1753, aged thirty-two, Smollett made a psychological diagnosis of his own temperamental weaknesses, just as in 1763 he sent to Dr. Anthony Fizès of Montpellier a medical diagnosis of his physical disabilities. In the latter he described one phase of his condition in the following sentence: "Systema nervosum maxime irritabile, orgamos patitur."[27] For this we have Smollett's own translation: "The nervous system being extremely irritable, undergoes a variety of spasms."[28] True as this was for him in the period of his chronic illness, it was also very characteristic of his disposition in the years we have surveyed. As to the good qualities of his friend (and of himself) Smollett was comparatively vague and incomplete except to insist that they overbalanced his

[25] See Smollett's *Plays and Poems* (London, 1777), p. xxvi, note.
[26] Quoted from the "Dedication" to *Count Fathom*.
[27] See Smollett's *Travels Through France and Italy*. With an Introduction by Thomas Seccombe. "World's Classics" [1919], p. 95.
[28] Quoted from Smollett's manuscript translation in the copy of the *Travels*, 1766, in the British Museum.

defects. This will be demonstrated as we follow him through his later years.

Although *Count Fathom* is quite free from recognizably personal satire, Smollett's indignation against certain groups is vigorously exhibited. This time it was not only the medical men but also the lawyers, especially the Templars, whom Smollett dissected, first in conjunction with the French abbés, in Chapter 22, and later, by themselves, in Chapter 37. Samples of his invective from these chapters are here presented:

> In a word, the abbés are a set of people that bear a strong analogy to the templars of London. Fools of each fabric, sharpers of all sorts, and dunces of every degree, profess themselves of both orders. The templar is, generally speaking, a prig, so is the abbé: both are distinguished by an air of petulance and self-conceit, which holds a middle rank betwixt the insolence of a first-rate buck, and the learned pride of a supercilious pedant. . . . Yet, I would not have it thought that my description includes every individual of those societies. Some of the greatest scholars, politicians, and wits, that ever Europe produced, have wore the habit of an abbé; and many of our most noble families in England derive their honours from those who have studied law in the temple: the worthy sons of every community shall always be sacred from my censure and ridicule; and while I laugh at the folly of particular members, I can still honour and revere the institution.[29]

Later in the novel, after an exposé of minor legal corruption, Smollett's attack on lawyers culminated in the following:

> His counsel behaved like men of consummate abilities in their profession; they exerted themselves with equal industry, eloquence, and erudition, in their endeavours to perplex the truth, browbeat the evidence, puzzle the judge, and mislead the jury.[30]

Both of these passages were linked up in an amusing way with Smollett's experience in the King's-Bench trial over the Gordon fracas in the Hilary term (*ca.* January 23 to *ca.* February 12), 1753. The connection is obvious when we recall Smollett's diatribe against Alexander Hume Campbell. This letter was dated February 23, 1753, some ten days after the close of the Hilary term, perhaps more than ten days after the end of the trial, and about a week after *Count Fathom* was advertised as published. In this epistle there are these sentences:

[29] Quoted from *Count Fathom*, Chap. 22.
[30] Quoted from *Count Fathom*, Chap. 37.

I could not divine the mysterious bond of union that attached you to Peter Gordon, Esq.[31] until you furnished me with the key to the whole secret, by that strong emphasis with which you pronounced the words, *Ferdinand Count Fathom.* Then I discovered the source of your good-will towards me, which is no other than the history of a lawsuit inserted in that performance, where the author takes occasion to observe, that the counsel behaved like men of consummate abilities in their profession; exerting themselves with equal industry, eloquence, and erudition, in their endeavours to perplex the truth, brow-beat the evidence, puzzle the judge, and mislead the jury.[32]—Did any part of this character come home to your conscience? or did you resent it as a sarcasm levelled at the whole bench without distinction? I take it for granted, this must have been the origin of your enmity to me; because I can recollect no other circumstance in my conduct, by which I could incur the displeasure of a man whom I scarce knew by sight, and with whom I never had the least dispute, or indeed concern.[33]

Campbell's sarcastic allusion in the King's Bench to *Count Fathom* does not necessarily mean that he had read that novel in the short period between its publication and the opening session of the trial because the estimated date of publication is only approximate. He might have read it, or he may only have heard about it. As Campbell was a very prominent figure in the Inner Temple[34] he certainly would have taken offense at Smollett's forthright remarks about the typical Templar and been led to make it as unpleasant as possible for Smollett in court. Little did Smollett dream when he wrote Dr. John Moore in 1755 that the "Cabal of the Campbells" would "always preponderate,"[35] and that he was again to be humiliated by Hume Campbell, later Lord Register of Scotland, in the Knowles libel case.

Though Smollett's satirical bent is shown in *Count Fathom*, there is also in this impressive novel the reflection of his strong humanitarian spirit. This is strikingly illustrated by his portrait of the generous Jew in the days of debate over the Jewish Naturalization Act. It also shines through his portrait of, and propaganda for, Theodore deNeuhoff, former King of Corsica,[36] who had been confined for debt in the King's Bench Prison since the end of 1749. It

---

[31] Smollett used the term, "Esq.," ironically.
[32] Cf. the passage quoted above.
[33] Quoted from *Letters*, p. 21.
[34] Campbell was elected Treasurer of the Inner Temple in 1750.
[35] *Letters*, p. 34.
[36] For the best account of this famous figure see André Le Glay, *Theodore deNeuhoff Roi de Corse*, Monaco and Paris, 1907.

is fairly certain that Smollett, who was never imprisoned because of poverty, went to visit Theodore and felt sorry for him. Such a feeling is clearly expressed in Chapters 39 and 40, where Smollett pointed out an analogy between Theodore and Belisarius, who had implored charity by repeating the phrase, *date obolum Belisario.*[37]

Not only was Smollett the satirist and the humanitarian in *Count Fathom*; he was also the moralist, the dispenser of literary quotations, and (in Chapters 20, 21, and elsewhere), the poetic forerunner of the romantic (Gothic) novel. But in spite of its varied moods, scenes, and characters, *Count Fathom* seems not to have been widely read in 1753. Just why this should have been so is not easily explained. Many readers in that year were busy pursuing the numerous tracts on the notorious case of Elizabeth Canning;[38] others were following the debates over the so-called Jew Bill. The chief reasons, however, for the small sale of *Count Fathom* were perhaps that its hero was too complete a monster and that this novel lacked the comic humor of *Roderick Random* and *Peregrine Pickle.* These two limitations were noted by Griffiths, who both praised and ran down *Count Fathom* in the *Monthly Review.*[39] He liked the story of Melville and Monimia but was (so he claimed) skeptical as to the instruction afforded the reader by the improbable and shocking diabolism of Fathom. He admitted that the book bore "strong marks of genius,"[40] but he missed the author's well-known comic humor. The latter he illustrated, however, by quoting practically all of Chapter 24 (the meeting in Paris of Sir Stentor Stiles and Sir Giles Squirrel). Except for Griffiths' review, the critics' reception of *Count Fathom* is not known, nor did Smollett leave any record of how he was affected by it. It is safe to assume, however, that he was deeply disappointed. At any

[37] It is worth noting that this sentence, which Smollett translates as "spare a farthing to your poor old soldier Belisarius," is the motto heading Horace Walpole's semi-ironic appeal for Theodore, published in *The World*, No. 8, Thursday, February 22, 1753, as by Adam Fitz-Adam. One who reads consecutively the appeal of Smollett and that of Walpole will see that Smollett was a sincere philanthropist, whereas Walpole was here playing a game of penny-tossing.

[38] See Lillian Bueno McCue, "Elizabeth Canning in Print" in *Elizabethan Studies and Other Essays in Honor of George F. Reynolds* (University of Colorado Studies, Series B. Studies in the Humanities, Vol. 2, No. 4 [Boulder, Colorado, 1945]), pp. 223-32. See also Lillian de la Torre, *Elizabeth is Missing; or, Truth Triumphant: An Eighteenth Century mystery*, New York, 1945.

[39] See the *Monthly Review*, VIII (1753), 203-14.

[40] *Ibid.*, p. 207.

rate, seven years were to elapse before he published another novel.

Because of the presumably small financial return from *Count Fathom*, because of fines and lawyers' fees, because of the loss of time entailed by law suits and the bankruptcy of a certain person who owed him £180, it is small wonder that in May 1753 Smollett had to borrow money from his friend Dr. George Macaulay. Previously he had been both a borrower and a lender. It is true that twenty letters by Smollett out of the seventy-two published by Professor Noyes mention his financial problems.[41] But this fact does not mean that Smollett was ever for any considerable time in acute financial distress. In the twenty-four letters which have been published since Professor Noyes' edition of the letters there is hardly a word about financial difficulties. And in his letter to Macaulay, just referred to, he declared that he was expecting any day from Mr. Bontein (his and Mrs. Smollett's business agent in the West Indies) "above 1000 l."[42] Now one thousand pounds was no small sum.[43] In fact Smollett's "poverty" has been greatly overstated, though it is true that, owing to his generous habits and his fairly expensive household (he had his manservant, Tolloush, and other domestic help, surely), his expenses often outran his and Mrs. Smollett's combined income. At such very unpleasant crises Smollett was obliged to write to some friend for a loan, and that type of letter had a better chance of being preserved than the sort of epistle more interesting to the average reader. But such financial emergencies were always successfully met.

In the lean months following the publication of *Count Fathom*, Smollett supplemented his medical fees by engaging in further undertakings—jobs for the booksellers he would have called them. This type of hack work is illustrated by the contract he signed May 5, 1753, with Robert Dodsley, James Rivington, and William Strahan, wherein he agreed to complete for the press on or before August 1, 1754, a new anthology of travels in seven volumes, "to contain in the whole one hundred sheets or thereabouts,"[44] for which he was to be paid one guinea and a half per

[41] This was pointed out by Professor Alice Parker in her article, "Tobias Smollett and the Law," *loc. cit.*, p. 546, n.4.

[42] *Letters*, p. 25.

[43] Whether this sum was restricted to income from investments or whether it was partly principal is not known.

[44] *Letters*, p. 23.

sheet. In other words, Smollett should have received prior to, or in, April 1756, when this seven-volume *Compendium* was finally printed,[45] some £155, or less, if he had hired assistants like Peter Gordon. It was hard-earned money, as is abundantly clear from Professor Martz's recent and very illuminating study of Smollett's extensive labors in it as presented in his *The Later Career of Tobias Smollett*.[46] In another contract, dated in May 1753, Smollett engaged himself to prepare for the press a book of travels by Alexander Drummond, brother of George Drummond, Lord Provost of Edinburgh.[47] This volume, handsomely printed and illustrated, and published in folio in 1754, was entitled *Travels through different Cities of Germany, Italy, Greece, and Several Parts of Asia, as far as the Banks of the Euphrates*. For his work on this book Smollett received at least 100 guineas,[48] as well as useful experience.

About June 1753, Smollett set out for Scotland to see his relatives and friends, after having been separated from them some fifteen years. He appears to have left his family in Chelsea during the five months or so of his absence.[49] Although his itinerary cannot be traced in detail, there are a few records of his activities preserved in Carlyle's invaluable *Autobiography*,[50] and in Moore's "Life," though Moore was responsible for the erroneous belief of Smollett's later biographers that he visited Scotland in 1755.[51] Having arrived in the Land of Cakes, Smollett went to see his mother, then living with his married sister Jean, Mrs. Alexander Telfer, on the estate of Scotstoun[52] in Peeblesshire. Moore, in the

[45] When published anonymously in 1756, in 7 volumes, the compilation was called *A Compendium of Authentic and Entertaining Voyages, Digested in a Chronological Series*.

[46] See Louis L. Martz, *op. cit.*, pp. [23]-64. See also George M. Kahrl, *Tobias Smollett, Traveler-Novelist*, pp. 80-86.

[47] For this distinguished Scottish worthy, see William Baird, "George Drummond: an Eighteenth Century Lord Provost," in *The Book of the Old Edinburgh Club*, IV (1911), pp. 1-54.

[48] See *Letters*, pp. 24-25.

[49] Evidence that his mother-in-law, Mrs. Leaver, remained in Chelsea exists in the fact that she made her will there July 25, 1753.

[50] See Alexander Carlyle, *op. cit.*, pp. 277-78.

[51] See "New Smollett Letters," *TLS*, July 31, 1943.

[52] For a sketch of Scotstoun in the nineteenth century, see William Chambers, *A History of Peeblesshire* (Edinburgh and London, 1864), p. 476. See also *A History of Peeblesshire*, eds. James Walter Buchan and the Rev. Henry Paton, M.A., 3 vols. (Glasgow, 1925-1927), III, 88 and 93, for a modern photograph and account of Scots-

COUNT FATHOM AND DON QUIXOTE

following passage, related how Smollett played a joke on her:

> With the connivance of Mrs. Telfer, on his arrival, he was introduced
> to his mother as a gentleman from the West Indies, who was intimately
> acquainted with her son. The better to support his assumed character, he
> endeavoured to preserve a very serious countenance, approaching to a
> frown; but while the old lady's eyes were rivetted with a kind of wild and
> eager stare on his countenance, he could not refrain from smiling: she
> immediately sprung from her chair, and throwing her arms around his
> neck, exclaimed, "Ah, my son! my son! I have found you at last!"
> She afterwards told him, that if he had kept his austere look, and con-
> tinued to *gloom*, he might have escaped detection some time longer; but
> your old roguish smile, added she, betrayed you at once.[53]

While in Scotland Smollett divided his time between Edinburgh and Glasgow and their vicinities. Carlyle recorded: "He
came out to Musselburgh[54] and passed a day and a night with me
and heard me preach. I introduced him to Cardonnel the Commissioner,[55] with whom he supped, and they were much pleased with
each other. Smollett has reversed this in his *Humphry Clinker*,
where he makes the Commissioner his old acquaintance.[56] He next
went to Glasgow and that neighborhood to visit his friends, and
returned again to Edinburgh in October, when I had frequent
meetings with him—one in particular, in a tavern, where there
supped with him Commissioner Cardonnel, Mr. Hepburn of
Keith,[57] John Home, and one or two more. . . . Cardonnel and I

---

toun, which Alexander Telfer purchased for his son Alexander in 1749 for about
£2000.
[53] Moore, "Life," p. cxxxvi.
[54] Musselburgh is an ancient regality in the parish of Inveresk, near Edinburgh.
[55] Identified as Mansfield [or Mansfeldt] Cardonnel. See James Paterson, *History of
the Regality of Musselburgh* (Musselburgh, 1857), p. 157 and n. Smollett sent his
compliments to Cardonnel in his letter to Carlyle, March 1, 1754. ("New Smollett
Letters" in *TLS*, July 31, 1943.) For further data on Commissioner Cardonnel, see
Gentleman's Magazine, XIV (1744), 109 (appointment as commissioner); *Book of the
Old Edinburgh Club*; and Carlyle's *Autobiography*.
[56] *Humphry Clinker*, Letter of Bramble, Edinburgh, July 18.
[57] The gentleman referred to was James Hepburn of Keith, an ardent Jacobite,
active in 1715 and in the Forty-Five. See Carlyle's *Autobiography*, ed. John Hill Burton, 1910 (where he is incorrectly indexed as Robert Hepburn of Keith), pp. 61,
242-43, 278. For this extraordinary person see also John Home's "The History of the
Rebellion" in his *Works*, ed. Henry Mackenzie, 3 vols. (Edinburgh, 1822), III, 72, 87,
[381]. Home's account of how he ushered Prince Charles into Holyrood Palace was
denied by Carlyle but is still current. (See John Harrison, *The History of the Monas-
tery of the Holy-Rood and of the Palace of Holyrood House* [Edinburgh and London,
1919], p. 231.)

went with Smollett to Sir David Kinloch's,[58] and passed the day, when John Home and Logan[59] and I conducted him to Dunbar, where we stayed together all night."[60] Such jaunts with such friends Smollett keenly enjoyed. With these Scottish figures—all colorful and attractive in their interests and achievements, Smollett escaped from his heavy Chelsea routine. While in Scotland, moreover, he received a very pleasing honor from the town council of Edinburgh by being admitted burgess and guild-brother "in the most ample form" on August 22, 1753.[61] Smollett probably received this honor in person.[62]

How much of his vacation Smollett spent in Glasgow can only be surmised from Moore's meager statement: "Dr. Smollett . . . visited various parts of Scotland, and particularly the city of Glasgow, where I had the pleasure of passing two very agreeable days with him and some of his old companions."[63] These companions included, presumably, the men to whom Smollett, writing to Moore in March 1754 wished to be remembered: the printer, Robert Urie; Dr. Robert Dick and Dr. Thomas Hamilton, professors at Glasgow University; Moore's partner, Dr. John Gordon; and Hugh Blackburn, a prominent merchant of the city.[64] With other persons now long forgotten Smollett reminisced, of course, about his youthful days in the vale of Leven, in the apothecarys' shops in Glasgow, and in the halls of the University. As he gazed on the old scenes, perhaps he "found every thing diminished" and "shrunk in its dimensions," as he did years later in France.

By November 28, 1753, he was again in the old harness, as is

[58] For Sir David Kinloch (ca. 1710-1795), of Gilmerton, Athelstaneford, Hoddingtonshire, see Carlyle, op. cit., passim. Sir David, the friend of John Home, was host in 1753 to Hume as well as to Smollett. A member of the Wig Club in Edinburgh in 1778, he was noted for his conviviality.

[59] Logan was the Rev. George Logan. See Carlyle, op. cit., pp. 244-47, and "New Smollett Letters," TLS, July 31, 1943.

[60] Quoted from Carlyle, op. cit., pp. 277-78.

[61] The date appears on the manuscript ledger of the Council Records (December 27, 1752-February 27, 1754), at the Office of the Town Clerk, City Chambers, High Street, Edinburgh. See also the Roll of Edinburgh Burgesses and Guild-Brethren, 1701-1760, ed. Charles B. Boog Watson (Edinburgh, 1930), p. 189. For the entry, see Kahrl, op. cit., p. 62.

[62] When I examined the ledger I was told by Miss Wood, who was in charge of it, that the entry for Smollett meant that he might have been present.

[63] Quoted Moore's "Life," p. cxxxvi.

[64] See Letters, pp. 29, 136-39.

[65] See Travels, ed. Seccombe, p. 48.

shown by the signed document relating to the copyright of Smellie's forthcoming volume.[66] A few weeks later he was seeking more funds, this time from his brother-in-law, Alexander Telfer.[67] Upon his return he must have finished his translation from the French of a collection of scientific essays from the pages of the *Journal Oeconomique*. Indeed it is conceivable that Smollett labored on this while in Scotland, as the translation, a volume containing over 500 pages, was off the press in February 1754. This work, published anonymously, and entitled *Select Essays on Commerce, Agriculture, Mines, Fisheries, and other Useful Subjects* Smollett referred to as "no other than a paltry bookseller's job, in which my name ought not to be mentioned."[68] We learn from the preface that this volume was "undertaken at the desire of several persons of taste and distinction." The group sponsoring it was headed by Archibald Campbell, third Duke of Argyll, if we may trust the word of Robert Bell of Philadelphia, who, in 1777 reprinted, along with other material, eight of the essays translated by Smollett.[69] Argyll's associates were perhaps some of the Commissioners and Trustees for Fisheries, Manufactures, and Improvements in Scotland at the time. It may be that while he was in Scotland Smollett was first asked to translate the *Select Essays*.

Along with this sort of work, Smollett pushed ahead in the winter of 1753-1754 with Drummond's *Travels*, Smellie's second volume, his own "History of the German Empire" (to appear years later in the *Universal History*) and with his ambitious translation of *Don Quixote*. That winter marked the beginning or intensification in Smollett's career of what he called "a sudden Transition from an active to a Sedentary Life of hard study and application, by which the Fibres were gradually relaxed & in consequence of reading and writing in a stooping posture, his Breast became affected."[70] From that time on, Smollett very gradually went down hill physically from tuberculosis. As he penned sheet after sheet in his study, his thoughts were still in Scotland. On March 1, 1754, he wrote

---

[66] *Letters*, p. 26.   [67] *Ibid.*, pp. 27-28.   [68] *Ibid.*, p. 28.

[69] See *Select Essays: Containing: The Manner of raising and dressing Flax, and Hemp . . . Collected from the Dictionary of Arts and Sciences, and from various modern Authors*, Philadelphia, printed by Robert Bell, 1777. There is a copy of this rare book in a private collection in the Department of Graphic Arts, Harvard University. For Bell's prefatory statement, see *Letters*, p. 137.

[70] Smollett's manuscript translation (in the British Museum copy of his *Travels*) of his own Latin diagnosis (*Travels*, ed. Seccombe, p. 96).

Carlyle, "I do not think I could enjoy life with greater relish in any part of the World than in Scotland among you and your friends, and I often amuse my imagination with schemes for attaining that degree of happiness, which however is altogether out of my reach."[71] On the same day, in a letter to Moore, he confessed that he was "so jaded" that he wrote with "infinite reluctance." Yet to Carlyle he ran on in a very gay and exuberant mood about the stolidity of English theatergoers; about a play which he had recently seen (Philip Francis' *Constantine* at Covent Garden); about the absurdities of contemporaneous tragedy; about the antics of John Moncrieff, formerly purser of a man-of-war but now an ambitious dramatist; and about his own multiple projects.

Of these undertakings the most ambitious, extended, and laborious was his translation of Cervantes. Nearly six years had passed since his letter to Carlyle, with its fears that the latter would regard the project as "a very desperate undertaking," as there were four translations already available.[72] But, Smollett had added, "I am fairly engaged and cannot recede."[73] In 1748,[74] and again in 1749,[75] his translation was announced as preparing for the press. Finally, on March 16, 1754, according to the *Public Advertiser*, Smollett issued his "Proposals" for printing the work by subscription, this being some two weeks after he wrote Carlyle (March 1) that the "proposals for my Translation of Don Quixote, are now printed and what with new cutts and the paper it will make a very grand appearance." Of the original proposals no copy is available, but their general provisions as advertised in the press are clear: the translation was to be in two volumes quarto, adorned with 28 new prints by Francis Hayman; subscribers were to pay down one guinea, and another upon the receipt of the books; such noblemen and gentlemen as intended to encourage the work were requested "to call for receipts, signed by Dr. Smollet" of the booksellers, A. Millar; T. Osborne; T. and T. Longman; C. Hitch and L. Hawes; J. Hodges; and J. and J. Rivington, at whose shops the

[71] "New Smollett Letters," *TLS*, July 31, 1943.
[72] Smollett probably had in mind translations by Shelton, Motteux, Wilmot, and Jarvis.
[73] See "New Smollett Letters," *TLS*, July 24, 1943.
[74] See *General Advertiser*, November 21, 1748.
[75] See *General Advertiser*, September 7, 1749.

proposals were available and where "the impression of 18 plates, already engrav'd," could be seen.[76] The printed proposals contained also a short specimen of the forthcoming translation, judging from an attack on them published February 28, 1755,[77] and entitled *Remarks on the Proposals lately published for a New Translation of Don Quixote . . . In a Letter from A Gentleman in the Country to a Friend in Town.*

The author of this anonymous and unfavorable notice of Smollett's proposals was William Windham (1717-1761),[78] father of the Hon. William Windham (1750-1810). In a shilling pamphlet, Windham sharply criticized the specimen of Smollett's translation which had appeared in his printed proposals. He found it very inaccurate and made caustic comment on "the consummate effrontery . . . of a man, who without any of the qualities requisite for a good translator, dares to publish his proposals and specimen, when there is so much a better translation existing than he is, or ever will be, capable of making."[79] The good translator, Windham insisted, was Jarvis.

Only a few days before Windham's pamphlet appeared, Smollett's *The History and Adventures of the Renowned Don Quixote* was announced by the *Public Advertiser* as published on February 25, 1755. No list of subscribers appears to have been printed. The two handsome quarto volumes, illustrated with 28 new plates designed by Francis Hayman,[80] were inscribed to Don Ricardo Wall, formerly Spanish ambassador to England,[81] in a brief dedication dated February 7, 1755. Preceding Cervantes' Preface to the Reader, Smollett inserted a short statement concerning his aims as

[76] My statement is a summary of what appeared in the *Public Advertiser*, March 16, 1754.

[77] See the *Public Advertiser*, February 28, 1755.

[78] See R. W. Ketton-Cremer, *The Early Life and Diaries of William Windham*, (London, 1930), p. 36, and p. 47 where his attack on Smollett is referred to. See also R. W. Ketton-Cremer, *Norfolk Portraits* (London [1944]), *passim*.

[79] See [William Windham], *Remarks*, 1755, p. 16.

[80] Hayman was one of the founders of the Royal Academy. His original drawings for Smollett's *Don Quixote* are in the Department of Prints and Drawings of the British Museum, according to J. T. Smith's *Nollekens and His Times* (London, 1920), II, 277.

[81] For Richard Wall (1694-1778) see *DNB*. It is possible that Smollett met Wall, but there is no record of any association. Wall had the reputation of being a lively and clever person.

translator and the care bestowed upon the work, which ran in part as follows:

> He has endeavoured to retain the spirit and ideas, without servilely adhering to the literal expression, of the original; from which, however, he has not so far deviated, as to destroy that formality of idiom, so peculiar to the Spaniards, and so essential to the character of the work. . . . Whatever may be the fate of the performance, he cannot charge himself with carelessness or precipitation; for it was begun, and the greatest part of it actually finished, four years ago; and he has been for some time employed in revising and correcting it for the press.[82]

The last sentence of this paragraph was omitted in the edition in four volumes, called the second edition, corrected, published in 1761, probably because it was misleading: Smollett began his translation in 1748, seven years before it was published. If it was finished for the most part four years before the dedication (dated February 1755) that is, in 1751, it is clear that he spent most of the summer of 1754 preparing it for the press, and that he was paid for the translation in 1749.[83]

In view of these facts the publication of *Don Quixote* in 1755 brought Smollett no immediate returns, though he had reason to be pleased to see it so beautifully printed[84] and illustrated. Neither did *Don Quixote* receive any noteworthy critical reception. Except for the fact that a sample of it appeared in the *Gentleman's Magazine*,[85] and that there was a short review of it in the *Monthly Review*,[86] this project upon which Smollett had spent so many hours created no stir. From Italy, Lady Mary Wortley Montagu, having heard of Smollett's forthcoming translation, wrote to her daughter, the Countess of Bute, January 1, 1755, "I am sorry my friend Smollett loses his time in translations; he has certainly a talent for invention, though I think it flags a little in his last work [*Count Fathom*]. Don Quixote is a difficult undertaking: I shall never desire to read any attempt to new-dress him. Though I am a mere piddler in the Spanish language, I had rather take pains to

---

[82] *The History and Adventures of Don Quixote*, 2 vols. (London, 1755), I, [xxi].
[83] See *Letters*, p. 32.
[84] I know of no evidence as to who printed it.
[85] See *Gentleman's Magazine*, XXV (1755), 101.
[86] See *Monthly Review*, XIII (1755), 196-202. According to Nangle, *op. cit.*, p. 74, this review was by Griffiths.

understand him in the original, than sleep over a stupid translation."[87] However, Smollett's translation became increasingly popular, judging from the several editions printed before his death and from the large number issued from 1770 to 1800.[88]

From February 1755, when the *Don Quixote* was published, to the end of that year we can only guess at the timetable of Smollett's labors. That he worked with amazing concentration is abundantly clear. There was the final editorial work to be done on the seven volumes of the *Compendium of Authentic and Entertaining Voyages*, published in April 1756;[89] the first draft, perhaps, of his comedy, *The Reprisal*; and the initial planning of his extended *History of England*. To these activities must be added what he called his "extensive Plan . . . for a sort of academy of the belles lettres," of which the *Critical Review* was "a small branch."[90]

Of Smollett's ambitious scheme for an academy of the belles-lettres, launched unsuccessfully in 1755, nothing specific is known, and yet it created some stir at the time. Dr. John Armstrong was probably consulted in this undertaking,[91] which Joseph Reed, a minor dramatist, sneered at four years later in the following attack:

> In the close of the Year 1755, a certain *Caledonian* Quack, by the Curtesy of *England*, call'd a *Doctor of Physick*, whose real, or assum'd Name was FERDINANDO MAC FATHOMLESS, form'd a Project for initiating and perfecting the Male-Inhabitants of this Island, in the Use and Management of the *linguary Weapon*, by the Erection of a *Scolding Amphitheatre*. For this Purpose, he selected, and engag'd, on weekly Salary, about a Dozen of the most eminent Professors of *Vociferation* in this Academy: but, after he had been at a considerable Expence, the unfortunate *Emperic*[92] could not get his Project licenc'd.
>
> The Doctor was greatly mortified at his unexpected Disappointment, but being resolved that *his own*, and the *Sisterhood's* Talents should not

[87] Cited from *The Letters and Works of Lady Mary Wortley Montagu*, ed. W. Moy Thomas, 2 vols. (London, 1887), II, 279.
[88] See the bibliography of Smollett by Professor Luella Norwood in *CBEL*, and also Jeremiah D. M. Ford and Ruth Lansing, *Cervantes, A Tentative Bibliography of his Works and of the Biographical and Critical Material Concerning Him* (Harvard University Press, 1931), pp. 43ff.
[89] See Martz, *op. cit.*, p. 16.
[90] *Letters*, p. 39.
[91] See my article, "Dr. John Armstrong," in *PMLA*, LIX (1944), 1033.
[92] This term meant a quack in physic or surgery.

be lost to the World, *he* set about publishing a periodical Work, called the *Hyper-Critical Review.*[93]

Allowing for the obvious exaggeration in this tirade, it is undeniable that Smollett envisaged a considerable organization involving a group of critics in the general field of the belles-lettres, or polite literature, as Dr. Johnson defined this term. It is also notable that the plan specified some sort of public meetings for the purpose of oral literary debates, for which a royal license[94] was desirable or necessary. Whatever it involved, this grandiose scheme for an academy proves Smollett's initiative and leadership in an attempt at organizing the study of literature. This, in turn, paralleled his efforts at compilation and synthesis in the field of history in a period which Professor Martz rightly terms an "Age of Synthesis."[95] It may be not wholly a coincidence that in 1755 young John Nesbitt, first cousin to John Wilkes, with whom Smollett was then intimate, published his *Essay on the Necessity and Form of a Royal Academy for Painting, Sculpture and Architecture,* a pamphlet of much significance in the debate over the need of a Royal Academy of Art.[96] It is also tempting to suppose that the series of important essays entitled "On the Study of the Belles Lettres," published in the *British Magazine,* July 1761 to January 1763 were promoted or written by Smollett in 1755: they are no longer held to be Goldsmith's work.[97] In any event Smollett's unsuccessful campaign for an academy of the belles-lettres proves that by the end of 1755 he began to exert much more leadership in London literary circles than has hitherto been realized by his biographers and critics, with the exception of Thomas Seccombe, who declared that "for a short period during the interregnum between Pope and Johnson he was a kind of literary Protector."[98] This period extended from about

[93] Quoted from [Joseph Reed], *A Sop in the Pan for a Physical Critick: in A Letter to Dr. SM*LL*T, occasion'd by A Criticism on a late Mock-Tragedy, call'd Madriga and Trulletta. By a Halter-Maker* (London, 1759), p. 5. For Joseph Reed, see *DNB* For his alleged amiability, generosity, and hospitality see *Scots Magazine,* XLII (1787), 529ff.

[94] Smollett was granted a royal license for his *British Magazine* in 1760.

[95] See Martz, *op. cit.,* p. 5.

[96] For John Nesbitt see two notes by W. Roberts in *TLS,* April 30, and May 21 1938.

[97] See Caroline F. Tupper, "Essays Erroneously Attributed to Goldsmith," in *PMLA,* XXXIX (1924), 325-42. See also Ronald S. Crane, *New Essays by Oliver Goldsmith* (University of Chicago Press, 1927), pp. xiv, xix.

[98] Quoted from Thomas Seccombe, *The Age of Johnson* (London, 1900), p. 171.

1756 to 1763,[99] when Smollett, owing to his physical condition, relinquished his tremendous literary labors and began his long and dauntless battle against disease. To the *Critical Review*, launched in 1756 as a vigorous branch of the project for an academy, and to other matters of the years of Smollett's supremacy as a critic and a successful writer, we now advance.

[99] Though Smollett dubbed Johnson "that great Cham of Literature" in 1759, the term suited him best after 1762: he received his pension that year, and founded the Literary Club in 1764.

CHAPTER IX

The Beginning of the *Critical Review* and *A Complete History of England*, 1755-1757

IN 1755 three new literary reviews were planned or actually published. The first to see print was the *Edinburgh Review* (1755-1756), whose editors limited their attentions to books and pamphlets published in Scotland. This lacked popular appeal, however, and expired after two numbers had been issued.[1] It was in 1755 that Dr. Johnson, while his *Dictionary* was printing, recorded in his memorandum book brief notes for his own periodical review, which he at first envisaged as "The Annals of Literature, foreign as well as domestick."[2] About May 1756 this monthly review became available to the public under the revised title of *The Literary Magazine, or Universal Review*. This periodical, weakened because Johnson stopped contributing articles to it, expired in 1758.[3] A third publication, the *Critical Review*, destined for an exceptionally significant life, was also projected in 1755. The man who did most to give it vitality and significance was Tobias Smollett. Its widely publicized plans and policies, its inauguration, its original board of projectors and reviewers, and its early reception —these matters, though not easy to determine, must be examined because they all shed light on Smollett, its presiding genius from 1756 to 1763.

On the front page of the *Public Advertiser* for December 30, 1755, appeared the following notice:

[1] For a brief account of this periodical see Walter Graham, *English Literary Periodicals* (New York, 1930), p. 212n.

[2] See Boswell's *Life of Samuel Johnson* (Humphrey Milford, Oxford University Press, 1924), 2 vols., I, 190.

[3] For details about this magazine see William P. Courtney and David Nichol Smith, *A Bibliography of Samuel Johnson, A Reissue of the Edition of 1915 Illustrated with Facsimiles* (Clarendon Press, 1925), pp. 75ff.

PROPOSALS
FOR PUBLISHING MONTHLY,
THE PROGRESS OR ANNALS
OF
LITERATURE AND THE LIBERAL ARTS

In a succinct and faithful Detail of the Performances on the Subjects of Theology, Metaphysics, Physics, Medicine, Mathematics, History and the Belles Lettres; which shall occasionally appear at Home or Abroad; together with an accurate Description of every remarkable Essay in the Practical Part of Painting, Sculpture, and Architecture, that may do Honour to modern artists of this or any other Kingdom.

This Work will not be patched up by obscure Hackney Writers, accidentally enlisted in the Service of an undistinguishing Bookseller, but executed by a Set of Gentlemen whose Characters and Capacities have been universally approved and acknowledged by the Public: Gentlemen, who have long observed with Indignation the Productions of Genius and Dullness; Wit and Impertinence; Learning and Ignorance, confounded in the Chaos of Publication; applauded without Taste, and condemned without Distinction; and who have seen the noble Art of Criticism reduced to a contemptible Manufacture subservient to the most sordid Views of Avarice and Interest, and carried on by wretched Hirelings, without Talent, Candour, Spirit, or Circumspection.

Urged by these considerations, they have resolved to task their Abilities, in reviving the true Spirit of Criticism, and exert their utmost Care in vindicating the Cause of Literature from such a venal and corrupted Jurisdiction.

They have no Connexions to warp their Integrity; they have no Prejudices to influence their Judgment; they will not presume to decide upon the Merits of a Work in an arbitrary Sentence unsupported by Evidence; they will not condemn or extol, without having first carefully perused the Performance; they will not affect to draw odious Comparisons, where there is no Resemblance or Relation; they will not invidiously seek to wrest the Sense, misinterpret the Meaning, or misquote the Words of any Author, who may fall under their Inspection; they will not exhibit a partial and unfair Assemblage of the Beauties or Blemishes of any Production; they will not venture to criticize a Translation, without understanding the Original, or fill up the page with long insipid Transcripts: In a Word, they will not commend with Reluctance, or censure with Hesitation; they scorn to act as Ministers of Interest, Faction, Envy, or Malevolence; they profess themselves indeed the Enemies of Dullness; but their favourite Aim is to befriend Merit, dignify the Liberal Arts, and contribute towards the Formation of a public Taste, which is the best Patron of Genius and Science.

They pretend to delineate the Plan of every Work with Accuracy and

Candour; to point out the Excellencies; hint at the Defects; and whenever they signify their Disapprobation; [*sic*] they promise to illustrate their Censure with proper Quotations, from which the Reader may appeal to his own Understanding.

In these Sentiments they have established a Correspondence with France, Holland, Germany, Italy and Spain; which will enable them to entertain their Readers with the Literary News of those different Countries, and to translate such Productions, as shall seem to bid fairest for succeeding in an English Dress.

The Work will be comprehended in a Pamphlet of six Sheets, to be published on the First Day of every Month, and the first Number make its Appearance on the first Day of February 1756.

What a provocative and bellicose manifesto this is, with its defiant attack on that "undistinguishing Bookseller," Ralph Griffiths, head of the *Monthly Review*, and all his pitiful hacks! What a fanfare proclaiming the long awaited knights-errant confidently poised to emancipate Criticism from the foul bondage of crass commercialism and to restore it to its rightful function as the creator of true public taste, that "best Patron of Genius and Science!" It was enough to make Alexander Pope stir in his grave. Was it all mere rhetorical pretension? Not by any means, for it expressed, although in an aggressive and tactless manner, the honest aspirations of the new and self-conscious editorial board, whose spokesman was the brilliant and irrepressible Smollett.

A month later in the same newspaper the foregoing proclamation was republished with one significant revision: "The Progress or Annals of Literature and the Liberal Arts" was changed to "The Critical Review or Annals of Literature."[4] In the same notice it was stated that the publication of the first number was "postponed till March, in expectation of some foreign articles."

On March 1, 1756, No. 1 of the *Critical Review* duly appeared. It contained seventeen articles on books published in January and February as prepared by an anonymous "Society of Gentlemen," and it was printed, presumably, by Archibald Hamilton, for R. Baldwin, at the Rose, in Paternoster Row. Priced at one shilling,[5] it contained ninety-six pages octavo size, and was probably covered

---

[4] See the *Public Advertiser*, February 2, 1756.

[5] The *Public Advertiser* for June 26, 1756, carried the following notice as part of its advertisement for the *Critical* to be published July 1: "Gentlemen may be served with the Critical Review Monthly delivered at their Homes in Towns at 1*s.* each month, by giving Notice to R. Baldwin, as above, and in any Part of Great Britain, by their Booksellers or the Newscarriers."

with conventional blue wrappers,[6] on which was printed the table of contents. Among the items reviewed were Thomas Sheridan's *British Education*, a work on oratory; Birch's *History of the Royal Society*; Shebbeare's *Third Letter to the People of England*; Murphy's farce, *The Apprentice*; and Foote's farce, *The Englishman Returned from Paris*. In addition there were brief notices of painting, sculpture, and foreign literature. In most of the reviews there was a liberal sprinkling of caustic comment; sometimes there was the conventional blending of commendation and adverse criticism. At the end of the issue the public was offered a sort of apologia, which ran, in part, as follows:

> If we have in this Specimen commended too lavishly, or condemned too severely; if we have omitted beauties, and exaggerated blemishes; if we have afforded any reason to doubt our taste or integrity; we profess ourselves open to conviction and reproof; and should any person take the trouble to demonstrate our errors and misconduct, we will endeavour to improve by his censure, and kiss the rod of correction with great humility.
>
> Far from thinking ourselves infallible in the art of criticism, we shall thankfully acknowledge any hints or assistance we may receive from the learned and ingenious of every denomination. We request the favour of *their* remarks; and, in a particular manner, address ourselves to the GENTLEMEN OF THE TWO UNIVERSITIES, for whom we profess the most profound veneration, and with whom we shall be proud to cultivate an occasional correspondence.

The charter members of the anonymous Society of Gentlemen who launched the *Critical*, formulated its initial policies, and wrote or revised its first reviews cannot all be identified with absolute certainty. They might be revealed if a marked file of this review should become available, but so far no such copy[7] has been located. Consequently we can offer only plausible suggestions as to the identities of the "four gentlemen of approved abilities," who

---

[6] No. XXVIII of the *Critical*, issued June 1, 1758, had conventional blue wrappers. See my article, "Rex Versus Smollett: More Data on the Smollett-Knowles Libel Case," in *Modern Philology*, XLI (1944), 221, n.4.

[7] The following sets of the *Critical*, if not destroyed, might be revealing: (1) A fourteen-volume run owned by John Wilkes and sold in 1764. (See *A Catalogue of the Valuable Library of John Wilkes, Esq. Sold May 3, 1764*, in the British Museum.) (2) A set owned about 1769 by Archibald Hamilton, Sr. (*ca.* 1720-1793), the printer of the *Critical*, in which according to Boswell he had marked the names of the contributors. (See *Private Papers of James Boswell*, ed. Pottle, VII, 189.) (3) A file of the *Critical* owned by Thomas Wright, the printer, in which he had prefixed the names of the writers. (See John Nichols, *Literary Anecdotes of the Eighteenth Century*, 8 vols. [London, 1812-1814], III, 399.) (4) A complete run of the *Critical* owned by Alexander Chalmers (1759-1834), and listed in the sale catalogue of his library.

"conducted" the *Critical* in August 1756, according to Smollett's own declaration in his letter to Moore.[8] One of this group was presumably Archibald Hamilton, Senior, eminent both as a printer and a person, as far as can be ascertained.[9] That Hamilton printed the *Critical* at its beginning is practically certain, but what share he had in shaping its policy or its reviews is not clear. A second member was probably Dr. John Armstrong, Smollett's friend and fellow-Scot, author of *The Art of Preserving Health*, and successful by 1756 both in letters and in medicine. Proof of his interest in the *Critical* is found in the following extract from his letter to John Wilkes, January 6, 1756:

> Smollett imagines he and I may both make Fortunes by this project of his; I'm afraid he is too sanguine, but if it should turn out according to his hopes farewell Physick and all its Cares for me and welcome dear Tranquillity and Retirement.[10]

Smollett's project was surely the *Critical*, which was, in turn, a branch of his abortive scheme for an academy of the belles-lettres. It is likely that Armstrong contributed to the early numbers of the *Critical*: one William Burnett complained on March 1, 1757 (in a letter to Caleb Whitefoord) that his poem, *One Thousand seven hundred and Fifty six*, was "miserably . . . mauled by Drs Hill, Smallet and Armstrong who are the writers of it" [*The Critical Review*].[11] Though Burnett appears to have been accurate in listing Armstrong and Smollett, there is no reason for accepting Dr. John Hill as an editor of the *Critical*: his *Naval History of Britain* was scoffed at in the *Critical* in November 1757 as "a raw, indigested, and ridiculous performance."[12] Armstrong and Hamilton, however, were probably two of Smollett's "four gentlemen of approved abilities."

The other two members of the committee of four who launched the *Critical* remain to be identified. The third was evidently the Reverend Thomas Francklin, M.A., Fellow of Trinity College, and Professor of Greek at Cambridge; the fourth was unquestionably Smollett himself. Though Francklin does not figure in Smol-

---

[8] See *Letters*, p. 39.
[9] See the account of Archibald Hamilton, Senior in the Appendix, pp. 330-31.
[10] Quoted from Br. Mus. Add. MS 30867, ff. 113-113a. See my article, "Dr. John Armstrong," *loc. cit.*, p. 1033.
[11] *Whitefoord Papers*, ed. W. A. S. Hewins (Oxford, 1898), p. 132. For the unfavorable review, see *Critical Review*, II (1756), 282.
[12] *Critical Review*, IV (1758), 426.

lett's available correspondence, and though it was subsequent to 1756 that he achieved some fame as the projector of a short-lived periodical, the *Centinel*, and as the translator of Sophocles and the author of plays and sermons, there are good reasons for assuming that he was one of the first writers in the *Critical*. Smollett's biographer, Robert Anderson, referred to Francklin as "one of Smollett's coadjutors in the *Critical Review*."[13] That Francklin contributed to the *Critical* was also stated by W. P. Courtney, his biographer in the *DNB*, and accepted by Professor Noyes, who suggested him as one of the four original founders.[14] Moreover, in the list of Francklin's works in the *Cambridge Bibliography of English Literature* reference is made to his "regular contributions" to the *Critical*.[15] More compelling than the above evidence, however, is the fact that Arthur Murphy placed Francklin among the *Critical* reviewers about 1757,[16] either as the result of private information or because Dr. John Shebbeare, attacking the *Critical* reviewers in his *Appendix to the Occasional Critic*, was severe on a "Greek Professor of Cambridge," their "late auxiliary."[17] These facts offer some proof that Francklin was writing for the *Critical* by 1757 at the latest.

Along with Francklin, Armstrong, and Hamilton came Smollett as the fourth, and the most dynamic promoter of the *Critical*. Rumors of his activity in it were soon circulating in London. Someone wrote to John Boyle, fifth Earl of Corke and Orrery, on June 5, 1756, that "Dr. Smallet is said to be concerned in the Critical Review."[18] About the same time Smollett's friend, Dr. Moore, had heard the rumor in Glasgow and received confirmation of it from Smollett in the latter's letter of August 3, 1756. It was Moore's opinion when he wrote Smollett's "Life" that his old friend "was prevailed on to undertake the conducting"[19] of the *Critical*. That

---

[13] Robert Anderson's *Life of Tobias Smollett, M.D.*, fourth edition (Edinburgh, 1803), p. 118n.

[14] See *Letters*, p. 148.

[15] See *CBEL*, II, 466.

[16] See what may be Smollett's review of Murphy's *Poetical Epistle to Mr. Samuel Johnson, A.M.* in *Critical Review*, X (1760), 320.

[17] See [Dr. John Shebbeare], *An Appendix to the Occasional Critic* (ca. November 1757), p. 7. For the date of this pamphlet, see James R. Foster, "Smollett's Pamphleteering Foe Shebbeare," *PMLA*, LVII (1942), 1082, n.110.

[18] Cited from Harvard MSS, Eng. 218.2, Vol. 5, f. 13, at Harvard University.

[19] Quoted from *The Works of Tobias Smollett*, ed. John Moore, M.D. (1797), I, xxvii.

Smollett did not inspect all the reviews, however, is to be inferred from his letter to Samuel Richardson, August 10, 1756, wherein he insisted that an unkind allusion to Richardson's prolixity had been printed in the *Critical* without his (Smollett's) "privity or Concurrence."[20] Although there is no way of determining Smollett's precise editorial powers or the number of his reviews in the early years of the *Critical*, it is a good guess that both increased as time passed. By January 1759, the infuriated Dr. James Grainger in his vituperative *Letter to Tobias Smollett, M.D.*[21] referred to Smollett's extensive reviewing, and to his public prestige as a critic:

> For, indeed, next to *Zoilus*, you Dr. *Tobias Smollet* are allowed to be the greatest of Critics. Were I to indulge myself in any Range, so innumerable are the Instances to be culled out of your Part of the *Critical Review*, in Proof of this general Opinion, that
>
>> To tell them would a Hundred Tongues require,
>> Or one vain Wits [*sic*] that would a Hundred tire.[22]

Despite the irony which saturates this passage, it may be accepted as good evidence of Smollett's extensive activities as a reviewer. From 1756 to 1758 Grainger had been a writer in the *Monthly Review*,[23] and hence interested in reading the pages of the rival *Critical*. He had, moreover, known Smollett personally[24] and had probably enjoyed Smollett's well-known hospitality.[25] Grainger's statement is borne out, furthermore, by the fact that Smollett confessed in a letter to Dr. Moore in 1762 that he was at that date "proprietor" of the *Critical*, but whether he was ever the sole proprietor is open to question,[26] as well as when he first became a sole or a joint proprietor. In the letter just mentioned, Smollett declared:

> Your conjecture is right in supposing I still write some articles in the Critical Review. . . . but the laborious part of authorship I have long resigned. My constitution will no longer allow me to toil as formerly.

[20] See *Letters*, pp. 40, 152-53.
[21] Grainger's *Letter*, a six-penny pamphlet, was published about January 30, 175. See the *Public Advertiser* of that date.
[22] Quoted from Grainger's *Letter*, pp. 1-2. The quotation is from Pope's *Essay on Criticism*, Part I, ll. 44-45.
[23] See Benjamin Christie Nangle, the *Monthly Review* (Oxford, 1934), p. 18.
[24] See James Prior, *The Life of Oliver Goldsmith, M.B.*, 2 vols. (London, 1837), 239.
[25] See *Critical Review*, VII (February 1759), 148.
[26] See Edward S. Noyes, "Another Smollett Letter," in *MLN*, XLII (1927), pp. 23 234.

Shortly before going abroad in the summer of 1763, Smollett furnished Richard Smith of New Jersey with a "genuine list" of his literary works, wherein he put down "Great Part of the Critical Review."[27] This surely indicates that he wrote scores of long reviews and short notices; hence it is conservative to predict that if and when a marked file of the *Critical* becomes available, Smollett will emerge as the leading reviewer in London for the period from 1756 to 1763.

From all this we feel confident that the original group of four gentlemen who launched the *Critical* on its stormy voyage were Hamilton, Armstrong, Francklin, and Smollett. Later on, of course, many others are known to have contributed reviews occasionally.[28]

In the first months of the *Critical*, the original contributors relished the comedy of repeated efforts to pierce the veil of anonymity which covered them. The satirical pen of Smollett is discernible in the following extract from a notice to the public printed at the end of the number for April 1756:

> The task of professed critics, who undertake to reform the taste of mankind, is like that of cleansing the *Augaean* stable; they must not only wade through dunghills of dulness, but also be exposed to the stench and stings of all the vermin hatched amidst such heaps of noisome pollution.
>
> The authors of the Critical Review, laid their account with this nuisance, when they first engaged in that undertaking; and therefore they are not alarmed to find the whole republic of literary grubs in uproar and commotion. . . . Every author finding himself smitten by an unseen hand, suspects his brother of the quill, and attacks him accordingly; while the spirit of criticism sits in the clouds, and like *Ariel*, in the *Tempest*, enjoys the contention she has raised among the children of dulness and impertinence. She sees them at loggerheads, like blind beggars for an alms. They revile, bespatter, and fasten upon each other, and *dunce meets dunce, and jostles in the dark*. One inveighs against a vain, meagre, exhausted hireling, as the invidious *inspector*[29] of his fame. Another accuses a crazy sculler in divinity,[30] as the *Zoilus* who makes *free* with his writings. A third declares war against a *Scotch* adventurer in wit and physic,[31] who hacks at *random* the reputation of his betters: While

[27] See *Letters*, p. 81.

[28] For other suggestions as to the earliest as well as the later reviewers, see *Letters*, pp. 148ff. and Claude E. Jones, *Smollett Studies*, University of California Publications in English, Vol. 9, No. 2 (University of California Press, 1942), pp. 96ff.

[29] This points to Dr. John Hill, though there is nothing else to indicate that he was connected with the *Critical*.

[30] This points clearly to the Rev. Thomas Francklin.

[31] Here is an obvious allusion to Smollett.

others denounce vengeance upon a little, lank *Hibernian* Poet,[32] who beats the bush for this ferocious North-Briton.—These worthies too, far from resenting the charge, seem proud of the suspicion they have incurred; for while their tongues disclaim the work, their significant nods, shrugs, and smiles, confess the imputation.[33]

But this sort of gaiety was soon to be succeeded by different editorial emotions as the reviewers became aware of the mounting hostility of outraged authors and rival periodicals. A few attacks on the *Critical* during its first year are significant. The March number of the *Universal Visiter and Monthly Memorialist* printed an assault on the *Critical* in the form of a letter, recently reprinted by Professor Jones, who suggests that the author may have been Christopher Smart.[34] In reply to this epistle the *Critical* reviewers asserted that they waged "no war with Bedlam and the Mint."[35] A more serious attack was printed in the *Gentleman's Magazine* for May 1756. The anonymous contributor began by waxing merry and ironical over the extended publicity given to the original Proposals of the *Critical*:

> The public has been prepared to receive this elaborate work with proper respect, by a long ostentatious advertisement, that, like another Goliah

[32] The description indicates Samuel Derrick. There is ample evidence that Little Derrick, the translator of Dryden, the poetaster who was Boswell's first guide through London, and who gained a kind of eminence as the successor of Beau Nash as Master of Ceremonies at Bath, was associated with Smollett about this time. The preface to Derrick's *A Collection of Original Poems*, London, 1755, was written by the author at Chelsea. In the Derrick Correspondence at the Victoria and Albert Museum, London, is a letter dated June 27, 1757, from Tho⁸ Harvie of Kingston, B.W.I., addressed to Derrick "at Doctor Smolletts Chelsea near London." In 1755 Smollett subscribed for Derrick's *Poems* mentioned above. In 1757 Smollett wrote Dr. Moore: "The little Irishman, about whom you express some curiosity, was my Amanuensis, and has been occasionally employed as a Trash reader for the Critical Review, but you are not to number him among my Companions nor indeed does his Character deserve any further Discussion." (*Letters*, p. 46.) It is quite likely that the "little Irishman" was Derrick, with some of whose disreputable ways and cronies Smollett could not have been in sympathy. Among the Derrick Correspondence referred to above is a manuscript list of Derrick's writings (Forster MSS 146, f. 92), in what appears to be his own hand. In this list is entered the following: "Critical Review, one vol at least." This seems to show that Derrick was not only Smollett's secretarial assistant for a time but that he actually wrote in the *Critical*, perhaps in its "Monthly Catalogue." For data on Derrick supplementing my own research I wish to thank Mr. William Hubert Miller for allowing me to read and utilize his unpublished Master's Thesis at Columbia University. It bears the following title: "Samuel Derrick, Boswell's 'first tutor in the ways of London . . . in all its variety of departments, both literary and sportive' and Master of the Ceremonies at Bath and Tunbridge Wells. His Life, and a Discussion of some Bibliographical Problems in Connection with his Works."

[33] Quoted from the *Critical Review*, 1 (April 1756), [287].

[34] See Claude E. Jones, *op. cit.*, p. 111.

[35] *Critical Review*, 1 (April 1756), [287].

[*sic*], has come forth "morning and evening, and presented itself more than forty days," with insult and defiance. The authors are said to be gentlemen, and not hirelings of booksellers, who censure and commend without either justice or mercy. But if their abilities to censure and commend the works of others be estimated by their own, perhaps their impartiality may be admitted, without alowing [*sic*] that they are better qualified for their undertaking than those whom they have treated with contempt.[36]

This was followed by adverse criticism of the method of presenting numerous scrappy extracts in the articles in the *Critical*, and by comment on the diction, obscurity, and printing errors in the first number.

That similar attacks multiplied during 1756 was a fact acknowledged by the editors of the *Critical* in the "Preface" to their second volume:

In spite of open assault and private assassination; in spite of published reproach and printed letters of abuse, distributed like poisoned arrows in the dark; the Critical Review has not only maintained its footing, but considerably extended its progress. The breath of secret calumny excites a spirit of inquiry and comparison, from which the work hath derived singular advantage; and the loud blasts of obloquy, instead of tearing it up, serve only to prove its strength and fix its roots the deeper.

The proprietors think it needless to make any apology for concluding this Second volume in five numbers. . . .

Encouraged by the favour of the public, which is the only patron they will ever solicit, their chief attention shall be devoted to the execution of their original plan: They will continue to exert that spirit and impartiality, by which they flatter themselves the Critical Review has been hitherto distinguished; and though they have conscientiously forebore to condemn any performance that seemed to have the smallest title to approbation; yet, as some raw authors have complained of their severity, they will for the future endeavour to distinguish between the imperfect rudiments of still-born genius, and the full-formed productions of hardened dullness.

Modesty, even though void of literary merit, may always claim their favour and assistance; but they desire to be at perpetual war with pride, insolence and presumption.

What could be more succinctly stated than this, and where could be found a more perfect display of Smollettian anger, assurance, and independence? It should be noted, moreover, that no claim is made that the *Critical* had met with any marked success.

Its immediate reception must be gauged, unfortunately, by the

[36] *Gentleman's Magazine*, XXVI (May 1756), 141-42.

data of hostile attacks, as we are ignorant of its circulation and of the verdict of the common reader. Though Smollett wrote Dr. Moore in August 1756 that it met with a "very favourable reception," there is probably much truth in inferences made in 1757 by Dr. Shebbeare that the *Critical* was not a profitable venture for its proprietors. As a sequel to his long, anonymous, and scurrilous blast against Smollett in *The Occasional Critic*, 1757,[37] Shebbeare produced at the end of that year a short anonymous pamphlet called *An Appendix to the Occasional Critic*,[38] which contained a comic announcement for financing the *Critical*, now reduced to great difficulties, according to Shebbeare, because of his exposé of it in his first pamphlet. Shebbeare's mock-proposal ran in part as follows:

> A Subscription for continuing the Critical Review. . . . All those who are inclined to support this laudable undertaking, may be assured that it is a work of great charity by calling at R. Baldwin's, the publisher in Pater-noster-Row, where subscriptions are taken in. The Authors being reduced to great difficulties by the unforeseen and inevitable accident of the Occasional Critic, the smallest sum will be gratefully received and public thanks given for it in the weekly papers.[39]

Following this is a list of subscribers headed by Garrick, who is put down for twenty marks and ten bawbees for "the liberty of playing the reprisal, p^d value."

More specific evidence that the *Critical* was unsuccessful as a commercial venture in its early years is furnished by the following extract from Grainger's *Letter to Tobias Smollett*, published in January 1759:

> To peruse a new Work with Accuracy, so as to give the Public a just Character of it, does, it must be owned, require some Time, of which,

[37] *The Occasional Critic, or the Decrees of the Scotch Tribunal in the Critical Review Rejudged: In which the Learning, Philosophy, Science, Taste, Knowledge of Mankind, History, Physic, Belles Lettres, and Polite Arts, the Candor, Integrity, Impartiality, Abilities, Pretensions, Performances, Designs, Etc. Etc. . . . of the Gentlemen Authors of that Work, are placed in a true Light* [1757]. Shebbeare's attack was occasioned by a review in the *Critical* of his *Third Letter to the People of England.* Smollett probably wrote this review. For details of the ensuing controversy see Foster's "Smollett's Pamphleteering Foe Shebbeare," *loc. cit.*, 1077ff.

[38] *An Appendix to the Occasional Critic, in which the Remarks on that Performance in the critical and monthly Reviews are examined, and the Authors of them shown to be equally illiterate and illiberal.* This pamphlet has a statement on p. 25 dated November 26, 1757, and it was published, apparently, in December 1757. There is a reference to it in the *Critical Review*, IV (December 1757), 552.

[39] Quoted from *An Appendix to the Occasional Critic*, p. 24. For additional quotations from *An Appendix* see *Letters*, p. 168.

those must be very thrifty, whose daily Bread depends on writing by the Hour Glass. You, Dr. *Tobias*, in particular, are so sensible of the Necessity of being an Oeconomist of Time, that . . . as the Work itself [The *Critical Review*] contributes little or nothing toward the heavy Article of House-keeping, so sick are you grown of it, that it can be proved, *"Authors have been solicited to send Characters of their own Works."*[40]

It was not until 1762 that Smollett began to be reimbursed for his losses in the *Critical,* according to his own statement in his letter to Dr. Moore.[41] For some six years, then, Smollett could have made little or no profit in return for his large investment of time and for his endless vexations created by a very large number of controversies[42] occasioned by reviews which he or others contributed. Yet Smollett was chiefly responsible for making the *Critical* the most brilliantly written and significant literary periodical of the mid-eighteenth, if not of the whole eighteenth century.

In addition to promoting the early fortunes of the *Critical,* Smollett worked with amazing persistence at many other literary ventures from 1756 to 1758. During these years his multifarious enterprises gradually broke down his health. He drove himself thus, largely because, prior to the financial success of his *History of England* in 1758, he was frequently in debt. He lacked funds not because his income (including what his wife received from the West Indies) was small, but because he was generous to the point of neglecting his family expenses. This fact is confirmed by Smollett's own confession to Dr. Moore in 1762:

> The public has always been a liberal patron to me since I commenced author. My difficulties have arisen from my own indiscretion. . . from a want of courage to refuse what I could not grant without doing injustice to my own family; . . . [and from] want of economy.[43]

Smollett's household expenses were unquestionably high. Dr. Grainger's unkind sneer that the *Critical Review* contributed "little or nothing toward the heavy article of House-keeping,"[44] prompted

---

[40] Quoted from Grainger's *Letter,* p. 7. For the extended reply to Grainger in the *Critical* see *Critical Review,* VII (April 1759), 141-58. For the reply to the quoted extract see *Ibid.,* 147-48. It is possible that Goldsmith wrote the reply. See Claude E. Jones, *op. cit.,* p. 95, n.8.

[41] See Noyes, "Another Smollett Letter," *loc. cit.,* p. 232.

[42] For an impressive list of attacks on the *Critical* from 1756 to 1771, see Claude E. Jones, *op. cit.,* p. 107.

[43] See Edward S. Noyes, "Another Smollett Letter," *MLN,* XLII (1927), 232. My text follows that of the Historical Manuscripts Commission (Laing Manuscripts, 1925, II, 433).

[44] Grainger, *op. cit.,* p. 7.

a vigorous reply, written perhaps by Goldsmith,[45] in the *Critical* in February 1759. In that long and violent mauling of Grainger the reviewer pointed out the following facts:

> With respect to the *heavy article of housekeeping*, we conceive Dr. James Grainger might, with great propriety, have avoided that reflection, unless he could prove that ever Dr. Smollett sollicited him to defray any part of his domestic expences. That Dr. Smollett does keep house, and lives like a gentleman, divers authors of the age can testify, and among the rest Dr. James Grainger, who has been hospitably treated at his table. . . . All those who are acquainted with Dr. Smollett know, that for every dinner he ever received, he has given fifty at least.[46]

This openhanded hospitality to "divers authors" is the subject of some memorable pages in *Humphry Clinker*, where Jerry Melford described dining with S—— [Smollett]:

> He lives in the skirts of the town, and every Sunday his house is open to all unfortunate brothers of the quill, whom he treats with beef, pudding, and potatoes, port, punch, and Calvert's entire butt-beer.[47]

In the extended account of Smollett's benefactions to struggling authors, from which this sentence is extracted, the reader is informed that S—— "did not know the value of money" but that "his pride was gratified in seeing himself courted by such a number of literary dependants," and that through "their information, he became acquainted with all the transactions of Grub-street, which he had some thoughts of compiling, for the entertainment of the public." And what a superb account Smollett might have written from personal experience with all types of eccentric authorlings— English, Irish, Scottish, and Italian—to whom he felt, and was, superior as a writer and as a "civilized" gentleman.

To maintain a genteel scale of living in Chelsea from about 1750 to 1763 in Smollett's wing of Monmouth House required a large annual outlay, estimated by Thomas Seccombe to have been between six and eight hundred pounds per year.[48] With the Smolletts and their daughter Elizabeth, there lived from about 1753 until her death in 1762, Smollett's mother-in-law, Elizabeth Leaver,[49]

[45] See Katharine C. Balderston, *A Census of the Manuscripts of Oliver Goldsmith* (New York, 1926), pp. 38-39, 51-52.

[46] *Critical Review*, VII (1759), 147-48, 151-52.

[47] *Humphry Clinker*, Letter of J. Melford, London, June 10.

[48] See Smollett's *Travels*, ed. Seccombe (World's Classics [1919]), p. xii.

[49] Mrs. Leaver wrote her will (recorded at Somerset House, London, "Caesar 883") at Chelsea, July 25, 1753. She died there December 6, 1762, and was buried in the

and possibly the two girls[50] who accompanied Smollett and his wife to France in 1763. Then, of course, there were servants, one of whom, Smollett's own man-servant, Alexander Tolloush, refused to leave him in 1763 after twelve years of loyal service.[51] In addition to large household expenses and numerous benefactions, Smollett spent money freely in other ways. He had his portrait painted by Willem Verelst in 1756, and later (presumably after 1764) by Nathaniel Dance. In both paintings he appears as the well-dressed doctor and gentleman of the period. He subscribed for books,[52] and possessed such luxuries as a very fine silver inkstand.[53] "He was now become a great man, and being much of a humorist, was not to be put out of his way," noted his friend Carlyle, who dined with him at Forrest's Coffeehouse in 1758.[54]

---

middle aisle of Old Chelsea Church. Before this church was bombed, the inscription over her grave was still legible and ran as follows:

Elizabeth Leaver
Ob Decr 6, 1762
Aetat 71

[50] See Smollett's *Travels*, ed. Thomas Seccombe (World's Classics [1919]), pp. xviii, 2, 46. On circumstantial evidence I suggest that these two girls were Miss Anne Curry, later Mrs. George Renner, and Miss Frances Lassells, granddaughter to Mrs. Leaver. See Smollett's *Miscellaneous Works*, ed. Anderson (Edinburgh, 1820), 6 vols., I, 189, 195.

[51] For Tolloush, see my article, "Rex Versus Smollett" in *Modern Philology*, XLI (1944), 223.

[52] Smollett subscribed for the following books:

1. Samuel Derrick, *A Collection of Original Poems*, London, Printed for the Author, 1755. Royal Paper Copy.
2. Samuel Boyce, *Poems on Several Occasions*, London, 1757. Royal Paper Copy.
3. [Miss Smythies], *The Brothers. By the Author of The Stage-Coach, and Lucy Wellers*, London, 1758. For information concerning the authoress, see Frank G. Black, "Miss Smythies" in *TLS*, September 26, 1935, p. 596.
4. [William Woty], *The Shrubs of Parnassus Consisting of a Variety of Poetical Essays, Moral and Comic by J. Copywell of Lincoln's-Inn, Esq.*, London, 1760.
5. Francis Fawkes, *Original Poems and Translations*, London, 1761. Copy on superfine paper.
6. Christopher Smart, *A Translation of the Psalms of David*, London, 1765.

[53] Captain Robert Langton Douglas (the Rev. Mr. Douglas referred to by Thomas Seccombe in his article on Smollett in the *DNB*) told me at his home in London in the summer of 1937 that he recalled vividly being in Leghorn in the 1890's. While there he purchased the painting of Smollett, done by an anonymous Italian artist, which now hangs in the National Portrait Gallery. And while in Leghorn he saw in the home of ladies named Fisher an exquisite silver inkstand with two inkwells, made, he conjectured, by some distinguished French silversmith. This inkstand, he was assured, had belonged to Smollett.

[54] See Alexander Carlyle, *op. cit.*, p. 355.

Such was the generous mode of living which Smollett maintained in Chelsea by dint of colossal labor for his publishers, and by virtue of occasional assistance from Mrs. Smollett's investments in the West Indies, from which, in 1756, for example, they were counting on over £1000 sterling, a portion of which was probably overdue.[55] As Seccombe very properly pointed out, Smollett's income from writing was greater than that of any other eighteenth-century writer with the exception of Voltaire.[56] Such a very favorable income must be emphasized, first, as a correction of the old notion that Smollett was for a long period on the brink of bankruptcy; and, second, as an explanation of why he was so proud of the independence which he enjoyed because the public, rather than any individual, was his liberal patron.

To maintain this independent status Smollett turned to a variety of projects published in 1756 and the years immediately following. The first was *A Compendium of Authentic and Entertaining Voyages, Digested in a Chronological Series* published in seven duodecimo volumes in April 1756. This work, according to Smollett's contract with Robert Dodsley, James Rivington, and William Strahan, was to appear August 1, 1754. The delay was probably due, in part, to the pressure of Smollett's other commitments. It appears from Professor Martz's revealing study of this compilation that Smollett as general editor, took his supervisory duties very seriously in selecting, condensing, and arranging the contents, and in achieving a clear and precise style, which, as Professor Martz showed, is very similar in many ways to that of Johnson.[57] This *Compendium* contained, in the fifth volume, "An Account of the Expedition against Carthagena," published anonymously, but in all likelihood contributed by Smollett;[58] to this he seems to have re-

[55] See *Letters*, p. 42. It is unlikely that the average annual return from Mrs. Smollett's investments was anything like £1000. However, by the terms of her mother's will made out in 1753, Mrs. Smollett was named practically sole heir of properties additional to those she already possessed. These she inherited in 1762. For Mrs. Leaver's will, see Appendix, p. 332.

[56] See *Travels*, ed. Seccombe, p. xi.

[57] For an excellent study of the *Compendium* see Louis L. Martz, *The Later Career of Tobias Smollett* (Yale University Press, 1942), Introduction, and Part I.

[58] This "Account" was first included in the collected works of Smollett by Robert Anderson in his edition of the *Miscellaneous Works* in 1800. (See that edition, I, lxxxix, where Anderson stated that the "Account" was omitted in the former editions.) For recent circumstantial evidence that Smollett compiled the account, see Louis L. Martz, "Smollett and the Expedition to Carthagena" in *PMLA*, LVI (1941), 428-46.

ferred seven years later in the list of his own "Productions," as "a
very small part of a compendium of voyages."[59] However, this
must be regarded as understatement: Smollett spent many laborious hours on the *Compendium,* for which, according to the terms
of the original contract, he was paid one guinea and a half per
sheet. At this rate he would have received about £160, a part of
which, no doubt, went into the pockets of his amanuensis.[60]

Smollett's indignation over the hard fate of the drudging compiler, and more especially of the swinking historian (he was in 1756
laboring over his own colossal *History*), was characteristically expressed in what was surely his review of Rolt's *History of South
America.*[61] In this article, appearing in March 1756, Smollett,
insisting that he censured Rolt not from spleen or private resentment, being unacquainted with him, placed the blame for such a
miserable performance upon obtuse and greedy publishers

> who cannot distinguish authors of merit, or if they could, have not sense
> and spirit to reward them according to their genius and capacity. With-
> out considering the infinite pains and perseverance it must cost a writer to
> form and digest a proper plan of history; compile materials; compare
> different accounts; collate authorities; compose and polish the style, and
> complete the execution of the work; he furnishes him with a few books,
> bargains with him for two or three guineas a sheet; binds him with
> articles to finish so many volumes in so many months, in a crouded page
> and evanescent letter, that he may have stuff enough for his money;
> insists upon having copy within the first week after he begins to peruse
> his materials; orders the press to be set a going, and expects to cast off a
> certain number of sheets weekly, warm from the mint, without correc-
> tion, revisal, or even deliberation. Nay, the miserable author must perform
> his daily task, in spite of cramp, colick, vapours, or vertigo; in spite of
> head-ach, heart-ach, and *Minerva's* frowns; otherwise he will lose his
> character and livelihood, like a taylor who disappoints his customer in a
> birth-day suit.[62]

How superbly Smollett has described for any generation the woes
shared by the ragged regiment of Grub Street and those higher up

---

[59] See *Letters,* pp. 81-82.

[60] In 1760, while engaged in the *Universal History,* another project of compilation,
Smollett complained because both he and his amanuensis were idle while waiting for
source books. (See *Letters,* p. 67.)

[61] See *Critical Review,* I (1756), 97-106. This review was declared to be Smollett's
by Shebbeare (*Occasional Critic,* 1757, p. 79), who applied its portrait of the miseries of a hack writer to Smollett himself. Professor Martz has assigned this review to
Smollett. (See Martz, *op. cit.,* p. 24, n.12.)

[62] *Critical Review,* I (1756), 97-98.

on the slopes of Parnassus, and what a revealing confession this is of his own feelings at the very time he was writing his annals of England.

From about 1755 through 1757 Smollett worked with tremendous energy on his *Complete History of England, Deduced from the Descent of Julius Caesar to the Treaty of Aix La Chapelle, 1748. Containing the Transactions of One Thousand Eight Hundred and Three Years.* Why Smollett undertook this extensive project is not at all clear. It was Chambers' opinion that he was induced to do it by a bookseller;[63] Professor Joliat has asserted that he wrote it purely as a commercial venture to outstrip Hume,[64] the first part of whose *History* had appeared in 1754. There is, however, no ascertainable proof for either of these views. Smollett's *History*, published in four quarto volumes, 1757-1758, and comprising over 2600 quarto pages, he is said to have completed in fourteen months,[65] a feat rarely equaled in the history of writing. The incessant pressure of this Herculean labor undermined Smollett's health and also kept him from the relaxation of social contacts. In August 1756, he complained in a letter to Dr. Moore that he was "so liable to Intrusion" from the situation of his house and the number of his friends that he had ordered his servant to deny him to all except those with whom he had "express Business."[66] Added to this grueling routine was repeated financial embarrassment, with threats of arrest from clamorous Chelsea tradesmen,[67] and the necessity of borrowing, not only for himself but also to assist one Mr. Hamilton, a starving friend.[68] Despite such annoyances, however, Smollett drove ahead in 1756 to meet his contract "to finish the History by Christmas."[69] About that time the first three quarto volumes were presumably printing. In April 1757 they were published,[70] and the *Public Advertiser* contained in its announcement the following information:

[63] Chambers, *op. cit.*, p. 94.
[64] See Eugène Joliat, *Smollett Et La France* (Paris, 1935), pp. 213-14.
[65] See Moore's "Life" in *Works* (London, 1797), I, clix-clx.
[66] *Letters*, pp. 38-39.
[67] *Ibid.*, pp. 37, 41-42. See also Smollett's letter to Dr. Macaulay, pp. 64-65. The manuscript of this letter, which I examined at the Scottish National Portrait Gallery, Edinburgh, is dated 1756, and not 1759.
[68] *Ibid., passim.*
[69] *Ibid.*, p. 42.
[70] According to the *Public Advertiser* for April 11, 1757, they were to be published "Thursday next," for £2/18/6 in boards, and for three guineas bound.

N.B. The author begs leave to inform the public that, finding the materials for the latter Reigns multiply upon his hands, he has extended his plan to a fourth vol. which begins with the Reign of William III & will end with the last treaty of Aix la Chapelle. This addition, which is already partly compiled, will be finished with all possible care, accuracy & despatch, and deliver'd to the purchasers of the work without any further expense, and a promissory note, under the proprietors' hands for that purpose, will be bound up at the end of the third volume.[71]

The fourth quarto volume thus announced was not published until about January 1758,[72] though Smollett wrote Dr. Moore in June 1757 that it was then in the press and scheduled for publication in three months.[73]

The quarto edition of the *Complete History* was printed for James Rivington and James Fletcher. Both the typography and the paper are superior, and in addition the books contain frontispieces by C. Grignion and J. Miller. The handsome appearance of the volumes must have pleased Smollett, who presented the first three of them to Garrick[74] and also to William Pitt,[75] to whom in most elegant prose the work was dedicated.[76]

In 1758 Smollett revised his *Complete History*, which began to appear that year in six-penny weekly numbers[77] and was soon after published in eleven volumes octavo. In September 1758 he reported with pride to Dr. Moore that the weekly sale of the pamphlets had increased to over ten thousand.[78]

Smollett's *History* met with a mixed reception in an age when most readers and most critics were unreasonably partisan in their political and religious attachments. It was violently attacked by certain Whigs and by the proprietors of Rapin's *History*. Smollett was of course called a Jacobite, and a Papist, and charged with serious historical inaccuracies and inconsistencies. Typical of these

[71] *Ibid.*
[72] It was dated 1758 and was reviewed in the *Critical* for January. See *Critical Review*, V (1758), 1-17.
[73] *Letters*, p. 47.
[74] For Garrick's letter acknowledging this gift, see my article, "Smollett and Garrick," *loc. cit.*, p. 240.
[75] For Pitt's letter of acknowledgment, see my article, "Smollett and the Elder Pitt" in *MLN*, LIX (April 1944), 251.
[76] Smollett's dedicatory address was dated at Chelsea, March 25, 1757.
[77] For some publicized details of this revised edition, see my article, "The Publication of Smollett's Complete History . . . and Continuation" in *The Library* (Transactions of the Bibliographical Society), XVI (December 1935), 297ff.
[78] *Letters*, pp. 54-55, 173.

onslaughts was a pamphlet written by Thomas Comber, A.B. of York and entitled *A Vindication of the Great Revolution in England . . . and of the Characters of King William and Queen Mary; Together with a Confutation of the Character of King James the Second; as Misrepresented by the Author of The Complete History of England; by Extracts from Dr. Smollett: To which are added, Some Strictures on the said Historian's Account of the Punishment of the Rebels in A.D. MDCCXV . . . and on the Eulogium given to the Complete History of England by the Critical Reviewers.*[79] Comber, a clergyman, and a relative of the Duke of Leeds[80] labored through one hundred and fifty pages of dubious argument to prove that Smollett's *History* (chiefly volume 4) was replete with papistical propaganda, and vitiated by numerous inconsistencies in its accounts of William, Mary, and James II. Smollett, he asserted, was "lost to all sense of shame,"[81] and probably wrote for the *Critical* the eulogium of his own *History* (volume 4). Though Comber preened himself on "having kept within the Bounds of good Breeding,"[82] his claim is certainly laughable.

A smashing reply to Comber appeared in the *Critical* for September 1758. Though this article purports to be written by reviewers other than Smollett, it is clear that he inspired it and whetted its edge. It is a very typical example of irony, invective, and slashing Smollettian style in reviewing, as the following excerpts demonstrate:

> Let us then see who are the professed enemies of that production [the History]: the sage, the patriot, the sedate Dr. Sh——re [Shebbeare]; the serene G——ths [Griffiths], and his spouse, proprietors and directors of the Monthly Review; the profound, the candid, the modest Dr. H-ll [Hill]; the wise, the learned, and the temperate Thomas Comber, A.B. whose performance we are at present to consider. This is indeed a formidable group of adversaries, enough to daunt the heart of any young adventurer in the world of letters; but the author of the Complete History of England has long been familiar with such seas of trouble. . . . We cannot rank the proprietors of R——n [Rapin], and other histories, among the personal enemies of Dr. S——tt; because they were actuated by the dictates of self-interest, to decry his performance. This, however,

---

[79] This pamphlet, as stated by Comber on p. 149, was written at York, April 10, 1758. It was listed in the *Public Advertiser* as published on June 12. Comber dedicated his opus to Pitt.

[80] See *A Vindication*, p. 11n.   [81] *Ibid.*, p. 48.   [82] *Ibid.*, p. 146.

they have pursued in the most sordid, illiberal, and ridiculous manner. they have caballed; they have slandered; they have vilified; they have prejudiced, misrepresented, and used undue influence among their correspondents in different parts of the Kingdom: they have spared neither calumny nor expence, to prejudice the author and his work: they have had the effrontery to insinuate in a public advertisement that he was no better than an inaccurate plagiary from Rapin. . . . Finally, finding all their endeavours had proved abortive, we have reason to believe they hired the pen of the Rev. Thomas Comber of York, A.B. to stigmatize and blacken the character of the work which has been to them such a source of damage and vexation. Accordingly, this their champion has earned his wages with surprising eagerness and resolution: he has dashed through thick and thin, without fear of repulse; without dread of reputation. . . .

Without giving ourselves or the reader the trouble of particularizing the animadversions contained in this pamphlet, which Dr. Sm——tt has not deigned to answer, we shall only mention a few circumstances in the beginning of it, which will convey a proper idea of our author's politeness, candour and veracity. . . . But, of all his [Comber's] impeachments the following article is perhaps the most flagrant. In page 8 he affirms, that the author of the Complete History of England represents the late and present king as inhumanly severe to the partisans of the house of Stuart.—In what part of the work are they so represented?—in no part of it. . . . He moreover brands Dr. Smollett as a partisan of the Stuart family; as a papist; and a prostitute. If that gentleman did not think it beneath him to take notice of such a despicable antagonist, he might punish him severely by the laws of the land, for this insolent piece of defamation. . . .

The inconsistencies which this formidable Zoilus [Comber] pretends to have found in the Complete History of England, will, upon candid examination, be found incontrovertible proofs of the author's impartiality. Attached to no party, and independent of both, he scorned to suppress any circumstance tending to the illustration of historical truth; to represent one prince all angel, and another all fiend, as they happened to patronize or discourage this or that party, or cabal. He found them mixed characters, and as such he has handed them down for the use of posterity.

Mr. Comber may always be assured, that it is not in his power to excite the indignation of the Critical Reviewers: there are some objects too contemptible to excite resentment. We should be glad, however, to know what those *most respectable* personages are, that we have treated with indecency. Those *most respectable* personages are Drs. Sh——e and H-ll, Gr——ths and his spouse; a groupe [*sic*], to which the Rev. Mr. Comber will make a very proper addition. We think we see this formidable band, forgetting the distinctions of party, sitting in close divan, animated with double pots, encouraged with double pay, by the right worshipful the proprietors of R——n, to renew their attacks against the Complete History of England. We shall prophecy, however, that the author of that work will never deign to take any public notice of what may be advanced against him by writers of their class. He considers them as little inconsiderable curs barking at the moon.[83]

How transparent it is from the temper of this invective that such contemptible curs as Mr. and Mrs. Griffiths, and the Drs. Hill and Shebbeare, though theoretically beneath the notice of the *Critical* reviewers, did not infrequently stir up within them and within Smollett the seething currents of anger situated not far beneath the otherwise unruffled waters of decorous serenity.

In the excoriation of Comber, only partially revealed above, the reviewer did not fail to point out that Griffiths employed "an obscure grub, who wrote in his garret, to bespatter the History of England."[84] This grub was not Goldsmith, but rather Owen Ruffhead. Both men wrote reviews of the *Complete History* in the *Monthly Review.*[85] Goldsmith, in a short tactful appraisal of the first three quarto volumes in the *Monthly* for June 1757, expressed the wish that Smollett had introduced more personal comment in his *History*, but praised its style. Ruffhead, the following April, was very severe in his extended review of the fourth quarto volume, alleging that Smollett was partial, inconsistent, and superficial, and that, although his style was elegant, spirited, clear, and florid, it was the characteristic of an able novelist rather than that of an accurate historian.

Opposed to the adverse criticism of the *History* were the glowing tributes to it in the pages of the *Critical Review.* The initial one, covering the first three volumes and appearing in the May issue of 1757, reprinted Smollett's "Plan" of his *History*, prefacing the first quarto volume. This "Plan" is a terse statement of Smollett's purposes as a historian. It was, he maintained, "the result of the most mature deliberation." Moreover, it had benefited by the "judicious Remarks" of Samuel Richardson[86] and, probably, of others. Smollett's announced aims are of prime importance not only in appraising his historical work, but in understanding his pride in it and consequently his sensitiveness to criticisms of it.

[83] Cited from the *Critical Review*, VI (September 1758), 226-39, *passim.*
[84] *Ibid.*, p. 227.
[85] See Benjamin C. Nangle, *The Monthly Review . . . Indexes of Contributors* (Oxford, Clarendon Press, 1934), p. 200.
[86] *Letters*, p. 41.

Therefore a résumé of his chief objectives is enlightening. First, Smollett disavowed any claim of utilizing any new source material. What he tried to do was to "retrench the superfluities" of earlier historians; "to compile an history, not compose a dissertation"; to "guard against that affectation of singularity which is so apt to betray an author into a labyrinth of vague conjectures, through which the truth often vanishes from his researches"; to be free from national jealousy, prejudice, and illiberal religious and political partiality; to consult the most authentic historians; to write "in a clear, succinct, nervous style"; and "to arrange his materials with accuracy and precision."[87] These goals, the reviewer judged, had been "very happily, faithfully and judiciously" reached. He then presented samples of Smollett's "characters" of the early monarchs. A second installment of this review appeared in the *Critical* for June 1757. Here the reviewer, while admitting that the work contained a few oversights and defects, lauded Smollett's candor and impartiality, his animated style, and the "tenderness of his nature,"[88] shown in his championing of virtue and humanity. Special emphasis was placed by the reviewer on the structure of Smollett's *History* as contrasted with that of earlier ones:

> One would imagine that those gigantic historians had never read the antients, nor imbibed the least idea of elegance and composition; for, their narrative is generally loose, shambling, and unequal; sometimes inflated to a meer tympany; sometimes emaciated into a consumption; patched with quotations, swelled with idle and impertinent reflections, encumbered with tedious notes of no importance, and stiffened with treaties, speeches, and acts of parliament. . . .
> The history, that now lies before us, is disencumbered of all such rubbish. It is a round firm compacted clue[89] of composition, which may be gradually unwound, without being ravelled or disordered.[90]

This very telling statement was probably contributed by Smollett himself: it certainly bears obvious marks of his hand.[91]

The final review in the *Critical* appeared in January 1758 and dealt with the fourth quarto volume. The reviewer, though con-

[87] The quoted phrases are from Smollett's Plan.
[88] *Critical Review*, III (June 1757), 483.
[89] Johnson defined *clew* as "thread wound upon a bottom; a ball of thread."
[90] *Critical Review*, III, 482.
[91] The remark about unwinding the clue of composition is similar to Smollett's dictum that in a well constructed novel, the hero unites the incidents and unwinds "the clue of the labyrinth." (See Smollett's dedication of *Count Fathom*.)

ceding marks of hurry and oversight in this volume, and referring to printing errors, was generally laudatory, and concluded with the following:

> We have said enough to express our approbation of this performance: a more particular eulogium on the work, might be ascribed to our partiality for a friend and collegue [*sic*].[92]

So much for the opinions of the pundits on Smollett's *History*. There now remain to be considered its impressive popular reception and Smollett's own extremely revealing comment on his finished work.

In September 1758 Smollett informed Dr. Moore that the weekly sale of the *History* in pamphlet form had increased to over ten thousand.[93] From this extraordinary circulation Smollett realized a very substantial sum: according to Anderson he cleared £2000 on the *History* and the *Continuation*.[94] For Smollett this meant, after 1758, comparative freedom from any acute financial difficulties.

The unprecedented sale of Smollett's *History* was due to several causes. First, it came out at a period when the public was increasingly interested in history. Smollett's publishers, moreover, advertised it very extensively in the press; in fact they did more than that by employing what Anderson called "uncommon arts" in promoting it. Their methods were first described (and perhaps exaggerated) by William Goodhugh, who divulged the following story:

> Smollett first published a History of England in 1757, and reprinted in 1758, in eleven octavo volumes; it was published in sixpenny numbers, of which twenty thousand copies were sold directly, [*sic*] this extraordinary popularity was created by the artifice of the publisher. He addressed a packet of the proposals to every parish clerk in England, carriage free, with half-a-crown enclosed, as a compliment, to have them distributed through the pews of the church, which being generally done, the pious people read the papers instead of listening to the sermon, and the result was an extensive demand for the work.[95]

Not only was the *History* uncommonly well publicized, but its six-

---

[92] *Critical Review*, v (January 1758), 17.
[93] *Letters*, p. 55.
[94] See Robert Anderson's "Life" in his edition of *The Miscellaneous Works*, 6 vols. (London, 1796), I, xxxvii.
[95] See William Goodhugh, *The English Gentleman's Library Manual* (London, 1827), p. 47.

penny form provided payment on the installment plan, a method which doubtless appealed to the public. But the intrinsic merits of the work itself were also largely responsible for its wide appeal. Smollett wrote a successful history because he had significant purposes which he executed with unusual ability. In other words he actually achieved to a large extent the objectives expounded in his plan. Without any pretense of creating philosophical history, found in some degree in Hume, Robertson, and Gibbon, he simply built up a masterly synthesis of historical fact, for which his work on his *Compendium* was an invaluable preparation. Here he far surpassed such historians as Oldmixon, Carte, and Rapin. Then, too, he was conscientious in consulting the best available authorities:[96] in spite of the amazingly short time (some fourteen months) which he spent on the *History*, he "turned over and consulted," to cite his own words, "above three hundred volumes."[97] Again, he tried for a high standard of accuracy: he spent, according to his own statement, "the best part of a year in revising, correcting, and improving the Quarto Edition."[98] But Smollett's *History* was not only well organized, well grounded, and carefully revised; it was written in prose at once masterly and readable. Furthermore, it seems to have been set forth from a relatively disinterested and objective point of view.

In the light of this, Smollett should have forgotten at times the irritation caused by adverse criticism of his *History*. After all, it brought him not only money, but prestige at home and in France, where Jean-Baptiste Targe translated it into French in nineteen volumes, 1759-1764.[99] How Smollett felt about central aspects of the *History* is shown in two letters written to friends in 1758. In January he wrote to Dr. Moore as follows:

> I was agreeably surprised to hear that my work had met with any approbation at Glasgow, for it was not at all calculated for that meridian. The last volume will, I doubt not, be severely censured by the West country whigs of Scotland. . . . Whatever may be its defects, I protest before God, I have, as far as in me lay adhered to Truth without espous-

[96] For example, as Professor Powell has shown, Smollett made good use of the Journals of the House of Commons. See L. F. Powell, "William Huggins and Tobias Smollett," in *MP*, XXXIV (1936), 187.

[97] *Letters*, p. 81.

[98] *Ibid.*

[99] For information on Targe's translation and its reception in France, see Eugène Joliat, *op. cit.*, pp. 213ff. and p. 257.

ing any faction, though I own I sat down to write with a warm side to those principles in which I was educated. But in the course of my Inquiries the whig ministers and their abettors turned out such a set of sordid knaves, that I could not help stigmatizing some of them for their want of Integrity and Sentiment.[100]

It is therefore apparent that it was Smollett's historical research as well as his natural indignation over the Whigs' harsh policy toward Scotland after the Forty-Five which led him to swing away from that party in whose principles he had been educated,[101] and to attack in the *History* the corruption of Sir Robert Walpole's administration.[102] Smollett's admission, as printed later by Anderson and Moore, that he commenced the *History* with "a warm side" for the Whigs may have occasioned the vicious and wholly preposterous falsehood that he approached the Earl of Shelburne, offering to write history partial to the Whigs on the condition that his work receive governmental patronage, and that upon being ignored he then wrote with a Tory bias.[103]

In July 1758 under the irritation of Comber's *Vindication*, Smollett furnished in a letter to his friend William Huggins[104] an extremely important statement, which reveals completely the pride which he felt in his qualifications and achievements as a historian. A part of this letter follows:

I think myself very much obliged to any Person who will take the Trouble to point out any Errors or Mistakes I may have committed in writing the History of England. I can safely say I had no other view in the Execution of that work, than historical Truth which I have displayed on all occasions, to the best of my Knowledge without Fear or affection. I have kept myself independent of all Connexions which might have affected the Candour of my Intention. I have flattered no Individual: I have cultivated no Party. I look upon the Historian who espouses a Faction, who strains Incidents or willfully suppresses any Circumstances of Importance that may tend to the Information of the Reader, as the worst

---

[100] *Letters*, pp. 50-51.

[101] Smollett's grandfather was an ardent Whig.

[102] See *Complete History*, quarto edition, Vol. IV, Book IX, Chaps. 5, 6, and *passim*.

[103] See C. H. Timperley, *Encyclopedia of Literary and Typographical Anecdote*, second edition (London, 1842), p. 703. Timperley's statement is ridiculous because William Petty, Earl of Shelburne, and first Marquis of Lansdowne (1737-1805), was, when Smollett was writing the *History*, a stripling at Oxford with no political influence whatever. See the account of Petty in *DNB*.

[104] For light on the friendship between Smollett and William Huggins, the translator of Ariosto, see L. F. Powell, "William Huggins and Tobias Smollett," in *MP*, XXXIV (1936), 179ff. Smollett had been on cordial terms with Huggins since 1756.

Column to the memory of Smollett, and the house in which he was born

First rate of 100 guns c. 1720

A New Song. About 1744
the earliest version of Roderick's lyric in *Roderick Random*

of Prostitutes—I pique myself upon being the only Historian of this Country, who has had Honesty, Temper[105] and Courage enough to be wholly impartial & disinterested. I may be allowed to speak so far in my own Commendation, considering how I have been treated in public and private, by Envy, Malice, and Ingratitude. When I said impartial, I ought to have excepted the Infirmities of human Nature in which I own myself involved. I have such a natural Horrour of Cruelty, that I cannot without uncommon Warmth, relate any Instance of Inhumanity.[106]

There is absolutely no reason to question the truth of this ringing declaration of Smollett's belief in, and practice of, these high ideals as far as he was humanly able to do so. And they are, obviously, some of the very important objectives of any reputable historian.

[105] The word *temper* as used here means moderation or calmness of mind. See Johnson's *Dictionary*.

[106] Quoted from L. F. Powell, *op. cit.*, pp. 185-86.

CHAPTER X

Success with *The Reprisal*, Revision of *Peregrine Pickle*; Controversies, 1757-1760

ABOUT 1756, the first year of the *Critical*, and a year of crushing labor on the *Complete History*, Smollett found time to whip up for the stage *The Reprisal; or The Tars of Old England*, a farce, produced in 1757 at the Theatre Royal, Drury Lane. This patriotic after-piece in two acts seems to have been written as military propaganda to revive English morale which, after the loss of Minorca, was at a low ebb.[1] Precisely why Garrick accepted *The Reprisal*, which is a very weak play, is not clear. The former bad feeling between him and Smollett must have been much improved by 1756. Possibly John Home, a friend of both, had brought about a better understanding. Then Smollett may have written the tribute to Garrick's acting, printed in the *Critical* for March 1756, which follows:

> We cannot mention Mr. *Garrick's* name, without observing, that we often see this inimitable actor, labouring through five tedious acts, to support a lifeless piece, with a mixture of pity and indignation; and cannot help wishing there were in this age good poets, to write for one who so well deserves them. . . . He has the art, like the *Lydian* king, of turning all that he touches into gold.[2]

There is no proof, however, that this praise preceded Garrick's acceptance of *The Reprisal*; it may have followed it. At any rate there is news in Smollett's letters to Dr. Macaulay (written November 24, 1756, and December 14, 1756) first that "the farce . . . is coming on immediately"; and in the later letter, that "Mr. Garrick, in a very civil letter, gave me to understand that it will

---

[1] See David Hannay, *Life of Tobias George Smollett* (London, 1887), p. 144. See also Oliphant Smeaton, *op. cit.*, p. 93.
[2] *Critical Review*, 1 (1756), 149.

be proper to defer the representation of my piece until after the holidays."[3]

The opening of *The Reprisal* on a Saturday was announced in the *Public Advertiser* for January 22, 1757: "At the Theatre Royal in Drury Lane, This Day will be presented a Tragedy call'd *Merope*. . . . To which will be added a new Comedy of Two Acts call'd The Reprisal; or The Tars of Old-England. The Principal Characters by Mr. Woodward, Mr. Yates, Mr. Palmer, Mr. Blakes, Mr. Usher, Mr. Johnson,[4] Mr. Beard, Mr. Jefferson, and Miss Macklin. Boxes 5 s. Pit 3 s. First Gallery 2 s. Upper Gallery 1 s." The same newspaper preserves the following record of subsequent performances in the spring of 1757:

Jan. 24, with *The Earl of Essex* (Mr. Ross, Mrs. Cibber, Mrs. Pritchard)
Jan. 25, with *The Mourning Bride* (Mr. Mossop, Miss Macklin)
Jan. 26, with *The Chances* (Mr. Garrick, Miss Haughton)
Jan. 27, with *Zara* (Mr. Garrick, Mr. Mossop, Mrs. Cibber)
Jan. 31, with *Zara* (Mr. Garrick, Mr. Mossop, Mrs. Cibber)
Feb. 1, with *Zara* (Mr. Garrick, Mr. Mossop, Mrs. Cibber)
Feb. 3, with *The Suspicious Husband* (Mr. Garrick, Mrs. Pritchard)
Feb. 21, with *Every Man in His Humour* (Mr. Garrick)
April 25, (by desire) with *Jane Shore* for the Benefit of Mr. and Mrs. Davies. (Mr. Garrick, Mrs. Cibber)
May 5, (by desire) with *The Inconstant* (Mr. Woodward, Mrs. Clive)

From Smollett's letter to Garrick, February 4, 1757 (printed below), it is seen that Smollett's benefit night was that of the sixth performance given February 1, according to the original playbill,[5] with Garrick starring in *Zara*. From the same letter it will appear that the great actor directed to some extent the rehearsals of *The Reprisal*, though ill for a time prior to January 24.[6] Smollett also attended the rehearsals: Arthur Murphy recalled how the author of *Roderick Random* made Woodward,[7] who played Block,

---

[3] See *Letters*, pp. 43, 64, 188.
[4] Printed "Mr. Johnston" in the list of the cast as given in the first edition of *The Reprisal*.
[5] See the original playbill in the Harvard Theatre Collection. Despite the record in the *Public Advertiser*, there could have been no performance of *The Reprisal* on January 31. Professor Dougal MacMillan lists no performances for that date. See his *Drury Lane Calendar* (Oxford, Clarendon Press, 1938), p. 54.
[6] In the *Public Advertiser*, January 24, 1757, we read: "We hear that Mr. Garrick is so well recovered as to be able to perform some Day This Week."
[7] For a print of the actor Henry Woodward (1711-1777) in the role of Mercutio, see George Paston's *Social Caricature in the Eighteenth Century* (London [1905]), Plate LXIV opposite p. 45.

the British sailor, "lie down, and whimper and cry, in a manner that gave no adequate idea of a British tar."[8] But we may be sure that Smollett had his way, for who knew as well as he did how tars behaved! Had he spent two years on H.M.S. *Chichester* for nothing? How amusing it would be to know what Smollett said, what Woodward felt, what Garrick thought, and what comment circulated among the cast!

After the initial run of *The Reprisal*, Smollett wrote to Garrick on February 4, 1757, a letter of appreciation which has only recently been published in full:

> You will give me leave to express my warmest acknowledgements for the frank and generous manner in which you received my Performance, and the friendly Care you have exerted in preparing it for the stage. I am still more particularly obliged by your allotting the Sixth Night for my Benefit, instead of the Ninth to which only I was intitled by the Custom of the Theatre, and your acting on my Night I consider as an additional Favour[.] To Crown all these Benefits, you will I hope, order the Piece to be acted occasionally, that it may have some Chance of being saved from Oblivion; but whether you shall think it proper to comply with this Request, or judge it convenient to let the Tars go to bottom, I shall ever retain the most gratefull Sense of your Friendship, and eagerly Seize every opportunity of manifesting that Sincerity with which I am
>
> Sir
>
> Your most obliged, & obed^t Servt
> T^s Smollett
>
> Chelsea Feby 4, 1757 ⎫
> Should it ever lie in my way to ⎪
> Serve Mr Garrick, I hope he will ⎬
> command me without Reserve: ⎪
> He cannot do anything that will ⎪
> more oblige his humble Servant.[9] ⎭

These lines show that Smollett and Garrick were fairly well reconciled. That Smollett was eager to remain in Garrick's good graces is revealed in an undated note sent at about the same time:

> Sir,
>
> Understanding from Mr. Derrick that some officious people have circulated reports in my name with a view to prejudice me in your opinion,

---

[8] Quoted from Arthur Murphy, *The Life of David Garrick, Esq.* 2 vols. (London, 1801), I, 313-14.

[9] Reprinted from my article, "Smollett and Garrick" in *University of Colorado Studies*, Vol. 2, No. 4. (Boulder, Colorado, 1945), p. 239. For the source of the text, see *ibid.*, n.23.

I, in justice to myself, take the liberty to assure you, that if any person accuses me of having spoken disrespectfully of Mr. Garrick, of having hinted that he solicited for my farce, or had interested views in bringing it upon the stage, he does me wrong, upon the word of a gentleman. The imputation is altogether false and malicious. Exclusive of other considerations, I could not be such an ideot [*sic*] to talk in that strain, when my own interest so immediately required a different sort of conduct. Perhaps the same insidious methods have been taken to inflame former animosities, which, on my part, are forgotten and self-condemned. I must own you have acted in this affair of the farce with that candour, openness, and cordiality, which even mortify my pride while they lay me under the most sensible obligation; and I shall not rest satisfied until I have an opportunity to convince Mr. Garrick that my gratitude is at least as warm as any other of my passions. Mean while I profess myself,

Sir,

Your humble servant,

T. Smollett.[10]

Shortly after this, Smollett saw to it that his publisher, James Rivington, delivered to Garrick the first three handsome quarto volumes of the *Complete History*, a gift which Garrick acknowledged in cordial terms,[11] in April. By other means, no doubt, the reconciliation flourished so that Garrick, on November 26, 1757, dispatched to Smollett the following epistle:

Sir,

There was a mistake made by our office keepers to your prejudice, which has given me much uneasiness. Though the expence of our theatre every night amounts to 90 L and upwards, yet we take no more from gentlemen, who write for the theatre, and who produce an original performance, than sixty guineas; they who alter only an old play, pay eighty guineas for the expence, as in the instance of *Amphitryon*. This occasioned the mistake, which I did not discover till lately. Though it is very reasonable to take four-score pounds for the expence of the house, yet as we have not regulated this matter, I cannot possibly agree that Dr. Smollet shall be the first precedent. I have inclosed a draught upon Mr. Clutterbuck for the sum due to you.

I am, most sincerely,

Your most obedient humble Servant,

D. Garrick.[12]

[10] Cited from *Plays and Poems written by T. Smollett, M.D.* (London, 1777), p. vi.
[11] For Garrick's note, see my article, "Smollett and Garrick," *loc. cit.*, p. 240.
[12] Quoted from Arthur Murphy, *op. cit.*, II, 299-300.

The total amount which Smollett realized from the staging of *The Reprisal* can only be conjectured: Professor Whitridge estimated the sum to have been about £150,[13] a plausible figure. Whatever the total was, it arrived most opportunely. Some of it, no doubt, covered the expense of having the play published in January 1757 during its short run at Drury Lane.[14]

That *The Reprisal* succeeded at all on the stage is surprising. Its run was probably due chiefly to effective acting and to its patriotic theme. In any event, it was mercilessly flayed by the reviewers, even the writer in the *Critical* confessing that Smollett lacked dramatic talent.[15] The brief and scathing comment in the *Monthly* follows:

> Calculated for the Meridian of Bartholomew-Fair; but by some unnatural accident, (as jarring elements are sometimes made to unite) exhibited eight nights at the Theatre-Royal in Drury-lane.[16]

The writer in the *Literary Magazine* declared that "the humor of the piece, if it has any, can only be *intelligible on board ship, where, it is said, the author spent most of his time.*"[17] The reviewer in the *Theatrical Review*, after finding *The Reprisal* an utter failure, added this interesting comment:

> I hear the author himself is come over to the public opinion, and acknowledges it to be a very indifferent performance; it is not only very indifferent, but the most indifferent that has appeared for years . . . and might be brought as an incontestible proof, by Mr. Garrick's friends, that, whatever people may say, he is not over-nice in the acceptance of works for the stage. I should not have been so severe on this farce, if the author's reputation had depended on it; but as he has wrote several other works that have met with the public approbation, I thought he might without any great detriment to his fame sacrifice this trifle to the utmost severity of criticism.[18]

[13] Arnold Whitridge, *Tobias Smollett*, Published by the Author (n.d., n.p.), p. 21.

[14] *The Reprisal* was published February 1, 1757, according to the *Public Advertiser* of that date. It was printed for R. Baldwin and sold for one shilling. Baldwin and William Strahan, who printed 1000 copies of *The Reprisal*, seem to have been joint partners in the copyright. See my article, "Smollett's Works as printed by William Strahan," *loc. cit.*, p. 288.

[15] *Critical Review*, III (February 1757), 160.

[16] *Monthly Review*, XVI (February 1757), 179.

[17] See the *Literary Magazine, or, Universal Review* (London, 1756-1758), II, 36.

[18] Cited from the *Theatrical Review: For the Year 1757, and Beginning of 1758* (London, 1758), pp. 48 ff.

Could it be that Smollett, who hoped in February 1757 that Garrick would revive *The Reprisal* occasionally, came later to admit its dramatic flaws? Possibly.

Despite these savage reviews, however, Smollett's farce did not immediately succumb to oblivion. Garrick brought it on again on February 23, 1757, and there were performances on April 25, April 27,[19] and May 5.[20] Surely these productions were most gratifying to the author. Smollett should have been pleased again that *The Reprisal* was produced in Edinburgh, August 20, 1759, and that the author of *A View of the Edinburgh Theatre during the Summer Season, 1759* (possibly young Boswell),[21] was so enthusiastic:

> We were very much entertained with *The Reprisal*. We must congratulate with *Doctor Smollet* on the Success of this little Piece, which, although it is but a slight, easy Sketch of his Pencil, carries plain Marks of the Hand of a great Master; and convinces us, that the Doctor can make his most leisure Hours subservient to the Diversion of the Public.[22]

A detailed investigation would probably confirm the conjecture that *The Reprisal* held a small but secure place on the stage longer than has hitherto usually been assumed. There are records of performances in America during Smollett's lifetime: in Philadelphia, in 1767;[23] and in New York, in 1768.[24] It was presented in Charleston in 1774[25] and at Kingston, B.W.I., in the 1780's,[26] and during that decade it was printed in an anthology called *A Collection of the most esteemed Farces and Entertainments Performed on the British Stage.*[27] It is not strange, then, that Anderson referred to it

[19] The original playbill (Harvard Theatre Collection) shows it given along with *Every Man in his Humour* for the benefit of Mr. Blakes and Miss Haughton.

[20] The original playbill (Harvard Theatre Collection) shows it given along with *The Inconstant* for the benefit of Mr. Rooker and Mrs. Cowper.

[21] See Frederick A. Pottle, *The Literary Career of James Boswell, Esq.* (Oxford, Clarendon Press, 1929), pp. 284ff.

[22] Cited from *A View of the Edinburgh Theatre during the Summer Season, 1759* (London, 1760), p. 49.

[23] See George O. Seilhamer, *History of the American Theatre Before the Revolution* (Philadelphia, 1888), p. 154.

[24] See George C. D. Odell, *Annals of the New York Stage*, Vol. I (Columbia University Press, 1927), p. 124.

[25] See Eola Willis, *The Charleston Stage in the XVIII Century* (State Company, Columbia, S.C.), p. 71.

[26] See Richardson Wright, *Revels in Jamaica 1682-1838* (New York, 1937), p. 106 and *passim*.

[27] This set was printed in Edinburgh. For *The Reprisal* see the second volume.

around 1800 as still a favorite after-piece.²⁸ And so it happened that many audiences on both shores of the Atlantic applauded its concluding song,²⁹ honoring the tars of Old England:

> While British oak beneath us rolls,
> And English courage fires our souls,
> To crown our toils, the fates decree
> The wealth and empire of the sea.

The success of *The Reprisal* is significant chiefly in terms of what it meant in satisfying Smollett's long ambition (extending back to 1739) to succeed in the theater, an ambition which he kept alive with a persistence rarely equaled in literary history. At last that goal was reached in 1757. It is no exaggeration to say that it meant a great deal to him in resolving the chief frustration of his literary career. It also involved a considerable reconciliation with Garrick.

Seeing *The Reprisal* at Drury Lane was but a brief interlude in Smollett's enormous labors in 1757 on the *History* and on other small jobs now largely impossible to ascertain. By June he wrote Moore that he was "so fatigued with the unremitting labour of the pen" that he began "to loathe the sight of paper."³⁰ So heavy was his schedule that he did not write one article for the March issue of the *Critical*.³¹ He had, however, found time in February to read and criticize a manuscript play written by his new friend William Huggins and had perhaps taken it to Garrick, though he confessed to the former that his "Interest with" Garrick was "very low."³² In August 1757 Smollett was in Bath, as is apparent from William Hunter's epistle addressed to him there and relating to *A Letter to the Author of the Critical Review.* How long Smollett remained in Bath is not known, but he had returned to Chelsea by October.

Although in Bath for a time in the summer of 1757, Smollett appears to have written for the *Critical* in July and in August on matters relating to the professional integrity of his friend Dr.

---

²⁸ See Robert Anderson's *Life* of Smollett, fourth edition (Edinburgh, 1803), p. 80. For further revivals of *The Reprisal*, see Smollett's *Works . . . with an Introduction* by W. E. Henley, 12 vols. (London, 1899-1901), XII, xi note.

²⁹ For the musical settings of the songs in *The Reprisal*, see my article, "Smollett's Verses and their Musical Settings in the Eighteenth Century," in *MLN*, XLVI (1931), 231.

³⁰ *Letters*, p. 48.   ³¹ *Ibid.*

³² See L. F. Powell, "William Huggins and Tobias Smollett," *loc. cit.*, p. 185.

William Hunter, who was attacked in the *Monthly Review* for June by Dr. James Grainger.[33] To this assault Smollett replied in the *Critical* for July,[34] in very severe terms. Enraged by this rejoinder, Dr. Grainger, it seems, wrote *A Letter to the Author of the Critical Review*,[35] charging Smollett with ignorance, falsehood, and scurrility. This pamphlet Strahan printed, charging the bill to Ralph Griffiths.[36] While Smollett was concocting his reply, he received from Hunter a short letter dated August 23, 1757, in part as follows:

> I thank you for all the kindness to me, and particularly for the last instance of your warm friendship: and I'm sorry that it must occasion some further trouble. I understand that you propose taking notice of a letter to the author of the Critical Review, and I dare say you will do it properly. That part of the letter that relates to yourself, I hope, will be flea'd and broil'd alive; for it is damn'd impudent. He pretends it was the writer, not the man, that stuck with him. Your friends and mine say, they think you can, from your own knowledge, contradict him in this. I suppose you know he was some time (about twelve months, as I have been told) out of his senses, and confined at Edinburgh. Our friends think this would be the best apology you can make to the public for his behaviour.[37]

Hunter was absolutely correct in predicting that Smollett would do a proper job in "taking notice of" the author of *A Letter*. It appeared very promptly in the *Critical* for August 1757 and is replete with Smollettian debate, invective, and vituperative name-calling: the author is held up as a complete idiot and for good measure is termed an impertinent cur, a good reptile, and a petu-

---

[33] See *Monthly Review*, XVI (June 1757), 555ff. The writer of this article was Grainger. (See Nangle, *op. cit.*, p. 156.)

[34] *Critical Review*, IV (July 1757), 42n. To this defense Hunter clearly refers in his letter to Smollett, August 23. See Smollett's *Miscellaneous Works*, ed. Anderson, 6 vols. (Edinburgh, 1820), I, 181.

[35] This pamphlet, printed for T. Field in Paternoster Row, was published August 19, 1757, according to the *Public Advertiser*. Its material suggests that its author is identical with the reviewer (Grainger) who attacked Hunter.

[36] In William Strahan's ledger (f. 116a) appears the following entry:

Ralph Griffiths Dr
Aug 1757
    Letter to the Author of the Critical Review,
2 Sheets
    No 25 .... 1/12/0
    Many Alterations in D⁰   14/0
    For one Ream of Paper for D⁰   12/0

[37] Cited from Smollett's *Miscellaneous Works*, 1820, ed. Anderson, I, 181. Was Grainger actually mad in Edinburgh, or did Hunter have someone else in mind?

lant grub. At the close of the review Smollett proffers the following charitable advice:

> Endeavour to acquire a more perfect knowledge of your own importance. Confine yourself within your own sphere. Let not your vanity and self-conceit provoke you to deeds above your prowess. Let not the acrimony and gall of your disposition, stimulate you to kick against the pricks. The gentleman at whom you level your leaden arrows, is malice-proof. *Recalcitrat undique tutus.*[38]

The whole controversy is typical of many in which Smollett played an angry role. Provided Grainger wrote *A Letter* (and it is fairly certain that he did), his excoriation in the *Critical* motivated the unusual rage of his *Letter to Tobias Smollett, M.D.*, 1759, already noted. And it led to a renewed intimacy between Smollett and William Hunter, as is evident from the latter's epistle, of November 18, 1757:

> Dr Sir
>
> I'm much obliged to you for the last instance of your regard. No mortal but my brother knows any thing of it; nor shall any body know. In the mean time I have been taking measures, and I think I am now ready. . . . I have wished to be able to wait upon you, but have not dared to stir. I'm affraid I may not for some days to come. What shall I do? Pray are you to be in Town in a day or two? Could not you and Mrs Smollett etc dine with us some day soon & I would send the chariot for you & with you. or I must get my brother to talk the matter over with you, or I must write you a long letter about; but then I cannot have your opinion so well; or must I risk some Lady's displeasure? That I will rather than not see you upon this occasion.
>
> I am Dr Sir with my best respects to your family your much
>
>   obliged
>
>   William Hunter[39]

Though the subject about which Hunter wished to consult Smollett remains somewhat cryptic,[40] this letter proves that Hunter felt him to be a trustworthy friend in an emergency. The fact is, however, that for some unknown reason the two men had been estranged at one time, according to what Hunter confessed in a letter

[38] Cited from the *Critical Review*, IV (August 1757), 152.

[39] Printed from the original manuscript in the Ridgway Library, Philadelphia (MSS Rush, Vol. 28, p. 49). The manuscript is endorsed, "London 18 Nov. 1757, Wm Hunter."

[40] Hunter must allude to his controversy with Drs. Donald and Alexander Monro, which was publicized in the pages of the *Critical*. See *Critical Review*, IV (1757), 225ff., 431ff., 523ff.

to Dr. William Cullen,[41] July 29, 1758. A portion of this epistle was quoted in an earlier context, but a few sentences from it will bear repetition:

> Smollett I know not what to say of. He has great virtues, and has a turn for the warmest friendships. I have seen him very little for some years. He is easily hurt, and is very ready to take prejudices. There had been a great shyness between him and me, which his very kind behavior to me when I was attacked by Douglass, Pott, and Monro, has as yet scarcely conquered, so that I cannot well say how you stand with him; but if I can make you friends I will most certainly.[42]

The eminent William Hunter's characterization of Smollett (Hunter knew him well in the 1750's) is of the greatest importance in appraising his personality in the heyday of his success as novelist, historian, dramatist, and critic. In stressing Smollett's great *virtues*, Hunter meant, presumably, his intellectual, as well as moral excellencies. And from direct experience Hunter knew the warmhearted, friendly side of his fellow Scot. Then there was a supersensitiveness, linked with a quick pride and rashness and readiness "to take prejudices," of all of which Smollett was quite aware in his self-portrait in the dedication of *Count Fathom*.

By the side of Hunter's portrait we place another, painted by his old friend Alexander Carlyle, who saw him in London in 1758:

> Robertson had never seen Smollett, and was very desirous of his acquaintance. By this time the Doctor had retired to Chelsea, and came seldom to town. Home and I, however, found that he came once a week to Forrest's Coffeehouse,[43] and sometimes dined there; so we managed an appointment with him on his day, when he agreed to dine with us. He was now become a great man, and being much of a humorist,[44] was not to be put out of his way. Home and Robertson and Smith and I met him there, when he had several of his minions about him, to whom he prescribed tasks of translation, compilation, or abridgment, which, after he had seen, he recommended to the booksellers. We dined together, and Smollett was very brilliant. Having to stay all night, that we might spend the evening together, he only begged leave to withdraw for an hour, that

---

[41] William Cullen, M.D. (1710-1790), was Professor of Chemistry at Edinburgh in 1758.

[42] Quoted from John Thomson, *An Account of the Life, Lectures, and Writings of William Cullen, M.D.* 2 vols. (Edinburgh and London, 1859), I, 549.

[43] Forrest's Coffeehouse was in Charing Cross, opposite Mews Gate. That he frequented this coffeehouse is evident from one reference to it in his letters.

[44] In the eighteenth century this term meant a person who gratifies his own humor, or, an eccentric, crotchety person.

he might give audience to his myrmidons; we insisted that, if his business [permitted], it should be in the room where we sat. The Doctor agreed, and the authors were introduced, to the number of five, I think, most of whom were soon dismissed. He kept two, however, to supper, whispering to us that he believed they would amuse us, which they certainly did, for they were curious characters.

We passed a very pleasant and joyful evening. When we broke up, Robertson expressed great surprise at the polished and agreeable manners and the great urbanity of his conversation. He had imagined that a man's manners must bear a likeness to his books, and as Smollett has described so well the characters of ruffians and profligates, that he must, of course, resemble them. This was not the first instance we had of the rawness, in respect of the world, that still blunted our sagacious friend's observations.[45]

This sketch, like Hunter's, is indispensable in creating something like a complete view of Smollett in 1758. Here we see him as a brilliant talker; as a "great man," insisting on having his own way; and as an urbane sophisticate, seeing (but not necessarily without sympathy) the comical aspect of his literary authorlings drudging under his supervision on such projects as the *Universal History*. It is not surprising that to the celebrated leader of the Dublin booksellers, George Faulkner, Smollett stood out among the luminaries of the age.[46]

Such was Smollett in 1757-1758 in the eyes of William Hunter, Alexander Carlyle, and George Faulkner. But there were times when, running short of funds, he turned to the dull drudgery of preparing for the press the manuscripts of relatively amateurish writers. This sort of ghost-writing in a financially lean period (in 1757 after his sojourn at Bath) is nicely illustrated by his letter to the printer, William Strahan, written at Chelsea, Monday, October 24, [1757]:

Dear Sir

As soon as I can spare a Day, I will let you know, & come to Town that you may not have the Trouble to come to the Country. I have perused the m.s. from D^r R--y, which is very sensible & correct; but, I cannot well prepare it for the Press, without having the Synopsis & L---s's Pam-

---

[45] Quoted from *The Autobiography of Dr. Alexander Carlyle*, ed. John Hill Burton (London and Edinburgh, 1910), pp. 355-56.

[46] George Faulkner, writing from Dublin, July 5, 1757, to Samuel Derrick, declared: "How happy you are in the pleasing, agreeable, polite, entertaining, and improving company of Dr. Hart, Mr Mrs [*sic*] Mallet, Dr. Smollett and the other shining Men of the Age with whom I very often wish to be." From the Derrick Correspondence in the Victoria and Albert Museum, Forster MSS, 146, Letter 40.

phlet, which I desire, may be sent out, & I shall take care to return them in good Condition. I am obliged to you for your kind Interposition with Dr Harvie. It is a very hard case that I should be troubled with Duns for very small Sums when there are actually fifteen hundred pounds Sterling at the most moderate Computation due to us at Jamaica. I will not forget D____ & am always

your obliged, humble serv^t &
Sincere friend T^s Smollett

Chelsea Monday
Octr 24.^{47}

Thus it appears that Smollett was asked to prepare for the press a manuscript of that worthy eccentric, Dr. John Rutty, author of the well-known *Spiritual Diary*, whose *Methodical Synopsis of Mineral Waters* received a friendly review in the *Critical*, in the issues for August and September 1757.[48] Rutty's book was, however, violently attacked by Dr. Charles Lucas in his pamphlet, *An Analysis of Dr. Rutty's Methodical Synopsis*, which was vigorously ridiculed in the *Critical* for August 1757 in a review which only Smollett could have written.[49] It looks, therefore, as if Dr. Rutty were planning a formal reply to Lucas. To prepare it for the press, Smollett wished to consult both Rutty's *Synopsis* and Lucas's *Analysis*. The latter he had presumably read but wished to examine again in order to deal adequately with Rutty's manuscript. Now in 1758 there were printed two pamphlets, one by Dr. Rutty and the other attributed to him, both of which were replies to Lucas, and in either or both of which Smollett may well have had a hand. The titles of these pamphlets, neither of which I have seen, are listed in the British Museum Catalogue, as follows:

1. John Rutty, *A free and candid Examination of a pamphlet* [by C. Lucas] *intituled, An Analysis of Dr. Rutty's Methodical Synopsis of Mineral Waters*. [By J. Rutty.] London, 1758, 8°
2. *The Analyser analysed* [Signed J. R., i.e. John Rutty?] *To which is added an Appendix* ... 1758, 8°.

[47] Printed here from a photostat of the original manuscript in the Pierpont Morgan Library, New York, by the kind permission of the trustees. On the verso of the letter is the address, written in Smollett's hand: "To Mr W. Strahan Printer in New Street." The text, as here given, varies from that printed by Professor Noyes (*Letters*, pp. 48-49), who did not have the benefit of a photostat.

[48] See *Critical Review*, IV (1757), 121-30; 242-56.

[49] See *Critical Review*, IV (August 1757), 160-62. The reviewer (? Smollett) asserts ironically that he is aware of "the personal virtues of the cool, the candid, the patriotical Dr. Lucas." Smollett, while in Bath in the summer of 1757, could have observed Lucas who, that year, was involved in a medical row at Bath.

Smollett's letter also brings to light his gratitude to the printer William Strahan for relieving his financial difficulties in October 1757. Evidence that Smollett felt free to appeal to Strahan appears in his letter asking him to exert pressure on Millar about borrowing money in January 1758.[50] In the spring of 1758 Smollett wrote and signed the following document, hitherto unpublished:

£100: 0: 0   London May 27, 1758
Thirty Days after Sight pay this my Second p
Exchange (my first not paid) to Mr William
Strahan or Order One hundred pounds Sterling
Value received, which place to account as p
Advice from   Your humble Servant

To Alex^r Telfer of Symington Esq^{r51}
at Mr. Edward Lothian's in Edinburgh[52]   T^s Smollett

About a month later Smollett sent to Strahan another communication, hitherto unpublished:

Dr Sir
          receive inclosed a note for £50. in a few days I shall be with you
—I have received good news from the East Indies[53] & am always yours—
                                    T^s Smollett
Chelsea
June 24. 1758[54]

These documents suggest much about the nature of Smollett's loans and the pleasant informality of his relations with Strahan. The last light on their friendship radiates from Smollett's letter written about a year later:

Dear Sir

   I should have answered the Letter you sent me some time ago; but conscious of my own Innocence with respect to some Insinuations therein contained, & of your Entertaining some Jealousy which I knew Time

[50] See *Letters*, pp. 9-10. From a study of a photostat of the original manuscript I should say that Smollett dated this letter 1758 instead of 1750.

[51] Alexander Telfer was the husband of Smollett's sister Jean.

[52] Printed from a photostat of the original manuscript in the Pierpont Morgan Library, New York, by the kind permission of the trustees. The document bears on the verso the following endorsement: "Will: Strahan."

[53] The source of Smollett's income from the East Indies remains mysterious.

[54] Printed from the original manuscript in the J. S. H. Fogg Collection of the Library of the Maine Historical Society, Portland, Maine, with the kind permission of the Librarian. The letter is addressed "To Mr Wm Strahan Printer in New Street by Fetter Lane."

and my Conduct would easily dissipate; I thought it would have been unnecessary to vindicate myself any other way, from a Suspicion I had not justly incurred. I can say with a safe Conscience, that with respect to Mr Strahan, I never once deviated from Those Thoughts which every honest man ought to entertain for an old friend to whom he has been essentially obliged: you will never find any Just Reason to believe me capable of acting in another manner. I rejoice as much as ever in your Prosperity, & only regret that you are so little connected with me & so much with some Persons[55] who I know to be my inveterate Enemies. The first, is not owing to any fault in me; nor do I impute the other to any abatement in your friendship for me, but to inevitable chances in the Course of Business —I wish you a great deal of Pleasure in your proposed Excursion; & shall take it kind, if when at Ed[inburgh], you will visit Commissary Smollett to whom & his Lady you will present my best respects. I repeat it that there is no Person on Earth who wishes you better, than does

> Dear Sir
> Your obliged friend & Servt
> T^s Smollett

Chelsea July 20, 1759[56]

This admirable letter, so free from any petty envy of Strahan's growing prosperity, and so revealing of the typical cause of much bad feeling between authors and printers, is the last extant correspondence between Smollett and the King's Printer,[57] to whom he felt "essentially obliged." He felt grateful to Strahan not only for his efficient printing of his works, and for loans, but also, no doubt, because Strahan was one of the partners in the copyright of the revised *Peregrine Pickle*.[58]

Late in 1757, presumably, Smollett revised *Peregrine Pickle*. The most compelling reason must have been that he felt embarrassed, in view of his reconciliation with Garrick, over material in the first edition ridiculing Garrick's acting. Moreover, there was gossip in 1757 that it was a profitable move for Garrick to produce

---

[55] These persons were probably Ralph Griffiths, Dr. James Grainger and the like, who wrote or inspired anti-Smollett pamphlets printed by Strahan.

[56] Printed from a photostat kindly furnished me by Mr. Alwin J. Scheuer of New York, whom I thank for his consent to publish.

[57] For light on William Strahan (1715-1785), see R. A. Austen-Leigh, *The Story of a Printing House, being a Short Account of the Strahans and Spottiswoodes*, second edition, London, Spottiswoode & Co., Ltd., 1912, and "William Strahan and His Ledgers. A Paper by R. A. Austen-Leigh, M.A. Read Before the Bibliographical Society, XVIII December MCMXXII," published in *The Library*, III (1922-1923), 261-87.

[58] See my article, "Smollett's Works as printed by William Strahan," *loc. cit.*, p. 287.

a play written by a leading reviewer, and also that Smollett still held his old grudge against the actor—all of which was awkward.[59] Other motives for the revision are implicit in Smollett's Advertisement (with its characteristic notes of injured pride, confession, and defiance) prefixed to his revised and altered edition, published in March 1758:

> At length Peregrine Pickle makes his appearance in a new edition, in spite of all the art and industry that were used to stifle him in the birth, by certain booksellers and others, who were at uncommon pains to misrepresent the work and calumniate the author.
>
> The performance was decried as an immoral piece, and a scurrilous libel; the author was charged with having defamed the characters of particular persons, to whom he lay under considerable obligations: and some formidable criticks declared, that the book was void of humour, character and sentiment.
>
> These charges, had they been supported by proof, would have certainly damned the writer and all his works; and even unsupported as they were, had an unfavourable effect with the publick: but, luckily for him, his real character was not unknown; and some readers were determined to judge for themselves, rather than trust implicitly to the allegations of his enemies. The book was found not altogether unworthy of their recommendation: a very large impression has been sold in England: another was bought up in a neighbouring kingdom: the work has been translated into the French language; and the demand for the original, lately encreased in England. It was the author's duty, therefore, as well as his interest to oblige the publick with this edition which he has endeavoured to render less unworthy of their acceptance, by retrenching the superfluities of the first, reforming its manners, and correcting its expression. Divers uninteresting scenes are wholly suppressed: some humorous scenes he has endeavoured to heighten, and he flatters himself that he has expunged every adventure, phrase and insinuation that could be construed by the most delicate reader into a trespass upon the rules of decorum.
>
> He owns with contrition that in one or two instances, he gave way too much to the suggestions of personal resentment, and represented characters as they appeared to him at that time, through the exaggerating medium of prejudice: but, he has in this impression endeavoured to make atonement for these extravagances. Howsoever he may have erred in point of judgment or discretion, he defies the whole world to prove that he was ever guilty of one act of malice, ingratitude or dishonour. This declaration he may be permitted to make without incurring the imputation of vanity or presumption, considering the numerous shafts of envy, rancour and revenge, that have lately, both in private and in public, been levelled at his reputation.[60]

[59] See *Letters*, p. 44.
[60] Cited from *The Adventures of Peregrine Pickle*, second edition, 4 vols. (London, 1758), I, [iii]-[v].

For the AUTHOR of the FARCE.
Acted but Once THIS SEASON.

AT THE

TheatreRoyal in *Drury-Lane,*

To-morrow, being *Tuesday* the 1st of *February,* ☞ *1757.*
Will be presented a TRAGEDY call'd

Z A R A.

Lusignan by Mr. GARRICK,

Osman by Mr. MOSSOP,

Nereftan by Mr. DAVIES,

Orafmin by Mr. BURTON,
Chatillion by Mr. BLAKES,
Melidor by Mr. SCRASE,

Selima by Mrs. DAVIES.

Zara by Mrs. CIBBER.

End of Act II. a COMIC DANCE, call'd
The *INDIAN PEASANTS.*
To which will be added *(Being the Sixth Day)*

The R E P R I S A L;

Or, The T A R S of *Old England.*
The PRINCIPAL CHARACTERS by

Mr. WOODWARD,
Mr. YATES,

Mr. *Palmer,*   Mr. *Johnson,*
Mr. *Blakes,*   Mr. *Beard,*
Mr. *Usher,*   Mr. *Jefferson,*

AND

Miss MACKLIN.

Boxes 5s. Pit 3s. First Gallery 2s. Upper Gallery 1s.
† No Persons to be admitted behind the Scenes, nor any Money to be returned
after the Curtain is drawn up.

Playbill of Smollett's *Reprisal*
(Courtesy of Harvard University Library, Theater Collection)

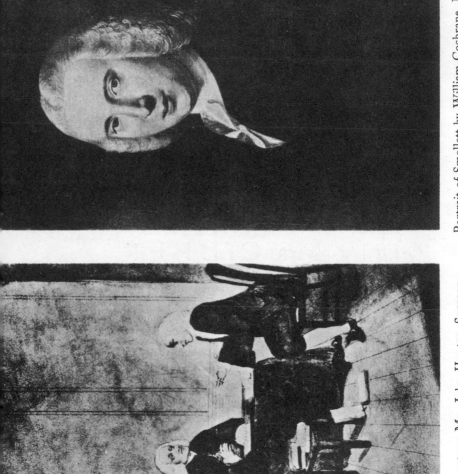

Smollett and the Hunters: Mr. John Hunter, Surgeon;
Dr. William Hunter; Dr. Tobias Smollett

Portrait of Smollett by William Cochrane. Date unknown
(Courtesy of the University of Glasgow)

In his careful study of Smollett's revisions of *Peregrine Pickle*,[61] Professor Buck showed that Smollett confined himself, in general, to excisions (the chief phase of his revision) and to marginal and interlineal corrections. Only once, according to Professor Buck, are there signs that Smollett wrote out a revision on a fresh sheet. Consequently the preparation of the new edition could have consumed relatively little of Smollett's time. One of the most significant matters in the revision was the excision from the 1751 edition of the satire on Garrick's acting.[62] Other alterations were not as successful in the opinion of some critics as Smollett claimed them to be, especially in realizing what he called "the rules of decorum." Certain desirable expurgations, however, were made.

The revisions in the "Memoirs of a Lady of Quality" strongly suggest the hand of Lady Vane, as was pointed out by Professor Buck[63] and acceded to by Professor Noyes.[64] Rather convincing evidence in favor of this theory lies in Smollett's undated note to the printer of the revised edition, which ran in part as follows:

> I have sent two copies of P. P. Vol. 3.—Lady V--e's story, you may compose from that which is incompleat in the other Parts . . . the remaining part of the 3ᵈ volume you will find corrected in the other copy. The fourth shall be done as soon as possible. . . . I wish you would send the proofsheets of Pickle to me to be corrected.[65]

Of these involved instructions I venture the following clarification:

> I have sent two copies of P. P. Vol. 3. Print Lady Vane's story from the copy wherein her story, only, is revised. Corrections for the rest of Vol. 3 you will find in the other copy. I will correct the fourth volume as soon as possible.

It certainly looks as if Smollett had revised his own copy of the third volume before Lady Vane's copy with her revisions reached him, and that not wishing to take time to transfer her revisions to his copy, or his revisions to her copy, sent along both of them to the printer, thereby making no effort to hide from him the fact of her revision.

In the note to his printer, just quoted from, he also wrote: "I

---

[61] See Howard S. Buck, *A Study in Smollett, Chiefly "Peregrine Pickle"* (Yale University Press, 1925), *passim*.

[62] *Ibid.*, pp. 90ff.   [63] *Ibid.*, pp. 45-47.   [64] *Letters*, pp. 169-70.

[65] Printed here from the original manuscript at the Harvard University Library. (Murdock MS 50).

will take care of Mr. Johnston's Papers & lick them up[66] in a very little time, for their appearance." Obviously Smollett was engaged in more ghost-writing.[67]

Meantime, from 1757 to 1760, Smollett certainly contributed heavily to the *Critical Review*, though under no necessity to turn in any specific number of pages per month. At the end of 1757, for example, his contributions fell off,[68] but that was an exception, it seems, to his general practice. A glimpse of his editorial methods is found in his note written in 1759 to Philip Miller, F.R.S., and Gardener of the Botanic Garden at Chelsea:

> Dear Sir
>
> If you are at Leisure I should beg as an addition to all your favours, your opinion of this late Performance of Hill's, which I send you with the Bearer, together with your Essay on the Papyrus: your other Book I shall transmit one of these days. If we could have your Thoughts on the method of producing double Flowers from single, in a few days, so that they could be inserted in the number for this month, it would be a double obligation on
>
> Sir
>
> your obliged, humble serv^t
> T^s Smollett[69]
>
> Chelsea Jany 20 1759

It is evident from this letter that Miller made an occasional contribution to the *Critical*. The "late Performance of Hill's," of which Smollett requested Miller's opinion was a new work by Dr. John Hill, entitled *A Method of Producing Double Flowers from a Single, by a Regular Course of Culture, Illustrated with Figures*, London, 1758. As an unfavorable review of this book appeared in the issue of the *Critical* for February 1759,[70] it is clear that Miller

---

[66] The manuscript reads *lick them up*, and not *link them up*. See *Letters*, p. 52.

[67] The Johnston here referred to may have been James Johnstone, M.D. of Kidderminster, whose *An Historical Dissertation concerning the malignant epidemical Fever of 1756* was published in London in 1758. It received no review in the *Critical*, but was favorably noticed in the *Monthly Review* for March 1758. See *Monthly Review*, XVIII (1758), 244-47.

[68] On January 2, 1768, he wrote Moore, "I have for some time done very little in the Critical Review." (*Letters*, p. 51.)

[69] This letter, of which the original manuscript is in my possession, was first printed (with my editorial comment) in the *London Times Literary Supplement*, June 24, 1944 (p. 312). In suggesting the watermark of Smollett's stationery as EKKBAINK I was inaccurate. Thanks to Professor A. T. Hazen, I now discover that it was GERREVINK, the mark of a well-known English stationery made in Holland.

[70] See *Critical Review*, VII (1759), 118-23.

submitted his opinion promptly, and that Smollett printed it, after adding, possibly, the opening paragraph and the final sentence. The review illustrates Smollett's handling of material which he customarily solicited from various experts.[71] Furthermore it may be inferred from the foregoing letter that the précis of the *Dissertation sur le Papyrus*, Paris, 1758 (by Count de Caylus) in the *Critical* for February 1759[72] was prepared by Smollett with Miller's assistance.

Smollett's numerous reviews were unquestionably the very life and spirit of the *Critical Review*. Through its pages vibrate Smollett's indelicacy, pugnacity, pride, satire, irony, and invective. One senses the immense vitality and gusto with which he carried on numerous and extended feuds with Griffiths, Grainger, Shebbeare, and many others. One feels that Smollett enjoyed hurling barbed insults at authors and authorlings in a period of hard-hitting, personal criticism. When such insults came back upon him, he protested violently, very thin-skinned and excitable as he was. Yet he must have realized that such warfare was a kind of public game, like the rumpus raised in a political fight, where much unseemly uproar leads to no very serious effects. In one instance, however, Smollett paid heavily for writing a libelous review. In May 1758, in the *Critical Review*, in his remarks on a pamphlet composed by Admiral Charles Knowles to vindicate his part in the unsuccessful expedition against Rochefort in 1757, Smollett released a heavy salvo against the Admiral's naval record and character:

> If Vice Admiral K——s had recollected a certain unsavoury proverb, perhaps, he would have saved himself the trouble of stirring up the remembrance of a dirty expedition, which has stunk so abominably in the nostrils of the nation: he might likewise have been more cautious of disturbing the quiet in which his own character was suffered to rest. But, some people are born for action, and would rather run the risque of hurting themselves, than allow their meddling talents to rust in idleness. It must be owned, however, for the honour of the gentleman whose work is under consideration, that though no man was ever involved in a greater number of scrapes and perplexities, yet he has always disengaged himself with a dexterity of address peculiar to himself. He has been compared to a cat, which, though thrown from the top of a house in twenty different attitudes, will always light on its feet; and to the arms of the

[71] See Claude E. Jones, *Smollett Studies* (University of California Press, 1942), pp. 87ff.
[72] See *Critical Review*, VII (1759), 168-69.

Isle of Man, which are three legs conjoined in ham, inscribed *quocunque scieris stabo*. We have heard of a man, who, without birth, interest, or fortune, has raised himself from the lowest paths of life to an eminent rank in the service; and if all his friends were put to the strappado, they could not define the quality or qualities to which he owed his elevation. Nay, it would be found upon enquiry, that he neither has, or ever had any friend at all; (for we make a wide distinction between a patron and a friend;) and yet for a series of years, he has been enabled to sacrifice the blood, the treasure, and the honour of his country, to his own ridiculous projects. Ask his character of those who know him, [and] they will not scruple to say, he is an admiral without conduct, an engineer without knowledge, an officer without resolution, and a man without veracity. They will tell you he is an ignorant, assuming, officious, fribbling pretender; conceited as a peacock, obstinate as a mule, and mischievous as a monkey; that in every station of life he has played the tyrant with his inferiors, the incendiary among his equals, and commanded a sq——n occasionally for twenty years, without having even established his reputation in the article of personal courage. If the service can be thus influenced by caprice, admiral K——s needs not be surprised at his being laid aside after forty years constant and faithful service.[73]

At this pulverizing blast, it is not surprising that the Admiral took umbrage. Archibald Hamilton, the printer, and Smollett were both sued for libel. During the prolonged legal action,[74] Smollett experienced worry and expense for nearly two and one half years, until in November 1760 he was confined in the King's Bench Prison. The highlights of this case will be introduced in due course.

Another review in the *Critical*, written, we may assume, by Smollett, led to the continuation of his controversy with Dr. Grainger. In the issue for December 1758[75] there appeared a very caustic criticism of the versification, diction, taste, and general inadequacy of Grainger's translation of the Elegies of Tibullus. The reviewer's attitude is unmistakably supercilious: he inquires whether or not one of Grainger's couplets might suggest "a scene like that of the *Bloody Bowl* in Hanging-sword-Alley." Grainger soon wrote to Bishop Percy, who had assisted him in the translation, that according to Millar, the publisher,

---

[73] Cited from *Critical Review*, v (1758), 438-39.

[74] For detailed studies of the libel case see Professor Alice Parker, "Tobias Smollett and the Law," in *Studies in Philology*, xxxix (1942), 545-58. See also my article, "Rex Versus Smollett: More Data on the Smollett-Knowles Libel Case," in *MP*, xli (1944), 221-27.

[75] *Critical Review*, vi (December 1758), 475-82.

our book was not condemned by the best judges; but Smollett has been at it in The Critical Review. He has a personal pique to me which upon this occasion has betrayed him into many false criticisms, delivered in very illiberal expressions. My friends strongly solicit me to expose him, to which I have no other objection than entering the lists with so unmannerly an adversary. Perhaps, however, I may give him a drubbing, which, if I stoop to, he shall remember it.[76]

The cause of Smollett's personal pique, to which Grainger referred, is not evident: the subsequent controversy reveals the fact that Smollett had entertained Grainger at Chelsea before he joined the staff of the *Monthly Review*. Then too, as we have seen, Grainger surely had a finger in *A Letter to the Author of the Critical Review*.

Smollett perhaps got wind of the drubbing which Grainger was preparing. At the end of the January issue of the *Critical*, the editors asked Grainger's pardon for small matters in their notice of his translation. On the same page, however, they announced their intention of chastising one "of the Owls belonging to the proprietor of the M--thly R----w."[77] On January 30, 1759, according to the *Public Advertiser*, Grainger's drubbing of Smollett was published. It took the form of a six-penny pamphlet of 25 pages, entitled *A Letter to Tobias Smollett, M.D. Occasioned by his Criticism Upon a late Translation of Tibullus*. Grainger's essay is a curious compound of irony and open rage. One of its informal pleasantries was calling Smollett good Doctor Tobias, and Dr. Toby. Grainger pointed out that Smollett's daily bread depended on his writing by the hour-glass. Sneering at Smollett's pretensions to learning and critical impartiality, Grainger complimented him on his "Conundrum Genius," his peculiar "Waggery," and his "high-flavoured Jokes and delicate Allusions." Thanks to the latter, declared Grainger, "any Reader of tolerable Sagacity can smell you out in your Annals of Literature." The more serious thrusts against the reviewer of his translation were summed up neatly in the *Gentleman's Magazine* for February 1759.[78]

A more than sufficient reply to Grainger's *Letter* came to the notice of all readers of the *Critical* for February 1759. In organization and style it is in Smollett's best manner. It is possible, how-

---

[76] Cited from John B. Nichols, *Illustrations of the Literary History of the Eighteenth Century*, 8 vols. (London, 1848), VII, 268.

[77] *Critical Review*, VII (1759), 88.

[78] See *Gentleman's Magazine*, XXIX (1759), 83-84.

ever, that Goldsmith contributed to it, as there is an authentic record of a lost manuscript by him called a "Defence of Dr. Smollet against Dr. Grainger's attack on him relative to the Criticism on Tibullus in the Critical Review."[79] However that may be, the review makes very lively and entertaining reading. One sample will suffice:

> Dr. James Grainger . . . has, in the Christian name of that gentleman [Smollett], found a very extraordinary fund of humour and ridicule. Had the parents of Dr. Smollett foreseen that this circumstance would turn out so much to his disadvantage, they certainly would have given him some other appellation than that of *Tobias*, which, with the unlucky diminutive Toby,[80] has been such a humorous source of triumph to his adversaries. We wonder that the facetious Dr. Grainger, and his witty coadjutors, had not ransacked the Apocrypha for the story of *Tobit*, in whose eyes the *sparrows muted warm dung*; and of his son *Tobias*, who went forth, and *his dog went with him*. What abundance of waggish things might have been said by this sprightly triumvirate, of Tobit's blindness, which even the physicians could not cure, of his altercation with his wife *Anna*, and of Toby and his dog! But, alas! Dr. James Grainger and his beef-eaters are but humble imitators, even in this species of wit. . . . Whoever looks into the works of that stupendous genius Dr. H-ll,[81] will see *Smollett* tortured into *Smallhead* and *Smallwit*. . . . After all, the dunces of the last age have been beforehand with all these worthies. They not only punned upon the denomination of *Alexander Pope*, but even wrote a poem against him, intituled *Sawney*. Think not, reader, we presume to compare Dr. Smollett, as a writer, with Mr. *Pope*:[82] we are sensible of the infinite disparity; but in one respect their fate is similar. They have been both abused, belied, and accused of ignorance, malice, and want of genius, by the confessed dunces of the age, at a time when their works were read and approved, at least, as much as those of any other cotemporary author.[83]

[79] See Katharine C. Balderston, *A Census of the Manuscripts of Oliver Goldsmith* (The Brick Row Book Shop, Inc., New York, 1926), pp. 38-39, 51-52.

[80] For the connotations of toby, see *NED*.

[81] Smollett is designated as Mr. Smallhead in John Hill's *The Inspector*, No. 14. Therein Hill, in his Vision of Licencing Hall, has Genius, one of the judges, tell Smollett (who inquires about "the novel he left there last month," *Peregrine Pickle*), that "until he understood more of Human Nature, and could distinguish better between Satire and Scurrility, he could not have the Leave of the Court to print again." After this speech, Smollett's four volumes are relegated to the Baker's Basket. As a result, Smollett threatens vengeance, whereupon he is ignominiously dismissed from the court. See *The Inspector Containing a Collection of Essays and Letters Lately published in a New Daily-Paper, called the London Daily Advertiser, and Literary Gazette* (London, 1751), pp. 75ff.

[82] In his quarto edition of *The Complete History of England* (Vol. IV, p. 517), Smollett termed Pope "the prince of lyric poetry, unrivalled in satire, ethics, and polished versification."

[83] Cited from *Critical Review*, VII (1759), 142-43.

After reading this, and knowing that Smollett either wrote it or approved it for publication, no one can say that he lacked a complete sense of humor. With this final shot, the Smollett-Grainger controversy closed. As a sort of aftermath, Bishop Percy, it seems, published a libel on Smollett in the *Impartial Review*, in November 1759.[84]

Another savage attack on Smollett came off the press in April 1759. This was delivered by Joseph Reed, who was incensed over the treatment which his mock-tragedy, *Madrigal and Trulletta* received in the *Critical* for August 1758.[85] Reed's pamphlet, *A Sop in the Pan for a Physical Critick*, has already been drawn upon for its reference to Smollett's efforts to establish some sort of Academy in 1755. In other respects its content is not important. It seems to have been ignored by Smollett.

During such controversies, Smollett took pleasure in 1759 in a friendly association with John Wilkes, to whom five of his letters written that year are extant. Perhaps it was Dr. John Armstrong, Wilkes' close friend in the 1750's who promoted their alliance. The Doctor prescribed for Wilkes' daughter Mary, who after 1756 boarded at a girls' school in Chelsea[86] where Smollett's daughter Elizabeth probably attended. In fact, Smollett through Armstrong, recommended a fashionable boarding school to Wilkes.[87] By 1759 Smollett knew Wilkes well enough to ask him to do what he could, through friends, to persuade Admiral Knowles to drop his prosecution of the printer of the *Critical* because of his libel. Smollett also approached Wilkes on behalf of Dr. Johnson in a letter of March 16, 1759, of which a few sentences merit quotation:

I am again your Petitioner in behalf of that great Cham of Literature,[88] Samuel Johnson. His Black Servant, whose name is Francis Barber, has

[84] I have been unable to consult a copy of this periodical, listed in R. S. Crane and F. B. Kaye, *A Census of British Newspapers and Periodicals, 1620-1800.* (See *SP*, XXIV, 141.) For references to the libel, see *The Letters of William Shenstone*, ed. Marjorie Williams (Oxford, 1939), pp. 530-31.

[85] See *Critical Review*, VI (August 1758), 168-70. The reviewer conjectured that Reed's piece "must have been a dismal three hours entertainment."

[86] This boarding school for girls was run by a Mrs. Aylesworth and a Madame Beete.

[87] On August 12 (no year stated, but *ca.* 1756) Armstrong wrote Wilkes: "Dr Smollet told me that the School you directed me to enquire about was a very reputable one and that a great number of young Ladies of the first fashion in England were educated there." (Br. Mus. Add. MS, 30875, f. 28.)

[88] Smollett's picturesque metaphor has been widely applied to Johnson.

been pressed on board the Stag Frigate, Capt. Angel, and our Lexicographer is in great distress. . . . You know what matter of animosity the said Johnson has against you, and I dare say you desire no other opportunity of resenting it than that of laying him under an obligation. He was humble enough to desire my assistance on this occasion, though he and I were never catercousins, and I gave him to understand that I would make application to my Friend Mr Wilkes who perhaps by his Interest with Dr Hay and Mr Elliot might be able to procure the Discharge of his Lacquey.[89]

Upon this request Wilkes acted promptly and effectively. Smollett's declaration that he and Johnson were never "catercousins" (intimates), implies some degree of mutual friendship and respect. It is very probable that Smollett entertained Johnson at Chelsea where the latter is known to have experimented on baking clay in the ovens of the Chelsea China establishment next door to Smollett's residence.[90] It is also clear that Johnson liked Smollett as a writer and as a man.[91]

In the spring of 1759 Smollett regretfully declined Wilkes' invitation to visit him at his fine country manor at Aylesbury, Buckinghamshire, pleading the excuse of a sore throat, and complaining of reading dull books and writing commentaries *invita Minerva*, a probable allusion to his labors in the *Universal History*.[92]

On June 2, 1759, Archibald Hamilton, printer and publisher of the *Critical*, appeared before Lord Mansfield and a jury to be tried for publishing the libel against Knowles; whereupon, as the legal record runs, "one Mr Tobias Smollet appeared in open Court and did acknowledge himself to be the Author and publisher"[93] of it. Then in the presence of those assembled, Smollett signed his name on the margins of the pages of the *Critical*[94] containing the libel. His script was a bit unsteady! As a result of these actions of Smollett, Hamilton was acquitted. Knowles then moved to prose-

[89] Cited from *Letters*, pp. 56, 174ff.

[90] See the communication, "Johnson at the Chelsea China Manufactory" in *Notes and Queries*, CLXXXVII (1944), 108.

[91] In 1785, James Beattie declared that Johnson "preferred Smollet to Fielding." See Sir William Forbes, *An Account of the Life and Writings of James Beattie, LL.D.*, 3 vols. (London, 1807), II, 375. Johnson's revision of a Latin epitaph written for Smollett is well-known.

[92] For the best account of Smollett's work in this compilation, see Louis L. Martz, "Tobias Smollett and *The Universal History*" in *MLN* (1941), 1-14; and the same writer's *The Later Career of Tobias Smollett* (Yale University Press, 1942), *passim*.

[93] Cited from my article, "Rex Versus Smollett," *loc. cit.*, p. 222.

[94] The separate issue for May 1758, with blue wrappers, and bearing the annotations of Knowles' lawyers, is preserved in The Public Record Office, London, K.B 1/14 Affidavits, Trinity Term, 32-33 George II.

cute Smollett,[95] but some seventeen months were to elapse before his final trial.

Sometime between June and October of this same year Smollett traveled to the Continent, as appears from his letter of October 30 to his good friend Dr. Macaulay, wherein Smollett is concerned over a draft drawn upon the former "from Flanders," in favor of a "Mr. Jamieson from Brussels."[96] It would seem that Smollett, alarmed over his asthma, sought rest and recuperation in a short trip. It was failing health, also, which led him at about this time to initiate a series of unsuccessful efforts to obtain a consulship in a warmer climate.[97]

By October 1759, Smollett described himself to Wilkes as "still an invalid."[98] His asthma and depression of spirits grew steadily worse, judging from his sad self-diagnosis sent to a dear friend in the West Indies, the following December:

> If I go on writing as I have proceeded for some years, my hand will be paralytic, and my brain dried to a snuff. I would not wish my greatest enemy a greater curse than the occupation of an author, in which capacity I have toiled myself into an habitual asthma, and been baited like a bear by all the hounds of Grub-street. Some people have flourished by imputed wit; I have suffered by imputed dullness. I have been abused, reviled, and calumniated, for satires I never saw; I have been censured for absurdities of which I could not possibly be guilty. . . . I perceive myself going down hill apace, and promise myself but a few years of enjoyment; I would therefore make the most of my time, and eagerly wish to see my friends about me. To tell you a secret, my constitution is quite broken: Since last May, I have hardly enjoyed one day of health: I am so subject to colds and rheums that I dare hardly stir from my own house; and shall be obliged to give up all the pleasures of society, at least those of tavern society, to which you know I have been always addicted.[99]

[95] For subsequent legal moves see Alice Parker, "Tobias Smollett and the Law," *loc. cit.*, and my article, "Rex Versus Smollett."

[96] The quoted phrases are from a copy of the original manuscript in The National Library of Scotland (MS 2207, f. 101).

[97] The concluding sentence of Smollett's letter to Dr. Macaulay, October 30, 1759, reads: "I long to know what steps you have taken with respect to Spain." See *Letters*, p. 63.

[98] Professor Noyes in his *Letters*, p. 62, was incorrect in printing "still enfeebled." See a facsimile of this letter to Wilkes published in Richard Garnett and Edmund Gosse, *English Literature, An Illustrated Record*, 4 vols. (New York and London, 1903-1904), III, 324.

[99] Cited from my article, "An Important Smollett Letter," in *RES*, XII (1936), 76-77. My original conjecture that Smollett was writing to Thomas Bontein is not valid. The recipient was, more probably, John Harvie, one of a numerous Harvie family, who acted in 1759 as agent for the Smolletts. On August 21, 1756, Eliz-

Here Smollett, at the age of thirty-eight in a mood of deep melancholy, underestimated his recuperative powers. In his remaining years (1760-1771), he was to undergo a slow but fluctuating physical decline, but his quick brain and tireless hand were to function for another decade, and his temperament was to be mellowed through suffering and endurance. He was to make the most of his time, a period longer than he anticipated.

---

abeth Leaver and the Smolletts granted a power of attorney to John Harvie, Alex Harvie, and Thomas Bontein, all of Kingston, for the purpose of selling Negro slaves. (Island Record Office, Spanish Town, B.W.I., Powers of Attorney, 44/102.) In Smollett's letters there are several allusions to the Harvies. Perhaps Smollett's friend, John Harvie, was related to the Dr. John Harvie of St. Ann's Parish, London, who was mentioned in the will of Dr. William Smellie. See Dr. John Glaister, *Dr. William Smellie and his Contemporaries* (Glasgow, 1894), pp. 327, 338. Dr. Harvie was identified by Peachey as the husband of Mrs. Smellie's niece. See George C. Peachey, *Memoir of William & John Hunter* (Plymouth, 1924), p. 62.

CHAPTER XI

Minor and Miscellaneous Writing;
Imprisonment;
Launcelot Greaves, 1760-1763

O N New Year's, 1760, was scheduled to appear the first number of another new six-penny monthly periodical, called the *British Magazine, or Monthly Repository for Gentlemen and Ladies*. Heralded in the press in December,[1] it doubtless was issued on time because Smollett was chiefly responsible for its arrival. This magazine had a run of seven years, 1760-1767.[2] In January 1760, Smollett applied for and secured a Royal License for his new magazine on the grounds that he had "been at great Labour and Expence in writing Original Pieces himself, and engaging Learned and Ingenious Gentlemen to write other Original Pieces" for it.[3] These activities had taken place, obviously, prior to December 1759.

Something may be conjectured as to the gentlemen whose services were engaged by Smollett for the launching of the *British*

---

[1] See *Lloyd's Evening Post and British Chronicle*, December 19-21, 1759. The *London Chronicle* ran its announcement, December 18-20. Therein the public was informed that the new periodical, dedicated to Pitt, was to be printed for James Rivington and James Fletcher at the Oxford Theatre, and also for H. Payne, at Dryden's Head, Paternoster Row, "by whom also Proposals are delivered."

[2] Complete bound-up runs of this magazine, such as that in the Yale University Library, are rare. For a photograph of a cluster of separate numbers in original condition, see Temple Scott, *Oliver Goldsmith Bibliographically and Biographically Considered* (New York, Bowling Green Press, 1928), p. 65.

[3] I have a photostat of Smollett's petition for a license, signed "Tobias Smollett" (P.R.O., State Papers Domestic, George II, 145), which shows that he applied for a Royal License "for the sole printing publishing and vending" of the *British Magazine*. See the *London Chronicle* for January 29-31, 1760, p. 106, for a public announcement about this license, in connection with the advertising of the second number of the magazine. For this license Smollett paid £6/7/6, perhaps more. This figure I owe to the kindness of Professor William M. Sale, who also obtained data on the date the license was granted (January 18, 1760). See, according to Professor Sale, P.R.O., State Papers Domestic, Exchequer Fee Books, Vol. 29; and Warrant Books after 1715, No. 371 (1748-1760), p. 497.

Magazine. One of them, perhaps, was Griffith Jones.[4] Another was possibly Samuel Derrick, some of whose verse appeared the first year.[5] A much more important figure was Oliver Goldsmith, who contributed some of his finest essays. As Goldsmith, before 1760, had reviewed Smollett's *Complete History* in the *Monthly Review*,[6] had complimented him in *The Bee*,[7] and had contributed to the *Critical Review*,[8] he was probably known personally to Smollett. In May 1760, Smollett wrote Samuel Richardson, whose character and work he admired,[9] the following appeal:

> I should think myself happy, if you would favour our Magazine with any loose essay, lying by you, which you do not intend for another sort of publication.[10]

Other prominent contributors to the new periodical, if such there were, remain anonymous, except Smollett himself.

In the *British Magazine* were first printed some of Smollett's short lyrics: "Ode to Blue-Ey'd Ann," composed, presumably, for his wife; "Ode to Sleep," perhaps originally a part of the lost opera, *Alceste*; the "Ode to Mirth"; a song, "To fix her—'twere a task as vain"; and possibly others, as suggested by Professor Buck, though attributing anonymous verse in the *British Magazine* to Smollett is a very hazardous procedure.[11]

The most novel feature of this periodical was that it purveyed to the public in monthly installments from January 1760 to December 1761 Smollett's novel, *The Adventures of Sir Launcelot*

---

[4] See article on Griffith Jones in *DNB*.

[5] See *British Magazine*, I (1760), 435.

[6] See *Monthly Review*, XVI (1757), 530. It is possible that Ralph Griffiths had a finger in this review. See Goldsmith's *Works*, with notes by J. W. M. Gibbs, 5 vols. (London, 1885), IV, 257n.

[7] See Goldsmith's *Works*, edition cited, II, 393-94.

[8] Goldsmith's conjectured reviewing for the *Critical* ran from 1757 to 1760.

[9] For Smollett's personal compliment to Richardson, see *Letters*, pp. 40-41.

[10] *Ibid.*, p. 66.

[11] See Howard Swazey Buck, *Smollett as Poet* (Yale University Press, 1927), pp. 52ff. The four poems which I have listed are assumed to be Smollett's solely because they were included in his *Plays and Poems*, 1777, by an anonymous editor. Professor Buck felt that Smollett must have written the "Ode . . . to the late Gen. Wolfe," printed in the February issue of the *British Magazine*. (See Buck, pp. 63-68.) As a matter of fact, this ode was printed in the *Scots Magazine*, XXII (January 1760), 32. The chances that Smollett wrote it are remote. Like most periodicals of that time, the *Scots Magazine* reprinted verse from London newspapers, such as the *London Chronicle*. The editors of the *Scots* reprinted in their issue for June 1760 the "Ode to Sleep" attributed to Smollett, which came out June 1, or thereabouts, in the June issue of the *British Magazine*.

Greaves, his first venture in fiction since *Count Fathom*, 1753, and the first considerable English novel ever to be published serially. There is no doubt that this feature gave the *British Magazine* some degree of popularity in 1760-1761. Goldsmith promoted both the magazine and the novel in his essay, "The Description of a Wow-Wow in the Country," printed in the *Public Ledger*, February 16, 1760, in the following passage:

> . . . we should certainly have had a war at the Wow-wow, had not an Oxford scholar, led there by curiosity, pulled a new magazine out of his pocket, in which he said there were some pieces extremely curious and that deserved all their attention. He then read the "Adventures of Sir Launcelot Greaves" to the entire satisfaction of the audience, which being finished, he threw the pamphlet on the table. "That piece, gentlemen," says he, "is written in the very spirit and manner of Cervantes; there is great knowledge of human nature, and evident marks of the master in almost every sentence; and from the plan, the humour, and the execution, I can venture to say that it dropt from the pen of the ingenious Dr. -----." Every one was pleased with the performance, and I was particularly gratified in hearing all the sensible part of the company give orders for the "British Magazine."[12]

This graceful compliment, as well as the varied appeal of the contents of the magazine seems to have brought it some success during its first year.[13]

Only a few days after Goldsmith's praise was being read in the coffeehouses of London, another compliment to Smollett saw print, this time in *Lloyd's Evening Post, and British Chronicle*. It took the form of an ode sent to the editor by "K,"[14] and is worth reprinting:

To Dr. Smollett

AN ODE

'Tis thine alone, O Smollett, to prepare
    The mental feast, that shall for ages hence
Delight as now, and soothe the sons of Care,
    With sweet repasts, of Science, and of Sense.

Thine is the pow'r, to touch, to rouze the soul;
    To guide each movement of the human heart;

---

[12] Quoted from Goldsmith's *Works*, edition cited, IV, 476.
[13] In the *Public Advertiser* for February 2, 1761, announcing the issue for January of that year, the editors (or perhaps the publishers) declared that the great success of their magazine demanded their utmost gratitude.
[14] I await suggestions as to the identity of "K."

To raise the passions, or their rage controul;
 And rule the bosom by thy magic Art.

Adown my cheek the tender social tear
 Steals unawares, when thy Monimia mourns:
Her sighs I feel, her soft complaints I share,
 As Love now melts, or Jealousy now burns.

But blood-ey'd Fury rends my throbbing breast,
 When faithless Fathom rises to my view;
When flushed with fraud, the villain stands confest,
 And unsuspected, plans his plots anew.

Again I sigh, again soft Pity flows,
 When noble Zelos, Honor's rigid son,
Opprest with grief, and stagg'ring with his woes,
 Recounts the triumph his revenge had won.

Such is thy skill, such is thy pleasing strain,
 Such is thy fancy, such thy Attic fire!
Entranced we read, what Critics can't arraign,
 What Age approves, and what the Fair admire.

But in thy Hist'ry, all thy Genius blooms,
 Old England's battles o'er again we wage,
Tread Cresci's plain, and follow Edward's plumes,
 And glow with Conquest, Liberty, and Rage.

There Truth appears in her transparent charms,
 How lovely she! when stript of Faction's veil,
When, undisguis'd, Kings take her to their arms,
 And rule with equity the Commonweal.

There shines thy Pitt (superior to all praise)
 The great Restorer of the British Name:
Th' historic Muse his dazzling Deeds displays,
 Records his virtues, and reflects his Fame.

Thee, Smollett, thee the sons of Science hail!
 Applaud thy clear, thy comprehensive page,
Nervous as Hyde, and accurate as Boyle,
 Warm as the Poet, sober as the Sage.

And lo! th' exulting Muse expands her wings:
 'Tis hers, to register the men divine,
Who trace the Source of Aganippe's springs;
 Or watch at Wisdom's adamantine shrine.

Ah, radiant Maid! thy raptures all infuse,
 Thy thrilling raptures let my bosom fire.
Be mine—the majesty of ev'ry Muse;
 Be mine—the music of the melting Lyre.

Immortal wreaths shall then my Smollett grace;
Immortal strains shall charm his pensive mind,
Such—as when Horace sung th' Augustan Race,
And changed to Gods those Conq'rors of Mankind.[15]

Smollett may well have squirmed a bit over this fulsome tribute, written by an enthusiast who restricted his praise to the beauties of *Count Fathom* and the *Complete History*. Yet this, together with Goldsmith's pleasant puff, was a welcome change from being baited like a bear by authors infuriated by reviews in the *Critical*.

For Smollett the spring of 1760 was inevitably clouded by the shadow of the constantly postponed libel trial.[16] Then there were other annoyances, such as that anonymous publication, *The Battle of the Reviews*, published probably in 1760.[17] In this mock contest between the forces of the *Monthly* staff, headed by Rehoboam Gruffy [Griffiths], and those of the *Critical*, led by His Typographical Highness [Hamilton], the *Critical* forces, though temporarily drugged, were saved by the medical skill of Sawney Mac-Smallhead [Smollett]; whereupon MacSmallhead had the misfortune to be arrested and imprisoned through Admiral K- - - - -s's Commission.[18] More important than the battle is the appraisal of MacSmallhead, who, the writer declared, knew medicine and had a taste for history and the belles-lettres, but, despite his acknowledged abilities was morally vague as a novelist, and emotionally prejudiced as a critic. Furthermore MacSmallhead's merit, the writer continued, was "quite tarnished by his Vanity; a Vanity, always fulsome and always odious."[19] It is not surprising that Smol-

[15] Quoted from *Lloyd's Evening Post, and British Chronicle*, VI (February 20-22, 1760), 179.

[16] See Alice Parker, "Tobias Smollett and the Law," in *SP*, XXXIX (1942), 552.

[17] *The Battle* is undated, but the mock fight described therein, occurred, according to the author, on the "Ides of March, in the year 1760." (See p. 156.) *The Battle* was printed in London for R. Marriner in the Strand. The *Public Advertiser* (May 14 and June 1, 1760) announced the following two-shilling pamphlet: *Bella Horrida Bella; or, The Battle of the Reviewers: Exhibiting among a Variety of curious and interesting Anecdotes, a faithful Portrait of the Characters of all the Reviewers, and their mighty Feats of Arms in a bloody and obstinate Battle that was fought between them on the Ides of March last. . . .* Printed for R. Marriner. This tract, which I have not seen, may be identical with *The Battle*. Neither of these pamphlets was reviewed in the *Critical* or in the *Monthly*. For brief comment on *The Battle*, see *Letters*, pp. 149-50.

[18] The latter part of the narrative may be imaginary, or it may have been a sort of supplement added after Smollett's imprisonment in November 1760.

[19] Quoted from *The Battle*, p. 112. On Smollett's ethics, the author declared that MacSmallhead's "Randoms and Pickles may stand excusable in the Time they were

lett's pride, which he himself lamented,[20] was exaggerated so un-pleasantly by this writer.

To continue with sidelights on Smollett in the spring of 1760, it is a safe assumption that he wrote extensively in the *Critical* at this time. It is all but certain that he reviewed *A Treatise on the Art of Midwifery*, an extraordinary attack on the theories of Smol-lett's friend, Dr. Smellie, by an equally extraordinary medical Amazon, Mrs. Elizabeth Nihell.[21] The review, tossed off with characteristic Smollettian gusto began as follows:

> If a pun may be allowed in discussing a ludicrous subject, we would advise Mrs. Nihell to take, for a motto, in the next edition of this work, should it ever attain a reimpression:
> Ex nihilo nihil fit!

The reviewer then commented in a superior and entertaining man-ner on Mrs. Nihell's writing, with the conjecture that "this good gentlewoman has employed some eructatious disciple of Paracelsus Bombast, to inflate her stile, and *bouncify* her expressions,"[22] which reminded the reviewer of the noisy oration of a medical mounte-bank's merry-andrew. The imagined harangue of the latter is memorable for its vigor and hilarity. After serious medical criti-cism the reviewer ended with an amazing list of Mrs. Nihell's "gigantic metaphors, foreign idioms, uncouth and affected words." All this provoked Mrs. Nihell into writing *An Answer*,[23] which received an ungentle notice in the *Critical* (issue of May 1760). These reviews (and many similar to it) Smollett undoubtedly dashed off with considerable pleasure as a release from drudging on the *Universal History*[24] and projecting his *Continuation of the Complete History of England*.

Smollett's proposals for his *Continuation* appeared in May

---

written: Sawney, no Doubt being then borne down by the Torrent of Ribaldry the late worshipful Justice Henry Fielding, Esq. poured upon him and others." In its moral emphasis and anti-Fielding tone, *The Battle* is like some of the writing of Dr. John Hill.

[20] See the dedication to *Count Fathom*.

[21] For information on Mrs. Nihell, see Kate Campbell Hurd-Mead, *A History of Women in Medicine* (The Haddam Press, Haddam, Connecticut, 1938), p. 475.

[22] This and the preceding quotation are from the *Critical Review*, IX (March 1760), 187.

[23] *An Answer to the Author of the Critical Review, for March, 1760. . . . By Mrs. Elizabeth Nihell, professed Midwife*. This item I have never located.

[24] References to Smollett's labor in 1760 on the *Universal History* are found in *Letters*, pp. 65-68.

1760.[25] About May 17, 1760, the first six-penny number of this new work was published. Forty weekly numbers were planned, and they were to be embellished with copper-plate engravings by Strange, Grignion, Ravenet, Miller and others.[26] Opposite the title page of the first published volume (1760) appeared an engraving of Smollett by Francis Aliamet, a good artist, who at that time probably lived in Chelsea.[27] This print of Smollett takes on especial interest as it must have met with his approval. Extensively advertised and generously illustrated, the *Continuation* (Vol. 1) was prefaced by highly characteristic remarks of Smollett to the public concerning the glories of the age (after the peace of Aix-la-Chapelle) to be comprehended, and concerning his own qualifications for the unusual project of chronicling contemporaneous events and personalities. A portion of the prefatory statement reveals no decline in Smollett's self-confidence, pride, and fighting spirit:

> Themes like these cannot fail to warm the heart, and animate the pen of the historian, who glows with the love of his country. Yet he will carefully avoid the imputation of enthusiasm. In the midst of his transports he hopes to remember his duty, and check the exuberance of zeal with the rigid severity of historical truth.
>
> This is the guiding star by which he hath hitherto steered his dangerous course; the star whose chearing radiance has conducted him safe through the rocks of prejudice and the tides of faction. Guiltless of all connexions that might be supposed to affect his candour, and endanger his integrity, he is determined to proceed with that fearless spirit of independence, by which he flatters himself the former part of the work hath been remarkably distinguished.... N.B. As many anonymous writers have been hired to abuse this work [*Complete History*] in printed papers and pamphlets, the author takes this opportunity of declaring, that if any person of character in the Republic of Letters shall think proper to censure this history in print, and set his name to his animadversions, he (the author) will answer them to the best of his power; but it cannot be expected that he

[25] The conditions for printing the *Continuation* in weekly numbers were publicized by May 10, 1760 (and perhaps earlier), in the *Public Advertiser*. Following the list of conditions was a statement informing the reader to consult the "Author's Address to the Publick," on the cover of the *London, Gentleman's, British* and other magazines. In its general substance this Address resembled, presumably, what is printed under the heading, "To the Public," at the beginning of the *Continuation*, Vol. 1, London, 1760.

[26] See *London Chronicle*, May 15-17, 1760, p. 479. See also my article, "The Publication of Smollett's Complete History . . . and Continuation," in *Transactions of the Bibliographical Society, The Library* (December 1935), pp. 300ff.

[27] According to Alfred Beaver, *Memorials of Old Chelsea* (London, 1892), p. 335, Francis Aliamet lived in Chelsea in 1763.

should employ his time in disputing with obscure, mercenary, and desperate scribblers, who enlist themselves under the banners of malicious interested calumny, and may be said to subsist upon the wages of assassination.[28]

What with weekly installments for the *Continuation*, and monthly installments for *Launcelot Greaves*, plus reviews for the *Critical*, labor on the *Universal History*, and growing apprehension about the libel trial, Smollett could have enjoyed little relaxation in his garden in June 1760. On June 6 the sheriff of Middlesex was ordered to arrest Smollett and take him to Westminster, June 25,[29] but whether or not such action was taken is not known. About the middle of June he received a curious letter written in Latin from one DeCedors asking for a loan.[30] Smollett preserved this epistle, possibly as a reminder that he had acceded to the request. Shortly thereafter, he seems to have escaped from London to return again to Scotland after an absence of seven years.

Smollett's visit to Scotland in the summer of 1760 is not recorded in any detail. It was not mentioned by either Moore or Anderson, nor is it alluded to in any available letter of Smollett. There are, in fact, only two reasons for believing that it took place. The first is implicit in Sir Walter Scott's statement that during the period of Smollett's composition of *Sir Launcelot Greaves*, "he was residing at Paxton, in Berwickshire, on a visit to the late George Home, Esq., and when post-time drew near, he used to retire for half an hour or an hour to prepare the necessary quantity of *copy*, as it is technically called in the printing-house, which he never gave himself the trouble to correct, or even to read over."[31]

---

[28] Quoted from *Continuation*, Vol. 1 (London, 1760), v-vi.

[29] See Alice Parker, *op. cit.*, p. 552.

[30] DeCedors' letter, dated "Londini 18 junii 1760" was sent to "Mr. Smollet Doctor, in Larance Street, next door to ye Cheney Manufactor Chelsea." The original manuscript is at the Ridgway Library, Philadelphia (MS Rush, Vol. 28, p. 50). DeCedors, in rather dubious Latin, declared that he lacked money enough to return to Paris, that he had been ashamed the other day to ask a favor, that he needed about two guineas, which, he swore, "per Apollinis numen," he would remit, once he reached Paris. DeCedors may have been the person whose French translation of Tassoni's *La Secchia Rapita* was published in Paris in 1758-1759. See the catalogue of the Bibliothèque Nationale, and Giorgio Rossi, *Studi e ricerche Tassoniane* (Bologna, 1904), p. 322n.

[31] Quoted from Scott's *Lives of the Novelists* (New York, 1872), p. 137. Scott's memoir of Smollett was originally prefixed to *The Novels of Tobias Smollett, M.D.* as the second volume of the so-called Ballantyne Novels, London and Edinburgh, 1821. The memoir comprehends pages i-xlii, and is dated Abbotsford, June 1, 1821. For the passage quoted, see p. xxiii.

But there is conclusive evidence against accepting any tradition that Smollett visited Home at Paxton House in 1760 for the sufficient reason that it was not yet constructed.[32] Then too, it is extremely improbable that George Home was Smollett's host anywhere in 1760 because at that time he could not have been much more than twenty years old.[33] Scott's statement, however, need not be completely rejected because young Home might well have seen Smollett at work on *Launcelot Greaves* on the estate of Scotston, the home of his brother-in-law, Alexander Telfer,[34] or in Edinburgh. The second and more conclusive piece of evidence that Smollett was in Scotland in 1760 is a record of his being made Burgess and Guild-Brother in Edinburgh, July 30, 1760. The memorandum runs in part as follows:

Edinbr 30th July 1760
Sederunt

Dn Hugh Inglis

John Carmichael   D.G.
Alexr Grant   O.D.G.

Tobias Smollett Esqr Doctor of Medicine Compearing is made Burges and Gildbrother of this burgh for the good services done by him to the interest thereof. Conform to an act of the Town Council of the date of these presents Likeas the Dean of Gild and his Council Conform to the said act Declare the said Tobias Smollet his admission as valid Effectual and Sufficient as if he had paid the whole dues in use to be paid by Unfreemen and gave his oath & ce.[35]

The presence in this entry of the word *Compearing* (meaning presenting one's self at a formal occasion) indicates clearly that Smol-

[32] The present owner of Paxton House, Mrs. Helen Home Robertson, has very kindly written me that she is positive that George Home did not live in Paxton House in 1760, and that she is extremely doubtful whether the construction of the house had even commenced at that time.

[33] George Home died at Paxton House, March 10, 1820. His obituary is in the *Scots Magazine*, LXXXV (1820), 295. The date of his birth is uncertain, but Mrs. Helen Home Robertson informs me that his mother, born in 1706, married *ca.* 1730, and that George was not her eldest child. Had he been born about 1740, he would have been eighty when he died. George Home, who became a Principal Clerk of the Court of Sessions, associated with the literati of Edinburgh, and contributed to the *Mirror*. It is Mrs. Robertson's belief that he did not succeed to Paxton House until 1795, or later.

[34] According to Mrs. Helen Home Robertson, the Homes were very friendly with the Telfers.

[35] Transcribed from the manuscript ledger of the Guild Register, 1744-1761, at the office of the Town Clerk, City Chambers, High Street, Edinburgh, with the kind assistance of Miss Wood.

lett received in person in 1760 the honor which had, it seems, been first awarded him in 1753.[36] As to the duration of Smollett's visit or the precise date of his return to London, nothing is known.

For the October issue of the *Critical* Smollett contributed, most probably, a review of Arthur Murphy's *Poetical Epistle to Mr. Samuel Johnson, A.M.* Therein Murphy had taken revenge against Thomas Francklin for disparaging in his *Dissertation on Antient Tragedy*[37] one of his (Murphy's) tragedies, perhaps *The Orphan of China*. The reviewer of Murphy's *Epistle* (Smollett?) regretted the controversy and wished that "for the sake of both, they would refer it to the decision of that gentleman to whom this epistle is inscribed; a gentleman whose candour is as universally acknowledged as his genius."[38] If Smollett wrote this, he was assuming the role of peacemaker as well as paying a generous compliment to the great Cham of literature.

Meantime the protracted series of legal moves manipulated by Admiral Knowles came to a dramatic climax when on November 24, 1760, Smollett was tried and convicted for his libel published in the May (1758) issue of the *Critical*. Though Lord Chief Justice Mansfield occasionally held sessions in Guildhall, the setting of Smollett's trial was presumably Westminster Hall.[39] In that magnificent fourteenth-century building,[40] haunted by the associations of old, unhappy, far-off trials, and in that august place where the rebel Lords of 1745 were heard and condemned, Smollett sat in the presence of the jury; the lawyers; Knowles, no doubt; and Lord Mansfield. The latter two, as well as Smollett, were Scotsmen, ambitious, pugnacious, and distinguished in their respective professions. Some of Smollett's feelings on that memorable occasion can be understood by virtue of a remarkable document addressed to Lord Mansfield and signed by Smollett, which runs as follows:

[36] See George M. Kahrl, *op. cit.*, pp. 62, 64.

[37] See *A Dissertation on Antient Tragedy*, n.d., n.p., quarto, 1760, p. 24, for an indirect slur on Murphy.

[38] Quoted from *Critical Review*, X (1760), 320.

[39] Early in November the Court of the King's Bench convened at Westminster Hall. (See *London Chronicle*, November 6-8, 1760, p. 454.)

[40] For a contemporaneous print of Westminster Hall, see *London and Its Environs* VI, 296. There is a good account of its history in Henry B. Wheatley's *London Past and Present*, 3 vols. (London, 1891), III, 483ff.

My Lord.

I beg to be indulged with a few Words in Justification of some parts of my Conduct which I apprehend have been misrepresented and misunderstood. This Indulgence I the more earnestly intreat as my Silence when last I was before your Lordship[41] may have been interpreted into Contumacy or Want of Respect for the Authority of this Court which I ever did and always shall revere with the most profound Veneration & Submissal[.] What might be imputed to me in this respect as a Crime was really my Misfortun[e]. My being produced in the Character of a Delinquent before such an awful Tribunal had such an Effect upon my Spirits that I was really deprived of the Power of Utterance.

It has been urged, My Lord, as a Proof of my Malignity & Contempt of the Law that when the Printer was prosecuted for the Paragraph which has been adjudged a Libel and the Cause was brought to a Hearing before your Lordship I took the advantage of an Expression dropped by one of Mr Knowles's Council and owned myself in open Court Author of that offensive Paragraph in Defiance of the Law & in order to involve Mr Knowles in the Expence and Trouble of a fresh Prosecution. Thus My Lord Have I been stigmatized for a Step which I humbly Conceive Your Lordship when my Motives are explained will ascribe to a good and honourable Intention; I understood that Mr Knowles had a double Action: An Action against the Author as well as the Printer of the Paragraph in Question. My Humanity and Friendship were interested for the Printer whom I had unwillingly involved in Trouble and I thought I could not in Conscience do too much for his Indemnification. Mr Knowles by the Mouth of his Council declared that if the Printer would give up the Author he would then withdraw the Prosecution from him. I had desired our Council to embrace this Proposal if it should be made. The Proposal was made and embraced accordingly [,] and then I was suddenly ordered to appear in Court so contrary to my Expectation so much against my Will that I was never so surprised and mortified in the whole Course of my Life; far from being in a Condition to shew any Contempt for the Law or the Prosecutor on that Occasion I was for some Minutes so discomposed that all my Faculties were suspended. The Endeavours that I used in the Sequel to effect an Accomodation and the offer I made to pay the Prosecutor's Costs will convince Your Lordship that the Charge of Obstinacy is unjust and that I had no Design to accumulate the Expence of Mr Knowles—That my subsequent Conduct with respect to this unhappy Affair has been unjustly branded with the Epithets—Malicious & obstinate appears from the Concessions I not only offered but actually made to the Prosecutor Concessions suggested by his own Solicitor[42] approved and recommended by his own Council as well

[1] Smollett may have appeared before Lord Mansfield on June 25, 1760.
[2] Probably John Chapone.

as by his particular Friend the late Lord Register of Scotland,[43] I agreed to pay a Considerable Sum of mony [sic] in Lieu of his Costs. I wrote a Letter asking his pardon in the Terms dictated by his own Friend the Lord Register: The Letter was written, signed, sealed and directed in presence of his own Solicitor and deposited in the hands of Dr Baylies[44] to be forwarded to M[r] Knowles whenever he should signify his Approbation and Desire of terminating the affair[.]

I shall trouble Your Lordship with nothing further on this Occasion than to declare my hearty Sorrow for having offended the Laws of my Country, my Readiness to make all the Atonement in my Power to the injured Party by any Concessions that shall be thought just, and my perfect Submission to your Lordship's Authority[.]

T^s SMOLLETT[45]

This dramatic appeal was presumably presented in court after his conviction either by Smollett or by his lawyer, and it was carefully prepared in advance, no doubt, for the obvious purpose of mitigating Mansfield's final sentence to be imposed a few days later.[46] In its temper, the appeal was properly submissive, as was, no doubt, the last letter of apology to Knowles, but writing such words was an extremely painful blow to Smollett's pride. In its content, the most surprising data relate to the prolongation of the old feud between Smollett and Alexander Hume Campbell,

[43] The Hon. Alexander Hume Campbell, M.P. for Berwickshire, was Lord Register of Scotland at the time of his death, July 19, 1760. He died at his house in Curzon Street, London. For an obituary notice see the *London Chronicle*, July 19-22, 1760.

[44] Presumably William Baylies, M.D., in 1760 Fellow of the Royal College of Physicians in Edinburgh. He was also one of the physicians to the King of Prussia. According to Robert Watt (*Bibliotheca Britannica*, Vol. 1), he died at Berlin, in 1787. Anecdotes of Baylies are found in *Mems. maxims and memoirs* (London, 1827), pp. 246-47, a book by William Wadd, surgeon extraordinary to the King. Wadd, who recalled Baylies as a very unusual character, stated that he had been an apothecary, and later a physician at Bath, and that he had a magnificent house in London. Baylies wrote on the Bath waters and on medical controversies at Bath, where Smollett may have met him. He does not figure in Smollett's available correspondence.

[45] This appeal to Mansfield is printed from a photostat of the original document in P.R.O., K.B. 1/14, Michaelmas Term, 1 George III. The signature is undoubtedly Smollett's, but the rest of the script is not in his clearly patterned handwriting. Smollett was apparently asked to sign this clerk's copy of his original manuscript. On the back of the folded document is written in still another hand, or hands, the following:

"London
The King
  agst Mr Howard Michas 1760. Barlow
Smollett   Waubolt [?]"

[46] It did have some effect on Mansfield. See Sir William Blackstone, *Reports of cases from 1746-1779*, second edition, 2 vols. (London, 1828), I, 268. At the end of a brief summary of the case is this sentence: "And Lord *Mansfield*, C.J. added, that his [Smollett's] submission had had its effect with the Court."

which began as early as 1752, when the latter infuriated Smollett by his insulting language and courtroom tactics. And now eight years later, Campbell, as Lord Register of Scotland, was the "particular Friend" of Knowles, and dictating the terms of Smollett's apology to the Admiral. How humiliating it all was! And how little comfort to Smollett to realize that his portrait of Knowles was largely justified by the Admiral's personality and conduct,[47] for, as Smollett knew, he was hopelessly caught in a criminal prosecution for disrupting the public peace.[48] As Professor Parker has very properly pointed out, he did not regard his libel as a real crime against society; indeed, he had no good reason for thinking so. But all he could hope for was that Mansfield would show some mercy in the sentence pronounced.

The actual penalty was sufficiently severe. Smollett was fined £100, sentenced to be imprisoned for three months, and obliged to give security for his good behavior for seven years, "himself in five hundred pounds with two sufficient sureties in two hundred and fifty pounds each," according to reliable records.[49] How Smollett met these monetary demands remains unknown, but there is no doubt that he was escorted to prison on or about November 28, 1760.

The King's Bench Prison, where Smollett spent some eleven weeks, was a block of buildings surrounded by a thirty-foot wall about a mile south of Westminster Bridge in St. George's Fields.[50] Opened as a new prison in 1758,[51] it contained comparatively comfortable quarters for non-bankrupt prisoners, like Smollett; and as he was confined there in an unusually mild winter,[52] he

[47] From all that I have been able to learn about Admiral Knowles, I should say that Smollett's article was, on the whole, fairly close to the truth.

[48] For the legal view of libel in 1760, see Alice Parker, *op. cit.*, p. 551.

[49] See my article, "Rex Versus Smollett," *loc. cit.*, p. 226, n.29, and Alice Parker, "Tobias Smollett and the Law," pp. 552-53 and n.37. For an excellent contemporaneous book on libel, see *A Digest of the Law Concerning Libels*, London, 1765. This volume has references to Smollett's case on pp. 81, 127.

[50] Some idea of the external appearance of the King's Bench Prison is given in the allegorical frontispiece to *English Liberty . . . a Collection of . . . Public Letters, Speeches, and Addresses*, of John Wilkes, London, n.d. [1769].

[51] A notice in the *London Chronicle*, November 7-9, 1758, p. 454 reads: "Yesterday the debtors confined in the King's Bench prison, Southwark, were removed to the new King's Bench prison, in St. George's Fields."

[52] A notice in the *London Chronicle*, January 6-8, 1761, p. 25 reads: "The season has been so uncommonly open and mild, that many pear trees in the gardens about this metropolis already appear in bloom, and many trees of the more forward growth are bursting into leaf."

appears to have led a tolerable life. Such an experience is reflected in his cheerful account of the spot in *Launcelot Greaves*, Chapter 20, first published in the *British Magazine* for July 1761:

> The knight . . . was, together with Captain Crowe, conducted to the prison of the King's-bench, which is situated in St. George's-fields . . . and appears like a neat little regular town, consisting of one street, surrounded by a very high wall, including an open piece of ground which may be termed a garden, where the prisoners take the air, and amuse themselves with a variety of diversions. Except the entrance, where the turnkeys keep watch and ward, there is nothing in the place that looks like a jail, or bears the least colour of restraint. The street is crowded with passengers. . . . Here are butchers-stands, chandlers-shops, a surgery, a tap-house well frequented, and a public kitchen in which provisions are dressed for all the prisoners gratis, at the expence of the publican. Here the voice of misery never complains, and, indeed, little else is to be heard but the sounds of mirth and jollity. At the farther end of the street, on the right hand, is a little paved court leading to a separate building, consisting of twelve large apartments, called state-rooms, well furnished, and fitted up for the reception of the better sort of crown-prisoners; and on the other side of the street, facing a separate division of ground, called the common side, is a range of rooms occupied by prisoners of the lowest order, who share the profits of a begging-box, and are maintained by this practice, and some established funds of charity. We ought also to observe, that the jail is provided with a neat chapel, in which a clergyman,[53] in consideration of a certain salary, performs divine service every Sunday.[54]

This rosy picture of prison life Smollett amplified by having Sir Launcelot, at the sight of the kitchen, express astonishment with uplifted hands over such a "comfortable asylum for the unfortunate." Smollett, however, did present in the twenty-first chapter of *Launcelot Greaves*, distressing scenes and a pathetic debtor to whom Sir Launcelot gave five guineas. But his assertion in the quotation cited above that "the voice of misery never complains" was surely an overstatement and, in general, Smollett played up the diversions of the prisoners rather than their hardships. Because of this fact Smollett was assailed a few years later in a rare pamphlet[55] for lacking humanity and charity, qualities

[53] The Rev. Leonard Howard, D.D., Rector of St. George the Martyr was appointed Chaplain of the King's Bench Prison in 1758. (See *Public Advertiser*, November 10, 1758.)

[54] Quoted from *The Adventures of Sir Launcelot Greaves*, 2 vols. (London, 1762) II, 158-60.

[55] This pamphlet, addressed to himself by Francis Vernon, Lord Orwell, the nephew of Admiral Vernon, was entitled *A Letter to the Right Honourable Lord Orwell . . . And to Philip Thicknesse, Esq. . . .* London, 1764. The pamphlet deals with Thick

which as a matter of fact he really possessed in abundant measure.

In the King's Bench Prison Smollett undoubtedly occupied a private apartment,[56] probably one of the so-called staterooms reserved for "the better sort of crown-prisoners," as he described them. There he was able to work at his many writing projects, leaving them at times to stroll around the prison streets, observing with his practiced eye the varied types of "licentious people," as he termed them, "amounting, with their dependants, to above five hundred."[57] Among these was his bitter detractor, "Doctor" Shebbeare.[58] Within the high walls was also confined the famous Italian tenor, Signor Tenducci, who because of debt had been incarcerated since June 1760.[59] There is a tradition that Smollett, while in prison, was so touched by this singer's plight that he paid his bills and so set him free,[60] but though Smollett may well have given him some money, there is doubt as to whether Tenducci

---

nesse's trial and conviction for a libel on Col. Vernon in 1762. Thicknesse, like Smollett, served his three months in the King's Bench prison. The passage relating to Smollett and the prison is of considerable interest:

"Since Mr. Thicknesse's enlargement, I had the curiosity to visit the prison, and to enquire what sort of accommodation there is for people of any fashion, who are so weak, or so wicked, to intitle themselves to be an inhabitant thereof; and I had the good fortune not only to see his apartments, but to meet with a very intelligent person, who gave me a tolerable good account of the prison, and its present inhabitants: An account so very opposite to that given by a celebrated Author, in the adventure of Sir Launcelot Greaves, that I cannot avoid embracing this occasion to express my surprise, that a man, who, if I mistake not, was himself a prisoner there, should have drawn a picture so very unlike the original. For, though there is a large, handsome, airy house, for the better sort of prisoners, called the State House, the upper part of which commands a fine prospect; yet the avenues to it are characteristic enough of a Gaol, and exhibit so many sons and daughters of woe, that a man must be void of all the sensible and susceptible emotions, of humanity and benevolence, who can eat, drink, and sleep, with any degree of content, amidst such a multitude of unfortunate people on one side, and such a banditti of reprobates on the other.—The inside of this Gaol seems to be extra-judicial; gaming, and all kinds of licentious behavior bear no restraint. For, though there is a very good Chapel, and the Chaplain has a very good salary to perform the service every Sunday, yet I find he scarce ever attends his duty, and very seldom appoints a deputy." (From *A Letter*, pp. 18ff.)

[56] From the *Public Advertiser*, November 10, 1758, we learn that "the apartments in the new King's Bench Prison are contrived so well, that each Prisoner, on the Master's and Common Side, has a Room allotted to his own Use."

[57] Quoted from *Launcelot Greaves*, Chap. 20.

[58] See James R. Foster, "Smollett's Pamphleteering Foe Shebbeare," in *PMLA*, LVII (1942), 1053ff.

[59] Tenducci was sent to prison June 6, 1760, for want of bail and for a bill of John Olivier as well as trespass charged by the same, according to P.R.O., Commitment Book, Prison 4/3, f. 84.

[60] See Robert Chambers, *Traditions of Edinburgh*, 2 vols. (Edinburgh, 1825), I, 9.

owed his liberation to Smollett.[61] It is, of course, just possible that Smollett wrote for the January issue of the *British Magazine*, 1761, the short and unimportant poem called "On Signior Tenducci's Singing Jubal's Lyre."[62]

It must be assumed that a good many of Smollett's "friends and acquaintances . . . visited him very attentively," as Anderson put it, while he was in prison: Garrick certainly did so,[63] but the names of any or all the others can only be surmised. Among his best friends at that time were Dr. Armstrong, in Germany with the army; John Wilkes; Dr. William Hunter; Archibald Hamilton; Dr. Macaulay; William Huggins; and Dr. Alexander Reid of Chelsea. Then there was a considerable group of his aides in the *Critical Review*, the *Universal History*, and the *British Magazine*, not to mention certain London publishers, and George Faulkner, the Dublin printer.[64]

Smollett, having been sentenced on November 28, 1760, for three months, was due to be freed at the end of February. He was released, however, somewhat earlier, as we know from the fact that his warm friend William Huggins of Headley Park, Hampshire, convalescing at Bath, wrote him on February 21, 1761, expressing the wish that "this finds my Inestimable Friend at his own Fire-side surrounded with his enraptured Family."[65] This indicates that Huggins thought that Smollett would be in Chelsea about February 23, an expectation probably fulfilled, because Smollett wrote him from Chelsea on the 25th, concluding his letter as follows:

> I offer my best Respects to Mrs Gatehouse, not forgetting our kind Land-lord of Wallop, whose Generosity made the Bells of Chelsea ring at my Deliverance.[66]

[61] The fact is that on February 23, 1761, Tenducci received special permission from his plaintiff to sing in Dr. Arne's *Judith*. (See *Public Advertiser* for that date. By this time Smollett may have been released.

[62] This has been suggested by Professor Jones. See *Notes and Queries*, Vol. 17 (February 1938), 152.

[63] See *Letters*, p. 70.

[64] Faulkner wrote from London, December 2, 1760, to Samuel Derrick, the out of town: "The Press hath received a fatal Wound through the Sides of Dr. Smollett, who, I am told, hath received Sentence from Lord Mansfield to be imprisoned for three months." (From the Forster MSS 146, No. 47, in the Victoria and Albert Museum, London.)

[65] See L. F. Powell, "William Huggins and Tobias Smollett," *loc. cit.*, p. 188.

[66] *Ibid.*, p. 189.

When Smollett's neighbors heard the bells of Old Chelsea Church ringing that day in February 1761, many of them recalled the "general illumination" with which, according to tradition,[67] they had greeted him almost exactly eight years before when he was freed from charges of assault in the lawsuit with Gordon and Groom.

By this tribute and by Huggins' very kind offer of his house[68] Smollett was deeply touched. He replied at once to Huggins at Bath, in part as follows:

> I have not been so deeply affected these many years, as I was when I received your last kind Favour—believe me, Sir, my Heart swells, & even my Eyes overflow, with Tenderness, when I now review the Contents— I flattered myself with the Hope of being able to present myself at your gate, unexpected, and Surprise you with my personal Congratulation on your Recovery— I hope to do it still— at present, Headly Park has no charms for me— I should miss my kind Landlord & be miserable. . . . I am perplexed and uneasy, & have no Joy in Liberty, while my good Friend is disordered or dejected— were I not tied down to the stake by periodical Publications, I would pay my respects to you in Somersetshire.[69]

It is clear from these words that Smollett had become deeply attached to William Huggins, that literary enthusiast and translator of Dante and Ariosto. Having received from Huggins about 1756 a copy of his translation of *Orlando Furioso*, Smollett returned the compliment by sending to Huggins in December 1756, his newly translated *Don Quixote*. Accompanying this gift was the following note:

Dear Sir,

I send my Spaniard to return the Compliment I have received by your Italian. Cervantes was a warm Admirer of Ariosto, and therefore Don Quixote cannot be dissagreable [*sic*] to a Lover of Orlando furioso[*sic*]. Though I do not pretend to compare my Prose with your Poetry, I beg

[67] In the "Life of Dr. Smollett" prefixed to *The Adventures of Peregrine Pickle*, vols., London, 1806, is found the first reference to this celebration. The author of he memoir was in all probability one William Watson, whose account of Fielding was published in 1807. From the same account of Smollett prefixed to an 1811 edition of *Peregrine Pickle* we quote: "There is a traditionary report, that, on this occasion, the inhabitants of Chelsea expressed their satisfaction by a general illumination." See *The Adventures of Peregrine Pickle*, 4 vols. (London, 1811), I, xi.
[68] See L. F. Powell, *op. cit.*, p. 188.
[69] *Ibid.*, p. 189.

you will accept of my Translation, as a mark of that Perfect Esteem with which I have the Honour to be

Sir,

Your most obed^t humble Servt

T^s Smollett

Chelsea Decr 7. 1756[70]

The next year Smollett proffered suggestions on Huggins' manuscript play and informed him that he had read part of his translation of Ariosto with pleasure. To Huggins, in 1758, Smollett wrote in defense of his historical account of the Fleet prison, the warden of which had been Huggins' father. From 1758 to 1761 there is a gap in the extant correspondence, and whether by 1761 Huggins and Smollett had met is uncertain. It is quite clear, however, that Smollett had a leading part in articles in the *Critical* from 1756 to 1759 defending Huggins as a translator and as an opponent of Thomas Warton.[71] That Smollett had been entertained by Huggins was certainly implied by Dr. Grainger in his *Letter to Tobias Smollett, M.D.* After jeering at Smollett's recommendation of a stanza from Huggins' translation of Ariosto, Grainger added:

> But the Translator of *Tibullus* has no Country Seat, some fifty miles from *London*; and if he had one, has been accustomed to too good Company, ever to dream of entertaining with Claret and Venison, such *Authorlings* as you know, in their Summer and Holiday Excursions.—*And have you still, no Connexions to warp your Integrity?*[72]

Another reference to Huggins' generosity to Smollett was recorded by the Rev. John Wooll, the biographer of Joseph Warton, in his note to a letter of Thomas Warton:

> Huggins was a very indifferent translator of Ariosto. . . . When the work was finished, Huggins sent to Smollet, who at that time managed the Critical Review, a fat buck; consequently the work was highly ap

---

[70] This note was first published by Professor Claude Jones. See his "A Smollett Letter" in *MLN*, L (1935), 242-43. I print here from a photostat of Smollett's manuscript furnished me by the New York Public Library. Their photostat is taken from a reproduction of the manuscript which appeared in a catalogue of the American Art Association, January 16-17, 1930. See item 242. For a rare print of Huggins done after Hogarth's painting, see Roderick Marshall, *Italy in English Literature* Columbia University Press, 1934. In this book there is interesting information on Huggins. See also Lacy Collison-Morley, *Guiseppe Baretti* (London, 1909), pp. 91ff.

[71] See *Critical Review*, I (May 1756), 374-78; III (May 1757), 385-98; I (July 1757), 83-85; VI (December 1758), 506-8; VII (February 1759), 150-51; 180; VIII (July 1759), 82-83.

[72] Cited from Grainger's *Letter* (London, 1759), p. 11. For Smollett's comment see *Critical Review*, VII (February 1759), 150 ff.

plauded: but the history of the venison becoming public, Smollet was much abused, and in a future number of the Critical Review retracted his applause.[73]

As it is unlikely that Wooll fabricated this story out of whole cloth, he probably got it from some unpublished letter of Thomas Warton, at one time intimate with Huggins.[74] To accept the story is not, however, to accept the accompanying error that Smollett took back his praise of Huggins' translation. But we must assume that Smollett had received some favors from his generous friend.

Granting all this, the emotion in Smollett's letter to the dying Huggins' son-in-law is nevertheless surprising:

> I can safely say that I never was more affected by the Loss of the nearest Relation, than I should be upon losing Mr Huggins whom I have ever loved with the most cordial affection.[75]

A few days after writing this, Smollett traveled to Nether Wallop to pay his final respects to his friend, who died July 3, 1761, aged sixty-five. On his return trip to Chelsea he suffered a cruel attack of asthma at Farnham, Surrey. He also examined "Viner's House" at Aldershot,[76] which was probably one of the properties of the jurist, Charles Viner, the benefactor of Oxford,[77] who had died in 1756. Viner's house he found unsatisfactory for his purpose. Perhaps he was seeking a retreat for a vacation, but nothing is known of how he passed the summer of 1761.

Meantime, on February 25, 1761, there appeared in the *Public Advertiser* proposals for a "New and Complete Translation of the Works of Voltaire" to contain "Notes Historical and Critical By T. Smollett, M.D. R. Lloyd, M.A. and Others." The inclusion of Lloyd's name was obviously an error, soon corrected.[78] The first and second volumes of *The Works of . . . Voltaire* were available in March and April respectively,[79] and by 1765 a total of thirty-

[73] See the Rev. John Wooll, A.M., *Biographical Memoirs of the late Revd Joseph Warton, D.D.* (London, 1806), p. 232.
[74] According to Wooll, Thomas Warton helped Huggins in the first draft of his translation. See Wooll, *op. cit.*, p. 232.
[75] See L. F. Powell, *op. cit.*, p. 191.   [76] *Ibid.*, p. 191.
[77] See *DNB*. There is a brief account of his foundation at Oxford in a review of Blackstone's *Discourse on the Study of the Law* in the *Critical Review*, VI (1758), 430-33.
[78] The *Public Advertiser*, February 26, 1761, in connection with its announcement of Lloyd's *Poems* ran a statement that "Mr. Lloyd is not concerned in any translation of Voltaire."
[79] See *Public Advertiser* for March 9, and April 1, 1761.

five volumes had appeared,[80] under the joint editorship of Smollett and Francklin. Smollett, as Professor Joliat has clearly indicated, seems to have annotated only the prose works of Voltaire; even so, it was a considerable undertaking, done with Smollett's customary care,[81] and, in a real sense another periodical assignment by which, in his own words, he was "tied down to the stake,"[82] whether in the King's Bench Prison or in his study at Chelsea.

Wherever he was between 1756 and 1763, Smollett seems never to have neglected his contribution to the *Critical Review*. To the issue for January 1761, he must have sent in while confined in the King's Bench Prison, the "Preface," occasioned by the fifth anniversary of the magazine, running in part as follows:

> Five annual revolutions of the sun are now performed since the Critical Review made its first appearance, under such peculiar auspices, that for the greater part of that time it has been exposed to the incessant hostilities of a combination of foes, that can hardly be paralleled in any other period of the annals of literature.
>
> It hath sustained all the complicated assaults of dullness, whose name is Legion; whose progeny spring up like the dragon's teeth which Cadmus sowed; whose heads, like those of the Hydra, are no sooner mowed down, than they regerminate as it were under the scythe, with the most astonishing increase. . . .
>
> Its supposed authors have been vilified in person, and assassinated in reputation. One gentleman, in particular, whose character stands in some degree of favour with the public, has been singled out as a victim, and galled by all the shafts of malignity. He has not only felt the rod of persecution and prosecution for opinions which he really broached, but he has been insulted in public abuse, and traduced in private calumny, by obscure authors whom he did not know, for criticisms he had not written on performances which he never saw. Peace to all such; they are now at rest, and we have no intention to disturb their ashes. Like the insects of a summer's day they have buzzed, and stung, and stunk, and expired; but like other vermin, the eggs they have deposited, may, by some revolving sun of success, be hatched for the propagation of the species. Be that as it will, such puny stings can have no longer any effect upon the Critical Review, improved and strengthened as it is, in age and constitution, schooled by its sufferings, as well as hardened by the opposition which it has undergone, and now fairly surmounted.[83]

[80] See *Public Advertiser* for March 1, 1765.

[81] For an excellent survey of Smollett's part in the new translation of Voltaire, consult Eugène Joliat, "Smollett, Editor of Voltaire," in *MLN*, LIV (1939), 429-36.

[82] See L. F. Powell, *op. cit.*, p. 189.

[83] Quoted from *Critical Review*, XI (January 1761), [i].

How self-conscious, superior, and bellicose all this is, and how well contrived to stimulate the incessantly hatching ephemeridae of ignorance and malice.

Naturally enough, the old buzzing and stinging continued. George Colman, who was probably not wholly delighted with the review of his *Jealous Wife*,[84] took offense at the review of Charles Churchill's *Rosciad*.[85] Word of this having reached Smollett, he wrote to Garrick in April 1761, that he was not the author of this review, and that he desired "to live quietly with all mankind, and, if possible, to be upon good terms with all those who have distinguished themselves by their merit."[86] But within a few weeks there came from the press Churchill's *Apology Addressed to the Critical Reviewers* with its powerful invective against both Smollett and Archibald Hamilton. The latter Churchill called a malicious concocter of falsehoods, and next proceeded to pour ridicule on Smollett as novelist, historian, dramatist, and critic, asking

> Who ever read the Regicide, but swore
> The author wrote as man ne'er wrote before?
> Others for plots and under-plots may call,
> Here's the right method—have no plot at all.[87]

Then in a Satanic portrait of all that was diabolical in reviewers, Churchill painted Smollett, the critic, as one

> Who spares no character; whose every word,
> Bitter as gall, and sharper than the sword
> Cuts to the quick,[88]

and as a monstrous hypocrite as well. It was an unscrupulous attack because Smollett had not reviewed the *Rosciad* at all. In fact, no more savage blow was ever struck at the qualifications and personal character of a leading reviewer. The reply to Churchill's *Apology* appeared in the *Critical* for May 1761, in its monthly catalogue, and surely Smollett shaped it for publication. As it is unusually revealing in its defense of the *Critical's* editorial policies, parts of it here follow:

[84] See *Critical Review*, XI (February 1761), 131-41.
[85] *Critical Review*, XI (March 1761), 209-12.   [86] *Letters*, pp. 69-70.
[87] See *The Poems of Charles Churchill* (King's Printer's Edition in 2 vols., 1933, ed. James Laver) I, 52.
[88] *Ibid.*, 57. There is no question but that Churchill was here attacking Smollett. In a copy of *The Apology*, London, 1761, with the marginalia of Horace Walpole (in the Harvard University Library), Walpole wrote "Dr Smollet" opposite this verse-portrait.

This is another *Brutum Fulmen* launched at the Critical Review by one Churchill, who it seems is a clergyman, and it must be owned has a knack at versification; a bard, who upon the strength of having written a few good lines in a thing called *The Rosciad*, swaggers about as if he was a game-keeper of Parnassus, and lays about him with his quarter-staff, *a tort et travers*, against friend and foe without distinction. His chief attack, however, is directed against the Critical Review, which he reviles in good phrase and poetical cadence, as a tribunal raised upon rancour, envy, and dulness; as a court consisting of malignant dunces, who employ the most scandalous arts to defame character, and crush rising merit in the bud. . . . We cannot, upon the severest review of our own conduct, charge ourselves with malice. . . .

Upon a revision of our processes, we find ourselves rather chargeable with an excess of lenity, in sparing sometimes the transgressions of modest dulness. We have, upon some occasions, even permitted a meagre ass to graze upon the common of Parnassus, until he hath become fat and wanton, begun to kick his benefactors, and disturbed the whole neighbour-hood with his braying. . . .

He [Churchill] moreover upbraids the reviewers with the guilt of stabbing in the dark, and with keeping their own persons concealed, that the injured may not know how to direct their resentment. The reviewers pass no censures, but in the face of day; censures, which if they are un-just, may be openly and fairly refuted by reason and argument, without any scurrility or recrimination. Common sense might have told him, that no man, supposing himself qualified for the office of a reviewer, would chuse to lay himself personally open to the illiberal revenge of every vul-gar dunce, or low bred railer . . . and common honesty ought to have suggested that it ill becomes the character of a clergyman to attack, re-vile, and bespatter those from whom he knows he never received the least injury or provocation. Such are the two writers[89] against whose works the apologist hath spouted his malevolence with open throat . . . exclaiming like a fanatic possessed, that they are the ministers of rancour, the very daemons of malignity. What reader of candour . . . will not im-pute all his obloquy to a spirit of recrimination operating in a weak mind inflamed by the sense of injuries sustained? But what will he think of the aggressor's urbanity and morals, when he is assured that neither of those gentlemen whom he has thus bedaubed were in any shape concerned in the article . . . that one of them[90] never in the whole course of his life wrote one single article in the Critical Review; and that the other, whose veracity stands above all suspicion, solemnly declared to the friends of the apologist, that he had no hand in reviewing the Rosciad. If he had writ the article, 'tis ten to one, but he would have frankly owned it, without any apprehension from the resentment of such a puny antagonist, who

[89] Smollett and Archibald Hamilton.
[90] Archibald Hamilton.

Monmouth House, Smollett's residence in Chelsea

Chelsea Old Church

must write many more poems as good as the Rosciad, before he will consider him as a respectable enemy.[91]

Laboring as he was at many tasks in the spring of 1761, Smollett still found time and energy to contemplate the writing of a history of Ireland. This new project was clearly referred to by several Irish celebrities. First, Charles O'Conor of Belangare alluded to it in a letter to his friend Dr. John Curry, a Dublin physician, May 12, 1761, as follows:

> If Smollet should deign to correspond with me on points of history relating to this island I shall point you out to him, after telling him who wrote the *Historical Memoirs.* . . . He is a man of very considerable historical abilities, and should he attempt writing our history, we should exert ourselves from all quarters to supply him with proper materials.[92]

In June 1761, O'Conor again returned to this matter,[93] and George Faulkner, the leading Dublin printer, wrote of it in London, May 14, 1761, in his letter to Samuel Derrick:

> I often see Lord Southwell, Mr. Mallet, Dr. Smollett, who all make friendly Enquiry after [you], and last week I dined with the last Gentleman at Salter's at Chelsea, in a very agreeable Sett of Company. The Doctor proposeth going to Ireland next Summer, and to spend a Year or two in that Country in Order to enable him the better to write that History.[94]

Faulkner by his phrase "next Summer" meant, presumably, the coming summer of 1761, and as there are no documents to show where Smollett was from July to October of that year, it is quite possible that he visited Dublin for a short stay during that period.[95] But gradually failing health forced him to abandon what seems to have been a lively desire to write a history of Erin.[96] Keeping up

---

[91] Quoted from the *Critical Review*, XI (May 1761), 409-11.

[92] Quoted from Historical Manuscripts Commission, Eighth Report, Pt. 1 (London, 1881), p. 469.

[93] *Ibid.*

[94] Printed from Forster MS 146, Letter No. 50, in the Victoria and Albert Museum, London.

[95] A letter of O'Conor to Curry, printed, perhaps inaccurately, as of July 21, 1762, announced that Smollett was coming to Dublin "to collect materials and encouragement for a history of Ireland." See Historical Manuscripts Commission, Eighth Report, Pt. 1, p. 471.

[96] Though Smollett's motives for writing Irish history may have been chiefly economic, it is possible that his interest in Ireland had been heightened by his recent association with Goldsmith. Since the latter's uncle, the Rev. Thomas Contrarine (who had died in 1758) was a good friend of Charles O'Conor, it would have been easy for Goldsmith to introduce Smollett to the O'Conor circle. Moreover it looks

with the edition of Voltaire, with *Launcelot Greaves*, with the *Critical*, and with the *Continuation of the Complete History*, and heaven knows what else, was more than enough for the rest of 1761.

The final chapter of *Launcelot Greaves* having appeared in the *British Magazine* (issue of December 1761), this novel came off the press in book form at the end of March 1762.[97] Little attention was paid to it by the reviewers. In the *Monthly Review*, it was greeted in its monthly catalogue with this single sentence, "Better than the common Novels, but unworthy the pen of Dr. Smollet."[98] It was praised for its characters, style, and "many fine strokes of genius, nature, and passion" by a writer in the *Library*;[99] and in the *Critical* it was commended chiefly for its characters, which, asserted the reviewer, are illustrative of "the genuine humour, satirical talents, and benevolent heart" of their creator.[100] These qualities, however, are not powerful enough to have led to much reprinting of this novel in Smollett's lifetime.[101] *Launcelot Greaves* does reflect, nevertheless, central social attitudes of Smollett: his opposition to the war in Germany;[102] his dislike of both political parties;[103] and his propaganda against the horrors of private madhouses.[104]

In March, just when *Launcelot Greaves* was published in book

---

as if Smollett by 1760 had met young Edmund Burke, because of evidence in a letter of O'Conor to Curry years later, in 1768. O'Conor wrote: "Counsellor Ridge, on his circuit, called upon me here t'other day, and eat a mutton chop with me; a worthy young gentleman, and most heartily your friend. He is well acquainted with Dr. Smollet one of the 'Critical Reviewers.' It was in a sitting with him that he and Mr. Burke put the *Memoirs* into his hands, and from that event proceeded the judgment published in the Critical Review." By the *Memoirs*, O'Conor referred to a volume called *Historical Memoirs of the Irish Rebellion in the year 1641*, for which he wrote the preface only, the rest having been written by his friend Dr. John Curry. The book was published in 1758 and given a very careful and generally favorable appraisal in the *Critical* for February 1761, probably by Smollett. The Counsellor Ridge alluded to by O'Conor was presumably John Ridge. For data about him see *Alumni Dublinenses*, Dublin, 1935, and also Dixon Wecter, *Edmund Burke and His Kinsmen*, University of Colorado Studies, Ser. B., Vol. I, No. 1 (Boulder, 1939), 54n., 76n., 78.

[97] For a newspaper announcement, see the *Public Advertiser*, March 30, 1762.

[98] *Monthly Review*, XXVI (May 1762), 391.

[99] *The Library: or, Moral and critical magazine*, London, II (May 1762), 262.

[100] *Critical Review*, XIII (May 1762), 428.

[101] See *CBEL*.   [102] *Launcelot Greaves*, Chap. 2.

[103] *Ibid.*, Chap. 9.

[104] *Ibid.*, Chap. 23. A Parliamentary committee reported in 1763 on the state of private madhouses.

form, Smollett wrote Wilkes, "I have been ill these three months: but hope Soon to be in a condition to pay my respects to Mr. Wilkes in Person."[105] His serious physical condition he described the following June in a letter to Dr. Moore: "I have had no attack of the asthma these two months; but I am extremely emaciated; and am afflicted with a leeking Catarrh, & cough all night without ceasing."[106]

Seriously ill as he was, Smollett was nevertheless persuaded, through means now unknown,[107] to write the *Briton*, a political weekly sheet in defense of Lord Bute's ministry, which appeared every Saturday from May 29, 1762, to February 12, 1763. For some eight months Smollett was caught up in the violent whirlpool of the most bitter political controversy, for which he was temperamentally unfitted. In general it brought about his complete rupture with Wilkes, and it led to his complete disillusion about William Pitt.[108] It also meant that Smollett, along with Bute, and other ministerial writers,[109] was the target of virulent anti-Scottish writing and the subject of satirical prints.[110]

From all this vexation and drudgery Smollett escaped, at times, in the summer and fall of 1762, first in Dover, and later in Southampton and Bath.[111] From Bath he dispatched the following signed appeal to the public (printed on the front page of *The Gazetteer and London Daily Advertiser* for October 7, 1762) concerning his stand on Pitt:

To the Printer
Sir,
    By a letter which I just now received from a friend at London, I am informed that I have been lately attacked in the Ledger, by some anonymous defamer, who, upon the supposition that I am author of a political paper called *the Briton*, taxes me with venality and inconsistency, for

---

[105] *Letters*, p. 73.   [106] *Ibid.*, p. 76.

[107] One conjecture is that Bubb Dodington recommended Smollett. For the best account of Smollett's part in the controversies centering in the Earl of Bute see Arnold Whitridge, *Tobias Smollett* (Published by the Author [1925]), pp. 56-79.

[108] For a summary of Smollett's views on Pitt, see my article, "Smollett and the Elder Pitt," in *MLN*, LIX (April 1944), 250-57.

[109] These are conjectured to have been Mallet, Shebbeare, Ruffhead, Cleland, Guthrie, and Murphy. See Smollett's *Works*, ed. Anderson, 6 vols. (Edinburgh, 1820), I, 78n.

[110] See Arnold Whitridge, *op. cit.*, p. 67.

[111] See Edward S. Noyes, "Another Smollett Letter," in *MLN*, XLII (1927), 232, and *Letters*, p. 77.

having in that paper, insulted Mr. Pitt, whom I had before deified in the dedication of my history of England.

I shall not give this unknown aggressor the satisfaction to declare that I have no connection with *the Briton* or any other paper whatsoever, written either for, or against the ministry: but I challenge him and all the world to prove me guilty, in one single instance, of venality, prostitution, or any other species of dishonour.

If it be imputed to me as a crime that I have blamed some parts of Mr. P---'s ministerial conduct, I plead guilty to the charge.

I inscribed the first part of my history to that gentleman as the most distinguished patriot of the day, who excelled all his cotemporaries in the powers of elocution, and exerted those powers in the service of his country; in stigmatizing a weak and corrupt administration, and particularly in exposing and opposing the absurdity and pernicious tendency of those German connections, which that administration had formed.

Though Mr. P--- as a M------r, afterwards adapted [*sic*] those very principles against which he had so long and so strenuously declaimed, I was surely under no obligation to follow his example; to renounce the maxims which I had always avowed, and violate my conscience out of respect to his character. I thought it my duty to sacrifice every personal consideration to historical truth; and therefore, in the course of my continuation, I freely censured some particulars of his conduct.

This being the true state of the case, I appeal to every man of sentiment and candour, whether the charge of apostacy, or inconsistency lies at my door; and whether the person, who has stabbed at my reputation in the public papers, is not actuated by the spirit of an illiberal assassin.

I am, Sir,

your humble servant.

T. SMOLLETT

Bath,
October, 3, 1762

In the summer of 1762, Smollett's health became alarming. "My constitution," he wrote Dr. Moore, "will no longer allow me to toil as formerly. I am now so thin you would hardly know me. My face is shrivelled up by the asthma like an ill-dried pippin, and my legs are as thick at the ancle as at the calf."[112] Aware of his need of a warm climate, he tried in vain in the summer for an appointment as physician to the army in Portugal.[113] At the end of the year he applied through his old friend John Home for a counsulship at Marseilles or Madrid, but nothing was forthcoming.

Added to failing health and frustrations was the bitter blow of

[112] Cited from Edward S. Noyes, "Another Smollett Letter," *loc. cit.*, p. 232.
[113] *Ibid.*

the illness and death of the Smolletts' only child, Elizabeth, aged fifteen. She died on April 3, 1763, the probable cause of her death being consumption, and was buried beneath the middle aisle of Old Chelsea Church beside her maternal grandmother, Mrs. Elizabeth Leaver, who had died the preceding December. Elizabeth Smollett is known to have been a very promising girl with a gift for writing verse.[114] Her untimely death overwhelmed Smollett and his wife "with unutterable sorrow."[115]

Broken in body and spirit, Smollett severed all his connections with the *Critical Review* and, in his own words, with "every other literary system,"[116] bade farewell to his London friends, and took his family to France in June 1763. This move he made with the hopes that travel would soften Mrs. Smollett's grief and that a mild climate would benefit his pulmonary weakness.[117] With a very heavy heart he wrote to Dr. William Hunter a farewell letter in which he confessed that he could not well stand the emotional shock of parting in person from his friends. Some tender farewells must have been said, however, in Chelsea, where he had lived for thirteen eventful years, and many notes, surely, were dispatched to his numerous friends in London. Among such should be mentioned Dr. Thomas Dickson of the London Hospital,[118] whom he had summoned to attend Elizabeth in her last illness. As he sailed for France, he was aware not only of physical weakness and domestic grief, but also of bitter resentment because he felt that he had been "traduced by malice, persecuted by faction" and "abandoned by false patrons," in a "scene of illiberal dispute, and incredible infatuation."[119] Frail, heartbroken, and bitter as he was, he could scarcely have dreamed of living another eight years or of being still destined to create his masterpiece, *Humphry Clinker*.

[114] For other details, see my article, "Elizabeth Smollett, Daughter of Tobias Smollett," in *RES*, VIII (1932), 312-15. There is, in my article, an error: on p. 314, ll. 6-7, for *Francesco Pera*, read *Giovanni Gentili*.

[115] *Letters*, p. 82.

[116] *Ibid.*, p. 96.

[117] See Smollett's *Travels*, Letter I.

[118] See the elegiac obituary of Dr. Dickson in *Gentleman's Magazine*, LIV, Pt. I (June 1784), 476.

[119] See Smollett's *Travels*, Letter I, paragraphs 2 and 3.

CHAPTER XII

The Search for Health in France and Italy;

The Travels, 1763-1766

ABOUT mid-June 1763, Smollett, accompanied by his wife, two young ladies,[1] and his servant Tolloush, sailed from Dover for France and Italy, where he was to remain, for the most part in Nice, until his return to England in July 1765. The traveling adventures of this party of five persons, and Smollett's commentary, so brilliantly set forth in his *Travels*, have been ably treated from various approaches by Thomas Seccombe,[2] Professor Joliat,[3] and Professor Kahrl.[4] On Smollett's social attitudes and essential personality his own story in his *Travels* sheds a flood of light.

After petty discomforts in the Channel crossing and at an execrable inn at Boulogne, Smollett found commodious rooms tolerably furnished, for three guineas a month. For this sum he and his party had the use of "four bed-chambers on the first floor, a large parlour below, a kitchen,"[5] and a cellar. There they remained from June to late September 1763.

For approximately the first six weeks of this period Smollett was without his books, which were held up on their arrival to be examined by the French authorities with an eye to anything in their contents "prejudicial to the state, or to the religion of the country."[6]

[1] One of the young ladies was Anne Curry, a native of Newcastle, later the wife of George William Renner, Smollett's agent in Leghorn. The other was perhaps Mrs. Leaver's granddaughter, Frances Lassells. She was called Miss Fanny by John Gray in his letters to Smollett (see Smollett's *Works*, ed. Anderson, 1820, I, 195, 202).

[2] See Smollett's *Travels Through France and Italy With an Introduction by Thomas Seccombe*, in The World's Classics [1919], pp. xviii-lx. See also Seccombe's bibliographical note on the *Travels* in Vol. XI of the *Works of Tobias Smollett*, with an introduction by W. E. Henley, 12 vols., London, 1899-1901.

[3] See Eugène Joliat, *Smollett Et La France* (Paris, 1935), pp. 111ff.

[4] See George M. Kahrl, *Tobias Smollett, Traveler-Novelist* (University of Chicago Press [1945]), Chap. VIII.

[5] *Travels*, Letter I.   [6] *Ibid.*, Letter II.

After correspondence with the Duchess of Douglas,[7] with Hume, and with Francis Seymour Conway, the Earl of Hertford, Smollett recovered his property through the agency of Richard Neville, who at that time was serving for Hertford as ambassador to France. As a result of this episode, we have the list of the books which Smollett carried to France, which I translate as follows:

Universal History Ancient and Modern	58 vols.
Complete History of England	8 vols.
Translation of the Works of Voltaire	25 vols.
Novels of Smollett	12 vols.[8]
Translation of Don Quixote	4 vols.
Works of Shakespeare	8 vols.
Comedies of Congreve	3 vols.
Critical Review	12 vols.
British Magazine	4 vols.

Complete System of Geography in folio
Some other books of entertainment in English,
    comedies and pamphlets
Homer, Sophocles, Virgil, Horace, Juvenal, Tibullus
Don Quixote in Spanish
Five Dictionaries: Greek, Latin, French, Italian, Spanish[9]

As this list was presumably written hastily and from memory by Smollett, it may be incomplete. Even so, it represents very well Smollett's love of the Greek and Latin classics and of Shakespeare, as well as his or Mrs. Smollett's attachment to his own compositions.

In addition to being without his books, Smollett suffered a setback in his physical condition shortly after reaching Boulogne. To remedy this he went for a daily plunge in the ocean until September, with what he felt to be some benefit, though when he left Boulogne, he was not sure that he should ever return to England.[10]

During his summer at Boulogne, Smollett, as appears from his

[7] Presumably Margaret Douglas, who married in 1758 Archibald Douglas, Duke of Douglas. The latter died in Edinburgh in 1761. See Martz, *The Later Career of Tobias Smollett*, 1942, p. 107.

[8] By 1763 Smollett's novels made up a total of ten volumes. As he carried with him the *British Magazine*, he may not have taken the two-volume set of *Launcelot Greaves*. If so, he probably took *Roderick Random*, *Peregrine Pickle*, editions of 1751 and 1758; and *Count Fathom*, all of which totaled twelve volumes.

[9] For the original list see A. C. Hunter, "Les Livres De Smollett Détenus Par La Douane à Boulogne en 1763," in *Revue de Littérature Comparée*, XI (1931), 763-67. See also Joliat, *op. cit.*, 249-53, for additional data.

[10] *Travels*, Letter III, and Letter V.

Travels, turned a critical eye on French manners. The noblesse he condemned as creatures at once useless, helpless, slothful, "without dignity, sense, or sentiment; contemptible from pride; and ridiculous from vanity."[11] The prosperous bourgeoisie he pictured as living in filth and as strangers to common decency. The laboring people he found ill-lodged, wretchedly fed, and victimized by tyrannous landlords. In general, Boulogne, like the rest of France, was in his opinion cursed with social injustice and ecclesiastical superstition.

These evils, however, did not prevent Smollett from enjoying life. He liked walking in the garden of a convent near the sea; he took pleasure in drinking tea in a charming summer-house belonging to Mrs. B---, a French lady, whose husband lived occasionally in London; he relished the good food of Boulogne—tasty veal, mutton, pork, turkeys, and fish, as well as good claret, white wine, and small beer; he regaled himself on a variety of fruits. Then there were pleasant social contacts: he felt himself lucky in meeting an elderly Scotsman of doughty deeds, General Paterson,[12] then on his way from Nice to England, who gave him a letter of recommendation to the English consul at Nice and advice on traveling in southern France; he enjoyed an excursion to Samers, a village on the road to Paris, with Captain L--- and Mrs. B---.[13] Finally, the Smolletts, shortly before leaving Boulogne, were the chief guests of honor at an elaborate banquet given by their French landlord. The food and company on this occasion Smollett described with remarkable gusto.[14]

While in Boulogne, Smollett must have dispatched numerous letters to friends in London and Scotland, only two of which are extant. In addition to his letter to Alexander Reid of Chelsea, dealt with earlier, he wrote one, August 11, to Dr. William Hunter, wherein he reported dining with General Paterson, and

---

[11] *Travels*, Letter IV.

[12] This officer was Sir James Paterson, brother of Sir Hugh Paterson, and a Lieutenant-General. See Alexander Drummond's *Travels* (London 1754), p. 33. The General died September 5, 1765, as appears in the following obituary: "At Bath, Sir James Paterson of the family of Bannockburn in Scotland, late a lieutenant-general in the army of the King of Sardinia, and governor of Nice. His corpse is brought to Scotland and interred at St. Ninian's, the burial-place of the family." From *Scots Magazine*, XXVII (1765), 502. For Smollett's other references to Paterson, see *Travels*, Letters III, X, and XIV.

[13] *Travels*, Letter V.　　　　　　　　　　[14] *Ibid*.

referred to William Hunter's well-known bibliomania, to his wish "to have every curious Book on the face of the Earth."[15]

About September 22, according to the *Travels*,[16] Smollett set out for Paris by way of Montreuil, Abbeville, and Amiens. In the French capital he remained for some two weeks. An extract from his own account of his life in Paris is delightfully revealing:

> I had desired a friend to procure lodgings for me at Paris, in the faux-bourg St. Germain; and accordingly we found ourselves accommodated at the Hotel de Montmorency,[17] with a first floor, which costs me ten livres[18] a day. I should have put up with it had it been less polite; but as I have only a few days to stay in this place, and some visits to receive, I am not sorry that my friend has exceeded his commission. I have been guilty of another piece of extravagance, in hiring a *carosse de remise*, for which I pay twelve livres a-day. Besides the article of visiting, I could not leave Paris, without carrying my wife and the girls to see the most remarkable places in and about this capital, such as the Luxemburg, the Palais-Royal, the Thuilleries, the Louvre, the Invalids, the Gobelins, &c. together with Versailles, Trianon, Marli, Meudon, and Choissi; and therefore, I thought the difference in point of expence would not be great, between a *carosse de remise* and a hackney coach. The first are extremely elegant, if not too much ornamented, the last are very shabby and disagreeable. Nothing gives me such chagrin, as the necessity I am under to hire a *valet de place*, as my own servant does not speak the language.[19]

All this shows that the Smolletts lived in considerable luxury in Paris. The visitors whom they received remain unknown. That they were entertained in the house of the Duchess of Douglas is certain,[20] and is perhaps indicative of other social activities. As Smollett in his *Travels* cried down French drama,[21] it is probable that he saw a few plays while there. In general, of course, Smollett discovered many outrageous defects among the Parisians, and noted that the cost of living had doubled since his previous visit.

Leaving Paris on October 13, 1763,[22] Smollett moved on via

---

[15] See *Letters*, pp. 86-88. Professor Noyes erred in thinking that this letter was sent to Dr. John Hunter, who, in marked contrast to his brother, was not known as a book collector. Nor was he intimate with Lord Hertford. See Jane M. Oppenheimer, *New Aspects of John and William Hunter* (New York, 1946), pp. 146-47.

[16] *Travels*, Letter V.

[17] In *The Gentleman's Guide in his Tour through France*, fourth edition (London, 1770), p. 233, the Hotel Montmorency, on La Rue Mazarine, is listed among the best hotels. Some other hotels in the Quartier St. Germain Des Pres were more expensive.

[18] The author of *The Gentleman's Guide* (p. 7), stated that a livre was equivalent to 10 pence. Smollett's rooms, therefore, cost him slightly over 8 shillings per day.

[19] *Travels*, Letter VI.   [20] *Travels*, Letter VIII.   [21] *Travels*, Letter VI.

[22] *Travels*, Letter VIII.

Dijon to Lyons, arriving there about October 19. For this expedition he hired a coach and set out with six horses and two postillions, in addition to his own servant Tolloush on horseback. Abominating the garlic in French cookery, he laid in a supply of tea, chocolate, cured neats' tongues, Bologna sausages, and fruit, in order to avoid the bad food of the inns. In Letter VIII of the *Travels* he declared: "My personal adventures on the road were such as will not bear a recital. They consisted of petty disputes with landladies, post-masters, and postillions." Fortunately for his reader, however, he described some very amusing episodes, the best being his scurvy treatment of a French seigneur unrecognizable as such because of his odd costume. Mortified over his breach of decorum, Smollett penned this memorable self-portrait:

> The truth is, I was that day more than usually peevish, from the bad weather, as well as from the dread of a fit of the asthma, with which I was threatened: and I dare say my appearance seemed as uncouth to him as his travelling dress appeared to me. I had a grey mourning frock under a wide great coat, a bob wig without powder, a very large laced hat, and a meagre, wrinkled, discontented countenance.[23]

The trip to Lyons was expensive: Smollett computed it at about forty *louis d'or*, i.e. £40 in English money.

At Lyons the cost of living was so alarming that Smollett stayed only a few days. There he was visited by the two young sons of Mr. Gustaldi, late minister from Genoa at London.

The next stage of Smollett's journey was from Lyons to Montpellier, where he arrived about the end of October and remained until November 13, 1763.[24] En route, Smollett enjoyed the summery weather, the meadow flowers, and the conversation of Joseph, his extraordinary muleteer, with his macabre anecdotes of Mandrin, the smuggler. During his stay at Montpellier Smollett must have met Sterne, who, with Mrs. Sterne, had arrived there by early October 1763[25] in search of health. Smollett, as is clear from his *Travels*, met Mrs. Sterne and from her heard the story of the sad plight of young Mr. Oswald,[26] who died of tuberculosis.

[23] *Ibid.*   [24] *Travels*, Letter XII.
[25] See Wilbur L. Cross, *The Life and Times of Laurence Sterne* (Yale University Press, 1929), p. 590, where Sterne, in a letter written at Montpellier, November 24, 1763, told of arriving there six weeks previously.
[26] *Travels*, Letter XI. The father of young Oswald, referred to by Smollett as "Mr. O----d, merchant in the city of London," was surely the distinguished Richard

Surely the Sternes were among the small group of English residents in Montpellier who, following a strict social convention, paid their respects to the Smolletts the day after their arrival.[27] As Smollett took rooms "in the high street"[28] in the city, and as Sterne had lodgings "on the hill,"[29] it is quite likely that the two novelists met more than once. It was in Montpellier, surely, that Sterne heard a few Smollettian complaints about traveling in France, which he remembered, and which, recalled no doubt when he read or heard of Smollett's *Travels*, led him to write the famous passage in his *Sentimental Journey*, wherein he called Smollett the "learned Smelfungus." Sterne, in his *Journey*, wrote of purely imaginary meetings with Smollett in Rome (where the latter termed the Pantheon "nothing but a huge cockpit"[30]), and in Turin (where he poured forth "a tale of sorrowful adventures") and advised the querulous traveler to tell them not to the world, but to his physician.[31]

In Montpellier, Smollett, harassed again by a cough, asthma, and fever, received medical advice from one Dr. Fitzmaurice and later approached the famous specialist there, Dr. Antoine Fizès, whom Sterne, too, probably consulted.[32] As Fizès had, among the English of Montpellier, a reputation for bluntness and insolence,[33] Smollett sent his *valet de place* to the doctor's house with a long description of his case written in Latin, as he probably dreaded being told the blunt truth in a personal interview. Highly disgusted because Fizès replied in French, Smollett declared in his *Travels* that Fizès either could not understand Latin or had not read his letter, that he misunderstood his case, and was, in short, a flagrant humbug.[34] Probably this was a considerable exaggeration.

Despite illness and his disillusion over Dr. Fizès, Smollett enjoyed Montpellier, where he was treated with great politeness by

---

Oswald, with whom Smollett corresponded. (See *Letters, passim*). He also acted as Mrs. Leaver's business agent. For a highly laudatory obituary of him, see *London Chronicle*, November 9-11, 1784, p. 464. Sterne referred to him in his letters.

[27] See *Travels*, Letter X.   [28] *Ibid.*

[29] See Wilbur L. Cross, *op. cit.*, p. 337.   [30] See *Travels*, Letter XXXI.

[31] See Sterne's *Sentimental Journey*, ed. Herbert Read (The Scholartis Press, London, 1929), pp. 46ff.

[32] See Wilbur L. Cross, *op. cit.*, p. 342.

[33] Benjamin Hutchinson, on the contrary, in his *Biographica Medica* (London, 1799, 2 vols., I, 302) stressed Fizès' politeness and elegance of manners.

[34] *Travels*, Letter XI.

Lieutenant-Colonel Tents, commander of the Irish regiment of Berwick. There he seems to have attended the concerts, and enjoyed its gay and sociable residents. In fact the very virtues of the place led him to move on: "I have not health to enjoy these pleasures," he wrote in his *Travels*, adding, "I cannot bear a crowd of company, such as pours in upon us unexpectedly at all hours; and I forsee, that, in staying at Montpellier, I should be led into an expense which I can ill afford."[35] From this it appears that the French, as well as the few English, in Montpellier, made much of their celebrated visitor.

On November 13, 1763, Smollett set out for Nice, arriving on the twenty-third of that month. Traveling in a mule-drawn coach he passed through Nismes, Tarrascone, Orgon, the suburbs of Aix, Brignolles, Le Luc, Le Muy, Frejus, and Cannes. In one small village Smollett was deeply moved when the landlady took him by the hand at parting, shedding tears and praying that God would restore him to his health. "This," asserted Smollett, "was the only instance of sympathy, compassion, or goodness of heart, that I had met with among the publicans of France."[36] At Brignolles, Smollett helped a young Irish priest with money and a letter of introduction to a fellow countryman in Montpellier. On the ten-day trip Smollett passed from wintry weather to a region east of the mountains of Esterelles where he saw an orange tree bearing ripe fruit. As usual, he raged at landlords and admired the romantic landscape. Upon reaching Nice he was welcomed by the English vice-consul, John Buckland,[37] who after a week or so lent him his lodgings. There were other congenial visitors.

At Nice, Smollett maintained his residence from November 1763 to April 1765,[38] being away only on his trip to Italy (from the beginning of September until about the middle of November 1764) and on a short excursion to Turin in February 1765.[39] From

[35] *Ibid.*, Letter x.　　　　　　　　　　[36] *Travels*, Letter xii.

[37] In the *Travels* Smollett referred to this person as Mr. B------d. John Buckland, an aged Lieutenant and native of London, acted after 1761 as the agent of Michael Ramsay, absentee consul. He had lived around Nice since 1730. For this information see Georges Doublet, "Les Consuls De La Nation Britannique A Nice, Aux xviiᵉ et xviiiᵉ Siècles," in *Les Anglais dans Le Comté de Nice et en Provence Depuis Le xviiiᵐᵉ Siècle* (Musée Massena, Nice, 1934), pp. 46ff.

[38] Smollett wrote Dr. William Hunter that he arrived at Nice, November 23, 1763; on this date came the first entry in his "Register of the Weather," printed at the end of his *Travels*. He concluded his entries on April 24, 1765.

[39] See *Travels*, Letter xxxviii.

his *Travels* we can extract many vivid and dependable details concerning his comfortable house, his activities, his health, and his impressions of Nice. Soon after arrival, he rented of one Corvesi for £20 a year an unfurnished "tenement" [house], which he described as "a ground floor paved with brick, consisting of a kitchen, two large halls, a couple of good rooms with chimneys, three large closets that serve for bed-chambers, and dressing-rooms, a butler's room, and three apartments for servants, lumber, or stores, to which we ascend by narrow wooden stairs. I have likewise two small gardens, well stocked with oranges, lemons, peaches, figs, grapes, corinths, sallad, and pot-herbs. It is supplied with a draw-well of good water, and there is another in the vestibule of the house, which is cool, large, and magnificent."[40] To furnish this place Smollett spent about £60, and to run this considerable establishment, he had a cook, a maid, an *aeconome*[41] [household manager], and probably occasional gardeners[42] as well as his servant Tolloush. Though not as formal as his Chelsea residence, it was, as Smollett would have said, quite tolerable.

Something of his activities in Nice he divulged in his *Travels*. There were rides on horseback, and, in cool weather, a daily tour of the streets and ramparts of Nice, taken at the noon hour, when the ways were not crowded.[43] About the first of May 1764, Smollett began taking his daily plunge into the ocean. In the summer of 1764, he hired a sedan chair to and from the beach, which was a mile from his house.[44] He complained because the heat from May to October deprived him of exercise. After his tremendous work-schedule in Chelsea, it must have been a comparatively idle life, and what writing he did, apart from correspondence, is not known, except that we have his word that he had no share in the political paper-warfare that raged in London,[45] and that he gave up thoughts of writing "a complete natural history" of Nice.[46]

By this relaxed life and by the easy climate Smollett's health was somewhat benefited. He was continually tormented, however, by recurring asthma, cough, and fever, and was no doubt suffering from a milder type of tuberculosis.[47] Added to this was what he

---

[40] *Travels*, Letter XVIII.   [41] *Ibid.*, Letter XXIV.   [42] *Ibid.*, Letter XX.
[43] *Ibid.*, Letter XXIII. Smollett reported that the population of Nice was 12,000, and that there were in the neighborhood of the city an additional 12,000 laborers.
[44] *Ibid.*, Letter XXIII.   [45] *Ibid.*, Letter XXVIII.   [46] *Ibid.*, Letter XXII.
[47] See Thomas Seccombe's Introduction to the *Travels*, edition cited, pp. xxxiii-iv.

described as a scorbutical eruption on his right hand, which troubled him after he arrived at Nice. In February 1764, he reported to Dr. William Hunter that he grew thinner and thinner,[48] and in the following June he was very ill[49] while at his *cassine*, or small house in the country. In general, from this time until his death, his physical condition was constantly fluctuating, but his physical afflictions never dulled the edge of his remarkable powers of observation.

His comments on the social culture of Nice were characteristically pointed. He bewailed the evils of its religion, its lack of taste and arts, its "gothic pride, Ignorance, and superstition."[50] There was nothing of interest in its libraries, private or public, and not even a bookseller, he declared.[51] Though he alluded to a printing press,[52] there were no newspapers or magazines printed there during his residence.[53] Despite the cultural flaws of Nice and its swarms of gnats and mosquitoes, Smollett admired its soft atmosphere, its abundant and excellent food, and its romantic flowers and scenery. A sample of his enthusiasm appears in the following:

> When I stand upon the rampart, and look around me, I can scarce help thinking myself enchanted. The small extent of country which I see, is all cultivated like a garden. Indeed, the plain presents nothing but gardens, full of green trees, loaded with oranges, lemons, citrons, and bergamots, which make a delightful appearance. If you examine them more nearly, you will find plantations of green pease ready to gather; all sorts of sallading, and pot-herbs in perfection; and plats of roses, carnations, ranunculas, anemonies, and daffodils, blowing in full glory, with such beauty, vigour, and perfume, as no flower in England ever exhibited.[54]

It was natural that Smollett, with all his love for the classics, longed soon after his arrival at Nice to see the glorious antiquities of Italy. He agreed, too, with his "worthy friend Dr. A---"[55] (probably Dr. Armstrong) that a sea trip would benefit his health. Consequently he began to work hard at Italian early in 1764

---

[48] See *Letters*, p. 90.
[49] For the reference to this illness, see *Travels*, Letter XXIV. It was probably at this time that Smollett feared that he was "in the last stage of a Consumption," as he expressed it over a year later in writing to Dr. Moore. See *Letters*, p. 97.
[50] *Letters*, p. 94.   [51] *Travels*, Letter XXI.   [52] *Ibid.*
[53] While at Nice in 1937, I was informed by Mon. Cappatti of the Nice Public Library that the first periodical of Nice, called *Courrier de Nice*, appeared in 1771.
[54] *Travels*, Letter XIII.   [55] *Ibid.*, Letter XXV.

hoping to be able to speak it within six months.[56] Early in September, then, he set out in a gondola, "rowed by four men, and steered by the patron" and accompanied by Mrs. Smollett, Miss Curry, "Mr. R---- a native of Nice" and one servant.[57] The party reached Genoa after hardships in seacoast inns. As Smollett carried recommendations to a well-bred lady in Genoa, he and Mrs. Smollett were treated most hospitably and were entertained "at her conversazione, which was numerous."[58]

From Genoa, Smollett journeyed on to Pisa where he enjoyed meeting gentlemen of taste and learning. As he carried a letter of introduction to one of the professors at the University of Pisa,[59] it is almost certain that he met some of the faculty, whose society he is known to have enjoyed later, in 1769.[60] In Pisa he was much impressed by the palaces; the Campanile, or leaning tower; and the great cathedral. Florence was the next city on the itinerary of the Smolletts, and there the traveling party lodged in the central quarter near the four bridges at an English house conducted by an English widow named Mrs. Vannini. During his days in Florence Smollett seems to have been a tireless sightseer of painting and sculpture. He also witnessed in September what was presumably the great annual procession of the Compagnia della Misericordia.[61] Before the end of September 1764,[62] Smollett was in Rome observing its impressive glories with characteristic excitement. On the return trip from Rome to Nice (by land and sea through Florence, Pisa, Genoa, Porto Mauritio, and San Remo), the Smolletts, delayed by the loss of a coach-wheel, encountered some appalling traveling, climaxed by a four-mile walk in mud around the city wall of Florence the night on which they finally entered its gates. Smollett, "wrapped up in a very heavy greatcoat" supported his wife, "a delicate creature, who had scarce ever walked a mile in her life" and "who wept in silence, half dead

[56] *Letters*, p. 92.
[57] *Travels*, Letter xxv. The "Mr. R----" sometimes spelled Mr. "R----i" in the *Travels*, could not have been Renner, who was a native of Bremen.
[58] *Ibid.*, Letter xxvi. In his *Letters from Italy*, second edition, London, 1767, p. 232, Dr. Samuel Sharp wrote: "the *Italian Conversazioni* differ very little from our *London* routs, being composed of card parties, and lookers on."
[59] *Travels*, Letter xxv.
[60] See my article on Dr. John Armstrong in *PMLA*, LIX (1944), p. 1047.
[61] *Travels*, Letter xxvii.
[62] In his *Travels*, Letter xxxi, Smollett referred to the unusually cold weather in Rome on the last day of September.

with terror and fatigue."[63] Eventually they reached Nice about the middle of November 1764[64] with no subsequent illness as the result of their adventures.

In the rainy weather from mid-November to mid-January 1765, Smollett enjoyed such "good health and spirits,"[65] that on February 7, 1765, he sallied forth on muleback over snow-covered mountains with his servant Tolloush on a jaunt via Coni to Turin. As Smollett's account of this trip is limited to a few details in Letter XXXVIII of his *Travels*, all we know of his stay in Turin is that he made his headquarters at the Bona Fama at one corner of the great Square, La Piazza Castello.

Some two months later, Smollett packed up for his return to England. Having placed his heavy baggage on board a ship at Nice, he set out about April 25, 1765,[66] traveling by easy stages through Aix, Avignon, Orange, Fontainebleau, Paris, to Boulogne, where he arrived, presumably in June.[67] Writing to a friend from Boulogne, Smollett declared:

> I am at last in a situation to indulge my view with a sight of Britain, after an absence of two years; and indeed you cannot imagine what pleasure I feel while I survey the white cliffs of Dover at this distance. . . . I am attached to my country, because it is the land of liberty, cleanliness, and convenience: but I love it still more tenderly, as the scene of all my interesting connections, as the habitation of my friends, for whose conversation, correspondence, and esteem, I wish alone to live.

On July 15, 1765, Smollett wrote from London (in Brewers Street by Golden Square) to his friend Dr. Moore, in part as follows:

> I am returned to England after an absence of two years, during which I have been more than once at the Brink of the grave—after all I have brought back no more than the skeleton of what I was; but with proper care that skeleton may hang for some years together. I propose to pass

[63] *Travels*, Letter XXXIV.

[64] The date of arrival in Nice was before the rainy period, which, according to Smollett's "Register of the Weather," commenced on November 16 because Smollett wrote in Letter XXXV as follows: "Since my return to Nice, it has rained the best part of two months."

[65] *Travels*, Letter XXXV.

[66] This date is inferred from the fact that Smollett's entries on the weather at Nice ended April 24, 1765. It is an odd fact, however, that the "Register of the Weather" as printed was described as "Kept at Nice from November 1763 to March 1765."

[67] This time is assumed from the fact that Letter XLI of the *Travels* is dated June 13, 1765.

Portrait of Smollett by an unknown Italian artist. About 1770
(Courtesy of National Portrait Gallery, London)

In the name of God, amen —

I Tobias Smollett late of the Parish of Chelsea in
Middlesex Physician declare what follows, to be my last
Will & Testament

I give and bequeathe to Mrs Anne Renner (late Curry)
wife of Mr George Renner merckt in Leghorne the sum of
Two hundred Pounds Sterling, as a small Token of my
esteem & Gratitude for her Friendship & attention to me
shewn in the course of my long Illness: this money to be payed
within one year after my Decease, either out of those sums of
money due to me in Jamaica upon Bonds which are in the hands
of Robert Graham Esqr my attorney Substitute in that Island, or
failing these, from the Rents & Profits of my Estate —

I give & bequeathe to my dear Wife Anne Smollett (formerly Lassells)
all my Estate personal & real comprehending Houses, warehouses,
wharfs, offices, wherries, Lands, Plantations, Enclosures, wells,
watercourses &c in, and about the Town of Kingston in Jamaica
& elsewhere; as also Slaves, mortgages, Bonds, sums of money
Rents, arrearages, claims &c; & all my Possessions & Effects whatsoever
moveable & immoveable; & all this Estate, & these Effects &c I
give, bequeathe, make over & convey in the most full & ample
manner to the said Anne Smollett my sole Administratrix,
her Heirs, Executors & assigns: This being in fact no more than
restoring what she freely & generously gave to me without her it
-ation or Reserve.

I constitute and appoint Mr Allan Auld merckt, Mr Archibald
Hamilton Senr, Printer, both of the City of London, & Robert Graham
& Thomas Bontein Esqrs of the Island of Jamaica Executors of this
my last will & Testament, written with my own hand on the stampt
Paper of this Country (having no English stampt Paper by me) this
Twenty fourth day of August in the year of our Lord one Thousand
Seven hundred & Sixty nine —

Signed, Sealed & Delivered   Ts Smollett
in the Presence of us
Richard Edwards
John Burslar
John Cooke
        Septr 24. 1769   Sir John Dick Bart His

Smollett's Will

the winter at Bath, and if I find that climate intolerable, I shall once more go into Exile, and never think of returning.[68]

These lines indicate that Smollett had no longer any illusions about his health. As it turned out, he was to live on—for some three years more in England and for about the same time in Italy.

It must be assumed that Smollett stayed in Brewers Street bordering Golden Square during the summer of 1765. In *Humphry Clinker* (Letter of Jerry, London, May 24) young Melford reported that Bramble and his group lodged "in Golden square, at the house of one Mrs. Norton, a decent sort of woman, who takes great pains to make us all easy." This appears to be a pleasant compliment to his landlady. Mrs. Norton was presumably the wife or widow of John Norton, surgeon, and inventor of Maredant's Antiscorbutic Drops, who had built a fine house on the south side of Golden Square.[69] Brewers Street by Golden Square, located a little north of Piccadilly, was close to St. James's Place, where Smollett's generous friend, Dr. George Macaulay, lived.[70] In Brewers Street Hume lived when Smollett arrived, and John Hunter was located in Golden Square at that time. Dr. William Hunter resided in Jermyn Street, a short distance to the south, and John Home lodged in Chapel Court, a little to the north. Golden Square, neat and improved about 1760,[71] was an attractive place which Smollett must have enjoyed, and a center from which he could easily call upon a number of his good friends.

Some of Smollett's activities in the summer of 1765 were divulged in his letter to Dr. Moore written November 13, wherein he stated that he had written a few articles merely for amusement, but that he had no "concern" in the *Critical Review*. He also reported that he had prepared his *Travels* for the press,[72] and that they were being printed. It appears that he was also completing the

---

[68] *Letters*, p. 94.

[69] See *Notes and Queries*, Vol. 169 (September 1935), 209. In Catalogue 325 issued by Pickering and Chatto, London, in 1941, appeared the following item: Norton, (John): *An Account of Remarkable Cures performed by the Use of Maredant's Antiscorbutic Drops, prepared by John Norton, surgeon in Golden Square*. London. Printed in the year 1772. Mrs. Norton's Moredant [*sic*] Drops, were advertised widely in the London press in the 1760's. See Charles Welsh, *A Bookseller of the Last Century* (London and New York, 1885), p. 22.

[70] See Macaulay's obituary in the *London Chronicle* (September 16-18, 1766), p. 274.

[71] See *London and its Environs Described*, 6 vols. (London, 1761), III, 47.

[72] *Letters*, p. 96.

fifth and final volume of his *Continuation of the Complete History of England*, published in October 1765.[73]

About the first week in October 1765,[74] the Smolletts went to Bath, and took lodgings on the South Parade. They were announced in *Pope's Bath Chronicle*, October 17, 1765, as having arrived along with Dr. Macaulay and his literary wife, Catharine Macaulay, both of whom were ill at the time.[75] It is quite possible that the Smolletts and the Macaulays traveled to Bath together and that they all lived on the South Parade, in the fashionable quarter, not far from the Abbey Church and the Baths. Smollett seems to have remained at Bath until February 1766, when, according to the *Gazetteer and New Daily Advertiser* (February 12, 1766) he went to Hot Wells, i.e. Bristol. The statement in that paper ran as follows:

> Dr. Smollett, who is now somewhat recovered of his indisposition, is gone to the Hot Wells, to complete the restoration of his health.

From the same newspaper, under date of March 7, 1766, we discover that he returned to Bath, a desperately sick man:

> We hear Dr. Smollet, who is returned from the Hot Wells to Bath, is now so dangerously ill at the last mentioned place, that it is thought he cannot possibly recover.

But he rallied during the following weeks sufficiently to start for Scotland, though he was in very precarious health.[76] Information about Smollett at this period is extremely limited because there are only two surviving letters for the year 1765 and none for 1766. We can guess that he read some of the new books, such as Goldsmith's *History of England, Traveller, Essays*, and *Vicar of Wakefield*; Percy's *Reliques*; and Walpole's *Castle of Otranto*. He must also have followed the periodicals with especial interest, particularly the issues of the *Monthly Review*, the *Critical Review*, and the *British Magazine*. He was amused, rather than enraged, per-

[73] See my article, "The Publication of Smollett's *Complete History* . . . and *Continuation*," in *Transactions of the Bibliographical Society, The Library* (December 1935), pp. 306ff.

[74] Smollett wrote Moore, November 13, that he had been in Bath for five weeks.

[75] In the *Gazetteer and New Daily Advertiser* for September 22, 1766, it is stated that Mrs. Macaulay will "very shortly indulge her country with a third volume of her beneficial history," delayed because of a year's illness of hers and her husband's.

[76] For Smollett's report to Dr. Moore of his health in November 1765, see *Letters*, pp. 96-97.

haps, by Cuthbert Shaw's attack on him in *The Race*, an imitation of the *Dunciad*, with satirical portraits of the leading booksellers and of many writers, such as Wilkes, Johnson, Murphy, and Churchill. This poem, appearing early in 1765, contained the following lines:

> Next *Sm-ll-t* came. What author dare resist
> Historian, critic, bard, and novellist?
> "To reach thy temple, honour'd *Fame*," he cry'd,
> "Where, where's an avenue I have not try'd?
> "But since the glorious present of to-day
> "Is meant to grace alone the poet's lay,
> "My claim I wave to ev'ry art beside
> "And rest my plea upon the *Regicide*.
>
> . . . .
> . . . .
>
> "But if, to crown the labors of my muse
> "Thou, inauspicious, should'st the wreath refuse,
> "Whoe'er attempts it in this scribling Age,
> "Shall feel the *Monthly* spite of *Critic* rage;
> "Thus spurn'd, thus disappointed of my aim,
> "I'll stand a bugbear in the road to *Fame*;
> "Each future minion's infant hopes undo,
> "And blast the budding honors of his brow."
>
> He said—and grown with future vengeance big,
> Grimly he shook his scientific wig;
> Then sullen stalk'd away, as if he meant
> Hereafter to fulfill the dire intent:
> Scar'd at the menace authors fearful grew,
> Poor *Virtue* trembled, and e'en *Vice* looked *blue*.[77]

This attack is typical of many leveled at Smollett after he was no longer regularly connected with the *Critical Review*.

In the spring of 1766, Smollett, accompanied probably by his wife and by Miss Anne Curry, took the northern road to Scotland. Something can be inferred as to the date of his departure from news items in the *St. James's Chronicle* and in the *London Chronicle*. In the former was printed the following (April 26-29, 1766):

> Dr. Smollet, who for some time past has been thought in the greatest danger, is at present so well recovered, that he is preparing to set out for Harrowgate, from whence he proposes going to Scotland to reside.

[77] Printed, with Shaw's footnotes omitted, from my copy of *The Race. By Mercurius Spur, Esq. . . .* London, 1765. For the text of the second edition of *The Race*, in which Shaw made changes and considerable additions, see *The Poems of Cuthbert Shaw and Thomas Russell*, ed. Eric Partridge, London, Dulau and Company, Ltd., 1925.

The *London Chronicle* (May 10-13, 1766) ran the following notice:

> Newcastle May 10. Dr. Smollett, who for some time past has been dangerously ill, is so well recovered, that he is preparing to set out for Harrowgate, from whence he proposes to go to Scotland to reside.

It has usually been assumed that Smollett began the trip about the first of April,[78] but judging from these notices, it was nearer the first of May. The statement in the *London Chronicle* that he was proceeding from Newcastle to Harrowgate is hard to account for. That he stayed for a short time in Newcastle may be partly owing to the fact that it was Miss Curry's native city,[79] where her relatives, even though she may not have accompanied him, might have entertained him. In any event it is clear that Smollett was in Edinburgh in June 1766.[80]

Meantime, the well-known *Travels through France and Italy* were published in London about May 8, 1766, "handsomely printed," as the public were informed, for R. Baldwin in Paternoster Row, the two volumes selling for ten shillings bound.[81] Containing, as the title pages announced, observations on character, customs, religion, government, police, commerce, arts, and antiquities, the contents were such as would naturally appeal to a large group of British readers. It is safe to say that the sale of the work was considerably stimulated by the fact that leading newspapers printed large extracts as soon as it was published.[82] There were also extracts and favorable notices in representative periodicals.[83] The usually hostile *Monthly Review* in an article by Dr. John Berkenhout[84] printed generous samples and concluded with praise:

78 See Kahrl, *op. cit.*, p. 120.

79 In the document recording the marriage of George William Renner and Anne Curry, she is described as "nata Castri novi (Newcastle dicti) in Anglia." See Montgomery Carmichael, "Tobia Smollett A Livorno," in *Liburni civitas; rassegna di attività municipale*, anno ix, fasc. 2 ([Livorno], 1936), p. 118.

80 See Anderson's "Life" in his edition of Smollett's *Works*, Edinburgh, 1820, I, 87.

81 *London Chronicle*, May 6-8, 1766, p. 461.

82 There were at least six long extracts from the *Travels* printed in the *London Chronicle* from May 8 to May 22. Samples also appeared in the *Gazetteer and New Daily Advertiser* (May 15), *Pope's Bath Chronicle* (May 15), and in the *Caledonian Mercury* at Edinburgh (May 14 and later).

83 The *Gentleman's Magazine* from May to July 1766 printed extracts in some thirty columns and recommended the *Travels* as both entertaining and useful. See also the *Universal Magazine* XXXVIII (May 1766), 259-63; and *British Magazine*, VII (1766), 265ff.

84 See Benjamin C. Nangle, *op. cit.*, pp. 4, 200.

We cannot take leave of the Doctor without thanking him for the entertainment we have received in the perusal of his travels; which, as they are
the work of a man of genius and learning, cannot fail of being useful and
instructive, particularly to those who intend to make the same tour.[85]

In addition to such widespread publicity we should not overlook
the favorable notice in the *Critical Review*.[86] As a result of all this,
and of the intrinsic appeal of the contents of the *Travels* to the
provincial reader who enjoyed, among other matters, Smollett's
brilliant though sometimes unfair generalizations upon French and
Italian manners, the work was several times reprinted in London
and Dublin, and was translated into German in 1767.[87]

To French and Italian readers the *Travels* were for obvious
reasons offensive. Professor Joliat has very ably expounded the
caustic reception of the *Travels* in France and has pointed out both
the fairness and the injustice in Smollett's generalizations on the
French.[88] Among the angry criticisms of the French, that of Mme.
Riccoboni in a letter to Garrick from Paris, November 14, 1767,
is surely typical:

Smollet est un *charming author*! vil gredin, qui ne connoit pas mieux les
moeurs de son pays que ceux de la France, et dont tous les ouvrages sont
detestables: oui, detestables.[89]

After the *Travels* there was widespread dislike of Smollett among
the French. Philip Thicknesse, who was in Boulogne between 1766
and 1768, printed the following statement, which is probably
reliable:

I forgot to tell you, that as I passed through Boulogne, I saw the young
gentleman who so kindly received, and hospitably entertained, Mr. S-------
and his family. This young man, whose youth and good offices ought to
have saved him from the Doctor's ridicule, is now pointed out to every
English and *Bretesh* traveller, as an object of contempt, because he was
picked out as a subject of satire, for rendering every civility that lay in his
power to the Doctor in the best manner he was able.[90]

[85] *Monthly Review*, XXXIV (June 1766), 429.
[86] *Critical Review*, XXI (May 1766), 321-29; (June 1766), 401-6.
[87] See Professor Luella Norwood's bibliography in the *Cambridge Bibliography of
English Literature*.
[88] See Eugène Joliat, *Smollett Et La France* (Paris, 1935), pp. 118ff., 128ff., 147ff.
[89] Cited from *The Private Correspondence of David Garrick*, 2 vols. (London,
1831-1832), II, 524.
[90] Philip Thicknesse, *Useful Hints to Those Who Make the Tour of France*
(London, 1768), p. 17.

Thicknesse referred to Smollett's handsome and obliging young landlord, Mon. B - - - -, who entertained the Smolletts at a banquet. Smollett, it is true, exposed Mon. B----'s vanity over his gallantries with women,[91] and described his uncle as "a facetious little man, who had served in the English navy, and was as big and as round as a hogshead."[92] This was not malicious satire; neither was it in perfect taste. It all shows, incidentally, that the French in Boulogne read or heard of the *Travels* though it was not translated into their language.

[91] See *Travels*, Letter II.
[92] See *Travels*, Letter V.

CHAPTER XIII
Final Years in England and Scotland, 1766-1768

EARLY in May 1766, Smollett, Mrs. Smollett, and probably Miss Anne Curry were on the northern road to Scotland. It is difficult to say how he obtained funds for this trip. His expenses in France and Italy had been unquestionably heavy—Thicknesse may not have been exaggerating when he estimated them to have totaled £2000[1]—and his literary earnings after his return to England cannot have been considerable. Neither did he ever have a pension from the government, though a rumor to that effect was publicized at various times.[2] His income, however, was considerably augmented by the estate bequeathed to Mrs. Smollett by her mother, Mrs. Leaver, who had died in Chelsea in 1762.[3] It was to this inheritance that Smeaton perhaps referred in his statement that Mrs. Smollett received about 1763 "a small legacy of £1200" from one of her relatives.[4] In general, it is reasonably certain that Smollett, thanks to the generosity of Anne Smollett, did not have to worry too much about traveling expenses after 1763.

[1] See Philip Thicknesse, *Useful Hints to Those Who Make the Tour of France* (London, 1768), pp. 30-31.

[2] When Shebbeare's supporters petitioned successfully for his pension about 1763, they included Smollett's name on a list of those who had already obtained one. (See John Forster, *The Life and Times of Oliver Goldsmith*, 2 vols., London, 1871, II, 388.) Again in 1763, Churchill in *The Author* wrote, "And what makes Smollett write, makes Johnson dumb," thus branding Smollett as a pensioner. Later, in the *Public Advertiser* (May 6, 1766), there appeared an anonymous communication, signed by "Project Prateapace," alluding falsely to Smollett's pension of £300 a year.

[3] Mrs. Elizabeth Leaver by the terms of her will, written July 25, 1753, and approved January 19, 1763, bequeathed small sums to her son, Edward Lassells, to her granddaughter, Frances Lassells, and £200 to Elizabeth Smollett "at her Age of twenty-one years," the interest thereof to be "applied towards her Maintenance and Education." Practically all of the residue of her estate she left to her daughter, Anne Smollett.

[4] See Oliphant Smeaton, *Tobias Smollett* (Edinburgh and London [1897]), p. 112. I suspect that some of Smeaton's vague and undocumented statements were based on unpublished letters to which he had access.

Having traveled via Harrowgate and Newcastle, as reported in the newspapers, Smollett arrived in Edinburgh about the first of June 1766,[5] and visited his mother, then living with his widowed sister, Mrs. Jane Telfer, whose town residence was in the Canongate, at the head of St. John Street. Their abode was described in 1825 by Robert Chambers as "the second flat [floor] of the tenement, facing the Canongate, entering by a common stair, behind, immediately within, and on the west side of the pend."[6] On high ground between St. Giles' Church and Canongate Church, Smollett's relatively new rooms[7] must have commanded a fine view of the country surrounding old Edinburgh, and he was close to spots formerly frequented by Allan Ramsay and by John Gay. It would have been an extremely happy reunion for Smollett had he enjoyed normal health, but he was very miserable. "A person who recollects of seeing him there," recorded Chambers, "describes him as dressed in black clothes, tall, and extremely handsome, but quite unlike the portraits foisted upon the public at the fronts of his works, all of which are disclaimed by his relations. . . . He was very peevish, on account of the ill health to which he had been so long a martyr, and used to complain much of a severe ulcerous disorder in his arm."[8]

It is impossible to determine the details of Smollett's activities in Edinburgh during his brief visit there in June 1766, or, for that matter, to be sure of how he passed his time in Glasgow, where he arrived about the end of that month. Dr. Moore was tantalizingly vague:

> [Smollett] having passed some time with his mother at Edinburgh . . . proceeded with his sister Mrs. Telfer, and his nephew a young officer in the army,[9] to Glasgow, from whence, after they had made a short stay,

[5] See Moore's "Life," p. clxxiv, and Anderson's "Life" in *Works*, 1820, I, 87. The *London Chronicle* (May 10-13, 1766) reported that Smollett was in Newcastle, "much improved" in health, and that he was going on to Harrowgate and Scotland.

[6] See Robert Chambers, *Traditions of Edinburgh*, 2 vols. (Edinburgh, 1825), I, 42-43 and 270-71. For a picture of this building, see Daniel Wilson, *Memorials of Edinburgh in the Olden Time* (Edinburgh, 1872), opposite p. 288.

[7] *Ibid.*, p. ii of "Corrections and Additions" printed at the end of Vol. I.

[8] *Ibid.*, I, 272. Most of the data in this passage Chambers received from Charles Kirkpatrick Sharpe, whose aunt apparently remembered Smollett at Bath, as well as at Edinburgh. See *The Letters of Sir Walter Scott and Charles Kirkpatrick Sharpe to Robert Chambers 1821-1845* (W. & R. Chambers, Limited [Edinburgh], 1904), p. 21.

[9] A younger son of Mrs. Telfer was a Major. See Chambers, *Traditions of Edinburgh*, I, 277.

I accompanied them to the residence of his cousin, Mr. Smollett of Bon-hill near Lochlomond.

I had never before seen Smollett but in the bloom of health, of a vigorous make, an elegant form, and agreeable countenance; and was much affected at the dismal alteration which had now taken place in his face and person. . . .

During the time of his stay in Scotland he was greatly tormented with rheumatic pains, and he was seized besides with an ulcer in his arm, which had been neglected on its first appearance, and afterwards resisted every attempt to heal it. These disorders confined him much to his chamber, but did not prevent his conversation being highly entertaining when he joined society.[10]

Smollett, then, despite his sufferings, still shone in society, but in what society? That Smollett's conversation was highly entertaining, however, suggests that he did have some enjoyment in Scotland and means that he was surely exaggerating when, looking back on this last visit the following February, he wrote Moore as follows:

I must own that I now find myself better in Health and Spirits than I have been at any time these seven years. Had I been as well in Summer, I should have exquisitely enjoyed my Expedition to Scotland, which was productive to me of nothing but Misery and Disgust. Between Friends, I am now convinced that my Brain was in some measure affected, for I had a kind of *Coma Vigil*[11] upon me from April to November without Intermission. In consideration of these circumstances, I know you will forgive all my Peevishness and Discontent; and tell good Mrs. Moore, to whom I present my most cordial Respects, that with regard to me she has as yet seen nothing but the wrong side of the Tapestry.[12]

[10] Moore's "Life," p. clxxiv.

[11] In the text as printed by Professor Noyes, the word, *Vigil*, is omitted. (See Moore's "Life," p. clxxviii.) The medical term, *coma vigil*, is defined by Webster as a "morbid condition occurring in certain diseases affecting the nervous system in which the patient lies unconscious but with open eyes." It is a curious fact that this malady was attributed to Pope in a review of Spence's *Anecdotes* [*Quarterly Review*, XXIII (1820), 427] as follows: "At length, Pope partook of a calamity not uncommon in the family of genius, and fell into that state of exhaustion, which Smollett once experienced during half a year, of a *Coma Vigil*; an affection of the brain, where the principle of life is so reduced that all external objects appear to be passing in a dream; a sort of torpid, indistinct existence." For Pope's symptoms, see the Rev. Joseph Spence, *Anecdotes, Observations, and Characters, of Books and Men*, ed. Samuel Singer (London, 1858), pp. 241-42.

[12] *Letters*, p. 100. Smollett's effective metaphor, "the wrong side of the tapestry," was employed by John Henry Newman: "seafaring men . . . see the tapestry of human life, as it were on the wrong side, and it tells no story." See Newman's *The Idea of a University* (London and New York, 1893), p. 136.

What Smollett, with a touch of wry humor, termed his *coma vigil* could not have been continuous. It has always been assumed that there is much reliable autobiography in the fictitious letters in *Humphry Clinker*[13] written at Edinburgh by Melford, Winifred, and Bramble. At any rate it is possible that many of the Scottish worthies and social events commemorated in those letters were seen and experienced by Smollett during his visit despite his invalidism. On this assumption we may be confident that Smollett attended the Leith Races, and the Hunters' Ball; that he dined with Mr. and Mrs. Mitchelson,[14] and saw Robert Cullen;[15] and that he rode out to Musselburgh for a glimpse of Mr. Cardonnel,[16] whom he had seen in 1753, and his old friend, Alexander Carlyle. And like his Bramble, Smollett very probably consulted the amiable and eminent Dr. John Gregory, who had recently settled in Edinburgh.[17] In addition to such well-known Edinburgh figures, there were in Edinburgh, that "hot-bed of genius," as Bramble called it, the two Humes,[18] Robertson, Smith, Wallace,[19] Blair,[20] Ferguson,[21] and Wilkie,[22] to cite Bramble's list. We can only guess as to how many of these literary luminaries Smollett enjoyed.

In June 1766, Smollett, accompanied by his sister and his nephew, Major Telfer, moved on to Glasgow to gaze for the last time on the scenes of his youth, education, and early friendships. There he stayed, presumably with Dr. John Moore, who had been in the 1730's his fellow medical apprentice with Dr. John Gordon. A local antiquarian, Mr. David Murray, assumes that

[13] See letters of Melford, Bramble, and Winifred written at Edinburgh, July 18, and those of Melford and Bramble dated August 8.

[14] Mr. Samuel Mitchelson, Writer to the Signet, who lived at Carrubbers Close, High Street. See Chambers' *Smollett*, 1867, p. 138 n.

[15] For Robert Cullen, afterwards Lord Cullen, see Henry Cockburn, *Memorials of his Own Time* (Edinburgh, 1856), p. 144. He was an extraordinary mimic.

[16] Commissioner Cardonnel. See Chambers' *Smollett*, p. 134n.

[17] See Dr. Alexander Carlyle's *Autobiography*, ed. John Hill Burton (London and Edinburgh, 1910), *passim*, and the article on Gregory in *DNB*.

[18] John Home, and David Hume.

[19] Robert Wallace, D.D. (1697-1771), author of *Characteristics of the Present Political State of Great Britain*, 1758, a book which Smollett probably reviewed in the *Critical Review*, v (April 1758), 283ff. For memoirs of Wallace, see Robert Chambers, *Biographical Dictionary of Eminent Scotsmen*, 4 vols. (Glasgow, 1835), IV, 391ff.

[20] Hugh Blair, D.D. (1718-1800).

[21] Adam Ferguson, LL.D., Professor of Moral Philosophy at the University of Edinburgh.

[22] William Wilkie (1721-1772), author of *The Epigoniad*.

Smollett "travelled to Glasgow by the recently established express, the 'Edinburgh Fly' which set out from John Paxton's at the White Hart in the Grass-market every morning at six o'clock and arrived at the Black Bull, Glasgow, between one and two o'clock, for dinner."[23] It may be, however, that Smollett, like Bramble, journeyed to Glasgow via Stirling and spent the night there. Arrived at Glasgow, Smollett made his chief headquarters at Moore's home on the north side of the Trongate, a little east of Nelson Street[24] until sometime in August.[25]

Smollett's activities around and within Glasgow can only be inferred. In the letters in *Humphry Clinker* written at Glasgow (or dealing with Glasgow) by Melford, Bramble, Lydia, and Winifred[26] there are descriptions of short trips to Hamilton, Paisley, and Renfrew, as well as the longer expedition to Loch Lomond and a trip thence to Inverary, and to the islands of Isla, Jura, Mull, and Icolmkill. Whether or not Smollett visited all these places is not absolutely certain, but remembering his love of traveling, and remembering, too, his realization in 1766 that his years were numbered, we may assume that he covered most of the itinerary above outlined. The only trip mentioned by Moore was that on which the latter accompanied Smollett to visit his cousin, James Smollett, the Commissary, at Cameron House, in the parish of Bonhill, and delightfully situated on the shores of Loch Lomond. The days passed in this Scottish Arcadia inspired Smollett's "Ode to Leven-Water," first published in *Humphry Clinker*. At Glasgow, Smollett may have been "complimented with the freedom of the town," an honor bestowed upon his Bramble. The latter met the distinguished Andrew Cochrane,[27] Provost of Glasgow; Mr. John Glassford,[28] the merchant-prince of the city; and Dr. John Gordon,[29] Smollett's former master. The chances are ten to one that

[23] See David Murray, *Early Burgh Organization in Scotland* (Glasgow, 1924) I, 458, n.1.

[24] *Ibid.*   [25] *Letters*, p. 99.

[26] See *Humphry Clinker*, Letters of Bramble, Cameron, August 28 and September 6; Letter of Melford, Argyllshire, September 3; Letter of Lydia, Glasgow, September 7; and Letter of Winifred, Grasco, September 7.

[27] For an account of Andrew Cochrane, see Moore's "Life," p. clxxxiii and Chambers' *Smollett*, p. 150 n.

[28] For John Glassford, see Chambers' *Life*, p. 151n. and John Rae, *Life of Adam Smith* (London, 1895), p. 90.

[29] In *Humphry Clinker* (Letter of Bramble from Cameron, August 28) Smollett called Gordon "a patriot of a truly Roman spirit." Moore ("Life," clxxxiii), stated

these leading citizens enjoyed conversing with Smollett and his host, Moore, in 1766. Then there was a small group to whom Smollett sent greetings some six months later in his letter to Moore, February 8, 1767: Moore's brother-in-law, Mr. Simpson,[30] the banker; Dr. Stevenson and Dr. Douglas;[31] and "honest Robin Urie," the printer, who had engaged in his craft while Smollett was a student at the University. There were doubtless many others. In addition to the pleasure of such social connections, Smollett, lured by his old love of the theater, could have seen *Hamlet*, and other plays presented while he was in Glasgow.[32]

Smollett left Moore's home in August 1766, and returned to Bath, probably following the route of his travelers in *Humphry Clinker* through Lanark, where he would have paid his respects to Mrs. Smellie,[33] and on south through Dumfries and Carlyle. By November his ulcer had spread over a part of his right hand so that he could not use it. Afflicted with pain and fever, he despaired of seeing the end of the winter and wished every night that he might die before morning. In this miserable condition he consulted the eminent surgeons, Drs. Middleton[34] and Sharp[35] at Bath, who approved of his own proposed course of treatment.[36] To his great astonishment he improved rapidly. His cure, he wrote Moore, was "looked upon as something supernatural," and by February 8, 1767, he felt better than he had for seven years.[37] This happy condition, however, did not persist, for in a letter

---

that Smollett, uneasy because Gordon had been identified with the character of Potion in *Roderick Random*, wished to do him full justice.

[30] See *Letters*, p. 219.

[31] *Ibid.*, pp. 219-20.

[32] See David Murray, *op. cit.*, p. 456n. Murray, in what seems to be an incomplete list of performances in Glasgow in June and July 1766, lists Farquhar's *Recruiting Officer*, a play which Smollett's nephew, Major Telfer, would have appreciated. Possibly Smollett saw in Glasgow the *Beaux Stratagem*, of which Melford planned an amateur performance in *Humphry Clinker*, Letter of Melford, October 14.

[33] See John Glaister, *Dr. William Smellie and his Contemporaries* (Glasgow, 1894), p. 116.

[34] According to Horace Walpole, Dr. Middleton was a Scottish physician who attended Lord Bute. See *Letters of Horace Walpole*, 16 vols., ed. Mrs. Paget Toynbee (Oxford, 1904), IV, 402, and V, 420.

[35] Dr. Samuel Sharp, who had just returned from Italy and published his *Letters from Italy*, London, 1766.

[36] Smollett dressed his ulcer with double mercurial ointment made without turpentine, took a dose of Van Sweeten's solution of corrosive sublimate every morning, and drank a quart of strong decoction sarsae every day. See *Letters*, pp. 99-100.

[37] *Letters*, p. 100.

written to Dr. William Hunter about two weeks later, he declared with a degree of dramatic exaggeration:

> I am almost stupified with ill Health, Loss of memory, Confinement & solitude; & I believe in my Conscience, the Circulation would have stopped of itself, if it was not every now & then stimulated by the stings of my Grub street Friends, who attack me in the public Papers.[38] Sometimes I am baited as a Dunce, then a ministerial Hireling, then a Liar, Quack & assassin—a Dunce I partly believe myself to be; but as to the other Epithets, I humbly concieve they are missapplied.[39]

That Smollett could joke about, rather than denounce, attacks on him in the press about 1767 shows the growth of his final and mellower mood so memorably manifested in *Humphry Clinker*. For Smollett the years 1767 and 1768 were necessarily transitional and crucial, and it is unfortunate that we have so few guiding facts for this period.

Such data as there are for Smollett's last two years in England will now be briefly presented. He lived after his return from Scotland until May 1768 or later, at Bath, on Gay Street.[40] In February 1767, he had the satisfaction of knowing that his *Travels* was reprinted.[41] This pleasure, however, was heavily counterbalanced by the rejection of his third application for a consulship abroad.[42] At an uncertain time he had approached the Earl of Shelburne, perhaps directly, but certainly indirectly through the Duchess of Hamilton and David Hume. The former appears to have written Shelburne twice,[43] and Hume had a personal conversation with him. Hume's reply to Smollett dated at London, July 18, 1767, stated only that both the consulships of Nice and Leghorn were pre-engaged.[44] But had there been no earlier applications for these

[38] For a list of typical attacks on Smollett in the *London Chronicle* for 1766, see *Letters*, p. 221.

[39] *Ibid.*, p. 102.

[40] Bramble in *Humphry Clinker* left his first-floor apartment on the South Parade, which he found excessively noisy, for a small house in Milsham Street, close to and parallel to Gay Street. (See Letter of Bramble, Bath, April 23.) Smollett may have left the South Parade, his residence in 1765, for a similar reason.

[41] See *London Chronicle*, February 19-21, 1767, p. 181.

[42] He had applied for the consulship at Madrid in Pitt's administration, 1758-1760, but was offered that of Nice, which he refused. In 1762 in Bute's administration he made a bid for the same office at Marseilles or at Madrid, with no success. See *Letters*, pp. 78-79.

[43] For Shelburne's belated reply to the Duchess of Hamilton, see Anderson's "Life" in his edition of Smollett's *Works*, 1820, I, 183-84.

[44] See *Letters of David Hume*, ed. J. Y. T. Greig (Oxford, 1932), II, 151-52.

posts, Smollett would never have received Shelburne's recommendation, as is evident in Hume's letter to John Crawford ("Fish" Crawford) written [July 20, 1767], which ran in part as follows:

My Dear Crawford

You have certainly mistaken the whole affair of Dr Smollet. Before I receiv'd Yours, I had spoke to Lord Shelburne at Smollet's Desire. His Lordship told me, not that the Person to whom he had promis'd the Consulship of Nice had got Intelligence of the new Engagement to Smollet, and was very unreasonable in his Demands of Satisfaction (which you imagine) but that his Lordship had long ago promised that Office to the Recommendation of the Spanish Ambassador and could not now depart from his Engagement. Besides, said he, how could I send Smollet to Nice? The people would rise upon him and stone him in the Streets on his first Appearance. I then mentioned the consulship of Leghorn. He said it was promised to a Friend or Relation of Dunning, the Lawyer. Besides, said he, how can I take on me the Patronage of a Person, so notorious for libelling as Dr. Smollet? I should disoblige every one whom he has abus'd. In short, I do not see any great hopes of Success from that Quarter.[45]

Shelburne's opposition to Smollett on political grounds the latter may have suspected, but Hume with characteristic kindness withheld it from him. Did Shelburne exaggerate in calling Smollett a notorious libeler? Not so much, probably, at least in the opinion of Admiral Knowles, in the judgment of many persons satirized in the novels and in the *Critical Review*, and in the estimation of certain influential Frenchmen offended by the *Travels*. Smollett's feelings over his failure to receive a diplomatic appointment in 1767 remain hidden. Any bitterness he harbored is thought to have expressed itself in the satire of the *Atom*, directed not against Shelburne, whose political independence he may have admired, but against a whole pack of other politicians from the 1750's onward.

In February 1768, in Smollett's last winter in England, appeared Sterne's *Sentimental Journey*, in which Smollett was scolded under the name of Smelfungus. In March there came off the press *Useful Hints to those who make the Tour of France* by Philip Thicknesse, who, convinced that Smollett had libeled in the *Critical* his earlier work, *Observations on the Customs and*

[45] Printed from the original manuscript in the Victoria and Albert Museum, London, MSS 275.

Manners of the French Nation (1766),[46] went out of his way to heap insults on him and on his *Travels*. In a score of bitter allusions, violently anti-Scottish and personal, Thicknesse assailed Smollett, calling him Toby, the martinet in literature, casting suspicion on the accuracy of his *Travels* (except his observations on Catholicism, which he admitted as just), and suggesting that the work be called "Quarrels through France and Italy for the cure of a pulmonic disorder, by T.S.M.D." Thicknesse, who may have heard rumors of Smollett's efforts to secure a consulship, recommended that he be made a governor in North America.[47]

To these jibes Smollett made no reply. Yet he was not idle in the spring of 1768. Dr. Sharp, at Bath, April 1, 1768, writing about his controversy with Baretti, penned the following to David Garrick: "Dr. Smollett is too ill, and too much engaged, to revise your pamphlet; and besides, he would have answered him himself, had Baretti been worthy of his pen."[48] Despite illness, Smollett's engagements may have taken him occasionally for a brief visit to London because Boswell assumed that he could meet him there in March 1768, and perhaps did so.[49] A further hint that Smollett was in London at intervals is found in his letter written at Bath, May 18, 1768, to Robert Salusbury Cotton of Crown Court, Westminster, which ran in part as follows:

[46] Thicknesse was notoriously given to sniffing personal injuries from afar. See *DNB*.

[47] "If I had any interest with the present l---ds of t--e, I would recommend Dr. S--- to one of the American governments. He is a very good hand at scolding, and it is a good air for pulmonic complaints. . . . it is possible he might favour the world with a natural history of the great continent of America. Methinks I should rejoice to see advertised 'A complete Natural History of America, by his excellency Toby S---, M.D.' or the puff in the Critical Review, with an extract from Governor S---'s observations on the customs and manners of the *Creek* and *Chickasau* Indians." From *Useful Hints* (London, 1768), p. 122.

[48] Cited from *The Private Correspondence of David Garrick*, 2 vols. (London, 1831-1832), I, 297.

[49] See Boswell's letter to Smollett written at Edinburgh, March 14, 1768, and first published from the original manuscript (now apparently missing) in the *Port Folio*, Philadelphia, 1801. This letter was reprinted by Anderson in his *Life of Tobias Smollett* (Edinburgh, 1806), p. 191, and again, with an error in its date, in the first volume of Smollett's *Works*, Edinburgh, 1820, p. 186. Boswell, disturbed because Mr. Douglas of Douglas had told him that Smollett had taken amiss a correction in the *Account of Corsica*, 1768, of an error relating to Paoli (in Smollett's *Continuation of the History of England*), assured Smollett that he intended no offense and asked for an interview.

Dear Sir

I have a very gratefull sense of your Kindness to Miss Curry when she was lately in London; & think myself much obliged to you and good Mrs. Cotton for all your expressions of Friendship and Regard. I shall never forget the chearfull Hours I have passed in your Company; & I regret very much my being at Such a Distance as not only interrupts our Society but prevents me from offering my advice, such as it is, to Mrs. Cotton, in the state of whose Health I take a Sincere Concern. . . . Pray, remember me to our friend Halford who I hear is still in a single state. if I had a little Health and spirits I would write a Ballad upon him intituled *the old Batchelor's Ditty*. If he will clap a Bagwig & a bit of Lace & come down to Bath, it shall go hard but I will buckle him for Life.[50]

In the spring of 1768 Smollett was engaged to some extent in completing and preparing for publication *The Present State of All Nations*, upon which he had been laboring at uncertain times since about 1760.[51] From advertisements of this work in the press[52] it is evident that it was originally published in weekly six-penny numbers, the first of which was issued about June 25, 1768. In the press notices and on the title pages of the bound volumes of this work in eight volumes, Smollett's name alone appears, though there is evidence that parts of it may have been the work of other hands.[53] The "Plan" of the work, however, prefixed to the first volume, and pointing out the merits of its precise organization, is in Smollett's own style. Another work long attributed to Smollett is *The History and Adventures of an Atom*, which, as it was published in 1769 after he had left England, we shall consider in more detail later. This opus was perhaps submitted for printing in the summer of 1768. To the matters of the composition of the "Ode to Independence" and of *Humphry Clinker* we shall turn later.

On August 31, 1768, Smollett, then in London, dispatched his last known letter to David Hume by a trustworthy bearer, Captain Robert Stobo of the Fifteenth Regiment of Foot,[54] then returning

[50] For the complete text of this letter, see my article, "More Smollett Letters," in *MLN*, XLVIII (1933), 248ff.

[51] See Louis L. Martz, *The Later Career of Tobias Smollett* (Yale University Press, 1942), pp. 104ff.

[52] See the *London Chronicle* (May 14-17, 1768), p. 479 and the *Public Advertiser* for May 17, 1768, and for June 13, 1768. See also the *London Chronicle* (June 11-14) and subsequent issues.

[53] See Martz, *op. cit.*, p. 106.

[54] See George M. Kahrl's pamphlet, "Captain Robert Stobo," Richmond, Va., 1941 (Reprinted from *Virginia Magazine of History and Biography*, Vol. XLIX, Nos. 2 and 3), p. 262.

to his regiment stationed, it seems, at Cirencester, Gloucestershire,[55] where Hume was at that time. In his letter, Smollett highly recommended the Captain, whom he had perhaps first met in London in July or August 1768, and something of whose character and career (as Professor Kahrl has shown) he utilized in creating Lismahago in *Humphry Clinker*.[56] The latter part of Smollett's letter ran as follows:

> With respect to myself, I am sorry that I cannot have the pleasure of taking leave of you in person, before I go into perpetual exile. I sincerely wish you all health and happiness. In whatever part of the earth it may be my fate to reside, I shall always remember with pleasure and recapitulate with pride, the friendly intercourse I have maintained with one of the best of men, and undoubtedly the best writer of the age;[57] if any judgment in distinguishing either character or capacity may be allowed to, dear sir, your very humble servant,
>
> T. Smollett
>
> Nos patriam fugimus: tu, Tityre, lentus in umbra
> Formosam resonare doces Amaryllida silvas.[58]

To this farewell tribute, which reached Hume as he was about to leave Cirencester, Hume replied at Ragley Hall,[59] September 21, assuring Smollett that he had enjoyed meeting Capt. Stobo, lamenting that Smollett must go into perpetual exile, and concluding as follows:

> I am sensible of your great partiality, in the good opinion you express towards me; but it gives me no less pleasure than if it were founded on the greatest truth; for I accept it as a pledge of your good will and friendship. I wish an opportunity of showing my sense of it may present itself during your absence. I assure you I should embrace it with great alacrity; and you need have no scruple, on every occasion, of having recourse to

---

[55] *Ibid.*, p. 263, n.57.

[56] See George M. Kahrl, *Tobias Smollett, Traveler-Novelist* (University of Chicago Press [1945]), pp. 132ff. On Stobo as a source for Lismahago, see also Louis L. Martz, *The Later Career of Tobias Smollett*, pp. 175ff.

[57] This praise outdoes Smollett's tribute in the *Continuation of the Complete History of England*, IV (1761), 127: "The field of history and biography was cultivated by many writers of ability, among whom we distinguish . . . above all the ingenious, penetrating, and comprehensive Hume, whom we rank among the first writers of the age, both as an historian and philosopher."

[58] *Letters*, pp. 103-4. The Latin verses are from Virgil's first Eclogue, ll. 4-5.

[59] Hume in his letter-heading wrote merely *Ragley*, an abbreviation of Ragley Hall, near Alcester, Warwickshire, the family seat of the Conways. The fact that Hume was at this time Undersecretary to Henry Seymour Conway, brother to the Marquis of Hertford, explains his visit to this country estate.

me. I am, my dear Sir, with great esteem and sincerity, your most obedient and humble servant,

David Hume[60]

These letters are the final and pleasant evidence of the durable friendship between Smollett and Hume.[61]

Of other farewell letters or visits of Smollett and his family no documented record remains. Certain activities, however, can be taken for granted. Smollett may have paid his final respects to the staff of the *Critical Review*, though he had had no proprietary interest in that periodical, as far as is known, since 1763. All the same, he may well have contributed an occasional article from 1763 to 1768, and surely he had followed its pages with interest. If there were no changes in the staff of the *Critical* from 1768 to 1770, then its reviewers in 1768 may have been those satirized in a pamphlet published in London in 1770 by T. Underwood, entitled *A Word to the Wise. A Poetical Farce, most respectfully addressed to the Critical Reviewers with An Apology to the Ingenuity of Mr. Hugh Kelly, for the Title of the Piece.*[62] In this tract, Underwood presents his "Dramatis Personae" as consisting of "General" Hamilton, "Captain" Guthrie, "Lieutenant" Robertson, and "Ensign" Thompson, plus Vulgo, a publisher, and Mungo, the General's *Devil*. According to Underwood, then, the staff of the *Critical* appears to have included Archibald Hamilton, William Guthrie,[63] the Rev. Joseph Robertson,[64] and Edward Thompson.[65] In *A Word to the Wise* there is no reference to Smol-

[60] See *Letters of David Hume*, ed. J. Y. T. Greig, 2 vols. (Oxford, Clarendon Press, 1932), II, 186.

[61] Hume, doubtless considering himself a greater historian than Smollett, was not unaware that the great popularity of the latter's *History* reduced the sale of his own. See Hume's *Letters*, ed. J. Y. T. Greig, 2 vols. (Oxford, Clarendon Press, 1932), I, 272, 302, and 359. But Hume continued to be cordial and helpful to Smollett.

[62] On the title page of this pamphlet, a copy of which is in the Bodleian Library, Underwood appears as "Late of St. Peter's College, Cambridge; Author of the Impartialist, Liberty &c &c." *The Impartialist* is a pro-Churchill tract, lashing in general terms both the *Critical* and the *Monthly*.

[63] William Guthrie, whose death was referred to in Underwood's *Word to the Wise*, died March 9, 1770. For his obituary see *Scots Magazine*, XXXII (1770), 167. Interesting details of his literary career are given by the Rev. Daniel Lysons in *The Environs of London*, Vol. 3 (1795), p. 265. Lysons stated that Guthrie "compiled some parts of the Universal History, and for several years carried on the *Critical Review*, with little or no assistance."

[64] According to the *DNB*, the Rev. Joseph Robertson contributed more than 2,600 articles to the *Critical Review* from 1764 to 1785.

[65] Captain Edward Thompson was a minor poet and the author of *Sailor's Letters*

lett and not much light is thrown on the status of the *Critical*,[66] but it may be assumed that Smollett was acquainted with all or most of its staff from 1766 to 1768.

Before leaving England Smollett may well have visited a club in London which met, according to Dr. John Armstrong at the Q Arms and where, early in 1770 he reported in a letter to Smollett the following: "Our little club at the Q Arms never fail to devote a bumper to you, except when they are in the humour of drinking none but scoundrels."[67] This suggests that Smollett at some time or other had been a member of a club which in 1770 convened at the well-known Queen's Arms Tavern in St. Paul's Churchyard.[68]

How Smollett spent his final days in London, or possibly in Chelsea, is at present quite beyond our ken. It was with a frequent sense of tragedy that he realized at the age of forty-seven that the years ahead of him were to be very few and filled with discomfort, and to be spent far from friends and enemies alike. Perhaps he pondered over the recent death of Sterne and had fleeting thoughts of Fielding's final voyage, of Richardson's former friendship, of Quin and Derrick both deceased, of Grainger gone with the ghost of Tibullus, and of Churchill now interred at Dover. Surely he was often dominated by the old stoical mood which he had voiced in 1761 in a letter to Garrick:

> I am old enough to have seen and observed that we are all playthings of fortune and that it depends upon something as insignificant as the tossing up of a half penny, whether a man rises to affluence and honours, or continues to his dying day struggling with the difficulties and disgraces of life. I desire to live quietly with all mankind, and, if possible, to be upon good terms with all those who have distinguished themselves by their merit.[69]

Written to his Select Friends in England, 2 vols., London, 1766. In 1769 he wrote a short poem called "Bon-Hill," containing a tribute to Smollett. This poem appeared in *The Muse's Mirrour* (London, 1778), I, 54-56. Thompson is said to have attacked Ralph Griffiths in a satirical poem called *The Demi-rep*, published in 1756.

[66] Underwood presented Pomposo Hamilton as lamenting the waning power of the *Critical*. Toward the end of the farce Thompson and Robertson went on a successful strike for an increase in wages.

[67] For Armstrong's complete letter, see Smollett's *Works*, ed. Anderson, 1820, I, 189-90. The date of this letter is from internal evidence 1770. The original manuscript is at the Ridgway Library, Philadelphia.

[68] In the passage quoted, Armstrong may possibly have written 2 *Arms*, but I think he intended Q Arms, and referred to the Queen's Arms Tavern. For an account of this tavern, see John Timbs, *Club Life of London*, 2 vols. (London, 1866), II, pp. 145-46.

[69] *Letters*, pp. 69-70.

But the old mood of fierce Swiftian indignation created by the spectacle of the many who without merit had grasped affluence and political honors could scarcely have been dormant within Smollett, especially when he may have remembered that unpublished manuscript about the adventures of an atom, which, filled with explosive energy and stench, he may have placed all neatly written on the desk of some London publisher. There was, however, still another mood, which, despite his illness, he could, fortunately for himself and lovers of literature, summon up for his psychological salvation—the mood of Shakespearean laughter over the comedy and farce of life. Such an attitude had already found vigorous expression, probably, in some manuscript packed with books to be taken abroad, a manuscript later to be completed as *The Expedition of Humphry Clinker*, a novel wherein he expressed the essence of much that he had experienced in his final years both in England and in Scotland.

CHAPTER XIV

Final Years in Italy; the *Atom* and *Humphry Clinker*, 1768-1771

SMOLLETT left England in the fall of 1768 as far as can be ascertained,[1] and traveled by an unknown route to Pisa, Italy. From that city he wrote to Dr. Armstrong, who, after considerable delay sent a reply from London, March 28, 1769, addressing him at Casa Lenzi, al Ponte grande.[2] From Armstrong's reply we learn that Smollett's letter had given the former and other mutual friends "much pleasure and entertainment." From subsequent paragraphs of Armstrong's letter the following extracts are illuminating:

> It is needless to say how much I rejoice in your Recovery—But I have all along had great Confidence in the vigorous Stamina with which Nature has blest you. I hope you may within a year or two, be able to weather out if not an English winter at least an English summer. Meantime, if you won't come to us, I'll come to you; and shall with the help of small punch and your Company laugh at the Tuscan dog days.
>
> I enjoy with pleasing Sympathy the agreeable Society you find amongst the Professors at Pisa. All countries and all Religions are the same to men of liberal minds. . . . Your Friends at Pisa envy our Constitution—I'm afraid we may in a short time be reduced to sigh after theirs. For the View at present all around us is an object of the most extreme Indignation Contempt and Horror.
>
> Meantime the infernal Spirit of the most absurd Discord, Erynnis blind and blundering in her Dotage, has not yet so universally poysond the *noble* mind of the publick as to engross it entirely to the clumsy dirty black-guard amusement and Exercises. For History still makes a Shift to waddle on, tho' it grows rather *a lame Duck*; And there are still jackdaws [to] swallow the green cheese of Tragedy, and the no less insipid Curd of your *new Comedy*. So much the better—all Trades would live, they say. . . .

[1] Seccombe's statement (in *DNB*) that he left in December 1769 is manifestly an error, and Smeaton's assertion (in his *Tobias Smollett*, p. 118) that he departed in December 1768 has no documentary support.

[2] Perhaps the Casa Lenzi was the same centrally located inn where Smollett lodged while in Pisa in 1764. See *Travels*, end of Letter XXVI, and beginning of Letter XXVII.

All the Friends you have mentioned are well, and desire to be kindly remembered to you. Your Health is never forgot in our Compotations. I am sorry to tell you that our Society has lost one worthy Member in Doctor Russel[3] who died some months ago of a malignant Fever. I beg you'll let me hear from you soon; and am, with my best Compliments to Mrs Smollett, at the same time never forgetting Miss [blank space] and Miss Currie

> My dear Sir
> Your ever affectionate Friend and
> faithful humble Servant
> John Armstrong[4]

In Armstrong's lines it is evident that Smollett, at the time he sent news from Pisa, felt that his health had improved, and that he was having some pleasant association with the faculty of the University, to one of whom he had taken a letter of introduction in 1764.[5]

A strange fact about this letter of Armstrong, written March 28, 1769, is its lack of any reference to *The History and Adventures of an Atom*, which had been advertised for several months and was published about April 1, 1769. It is odd that Armstrong did not seem to know that his friend wrote it. This violent and unpleasant political satire is attributed to Smollett chiefly on the grounds of internal evidence. Moreover, the publicity given to the *Atom* prior to its publication as well as the genesis of the tradition that Smollett wrote it, are both unusual enough to merit a brief survey. The record in the newspapers and periodicals is peculiar: in December 1768, the *Atom* was announced as forthcoming in a few days and as printed for J. Almon opposite Burlington House in Piccadilly.[6] The *Universal Magazine* for December entered it erroneously among the books appearing that month and specified Almon as its publisher.[7] In February, moreover, the *Atom* was advertised again as to appear in a few days, but now as printed for G. Kearsly, at No. 1 Ludgate Street.[8] Finally the work

---

[3] Perhaps Dr. Thomas Russel. See *Letters*, pp. 86 and 210.

[4] These extracts are printed from the original manuscript of Armstrong's letter, by the kind permission of the Pennsylvania Historical Society, Philadelphia. For a complete but not always accurate text of the letter, see *Works* of Smollett, ed. Anderson, 1820, I, 187-89.

[5] See *Travels*, Letter xxv.

[6] See *London Chronicle*, December 6-8, 1768, and the *Whitehall Evening Post* of the same date.

[7] See the *Universal Magazine*, XLIII (December 1768), 335.

[8] See *London Chronicle*, February 7-9, 1769.

was proclaimed as forthcoming on Saturday, April 1, 1769,[9] and this time as printed for Robinson and Roberts, Paternoster Row, and for these publishers it was released, apparently on the day scheduled. All this is rather extraordinary. It is possible that the first publisher mentioned above, John Almon, refused to be connected with the *Atom* because he feared that its contents would lead to his being sued for libel. Again it is possible that, as the warm friend of Wilkes, Almon refused it because he suspected that it was written by Smollett, whom Wilkes had, in 1763, violently attacked.[10] Why G. Kearsly, printer of the *North Briton*, was scheduled to publish it is as inexplicable as why Robertson and Roberts accepted it. But how could Armstrong (if he even suspected that Smollett wrote the *Atom*) fail to report to him something of this newspaper publicity?

Armstrong was not alone in remaining silent about the *Atom*. Not one of Smollett's correspondents, as far as we know, ever mentioned it, nor did Smollett or his wife ever refer to it in any surviving letters. How are these facts to be explained? We may assume that Smollett, like the mysterious "Junius," desired the absolute concealment of his authorship. This would be understandable had Smollett been in England when the book was published, for, even though his publisher might have agreed to be solely responsible in the event of legal action for libel, Smollett might still have feared subsequent punishment. But Smollett was in Italy and hence beyond the reach of the law. We may again assume that Smollett, like "Junius," was extraordinarily successful in maintaining absolute silence. But such a conspiracy of silence would have been especially difficult to achieve because the manuscript of the *Atom* seems to have passed through the hands of several publishers, with none of whom Smollett had had any known dealings and in none of whom is there any reason to suppose he could have trusted. Is it, indeed, possible that Smollett did not write the *Atom* at all? How was the public led to believe that he wrote it?

Perhaps the earliest attribution of the *Atom* to Smollett is found in the *London Chronicle* (April 8-11, 1769), p. 341, where extracts from the novel were introduced by the following statement:

[9] See *London Chronicle*, March 25-28, 1769, and April 1-4, 1769.
[10] See [J. Almon], *A Review of Lord Bute's Administration* (London, 1763), pp. 53-55.

This work, which is attributed to the Author of Roderick Random, is a satirical political history of the publick transactions, and of the characters and conduct of some great men in a certain kingdom, to which the Author has given the name of Japan, during the late and present reigns.

In the *Political Register, and Impartial Review* (IV, 1769, pp. 389-90), in a portion of its index, there is another account, written perhaps by its editor, John Almon, describing the *Atom* as

. . . a political, satirical and moral romance said to be written by Dr Smollet, but falls so far short of the graceful simplicity and lively entertaining humor of his other performances of the same kind, that we could not give credit to it did we not perceive a political transformation in the atom which points out the author to those that are in possession of the list of ministerial writers.

The foul, abusive, degrading character given of the late k--- . . . is mean, malevolent and unpardonable; but be it remembered that the supposed author was a prisoner in the king's bench during the late k---'s reign, which he will never forget; nor forgive the ministry at that period, whose characters are vilely mangled in this work, to gratify keen resentment.

No suggestion, however, that Smollett wrote the *Atom* appeared in notices of this work in the *Gentleman's Magazine*,[11] the *Monthly Review*[12] or the *Town and Country Magazine*,[13] in all of which the book was both praised and adversely criticized. In the *Critical*, however, there was nothing but praise, which concluded as follows:

We are unwilling to be more particular in our account of this truly original piece of humour, for reasons that may be easily guessed; but we must conclude, by saying as Shakespeare does of music, that the man who does not love and relish this performance, has no wit in his own composition.[14]

Here, the reviewer's unwillingness "to be more particular" may have arisen from fear of libel. His glowing praise, however, may be construed as partiality toward what he felt or knew to be Smollett's work.

From these reviews, and perhaps from other similar ones, arose the belief that Smollett wrote the *Atom*. Yet the author of the memoir of Smollett in the 1777 edition of his *Plays and Poems*

---

[11] *Gentleman's Magazine*, XXXIX (April 1769), 200-5.
[12] *The Monthly Review*, XL, 441-55. This review was probably written by John Hawkesworth. See Nangle, *op. cit.*, p. 125.
[13] *Town and Country Magazine* for May 1769, p. 269.
[14] Cited from the *Critical Review*, XXVII (May 1769), 369.

did not include it among the list of his works. In the edition of Smollett's *Works* published in 1790, however, the editor, though he did not print the *Atom*, asserted that Smollett wrote it.[15] His statement was the chief reason, we suspect, that caused Moore and Anderson to accept it as Smollett's, as have later biographers, editors, and readers.

The *Atom* does contain in its method and material much that is Smollettian. The satire is obviously what Smollett felt like writing at that time. Yet it should be remembered that we lack the external evidence necessary to prove conclusively that he wrote it.[16]

It is assumed that Smollett was still in Pisa to receive a letter sent there by one W. Kettilby,[17] who wrote from Marseilles, April 29, 1769. In his greeting, Kettilby, an invalid who had lived in Bath, expressed the hope that he would see Smollett in Pisa the following September; but by that time, as we shall see, he was elsewhere.

On June 5, 1769, Smollett, Mrs. Smollett, and Mary Vannini were witnesses at Florence of the wedding of George Renner and Anne Curry. Whether Smollett went to Florence expressly for this wedding or whether he was living there at the time is a question. The document recording the above wedding follows:

> Ego infrascriptus fidem facio me post imploratam Divini Numinis benedictionem, ritui Ecclesiarum Protestantium convenienter, sacro matrimonii vinculum junxisse virum egregium Dnum Georgium Gugliel-

---

[15] The editor stated it as follows: "The Doctor has satirized all his political enemies in the Adventures of an Atom—a work abounding with wit, and which was originally intended for this collection—but the satire is now so little understood (without which it could not possibly be relished) that the editor was advised to omit it.—It properly belongs to his political works." Cited from *The Works of Tobias Smollett*, 6 vols. (Edinburgh, 1790), I, vi, footnote 1.

[16] Smollett's authorship of the *Atom* might be proved conclusively if it could be demonstrated beyond any doubt that he annotated a copy of the *Atom* alleged to contain his marginalia, which once belonged to Jerome Kern, and which was sold in 1929. See *Catalogue 2311, The Library of Jerome Kern (Part Two), Sold January 21, 22, 23, 24, 1929*. The Anderson Galleries, New York, 1929, Item 1123. This copy of the *Atom* was, in 1946, in the possession of the Rosenbach Company, Philadelphia.

[17] The original manuscript of Kettilby's letter is at the Ridgway Library, Philadelphia (MSS Rush, Vol. 28, p. 51). It was addressed to "A Monsieur, Monsieur Smollett, Gentilhomme Anglais, a Pisa, En Tuscane, Italie." This manuscript, together with others, was sent by the Rev. Thomas Hall, Chaplain of the British Factory at Leghorn, to his kinsman Dr. Benjamin Rush of Philadelphia in 1795. This is clear from Hall's letters to Rush preserved in the Ridgway Library (MSS Rush, Vol. 34, pp. 1-35). Hall acquired some of the manuscripts in Smollett's trunk after the death of Mrs. Smollett in 1791.

mum Renner Bremensem, qui multis abhinc annis mercaturae exercendae causa Liburni in Etruria degit, cum praestantissima virgine Anna Curry nata Castri novi (Newcastle dicti) in Anglia, testibus adhibitis viro excellentissimo doctore Tobia Smollett, ejusdem uxore Anna nata Lasselo [*sic*], et denique Dna Vannini nata Boyd quorum nomina infra subjiciuntur.—Actum Florentiae in Etruria Non. Jun. N.S. MDCCLXIX, et ut publicum quoddam hujus rei documentum extaret, insertum quoque reperietur in registro ut vocant ecclesiastico coetus britannici qui degit Liburni.

In ulteriorem denique fidem manum sigillumque adpono.
(L.S.) Johannes Frederico Bryer
Verbi Divini Minister in Ducatu Wirtembergensi.
Testes: Ts. Smollett—Anna Smollett—Mary Vannini.[18]

Smollett's references in the *Travels* to Anne Curry will be recalled, and we shall hear more of her and of George Renner.

It is likely that Smollett experienced a sharp fluctuation in his illness in June or early July 1769, because a false report of his death reached England and was publicized on August 1, 1769 in the *London Chronicle*:

Some letters from Turin mention the death of Dr. Smollet, the ingenious Biographer and Historian, which happened at Massa Carrara the beginning of last Month.[19]

This error was rectified in the *London Chronicle* several days later as follows:

The report of the death of Dr. Smollet is groundless, the last post having brought letters from him, which mention that he is in better health than for years past.[20]

The dissemination of a similar false report in Europe accounts, no doubt, for the fact that we find it stated in W. C. S. Mylius' memoir of Smollett, written about 1785, that his death "erfolgte zu Massa Carara am lezten [letzen] Jun. 1769."[21]

On August 24, 1769, Smollett wrote his will in a hand that betrayed no trace of physical weakness, and in his usual succinct style:

[18] Quoted from Montgomery Carmichael, "Tobia Smollett A Livorno," in *Liburni civitas; rassegna di attività municipale*, anno IX, fasc. 2 ([Livorno], 1936), p. 118.
[19] See *London Chronicle*, July 29-August 1, 1769, p. 110.
[20] See *London Chronicle*, August 3-5, 1769, p. 122.
[21] See *Peregrine Pickle*, Neue Auflage, 4 vols. (Berlin, 1789), I, xxix. Mylius' "Vorbericht" is of unusual interest in revealing Smollett's popularity in Germany.

In the name of God, Amen—
I Tobias Smollett late of the Parish of Chelsea in Middlesex
Physician declare what follows, to be my last Will & Testament
I give and bequeathe to Mrs Anne Renner (late Curry) wife of M^r
George Renner merch^t in Leghorne, the sum of Two hundred Pounds
sterling, as a small Token of my Esteem & Gratitude for her Friendship
& attention to me shewn in the course of my long Illness: this money to
be payed within one year after my Decease, either out of those sums of
money due to me in Jamaica upon Bonds which are in the hands of Robert Graham Esqr my attorney substitute in that Island; or failing these,
from the Rents & Profits of my Estate—

I give and bequeathe to my dear Wife Anne Smollett (formerly Lassells)
all my Estate personal & real comprehending Houses, Warehouses,
Wharfs, offices, wherries, Lands, Plantations, Enclosures, wells, watercourses, &c in, and about the Town of Kingston in Jamaica & elsewhere;
as also Slaves, Mortgages, Bonds, Sums of money, Rents, arrearages,
claims &c; & all my Possessions & Effects whatsoever moveable & immoveable; & all this Estate, & these Effects &c I give, bequeathe, make
over & convey in the most full & ample manner to the said Anne Smollett
my Sole Administratrix, her Heirs, Executors, & assigns: this being in fact
no more than restoring what she freely & generously gave to me without
hesitation or Reserve.

I constitute and appoint Mr Allan Auld merch^t, Mr Archibald Hamilton
Senr, Printer, both of the City of London, & Robert Graham & Thomas
Bontein Esq^rs of the Island of Jamaica Executors of this my last will &
Testament, written with my own hand on the stamped Paper of this
Country (having no English stamped Paper by me) this Twenty fourth
day of August in the year of our Lord one Thousand Seven hundred &
Sixty nine—

T^s Smollett[22]

Through the legal terminology of this document there burns the
flame of Smollett's gratitude to Anne Renner and of his true affection for his wife.

By October 1769, Smollett, as Dr. Armstrong understood it,
was in Leghorn. At least the latter dispatched a letter to him at
that seaport in care of Renner, who may well have procured a place
there or nearby for his friend. Parts of Armstrong's letter reflect
topics in Smollett's last correspondence in 1769:

[22] Smollett's will is here printed from a photostat of the original manuscript in the
Principal Registry of the Probate Divorce and Admiralty Division of the High Court
of Justice at Somerset House, London. This will was signed, sealed, and delivered,
September 21, 1769, in the presence of Richard Edwards, John Burstall, and John
Cooke.

London, Oct. 10th, 1769

Dear Doctor

Your letter of Sept. 6th came to hand on Sept. 23rd and according to my calculation you'll receive this upon the 27th of the present month, with the kindest Salutations of all your friends here. Notwithstanding all you tell me, I have still such confidence in your Stamina that I hope to enjoy a pleasant ramble with you through several parts of Italy next Spring. It is my serious Intention and if neither Bob (or Rob) Smith who is I don't know where, nor Gov. Bell who is somewhere in France, will lend me their Company I'll come alone—I am but lately returned from a most agreable Excursion through South Wales with two Friends who remember you with particular regard (Mr. Forbes and Dr. Murdock).[23] . . . D. Maccullo[24] came here only for a trip and returned to Airshire after a stay of a few weeks. I was sorry to hear two days ago that your Friend and Agent Mr. Th. Bunting[25] very lately died of a Dropsy at Jamaica. . . . I wish you could without fatiguing yourself employ or amuse a little time upon the dramatick subject you mention. . . . I send my best wishes to Mrs. Smollet and the Lasses, with much joy to Mrs. Renner.[26]

How characteristic it was of Smollett's passion for the theater that in his last years he was interested in a dramatic subject.

It is chiefly by the indirect light of a handful of letters written to Smollett, reinforced by four not very revealing letters of his own, that we can perceive the mere outline of his final months in Italy, from 1770 to September 1771. In January or February of the former year he was in Pisa, as is divulged by a reference to him in a letter written by Sir Horace Mann at Florence to Horace Walpole, dated February 17, 1770.[27] "I was at Pisa," reported Mann, "when that paper [Johnson's *False Alarm*] came in. I sent to Smollett, the author, who is settled there for his health. He ap-

[23] Probably the Rev. Patrick Murdock, the college friend of James Thomson.

[24] Armstrong referred to David Maccullo, surgeon, who as Smollett's friend had business dealings with Mrs. Leaver.

[25] Armstrong referred to Thomas Bontein, Esq., identified as the second son to Mr. Bontein of Boglass in Stirlingshire and a relative of Robert Graham by Professor William Richardson in a letter to Smollett's biographer, Anderson. (See manuscript letter of Richardson in the National Library of Scotland, MS 22.4.13, ff. 134-134 verso.) Smollett appointed him as an executor of his will, not knowing that he died at Kingston in July 1769. The following obituary was printed in the *London Chronicle* for October 17-19, 1769 (p. 382) as a bulletin from Kingston, Jamaica, under date of July 22: "A few days ago died at his penn" [i.e. country house] "near Salt Ponds, Thomas Bontein, Esq; a Gentleman who had filled several public offices in this island."

[26] For the complete text of this letter see my article, "Dr. John Armstrong," in *PMLA*, LIX (1944), 1048-49.

[27] This date I owe to the kindness of Mr. Warren H. Smith, who is assisting in the preparation of the Yale Edition of Horace Walpole's correspondence.

proved much both of the stile and the method of treating the subject and seemed persuaded that Johnson was the author of it."[28]
As Mann wrote Walpole from Pisa on January 14 and on February 2, 1770,[29] he must have seen Smollett there in one or both of
those months.

By the spring of 1770 Smollett had moved to his country villa
near Leghorn, in which city it is known that he had dinner in May
with Dr. John Armstrong. Smollett's villa, called Il Giardino,
was situated in the parish of Antignano about three miles south of
Leghorn[30] on the slope of a mountain called Monte Nero, where
there were both a resort and a convent bearing the same name. In
his letter to Caleb Whitefoord, May 18, 1770, Smollett declared:
"I am at present rusticated on the side of a Mountain that over-
looks the sea, in the neighborhood of Leghorne, a most romantic
& salutary Situation."[31] Smollett was not exaggerating. Fortunately
we have a trustworthy description of the location, beauty, and associations of Smollett's house written by a Scottish traveler, Alexander Malcolm, in 1827, at which time it was one of a number of
villas belonging to the merchants of Leghorn. Malcolm's account
follows:

> I learned that in one of them Lord Byron had resided six weeks with
> his fair Countess Guiccioli. . . . But of all these villas . . . there is none to be
> compared in point either of situation or elegance with the last abode of
> Smollett. You may hire a gig to go this distance [from Leghorn to the
> vicinity of Monte Nero] for tenpence, and after winding around the
> mountain for some distance, the place bursts upon you all at once, and
> certainly nothing on earth can be more truly romantic. It commands a
> divine view of the Mediterranean with the Islands of Gorgona and Elba
> on the right and left, and the snow-capped mountains of Corsica between,
> in the distance. There is also a delightful stream which skirts the front of
> the house, almost as transparent as Smollett's own poetry-inspiring Severn
> [*sic*]—and the road for five or six miles beyond, in the direction of Rome,
> forms one of the most charming rides in the country. The apartments of
> the house . . . are plain but lofty, and without that air of comfort or snug-
> ness which is so essential with us. You may guess the state of my feelings,
> however, the feelings of a countryman and an ardent admirer of his
> genius when I was shown the very bed where the poet's eyes were closed

[28] The text of this extract from Mann's letter is that printed in 'Mann' and Manners at the Court of Florence, 1740–1786, by Dr. Doran, 2 vols. (London, 1876),
II, 218, with minor corrections supplied by Mr. Warren H. Smith.

[29] For the dates of these letters I am indebted to Mr. Warren H. Smith.

[30] For the location of Smollett's villa see Montgomery Carmichael, *op. cit.*, *passim.*

[31] *Letters*, p. 106.

forever upon all terrestrial things, and also when the identical studium was pointed out in which his last and most humorous work was begun and finished. The premises are now occupied by a rich bookseller of Leghorn who takes apparently a mighty pride in detailing his *Smollett's reminiscences*; and who boasts with much truth but some vanity, that the place is just such a one as any poet or philosopher might select either to live or to die in.[32]

The elegance of Smollett's villa is suggested by other considerations. Carmichael, the best historian of his final residence, believed that Il Giardino was, in 1770, a grand-ducal property. About 1820, according to Carmichael, it belonged to the Niccolai Gamba family. Later the Sampieri family possessed it. By 1898 it was held by one Eugenio Niccolai Gamba, who supposedly occupied the room where Smollett died. Hence the house was called the Villa Gamba, or, Il Giardino, in the photograph made available in 1936 by Carmichael.[33] One can sense that Smollett loved this villa with its mountain stream which recalled the Scottish Leven of his boyhood; that he enjoyed the glorious vista of the Mediterranean which evoked old memories of his months on the stormy Atlantic, and of his years by the quiet Thames.

In Il Giardino, according to long-standing Italian tradition, Smollett worked on his last and finest novel, *The Expedition of Humphry Clinker*. To this tradition recorded by Vivoli in 1844,[34] the Sampieri family may have contributed reliable data because Smollett was asked to be guest of a member of that family shortly before his death.[35] At any rate, since there is no alluson in any let-

[32] Cited from Alexander Malcolm, *Letters of An Invalid from Italy, Malta, and The South of France* (London, William Clowes & Sons, Limited, 1897), pp. 156ff., from Letter XIII, Leghorn, June 10, 1827.

[33] For Carmichael's data, see his communication, "Smollett: His Death and Burial," in *Notes and Queries*, 9 Ser., 1 (1898), 309-11. For the photograph see Carmichael, "Tobia Smollett A Livorno," *loc. cit.*, p. 117.

[34] *Ibid.* See also Carmichael, "Tobia Smollett A Livorno," *loc. cit.*, p. 116. Carmichael referred to Dr. Giuseppe Vivoli's *Annali di Livorno*, 4 vols. (Livorno, 1844), II, 298. This work I have not examined.

[35] In a letter to Smollett written August 25, 1771, by one Stanislas Marie de la Lena there is a postscript headed "Pont au Serrail." On the manuscript of this letter someone (perhaps Mrs. Smollett) wrote "Bagno di Lucca 25 Aug. 1771." Hence the "Pont au Serrail" referred, obviously, to Ponte a Serraglio, a small resort near the Baths of Lucca, from which the Smolletts were planning to set out on Monday, August 26, 1771 (see *Letters*, p. 109). Mme. de la Lena, who was proposing to Smollett a new treatment for asthma, included in her P.S. the following: "Je viens de scavoir, que vous êtes pour aller a une maison de Plaisance de Monsr Sampieri." Where Sampieri's villa was located is not clear, but certainly Smollett had planned

ters by or to Smollett to the place or date of the composition of *Humphry Clinker*, it has always been, and must still be, assumed that a part of it, at least, was written in Italy. There is every likelihood, therefore, that he completed his last novel at his villa, Il Giardino. There are, however, some reasons for believing that the first two volumes of *Humphry Clinker* and possibly a portion of the third were written (in a first draft, at least) at London and Bath from 1765 to 1768.[36] But it was in Italy that the whole work was probably improved, cast into final form, and concluded in 1770. By January 1771, the printers were setting the type,[37] and after some delay it was issued about June 15, 1771,[38] in three volumes, priced at nine shillings bound, and printed for W. Johnston in Ludgate Street and B. Collins of Salisbury. From the fact that *Humphry Clinker* was in the press in January 1771, and in view of Smollett's proposing to Dr. Armstrong in May 1770 a "ramble somewhere to the south of France" it would appear that the novel was completed early in 1770.[39]

As Smollett looked through the manuscript for the last time, he was able to recollect in relative tranquillity the many vivid personal experiences and impressions which still make this novel live. Through his mind there flashed a remarkable series of scenes and characters: the dinners at Chelsea for authorlings where he

---

to go there. For a part of the text of Mme de la Lena's letter, see my *Study of the Final Period of Tobias Smollett*, MS Dissertation in Yale University Library, pp. 269ff. A Colonel Sampieri was one of the regents of Corsica appointed by the famous King Theodore (see *Memoirs of Corsica . . . By Frederick, Son of Theodore late King of Corsica*. London, 1768, p. 142). Smollett probably met this or some other Sampieri through George Renner, who in 1745 was appointed by Theodore as Consul to Leghorn. Renner's "Patent" from Theodore is at the Ridgway Library, Philadelphia, MS Vol. 967 F.

[36] For some details, which are too numerous to be presented here, see my *Study of the Final Period of Tobias Smollett*, MS Dissertation in Yale University Library, Chap. III, which, however, needs augmenting and revising.

[37] The *London Chronicle* for January 19-22 and also for January 22-24, 1771, ran the following announcement: "In the Press, and speedily will be published, In Two Volumes. The Expedition of Humphrey [*sic*] Clinker. By the Author of Roderick Random. Printed for W. Johnston, in Ludgate-street." This publicizing of a two-volume format was probably a slip, as the work was first issued in three volumes.

[38] The announcement of publication as given in the *London Chronicle* for June 15, 1771, was in part as follows: "This day was published In Three Volumes, Price bound 9 s The Expedition of Humphrey [*sic*] Clinker . . . By the Author of Roderick Random. Printed for W. Johnston, in Ludgate-street; and B. Collins at Salisbury."

[39] In the normal course of events, to transport the manuscript to London, to find a publisher, and to close a contract would have required several months. For Smollett's hope of traveling in France, see his *Works*, ed. Anderson, 1820, I, 191.

was both irritated and amused, like Bramble, by his assistants, disguised in the novel under such pseudonyms as Dick Ivy, Wat Wyvil, Lord Potatoe, and Tim Cropdale;[40] politicians, like Newcastle and Charles Townshend, whom he had perhaps observed; Ranelagh and Vauxhall and the streets of London filled with luxury and corruption; Bath, with its celebrities, such as Quin and Derrick, both of whom he presumably knew there; and Bath with its hordes of upstarts, and (in his own words) with its

> Clerks and factors from the East Indies, loaded with the spoil of plundered provinces; planters, negro-drivers, and hucksters, from our American plantations, enriched they know not how; agents, commissaries, and contractors, who have fattened, in two successive wars, on the blood of the nation; usurers, brokers, and jobbers of every kind; men of low birth, and of no breeding, have found themselves suddenly translated into a state of affluence, unknown to former ages; and no wonder that their brains should be intoxicated with pride, vanity, and presumption. Knowing no other criterion of greatness, but the ostentation of wealth, they discharge their affluence without taste or conduct, through every channel of the most absurd extravagance; and all of them hurry to Bath, because here, without any farther qualification, they can mingle with the princes and nobles of the land. Even the wives and daughters of low tradesmen, who, like shovel-nosed sharks, prey upon the blubber of those uncouth whales of fortune, are infected with the same rage of displaying their importance. . . . Such is the composition of what is called the fashionable company at Bath; where a very inconsiderable proportion of genteel people are lost in a mob of impudent plebeians, who have neither understanding nor judgment, nor the least idea of propriety and decorum; and seem to enjoy nothing so much as an opportunity of insulting their betters.[41]

Among the clerks and factors from the East Indies "loaded with the spoil of plundered provinces" there was one figure whom Smollett designated as Paunceford in *Humphry Clinker*. We will digress in order to identify him. This person, who had received substantial aid from Mr. Serle [Smollett], did nothing to repay in any manner his heavy obligations. Consequently Smollett branded him unforgettably in *Humphry Clinker*,[42] as a contemptible snob and ingrate, and could not have failed to have him in mind

[40] See *Humphry Clinker*, Letter of Jerry, London, June 10, for the complete roster of Grub Street writers as presented by Smollett. Although it is hazardous to guess at the names of the real authors here satirized, I venture the suggestion that by Wat Wyvil, Smollett meant the minor poet William Woty.

[41] *Humphry Clinker*, Letter of Bramble, Bath, April 23.

[42] *Ibid.*, Letter of Jerry, Bath, May 10.

when he wrote the final strophe of his memorable *Ode to Independence*, beginning,

> In Fortune's car behold that minion ride;
> With either India's glittering spoils oppress'd.[43]

The first attempt to illuminate the Paunceford incident is found in a memoir of Smollett by Alexander Chalmers, who reported the following on the strength of data supplied by Archibald Hamiltŏn:

> Paunceford was a John C--l, who was fed by Smollett when he had not bread to eat, nor clothes to cover him. He was taken out to India as private secretary to a celebrated governor-general, and as essayist; and after only three years absence, returned with forty thousand pounds. From India he sent several letters to Smollett, professing that he was coming over to lay his fortune at the feet of his benefactor. But on his arrival, he treated Smollett, Hamilton, and others, who had befriended him, with the most ungrateful contempt. The person who taught him the art of essaying became reduced in circumstances, and is now (1792) or lately was collector of the toll on carts at Holborn Bars. C--l never paid him, or any other person to whom he was indebted. He died in two or three years after at his house near Hounslow, universally despised. At the request of Smollett, Mr. Hamilton employed him to write in the Critical Review, which with Smollett's charity, was all his support, previously to his departure for India.[44]

This account is unquestionably accurate in some of its detail, but in one crucial point it is erroneous: Paunceford was not John C--l, but Alexander Campbell, who according to the records of the India Office, London,[45] arrived at Fort William, Bengal, in September 1763, as junior merchant and essay-master. In 1764, Campbell

---

[43] For conjecture on the date of the composition of the *Ode* see Howard S. Buck, *Smollett as Poet* (Yale University Press, 1928), pp. 71-72. For conclusive proof that Smollett wrote the *Ode*, see Luella F. Norwood, "The Authenticity of Smollett's *Ode to Independence*," in *RES*, XVII (1941), 55-64.

[44] Cited from the *Works of the English Poets*, ed. Alexander Chalmers, XV (1810), 550. This passage has been many times reprinted.

[45] In 1937, upon arriving at the India Office, London, I was kindly shown by Mr. W. T. Ottewill, Superintendent of Records, a work by James M. Holzman entitled *The Nabobs in England: A Study of the Returned Anglo-Indian 1760-1785*, published in New York in 1926. This book greatly expedited my research, as it furnished (p. 136) a summary of Alexander Campbell's activities in Bengal and also gave the date of his death (1781) and facts from his obituary. My statements concerning Campbell's status in Bengal, his promotions, and the date of his departure from India are taken from the following records at the India Office:
   (1) Manuscript Ledger, Bengal Civil Servants 1760-1783, under List of the Honble Company's Covenanted Servants . . . Bengal, for the years 1763 to 1767.
   (2) Manuscript Volume, Range 1, Vol. 41, folios 12, 46, 1014, 1017-1019.

became mint-master, and by 1767 he was Secretary of the Select Committee, or council, headed by Verelst, at Fort William. Resigning in 1767 because of poor health, Campbell sailed from India, December 31, 1767, on the *Europa*, presumably reaching Bath in the spring of 1768, where, in line with his subsequent reputation, he treated Smollett with extraordinary ingratitude. That Campbell amassed a fortune in India cannot be doubted: he was charged with gross corruption in 1772 in the following newspaper attack:

> A Correspondent observes that the Select Committee will have a glorious Field of Inquiry when they come down to the year 1765, when the current Coin in Bengal was tampered with. Campbell, the master of the Mint, in the Course of three Years, sent home Sixty Thousand Pounds several Times told; and yet he was not at his setting out worth a Groat. This shews that a Critical Reviewer[46] will act with the same Honour when the Fate of a Nation and the happiness of Millions are at Stake as when the Character of an Author is in Question.[47]

Whether Campbell was guilty of illegal actions is uncertain. In his portrait of Paunceford, Smollett declared: "I don't find that he is charged with any practices that the law deems dishonest."[48] Whether or not Campbell was subsequently prosecuted remains uncertain. He died in 1781.[49] His callous ingratitude Smollett, naturally enough, could not recall without indignation, when he satirized him (in 1768 or later) in the *Ode to Independence*, as well as in *Humphry Clinker*.

But Smollett in 1770 was not living entirely in the past. He enjoyed some London newspapers which were sent to him by Caleb Whitefoord, the inventor of cross-reading, and the friend of Goldsmith. In his letter of acknowledgment he concluded as follows:

> Pray, who is *old Slyboots*?[50] is not *Junius* supposed to be Burke? what is

[46] There is no evidence that Alexander Campbell wrote leading reviews for the *Critical*; his work for Smollett remains a mystery.

[47] Cited from the *Public Advertiser*, July 18, 1772.

[48] *Humphry Clinker*, Letter of Jerry, Bath, May 10.

[49] Campbell's obituary in the *St. James's Chronicle*, October 6-9, 1781, ran as follows: "Wednesday the 26th of September, at Lewell-House, near Chudleigh in Devonshire, Alexander Campbell, Esq. of Worton in Middlesex, formerly one of the Council at Bengal." According to C. Greenwood's Map of the County of Middlesex, London, 1819, Worton House was near Hounslow.

[50] Old Slyboots was the *nom de plume* of James Scott, D.D. (see *DNB*). Articles by Old Slyboots appeared in the *London Chronicle* during March, April, and May 1770.

become of Mr⁸ Macaulay? they say she has been obliged to retire; for what reason I know not.—Do pray throw away half an hour in giving me the political anecdotes of the Times, & direct a Monsʳ Monsʳ Smollett, chez Monsʳ Renner Negotiant a Livourne. In the mean Time wishing you every Comfort & Consolation that this rascally Age affords, I am with great affection & Esteem

Dear Sir

Your very humble Servᵗ

T⁸ Smollett

Monte-Nero
May 18, 1770⁵¹

In May 1770, Smollett, as has been noted, dined in Leghorn with Dr. John Armstrong, who immediately traveled on to Rome. From this city he wrote a short note to Smollett, June 2, 1770, expressing his keen pleasure at the prospect of returning to him soon, and adding: "As you talked of a ramble somewhere to the south of France, I shall be extremely happy to attend you." This scheme was never carried out, but that Smollett even contemplated it is evidence of his unfailing love of travel and of his optimism over his health in the spring of 1770.

The Smolletts entertained Armstrong for some two weeks in July 1770, but no details of Smollett as host have survived. Armstrong, who wrote Mrs. Smollett in 1775 that the fortnight he passed was "one of the favourite Morsells"⁵² of his life, printed in his *Short Ramble* only a disappointingly meager reference to "having enjoyed above a fortnight of domestic Happiness with a worthy old Friend, in the agreeable society of two small Families who lived most cordially together on the Side of Monte Nero, a romantic Mountain, which affords great variety of Situation to a number of little Villa's and looks over the Sea at about the distance of four English miles from Leghorn."⁵³

Smollett was also visited by one John Gray,⁵⁴ a minor author, either in the fall of 1770 or the spring of 1771. Three of Gray's

---

⁵¹ *Letters*, p. 106.

⁵² See my article, "Dr. John Armstrong," *loc. cit.*, p. 1051.

⁵³ Cited from *A Short Ramble Through Some Parts of France and Italy* by Lancelot Temple, Esq. [John Armstrong] (London, 1771), p. 51.

⁵⁴ This John Gray was associated with William Guthrie and others in writing *A General History of the World, from the Creation to the Present Time*, 12 volumes, London, 1764-1767.

garrulous letters to Smollett[55] are preserved, but they shed more light on Smollett's friends than on his own status.

In December 1770, Smollett was naturally saddened by hearing of the death of his mother in faraway Scotland.[56] He recalled, of course, their farewells in 1766 and her prophecy that summer that if she died first, he would not be long in following her.[57] At that time she is said to have had "a strong understanding, and an uncommon share of humour."[58]

Of Smollett's last months little remains to be recorded. He wrote in January 1771 to his nephew, Alexander Telfer,[59] of the recent and severe earthquake in Leghorn, which caused most of the inhabitants to flee from the city, declaring characteristically:

> I could hardly keep my own family within Doors; but, for my own part, I thought it was better to run some small risque of being smothered quietly in my own warm bed, than expose myself to certain Death from the Damps of a dark Winter night, while the cold was excessive.[60]

The very day on which he wrote these words, he sent a letter to Dr. John Hunter, in which, as one medical man to another, he joked grimly about his physical condition:

> With respect to myself, I have nothing to say, but that if I can prevail upon my wife to execute my last will, you shall receive my poor carcase in a box, after I am dead, to be placed among your rarities. I am already so dry and emaciated, that I may pass for an Egyptian mummy, without any other preparation than some pitch and painted linen; unless you think I may deserve the denomination of a curiosity in my own character.[61]

And yet Smollett was not bedridden during his final months. In the spring of 1771 his health was better; at least John Gray was

[55] Gray wrote three letters to Smollett: (1) from Florence, November 15, 1770, original manuscript at the Ridgway Library, Philadelphia; (2) from Genoa, March 23, 1771, original manuscript at the Massachusetts Historical Society, Boston; (3) from London, July 8, 1771, original manuscript not located. The last two of these letters were printed by Anderson in his edition of Smollett's *Works*, 1820, I, pp. 192ff. and pp. 195ff.

[56] The death of Smollett's mother was recorded in the *Scots Magazine*, XXXII (1770), 631, under date of November 7, 1770, as follows: "At Bonnytown, near Edinburgh, Mrs. Barbara Cuningham, relict of Mr. Archibald Smollet." The Bonnytown here mentioned was probably the estate of Bonington in the parish of Ratho, Edinburghshire, owned in 1793 by William Cunningham. See the *Statistical Account of Scotland*, Vol. 7 (Edinburgh, 1793), p. 263. If Anderson was correct in stating that she was seventy-two years old in 1766, she died at the approximate age of seventy-six.

[57] See Chap. I.
[58] See *Works* of Smollett, ed. Anderson, 1820, I, 88n.
[59] See *Letters*, p. 228.   [60] *Ibid.*, pp. 107-8.   [61] *Ibid.*, pp. 108-9.

led to think so, for he wrote from Genoa March 23rd: "I shall be happy to hear from you at Turin ... particularly to have the agreeable news of your health daily more confirmed."[62]

His last Italian summer Smollett spent with his wife at the Baths of Lucca, some fifteen miles from Lucca. There he received on June 15 a letter from Mme. Stanislas de la Lena containing manuscripts for him to read. The writer also requested an interview and enclosed "quelque Fleur a Madame, ayant sceu par mon Frere qu'elle en faisoit recherche pour peindre en miniature."[63]

In Lucca Baths, then, the Smolletts remained until late August. While there he had sufficient vigor to work on some revised or abridged edition of the *Universal History*.[64] Mrs. Smollett in 1773 declared that he "work'd on the Universal History 3 months at Lucca besides what he did here [at Leghorn]."[65] Along with this old-time drudgery, however, Smollett probably experienced an author's pleasure of receiving his ten complimentary sets of *The Expedition of Humphry Clinker*,[66] which, having been published in London, June 15, 1771, should have reached him in July or August.[67] The two hundred and ten pounds for the copyright[68] had perhaps arrived earlier. At any rate, the attractive appearance and print of the three pocket-volumes should have pleased him. Equally gratifying, we hope, were the comments received from his friends—from friends, that is, who wrote promptly. One of these was John Gray, whose remarks in his letter to Smollett written at London, July 8, some three weeks after *Humphry Clinker* was issued, are of real interest:

> I have read the Adventures of Humphry Clinker with great delight, and think it calculated to give a very great run, and to add to the reputation of the author, who has, by the magic of his pen, turned the banks of Loch Lomond into classic ground. If I had seen the MS. I should like to have

[62] *Works*, ed. Anderson, 1820, I, 195.
[63] Cited 'from the original manuscript in the Ridgway Library, Philadelphia, MSS Rush, Vol. 28, p. 46.
[64] See Louis L. Martz, *op. cit.*, p. 8.
[65] See my article, "Ann Smollett, Wife of Tobias Smollett," in *PMLA*, XLV (1930), 1041.
[66] See Charles Welsh, *A Bookseller of the Last Century* (London and New York, 1885), p. 357.
[67] Seccombe (in *DNB*) stated, without offering documentary proof, that "Smollett had the satisfaction of seeing his masterpiece in print but not of hearing the chorus of praise that greeted it."
[68] See Charles Welsh, *op. cit.*, p. 357.

struck out the episode of Mr. Pouncefort.[69] The strictures upon Aristarchus[70] are but too just; shallow judges, I find, are not so well satisfied with the performance as the best judges, who are lavish in its praises. Your half-animated sots say they don't see the humour. Cleland[71] gives it the stamp of excellence, with the enthusiastic emphasis of voice and fist; and puts it before anything you ever wrote. With many, I find, it has the effect of exciting inquiries about your other works, which they had not heard of before. I expected to have seen an account of it in both Reviews, but it is reserved for next month.[72]

It is unlikely that Smollett read many reviews of *Humphry Clinker* or was even aware of the very extensive publicity which the book quickly received in England and Scotland.[73] Neither could he foresee that a German translation of it was to appear in 1772 and that an extraordinary number of reprints were to be issued in the British Isles from 1771 to 1800. He knew, of course, of his indomitable creative labor in writing it when he was exasperated by fever, coughing, and the infection on his hand. Mrs. Smollett well remembered that: "it Galls me to the Soul," she wrote in 1773, "when I think how much that poor Dear Man Suffered while he wrote that novel, and that all his pains & part of his Life was to be expended to Serve Such an unworthy & dishonest wretch, who has neither Honour nor probity in him."[74] Whether or not Smollett realized that he had created his masterpiece is an open question.

Just as Smollett was about to leave Lucca Baths, on August 26, 1771, he probably received another letter from Mme. Stanislas de la Lena written on the 25th. In this epistle she urged Smollett, who, she had heard, was going to "une maison de Plaisance [i.e. villa] de Monsr Sampieri" to try her treatment for asthma, a remedy which, she urged, had produced remarkable results for her friends.[75] Whether or not Smollett visited Sampieri is not

[69] See *supra*.
[70] Gray referred to an arrogant, dogmatic author depicted under the name Aristarchus in *Humphry Clinker*, Letter of Bramble, London, June 2. The identity of Aristarchus is not established.
[71] Presumably John Cleland (1709-1789).
[72] Cited from *Works*, ed. Anderson, 1820, I, 196-97.
[73] For a study of the contemporary reception of *Humphry Clinker*, see my "Study of the Final Period of Tobias Smollett," MS Dissertation in Yale University Library, Chap. II.
[74] Cited from my article, "Ann Smollett, Wife of Tobias Smollett," *loc. cit.*, pp. 1041-42. Mrs. Smollett referred to William Johnston, one of the publishers of *Humphry Clinker*, who was, or pretended to be, in financial straits about 1773.
[75] For portions of Mme. Stanislas de la Lena's letter see my "Study of the Final Period of Tobias Smollett," MS Dissertation in Yale University Library, pp. 269-71.

known, any more than what was his response to the suggested treatment for asthma. At any rate, Smollett's last available letter, written most likely to George Renner, shows what his plans were on August 21, plans which demonstrate that he still possessed considerable physical strength. Parts of this letter here follow:

> We shall Set out from hence on monday morning, & lie at Pisa, & on Tuesday we propose to take pot Luck with you at Leghorn; so that we may proceed to the Giardino in the Evening. . . . The Baggage we shall Send to Leghorn by the Canal; & when we arrive we shall be able to judge what must be forwarded to the Giardino where I hope you will remember to make Some Provision of wine—we shall have the best part of a Barrel to our friend Domenicho who has not yet received the printed Cotton but I suppose it will come to hand this day or to-morrow. Pray, remember us to Nanny & Kitty, Capt St Barbe & all friends & excuse this fresh Trouble from
>
> Dear Sir
Yours always
>
> Lucca Baths   T^s Smollett
Wednesday, Augt 21[76]

Even though these plans may have been postponed by a visit at the villa of Sampieri, we must believe that Smollett arrived by September at his own villa, Il Giardino. His friends, we fancy, welcomed him upon his return and were quite unprepared for the violent attack which seized him before mid-September and caused his death on the seventeenth of that month. That for a long time his vitality gradually ebbed away is no longer wholly credible; like a man-of-war, weakened, to be sure, by hard service, but still seaworthy for a season, he was swept down by an unexpected and overwhelming blast. The primary cause of his death appears to have been an acute intestinal infection. Such a disorder was reported in certain London and Edinburgh newspapers[77] and is con-

---

[76] *Letters*, pp. 109-10.

[77] The numerous accounts of Smollett's death in the newspapers are conflicting, as is natural, because they were based, obviously, on the informal and subjective reports of letter-writers. Hence they varied as to the cause and place of his death. Announcements that he died at Pisa arose, presumably, from the fact that the report was sent from that city. Reports that he died after a long illness resulted from a mere jumping to that conclusion. *The Middlesex Journal, or, Chronicle of Liberty* (October 24-26, 1771), a paper over which Archibald Hamilton had some supervision, reported that Smollett died, near Leghorn on September 17 and that he was interred on the 19th in the English burying ground. It also stated that he had spent most of the summer at the Baths of Lucca, and that, on his return to his house on the seacoast he was "seized with a disorder in the intestines, which carried him off in a few days." A similar account appeared in the *Edinburgh Evening Courant*, October 28, 1771.

firmed by the diary of Dr. Gentili, who visited him during his last illness. Gentili's entries follow:

> M. Smollet di a. [nni] 50 uomo di talento—Istorico 1772 [1771?] sett. [embre] asmatico soffre coliche—vigilie diarrea convulsioni febbre, ha del vigore, temperamento focoso, non vuol bevere.

> Visitato il sab. [ato] sera del di 14 sett. [embre] la p. [rima] volta—Il Dr. Garden il 15 propone i vescicanti, temperam. [ento] focosissimo, e ardenta. Egli ha una scabbia—come ortefica.

> Si dubita, che le nuove stanze di S.P. l'abbiano infettato. Le sue parenti sane.

> Muore asmatico, e consunto—senza volersi da aiuto. La notte del 17 sett. [embre] spira. Gli fu ordinato un cardiaco di vin di Reno ac. [qua] di can. [nella] zucch. [erata]. Uomo di talento svegliato sofferente gli acciacchi della vita umana, ma quasi misantropo.

> E vissuto con la moglie 18 [anni] in perfetta armonia dalla quale ottenne una figlia che poetava. Era di temp. [eramento] molto ardente e collerico —ma riflessivo e dedito agli studi politici e istorici.[78]

This entry may be translated as follows:

> M. Smollet aged 50, a man of historical talent. 1772 September, asthmatic, suffers from colic, chronic diarrhea, convulsions, fever. He has vigor, fiery temperament, will not drink. Visited for the first time on Saturday evening 14th September. Dr. Garden on the 15th prescribed vesicatories. He has a scabrous condition as in skin disease.

> They suspect that the new rooms of S.P. have infected him. His parents [were] healthy. He died asthmatic and consumptive without trying to help himself. The night of September 17th he expired. He had been ordered a cordial of Rhine wine with cane sugar. A man of matured talent enduring the blows of human life, but almost misanthropic. He lived 18 years in perfect harmony with his wife by whom he had a daughter who wrote poetry. He had a very ardent and choleric temperament but was reflective and devoted to political and historical studies.

It must be presumed that Smollett was interred in the English burying ground at Leghorn. For a time there was no monument to mark his resting place, a fact which troubled his widow, who wrote in her letter to Archibald Hamilton in May 1773 that amid her many causes of uneasiness she had

> the particular one, to reflect that my dear Smollett has never yet had [a] monument rais'd up to his memory, which in this Country is look'd at with astonishment, the more so as his Reputation was so well Known; I

[78] Printed from an exact transcript of Gentili's manuscript diary, Biblioteca Riccardiana, 3298cc. 74ᵃ-75ᵃ.

really think it would be a triffiling expence to His Cousin or Nephew to do it for him. God knows I am very little able to Spend,[79] but if you think none of them will give that last mark of regard to so worthy a Relation, I shall at all events do the best in my power, and even then, I have not among so many Friends any one who has wrote an epitaph to his memory; let me beg Sir as a true Friend to the Deceased, try what you can do with all speed, for it is the Dayly Chatt, why it has been so long Deferred. the Commissary wrote me he would put up a pile near Leven, but still that does not answer, for where his body lies, there certainly ought to be the Chief Monument. the expence will be about 40 Guineas, a very poor Sum to those who have large Estates.[80]

As a result of Mrs. Smollett's plea, a plain pyramidal monument was erected in 1773 in the Leghorn cemetery. For this, Dr. Armstrong is supposed to have furnished the inscription.[81] Regularly in the years following 1773, we have records of the comments of travelers who visited Smollett's grave in Leghorn. In 1791 Anne Smollett and in 1811 Anne Renner were buried in the same cemetery. Meantime, in 1774, a column was erected by James Smollett of Bonhill on the banks of the Leven, near Dalquhurn, Smollett's birthplace. At some uncertain time, moreover, Smollett's Italian admirers[82] bestirred themselves. In 1818, there appeared in the *Gentleman's Magazine* a remarkable reference to Smollett's

[79] To get an exact notion of the financial status of Anne Smollett in 1773 is quite impossible, as we do not know how extravagant or conservative she was in her financial outlay. It is clear, however, that the income from the West Indies was falling off even before Smollett's death. (See Appendix for the letter of Robert Graham of Gartmore written to Smollett in August 1771.) Further light on Anne Smollett's income is found in letters of Robert Graham to her and others, from 1778 to 1791 as printed in my "Study of the Final Period of Tobias Smollett," MS Dissertation in Yale University Library, pp. 289ff. Much of her property was destroyed by a fire in Jamaica in 1782, but thanks to the Renners of Leghorn and other friends, she was never destitute. See my article, "Ann Smollett, Wife of Tobias Smollett," in *PMLA*, XLV (1930), 1035ff. For her will, see my "Study of the Final Period of Tobias Smollett," MS Dissertation, pp. 273ff.

[80] Cited from my article, "Ann Smollett, Wife of Tobias Smollett," *loc. cit.*, p. 1041.

[81] See *Works* of Smollett, ed. Anderson, 1820, I, 94, 203.

[82] That Smollett enjoyed influential Italian friends is clear from a letter written in November 1771 by an "English Gentleman in Italy to his Friend in London." The following extract from the letter in question was sent by "W. W.," perhaps the poet, William Woty, to the *Town and Country Magazine*, III (December 1771), 651:
"You no doubt, long before this time, have heard of the death of Dr. Smollett. I sincerely regret the loss of this ingenious gentleman. I was in hopes of being honoured with his friendship during my residence in Italy, which would have been a valuable acquisition. He was much caressed by the princes and literati of this country, and whose [sic] death is no less generally lamented."

"tomb" on the banks of the Arno between Leghorn and Pisa.[83] The following year the *European Magazine* contained a detailed account of a high octagonal tomb and printed the Italian, Latin, Greek, and English inscriptions engraved on four marble slabs placed within it. Within it, too, was a marble table surrounded by stone seats, and thereupon, according to the account, the officers and crews of British vessels stopping at Leghorn did homage to Smollett in "*sacrifices* of the finest fruit, and copious libations of the most generous *lachrymae christi* wine."[84] Though the location of

[83] *Gentleman's Magazine*, LXXXVIII (1818), 267.

[84] See *European Magazine* for December 1819, pp. 512ff. The inscriptions which follow are taken from Smollett's *Works*, ed. Anderson, 1820, I, 97ff., with a supplementary note furnished by the correspondent in the *European Magazine*.

Italian Inscription

Stranger! respect the name of Tobias Smollett,
An Englishman,
A man of letters and playful genius.
He died
Contented in Tuscany.
His soul
Requires your prayers.

J.B.

Latin Inscription

He knew everything—he loved every one.
Familiar with past
and
Present ages,
His works merit a place by the side
of
Boccaccio
Pray for his soul.

S.

Greek Inscription

Here Smollett rests,
A Citizen of the world,
A Xenophon and an Hippocrates,
A Terence and a Boccaccio.
If he had
A native country, it was this;
For her
He chose to die:
I was his friend.

J. Pallionietta

English Inscription
'*Patria cara carior liberta*'

The great historian of his day,
Who rivall'd all but Hume below,
Thou tread'st upon his lowly clay;
Then let thy tears of rapture flow.
The *first* of novelists he shone,

such rites remains undetermined, the inscriptions—and perhaps the memorial structure itself—are true signs that Smollett was not forgotten in romantic Tuscany. Neither has he been forgotten since 1771 in his native Scotland[85] nor in many other lands. In our time, two centuries after the printing of his earliest works, we predict without hesitation that the spirit of his vital personality and the appeal of his notable literary power will long outlive his more perishable monuments.

The *first* of moralists was he,
Who Nature's pencil waved alone,
And painted man as he should be.
Dumbarton's vale in life's gay prime
Cherish'd this blossom of the North,
Italia's sweet and favoured clime
Enshrines in death the man of worth.

J.H.B.

As a note to the English inscription the correspondent added: "the initials J.H.B. I have heard interpreted as James Hay Beattie."

Though J. Buchan Telfer did not refer to these inscriptions, he was led in 1898 by the reference in the *Gentleman's Magazine* (above noted) to doubt that Smollett was buried in Leghorn. For the controversy between him and Montgomery Carmichael see *Notes and Queries*, 9 Ser., I, 201-2; 309-11, and 510-11. Although it is reasonably certain that Smollett was buried in the cemetery at Leghorn, the origin and subsequent fate of the "tomb" and its inscriptions somewhere on the banks of the Arno still remain a considerable mystery.

[85] In 1774, Smollett's cousin, James Smollett of Bonhill, erected a round column on the banks of the Leven a short distance from Dalquhurn, the novelist's birthplace. For the inscription, in which Dr. Johnson had a hand, see the Appendix.

CHAPTER XV

A Concluding View of Smollett's Personality

WE hope that the reader of the preceding chapters has been able to see clearly the various traits of Smollett in the evolving and dramatic stages of his career. There remain, however, a few concluding observations which we are impelled to offer in the desire to illuminate still further certain facets of his personality.

The first half of Smollett's life illustrates the very familiar pattern of the proud, sensitive, independent, and gifted youth fighting his way to recognition under the harsh handicaps of relative poverty. From personal experience Smollett felt the reality of the well-known couplet in Johnson's *London*:

> This mournful truth is ev'rywhere confessed,
> SLOW RISES WORTH BY POVERTY DEPRESSED.

How well Smollett knew the truth of the Horatian line which he chose for the title page of *Roderick Random*:

> *Et genus & virtus, nisi cum re, vilior alga est.*[1]

Like Horace he sensed that without money both birth and capacity are more worthless than seaweed. Repeated reflections on this realistic axiom also prompted him to select for the title page of his *Regicide* passages from Euripides[2] and Juvenal[3] which echoed the same mournful theme, namely that a poet can be great only when free from the bitter anxiety and conflict generated by poverty. The economic struggles of young Smollett are again reflected in a couplet from his *Advice*:

> Too coy to flatter, and too proud to serve,
> Thine be the joyless dignity to starve.[4]

These lines reveal that young Smollett was "coy," that is, reserved, not naturally given to familiarity with strangers. This coy-

---

[1] Horace, *Sermones*, 2, 5, 8.   [2] Euripides, *Suppliants*, 180, 184.
[3] Juvenal, *Satire* VII, ll. 56ff.   [4] *Advice*, ll. 235-36.

ness was a concomitant of his pride and independence. Like Burns, he was "owre blate to seek, owre proud to snool."

Young Smollett also possessed a very tender conscience. There is undeniable self-revelation in the fervid tribute to conscience in his lines from *Advice*, worth citing again:

> Hail, sacred Pow'r! my glory and my guide!
> Fair source of mental peace, what e'er betide;
> Safe in thy shelter, let disaster roll
> Eternal hurricanes around my soul;
> My soul serene, amidst the storms shall reign,
> And smile to see their fury burst in vain![5]

The realization of the proud and impassioned vow of the final couplet is given to few; certainly it was not often achieved by Smollett in the frequent storms of his life. His smiles appear to have been more often satirical or sardonic than serene. Moreover, his guiding conscience, glorified in the foregoing verses, was not for him—how could it be?—a source of self-satisfied peace of mind. On the contrary, it induced a frequent mortification of his pride and inflammability and gradually confirmed his strong instincts of tender humanitarianism.

It is obvious that most of our concluding generalizations on Smollett must be derived from what he became in his mature years. There were in Smollett, as in many other dynamic and complex personalities, two powerful forces, at times mutually antagonistic, but, in the long run, essentially interlocking and complementary. In many respects Smollett aspired to be, and was, a typical rationalist, a typical satirist, and a conventionally aristocratic gentleman of the mid-eighteenth century. At the same time, he was, in many respects, a man of ebullient and violent feelings which often escaped from the leash of reason; a person repeatedly unconventional for his times in romantic self-confession; and a very generous humanitarian. Curiously enough, something of the spirit of each of these contrasting forces in Smollett is expressed in lines which he remembered from Juvenal and found appropriate for the title page of *Count Fathom*:

> Materiam risus, [*sic*] invenit ad omnes
> Occursus hominum. . . .

[5] *Ibid.*, ll. 229-34.

Ridebat curas, nec non et gaudia vulgi;
Interdum et lachrymas fundebat.[6]

We offer the following translation: Food for laughter he found in all his meetings with men. He laughed at the worries and even at the joys of the rabble; at the same time he shed tears. This description of the man capable of both laughing at, and being moved to tears by crowds of people may have impressed Smollett because he felt—and with considerable justification—that it fitted his own moods. At any rate, we shall now consider each of these dual aspects of Smollett.

His frequent attacks on enthusiasts and fanatics indicate that he recognized the great value of rational control over emotion. Moreover, he was not, like Fielding, a follower of Shaftesbury's theories of innate goodness. Consider this sarcastic passage from the fifty-third chapter of *Count Fathom*:

> When a physician becomes the town talk, he generally concludes his business more than half done, even though his fame should wholly turn upon his mal-practice; insomuch that some members of the faculty have been heard to complain, that they never had the good fortune to be publicly accused of homicide: and it is well known, that a certain famous empiric of our day never flourished to any degree of wealth and reputation, till after he had been attacked in print, and fairly convicted of having destroyed a good number of the human species. Success raised upon such a foundation would, by a disciple of Plato, and some modern moralists, be ascribed to the innate virtue and generosity of the human heart, which naturally espouses the cause that needs protection: but I, whose notions of human excellence are not quite so sublime, am apt to believe it is owing to that spirit of self-deceit and contradiction, which is, at least, as universal, if not as natural, as the moral sense so warmly contended for by these ideal philosophers.

Elsewhere Smollett expressed his dislike for "wrongheaded" Platonists.[7] As a doctor and as a very keen observer of life, he witnessed numerous examples of innate depravity. The vicious conduct of Pickle and Fathom, so realistically and ruthlessly portrayed, show again that he had no soft view of human nature. In the seventy-second chapter of *Peregrine Pickle* the misanthropic Crabtree declared:

---

[6] Juvenal, *Satire* x, ll. 47ff. The sentence, "Interdum et lachrymas fundebat," does not follow, in Juvenal, the preceding verses; nor have I discovered its source. Smollett possibly remembered it from some Latin author, or he may have invented it.
[7] See Smollett's *Letters*, p. 60.

I have learned that the characters of mankind are every where the same; that common sense and honesty bear an infinitely small proportion to folly and vice; and that life is at best a paltry province.

It is clear that at certain periods in his life Smollett accepted the validity of Crabtree's generalization on human nature.

Like Dr. Johnson, Smollett was a firm believer in decorum, social order, and subordination. Following the aristocratic code he was scrupulously polite to his social equals or superiors, but disliked the rabble and was perhaps sarcastic and dictatorial at times toward his assistant literary hacks. He confessed his pride in being free from the irregularities or eccentricities in manners and dress affected by many writers of his day and disciplined himself to work regularly on colossal literary projects. He probably tolerated no romantic nonsense from his hirelings. In appearance, Smollett was the conventional gentleman: as is evident in the paintings by Dance and Verelst, his attire was genteel. Had Richardson, Fielding, Johnson, Sterne, and Smollett been judged in 1750 or 1760 by a connoisseur of the externals of gentility, he would with no hesitation have awarded first place to Smollett. Furthermore, in the role of a host at Chelsea Smollett was the typical gentleman. To his unfortunate brothers of the quill he served on Sundays, "beef, pudding, and potatoes, port, punch, and Calvert's entire butt-beer,"[8] but let no one suppose that he offered such plebeian fare to his close friends. Any reader of his *Travels* knows that he was very fastidious in his food and beverages. Additional aristocratic features of Smollett appear in his growing political Toryism, and in his shift from the Presbyterianism of his youth to his association with the Church of England in Chelsea. However, the complete personality of Smollett was not confined within the conventional moulds which shaped the typical rationalist and gentleman of his period.

By far the most dominant trait of Smollett was his perfervid, ebullient temperament, an inherited Scottish characteristic aggravated by his economic struggles and by his protracted invalidism. There were in Smollett violent emotional tensions impossible wholly to account for or to analyze. These central conflicts he repeatedly confessed. In his letter to Carlyle in 1749 he revealed what he called the "Weakness and Leakiness" of his disposition.

[8] See *Humphry Clinker*, Letter of Jerry, London, June 10.

He was passionate in speech, explosive in action, highly irascible in sarcasm and invective. These excesses made him often uneasy and remorseful. Very unusual is his preface to *Count Fathom* wherein he diagnosed his unhappy pride, obstinacy, and jealousy. And there is a direct and romantic confession of his faults in *Humphry Clinker*.[9]

In his extreme generosity Smollett was obviously the man of feeling. He was sooner disposed, according to his friend Dr. Moore, to help those who could never return his favors than those who might later serve him. In charitable activities he appears to have surpassed all his literary contemporaries, with the possible exception of Dr. Johnson. Both men were perhaps influenced by new doctrines on charity operating in the reign of George III,[10] but as Smollett did not theorize on the subject, his giving was probably largely instinctive. The following anecdote is a pleasant illustration of his impulsive charity:

> A beggar asking Dr. Smollet for alms, he gave him, through mistake, a guinea. The poor fellow, on perceiving it, hobbled after him to return it; upon which, Smollet returned it to him, with another guinea as a reward for his honesty, exclaiming at the same time, "What a lodging has honesty taken up with."[11]

Another anecdote sheds light on Smollett's kindness toward Derrick, sometime King of Bath:

> Derrick's poverty was at some times so great, that he had neither shoes nor stockings that were wearable. Being in this situation one day at Forrest's Coffeehouse, Charing-cross, he retired several times to the Cloacinian Temple to coax his stockings, which wickedly displayed every few minutes such conspicuous holes, as put even the King out of countenance. Doctor Smollet was present, and perceiving this embarrassment, said to him, "Why, Derrick, you are certainly devilishly plagued with a looseness, or else you would not repair so often to the cabinet?" Derrick thought to get rid of the observation by a joke, and, in exposing his poverty, obtain a pair of good stockings, as there was no stranger in the room. —"Egad, Doctor," said he, "the looseness is in my heels, as you may plainly perceive." "Faith, Derrick," said Smollett, "I always thought so, for your feet stink damnably." The misfortune was, the observation was but too true. However, the Doctor, to make him some reparation for the severity

[9] *Ibid.*

[10] See W. S. Lewis and Ralph M. Williams, *Private Charity in England, 1747-1757* (Yale University Press, 1938), *passim.*

[11] See *Anecdotes of Books and Authors* (London, 1836), p. 163.

of his jest, took him home to Chelsea, gave him a good dinner; and, upon his departure, slipt a guinea into his hand, to equip his legs and feet for next day.[12]

Such instances of generosity were probably very common, in view of the many better known references to his charities modestly referred to in his letters and portrayed indirectly in his works. His Peregrine, for example, relieved poverty "by stealth,"[13] and so, it seems, did Smollett. "The liberal hand of charity," declared Mr. Felton in *Launcelot Greaves*, "should be extended to modest want that pines in silence, encountering cold, nakedness, and hunger, and every species of distress."[14] Such was Smollett's own belief and practice.

Smollett's warm and generous instincts were also expressed in other ways. Like Dr. Johnson[15] he saw the need of social reform. Both men recognized the injustice of jailing debtors, and the evil and futility of the wars of the mid-century. They agreed on the frightful injustice of many instances of capital punishment.[16] Both advocated governmental aid for worthy writers.[17]

It should never be forgotten that Smollett was warmhearted toward his family, his relatives, and his associates, that he won and kept the devotion of his servant Tolloush, and that, despite his violent quarrels, he enjoyed many and distinguished friends.

What we know of Smollett does little to clarify his private attitude toward religion or his philosophical outlook. That he attacked Catholicism, inveighed against Protestant fanatics and hypocrites, made his Bramble rather sympathetic toward Methodists, and, as a citizen of Chelsea was associated with the Church of England—these facts do not supply a satisfactory answer. Neither do they validate the view (sometimes asserted) that he entirely lacked any feeling for religion. He has, of course, been called a Pagan. He has been termed a Stoic. He has been branded

[12] Cited from *Nocturnal Revels: or, the History of Kings-Place and other Modern Nunneries . . . By a Monk of the Order of St. Francis*, 2 vols. (London, 1779), I, 22-23. A copy of this work is in the British Museum.

[13] See *Peregrine Pickle*, Chap. 89.

[14] See *Launcelot Greaves*, Chap. 21.

[15] See Professor Bertrand H. Bronson's excellent study of Johnson in his *Johnson Agonistes & Other Essays*, Cambridge University Press, 1946.

[16] For Smollett's views, see his *Continuation of the Complete History of England*, Vol. I (London, 1760), p. 125.

[17] For Smollett's views, see his *Continuation of the Complete History of England*, Vol. v (London, 1765), pp. 27-28.

as a misanthropist. Such labels are not very illuminating. How his private views were influenced by Voltaire or by Hume has not been discovered.

There are clear signs in his essay on the waters of Bath of his skepticism concerning conventional medical theories and practice. This attitude is humorously set forth in the following excerpt from the fiftieth chapter of *Count Fathom*, where Fathom declared that "a physician without practice had one comfort to which his brethren were strangers, namely, that the seldomer he had occasion to prescribe, the less he had upon his conscience, on account of being accessory to the death of his fellow-creatures." It is likely that Smollett had his reservations about the efficacy of medicine. On his deathbed, Commodore Trunnion declared: "Here has been a doctor that wanted to stow me choakful of physic; but, when a man's hour is come, what signifies his taking his departure with a 'pothecary's shop in his hold."[18]

Trunnion's stoicism Smollett appears to have demonstrated in the manner in which he himself faced death. Dr. Moore asserted, probably on good authority, that, "although he [Smollett] did not trip along as gaily as Sterne did when Death was at his heels, yet he feared him as little, and met him at last, no distant date, with as much composure as any man ever did."[19] We read in Dr. Gentili's manuscript diary that Smollett faced death "senza volersi da aiuto," that is, without trying to help himself. "All is well, my dear" were his last words, according to his biographer, Oliphant Smeaton, who possibly took them from some unpublished letter sent to Scotland by his widow. It is indeed likely that in his final days Smollett realized much of the spirit of the stoical sentiments expressed in *Peregrine Pickle* by the physician:

> . . . a man of virtue and common sense could not possibly be afraid of death, which is not only the peaceful harbour that receives him shattered on the tempestuous sea of life, but also the eternal seal of his fame and glory, which it is no longer in his power to forfeit and forego.[20]

[18] Cited from *Peregrine Pickle*, Chap. 73.
[19] Cited from Smollett's *Works*, ed. Moore, 8 vols. (London, 1797), I, clxxi-clxxii.
[20] Cited from *Peregrine Pickle*, Chap. 64.

CHAPTER XVI
Smollett's Contribution to the English Novel

IT is a truism sometimes overlooked by readers, and by scholars as well, that the biography of a creative genius is only a necessary means toward a richer end, namely the maximum understanding and enjoyment of his works. Out of the works arises the wish to know the writer's life; out of the life springs, or should spring, a lively desire to return to that original achievement without which there could have been no significant biography. It is therefore appropriate to append to our account of Smollett's life an appraisal of his contribution to the English novel.

In this survey of Smollett's creative writing the intent is to focus on his novels, omitting *The History and Adventures of an Atom*, his translations, compilations, and historical works. No attention will be paid to his plays, which as literature are negligible; neither will there be any further notice given to his reviews, which for the most part are unidentifiable and inaccessible. As for his satirical verse, it must be said that it lacks enduring literary qualities. His occasional lyrics, which possess some charm and feeling, will not be dealt with, except incidentally. It is by virtue of his best novels that Smollett is still read and enjoyed.

The critics of Smollett have occasionally ignored the fact that he set out as a serious satirist with definite moral purposes. He commenced his literary career by producing satirical verse, and in writing his first novel he turned to another medium of expression without altering his satirical aim. *Roderick Random*, he declared to his friend Alexander Carlyle, was "intended as a satire on mankind." As it turned out, this novel, like *Advice* and like *Reproof*, also included, because of the author's propensity for libel, some thinly veiled satire on individuals, following the old satirical tradition exemplified by Dryden and by Pope. In subsequent novels Smollett's practice went far beyond a general satire on mankind to include libelous portraits of many leading London figures, such as Rich, Lyttelton, and Garrick, as well as other minor personalities now difficult or impossible to identify. As young Smollett, however, was an idealist at heart, he also announced in his preface to *Roderick Random* his desire to arouse "that generous indignation which ought to animate the reader against the sordid and vicious disposition of the world." It is reasonably clear, therefore, that young Smollett aspired to become through the medium of the novel another Swift or another Pope. Furthermore, it is obvious that he intended in *Roderick Random* to furnish a generous amount of comic entertainment, so that his novel would appeal to a large group of readers. In general, Smollett's purposes in all his novels conformed to the conventions of the mid-eighteenth century: the ends were instruction and reform through satire, as well as entertainment.

The materials commonly utilized by Smollett in his novels may be considered with profit, even though viewed for the moment in an artificial isolation from the method and temper with which he handled them. From *Roderick Random* on to *Humphry Clinker*, his novels are crowded with type-characters, presented in more profusion than in any other eighteenth-century novelist. Some, like Morgan, are derived from Shakespeare;[1] others seem to be descended from the humor-types found in Ben Jonson, on the Restoration stage, or in later comedy. Professional, occupational, national, rural, and urban types all abound, usually as vehicles of social satire. Of all these the most memorable, of course, are the nautical types, which Smollett was the first to introduce into the novel. Interspersed with what are apparently purely fictitious figures are numerous characters drawn largely from life but often impossible wholly to identify. And scattered throughout Smollett's novels are a host of actual personalities ranging from powerful politicians, authors, and actors down to obscure artists, Grub Street writers, and medical men. It is an extremely extensive and varied human panorama.

Together with a multitude of people, Smollett presented an unusual number and variety of actual localities. Between the covers of his novels he introduced many famous London coffee-

---

[1] See George M. Kahrl, "The Influence of Shakespeare on Smollett" in *The Parrott Presentation Volume* (Princeton University Press, 1935), p. 413.

houses, taverns, pleasure-gardens, and other social centers. Then there are, in addition to well-known towns and cities in *Humphry Clinker*, frequent glimpses of roads, inns, and travelers' resorts not only in England, Scotland, and Wales, but also in France, Flanders, and Holland. In Smollett, more than in any other eighteenth-century novelist, the reader senses a panorama of places.

Smollett's *locales* are almost invariably occupied by people, but there are a few exceptions, such as the Scottish Highlands, filled, as Bramble expressed it, with "sublimity, silence, and solitude." But such scenes, like that of the nocturnal forest in *Count Fathom*, are very rare. Here Smollett was the first novelist to utilize a scene in nature in order to create a powerful effect of romantic (Gothic) horror, as many critics have pointed out.

No examination of Smollett's subject matter is complete without some comment on the considerable amount of material in his fiction, which his friend and biographer Dr. Moore termed indelicate, an epithet tactfully echoed by Dr. Anderson at the beginning of the nineteenth century. Sir Walter Scott objected to what he termed the "extreme licence" of certain scenes in the first edition of *Peregrine Pickle* and felt that Smollett's revisions were not sufficiently drastic. It is hardly surprising therefore that certain Victorian readers and critics found Smollett's scatology and his other frequently noisome satirical data definitely immoral. Professor David Masson, on the other hand, writing in 1859, admitted that there were passages in Fielding and Smollett "which we should not like to see read by 'young ladies in white muslin,'" thought it "a pity," and did not absolve these novelists from all blame, but he insisted that there were "tons of literary matter" of the sort written by Fielding and Smollett which are "very innocent and very instructive for veteran philosophers in broadcloth, for medical and moral students, and for plain rustics in corduroys," and that it could "hardly be supposed . . . that the novels [of these men] could be intrinsically immoral."[2] This point of view is eminently sensible. Quite acceptable, also, is the following judgment of David Herbert, editor of Smollett about 1880:

[2] Quoted from David Masson, *British Novelists and Their Styles* (Boston, 1859), p. 140.

Smollett is, properly understood, the greatest realist in our language. The spirit of truth was the soul of his fancy. If there is lowness in his writings, it is because there is lewdness in men and women. Swift says:—

As Rochefoucault his manners drew
From nature, I believe them true:
They argue no corrupted mind
In him—the fault is in mankind.[3]

These views of Masson and Herbert certain later critics have found unsatisfactory because they have detected in Smollett what the poet William Henley called a "natural deliberate indecency," a phrase repeated by H. W. Hodges in his introduction to the Everyman Edition of *Roderick Random*. That Smollett was indecent for indecency's sake cannot be conclusively proved by any objective evidence. Furthermore, the known facts of his life are against any such view, as are the considered opinions of such critics as the late Ernest A. Baker,[4] the late Oliver Elton,[5] and Mr. Herbert Read.[6] The fact is that Smollett is not seductive, obscene, erotic, or pornographic by any valid definition of those terms.

It is also pertinent to consider the various techniques by means of which Smollett gave form, emphasis, and point to his material. In narrative method he followed, in general, the well-known picaresque pattern of LeSage. Smollett was obviously lacking in any achievement of a well integrated dramatic plot. He was an excellent storyteller only in presenting the brilliant, short, and relatively isolated episode, of which there are hundreds to exemplify the fecundity of his inventive power. He also contrived to keep his narrative moving, very rarely interrupting it to indulge, like Fielding, in either editorial comment or moral digression. In *Humphry Clinker* he developed something new in the epistolary method: he had his various letter writers present multiple reactions to their traveling experiences.

In the creation of character, Smollett's most frequent method involved his well-known caricature, which incorporated a considerable and sometimes extreme degree of physical exaggeration and

[3] Quoted from *The Works of Tobias Smollett*, ed. David Herbert (Edinburgh, 1881), p. 22.
[4] See Ernest A. Baker, *The History of the English Novel*, Vol. 4 (London [1930]), p. 239.
[5] See Oliver Elton, *A Survey of English Literature 1730-1780*, 2 vols. (London, 1928), I, 207ff.
[6] See Herbert Read, *Reason and Romanticism* (London, 1926), pp. 201ff.

distortion, both in appearance and in action. Yet Smollett did not always exaggerate as much as it may seem to the modern reader. To effect his social satire he focused on human oddities and eccentricities in action, costume, and speech, all of which were more in evidence in his day than they have been, on the whole, in more recent times. It is now conceded that Smollett's depiction of life in the British Navy in 1740 departed very little if at all from reality. In his descriptions of places, London and Bath for example, Smollett was undoubtedly as accurate in his realism as he was graphic and entertaining. In depicting both persons and places he had a remarkable eye for exact and concrete detail.

Another aspect of Smollett's method in presenting life is that he did not continually concentrate upon sordid and evil types of humanity. His practice of inserting complimentary portraits in the rogues' gallery of his verse satires, *Advice* and *Reproof*, he continued throughout all of his novels. These portraits, as found in his fiction, are usually those of actual persons whom Smollett knew and admired. It will be remembered that Fielding in *Tom Jones* followed the same practice on a very much smaller scale. The presence of such complimentary portraits results in an effective contrast between them and the rascally types, which illustrate the predominantly vicious human nature set forth. Smollett occasionally gains variety in still another way. Interspersed within his extensive catalogue of minor characters and short and loosely connected episodes, there are a good many passages which contain thinly veiled or unmistakable autobiography. The latter, which we have already utilized in the pages of his biography, consist of his verses, his self-portrait as host to his understrappers at Chelsea, and his attempts to vindicate himself in the eyes of his readers. All these passages, together with Smollett's own vigorous satirical attitudes, produce upon the reader a definite impact of the man within his works. His personality thus felt in the pages of his novels is not invariably engaging, because of his irritation over the human scene and because of the powerful savagery and cynicism which are often intermingled with his comic moods. These qualities have had their definite effect upon his critics.

By and large, the critics of the last century have not been very favorable to Smollett, as Mr. Fred W. Boege has clearly demonstrated in his recent book, *Smollett's Reputation as a Novelist.*[7] The impressive ability of the author of *Roderick Random* to irritate as well as to amuse his readers was not interred with his bones. Smollett's character has long been criticized adversely, and the irascible but kindly Matthew Bramble would have been more outraged than entertained, it is certain, by the attacks made by such critics as Garnett and Gosse, Legouis and Cazamian, William Henley, Ernest A. Baker, Harold Child, Mr. Norman Collins, and Professor Edward Wagenknecht. There has usually been a tendency, not justified by what is now known of his character, to attribute to Smollett the vices of the unheroic Roderick, Peregrine, and Fathom. Consider, for example, the silly and irresponsible statement made by J. C. Squire that Smollett was "no fit man for Fielding to dine with, and not of his rank."[8] In the frequent critical comparisons of Smollett and Fielding as men and writers Smollett's claim to be a serious and moral satirist has been looked upon with skepticism or even denied on grounds that are largely subjective. Such fundamental errors should be avoided by the critic who seeks to be fair to Smollett's literary contribution to the novel. It must be granted that Smollett has an honest desire to improve society and that he did not love brawls and rascals, though he made both extremely ludicrous, full-blooded, and laughable, and no doubt enjoyed them as fictitious creations. Smollett had his obvious weaknesses, such as pride and an excessive temper, but there are no ascertainable facts in his life to prove that he was malicious or mentally debased. But the critics of Smollett, despite their occasional slurs upon his personality, have found much to praise in his literary achievement. Rather than to attempt any summary of critical opinion on the novels of Smollett during the past century, we propose to state as objectively as possible our own appraisal.

It is going too far to assert that Smollett lacked all sense of narrative form: he was obviously following the convention of the loose picaresque structure, and he knew what he was doing.[9] Consequently he stressed the single episode rather than any unified whole. His method, however, is somewhat tedious to modern

[7] See Fred W. Boege, *Smollett's Reputation as a Novelist* (Princeton University Press, 1947), p. 146 and *passim*.

[8] See *The Living Age* (February 1926), p. 380.

[9] On this point, see Rufus Putney, "The Plan of *Peregrine Pickle*" in *PMLA*, LX (December 1945), 1051-65.

readers, who are predisposed to expect a more dramatic narrative pattern. Smollett's long series of episodes, similar in their general subject matter and satirical mood, except where they reveal his liveliest characters, become monotonous as narrative, despite the tireless vigor of the style. This is not always true: the initial portions of *Roderick Random* and of *Peregrine Pickle* are exceptions, as is *Humphry Clinker*, where the epistolary form and the material contribute variety. It is not in narrative power, but rather in his achievement of the ludicrous and the farcical in character and in action that we find one of Smollett's chief distinctions. After all, it is his power to provoke laughter that has, among other merits, kept Smollett alive. The quality and degree of laughter stimulated by his novels has always been a subjective matter, depending no doubt on subtle psychological factors within the reader. Hazlitt and Thackeray were especially impressed by Smollett's comic powers, as was the poet Henley. Smollett's *vis comica* also appealed to eighteenth-century Germany. W. C. S. Mylius, translator of the German edition of *Peregrine Pickle* published in Berlin in 1789, lauded its comic power, adding that a famous London physician (unfortunately unidentified) had the pleasant habit of writing on his prescriptions: "*Recipe* every day for a few hours several pages of Peregrine Pickle."[10] The Scottish quality in Smollett's sense of the comic has never been sufficiently recognized. Professor Wallace Notestein, in his recent and delightful book, *The Scot in History*, writes as follows on the subject of Scottish humor:

> There are three fairly old Scottish traditions of humor, the humor of the fantastic or grotesque, the humor of satire, and the humor of rollicking high spirits.[11]

All of these traditions Smollett exemplified with rich prodigality in Bowling, Morgan, Trunnion, Bramble, and Lismahago, who are among his greatest creations. It would seem that Smollett's *vis comica* ought to be especially appreciated among the Scots. Andrew Lang in his *Pickle the Spy* wrote of a Scottish secret agent so attracted to Pickle that he assumed that name as his *nom de guerre.*

[10] Translated from *Peregrine Pickle*, Neue Auflage, 4 vols. (Berlin, 1789), I, [ix].
[11] Quoted from Wallace Notestein, *The Scot in History, A Study of the Interplay of Character and History* (Yale University Press, 1947), p. 328.

At any rate, there is a wonderful comic quality in these characters and unsurpassable gusto and vitality in all their speeches and actions.

Smollett's prose style has won the acclaim of his most prominent critics, such as Seccombe, Saintsbury, Professor Wilbur Cross, the late Oliver Elton, Mr. Herbert Read, and Professor Louis L. Martz. The latter has rightly contended that Smollett's final style in *Humphry Clinker* shows in its simplicity, succinctness, and precision the effects of his long labors on historical compilation, whereas his early style is relatively elaborate, expansive, and turgid.[12] In general, Smollett's style in his novels is invariably clear, nervous, strong, fluent, rhythmical, and often idiomatic. It is free from eighteenth-century Scotticisms, and it bears the personal impress of his moods and manner of thinking. At its best it is a very fine and cultivated example of eighteenth-century prose.

Smollett's powers of characterization have already been alluded to in connection with his brilliant comic achievements. His finest characters are his nautical men; next in order come Matthew Bramble and Lismahago. In the creation of the latter and of the immortal Trunnion, Hatchway, and Pipes he appears to have taken numerous hints from actual persons, as Professor Kahrl has shown.[13] In Bramble, he drew heavily upon his own personality. Like Fielding, Smollett was relatively weak in the creation of women characters, as we shall show later. To do justice to his protagonists, Random, Pickle, Fathom, and Greaves would require an extended essay, as would any discriminating analysis of his numerous satirical and caricatured portraits. On the whole, despite Smollett's method of exaggeration in appearance, action, and speech, his characters are essentially real, more so in fact than his Victorian critics were willing to admit.

In the final analysis, it is in his own peculiar combination of vivid episode, comic character-creation, and style that Smollett makes his greatest contribution to the novel. Though one may grow weary at times in Smollett, after following for hours the series of episodes, which, like a long row of hurdles are lined up on the course of the picaresque obstacle race run by Roderick, Pickle, and

---

[12] See Louis L. Martz, *The Later Career of Tobias Smollett* (Yale University Press, 1942), p. 16.

[13] See George M. Kahrl, *Tobias Smollett, Traveler-Novelist* (University of Chicago Press [1945]), Chap. 3.

Fathom, it is not because the episodes, experienced singly, lack human reality or exciting action. The very rapidity and explosive energy in their action, character, and style may induce a temporary numbness. A law of diminishing returns operates upon one who tries to imbibe too much at one time of *Roderick Random* or *Peregrine Pickle* in sections where the Punch-and-Judy-show violence prevails. Taine disliked the "common brandy" in *Roderick Random,* but in this novel Arthur Machen enjoyed what seemed to him like the Irish Potheen,[14] an undeniable element in the earlier work of Smollett, which has not always pleased the French or the Romantic palate. This quality, however, is not so much in evidence in his last novel, *Humphry Clinker.*

To deal at length with the characteristic merits and admitted defects of each of Smollett's novels would be to repeat critical points which we have already stated and to extend unduly the length of this final chapter. Nevertheless a brief and general appraisal of each novel will now be furnished.

In Smollett's *Roderick Random,* so avidly read upon its appearance two centuries ago, the modern reader will look in vain for the aesthetic, intellectual, or spiritual aspects of life. On the contrary he will be exposed to much rascality, ugliness, and brutality still alive today, however, under one modern guise or another. Neither will the reader experience a dramatic ordering of the actions, such as is found in *Tom Jones.* Instead, he will be led through a chain-like linkage of relatively short episodes, many of them set forth with great gusto and gaiety. Contrasted with the roistering but not abhorrent hero, Roderick, his clown-like valet Strap, and a varied host of solid rascals, there stands out a truly memorable trio of vital and likable nautical figures—Morgan, Bowling, and Rattlin—such as had never appeared previously in English literature. For most readers the immense spirit and reality of these characters have been, and still remain, the chief glory of the book. However, for the special student of Smollett and his times, *Roderick Random* has other engaging merits. First, it provides many hints of Smollett's youth, naval experience, travel, and of his courtship of Anne Lassells. Furthermore, its action takes place on a huge international setting, including Scot-

---

[14] See *The Expedition of Humphry Clinker* with an Introduction by Arthur Machen, Modern Library Edition (New York [1929]), p. vi.

land, England (chiefly London), France, and the West Indies, although the settings are not usually delineated with as much detail as are those in the later works. Its naval settings and characters are by common consent its most unique contribution and permanent merit.

Generally speaking, Smollett's second novel, *Peregrine Pickle*, is an extension and intensification of the materials and methods of *Roderick Random*. In its revised form, which is the only easily accessible version—the first edition was some seventy pages longer —it is an astonishing mélange, with its lengthy inset memoirs of Lady Vane, its extended story of Daniel MacKercher, its satirical portraits, its varied gallery of characters, and its endless episodes crammed with slapstick adventure, practical jokes, and dull amours. Peregrine is more mature in trickery and ruffianism than Roderick, and Smollett's satire is correspondingly heavier, more cruel, and more misanthropic. Heightened and intensified also is the caricature, which here becomes fantastic, grotesque, and almost poetic. As in *Roderick Random*, the greatest characters are the nautical figures, Trunnion, Hatchway, and Pipes, who dwell together in their garrison in Cheshire. This group, which inspired Sterne's Uncle Toby and Corporal Trim, are surely equal and perhaps superior to the salty tars in *Roderick Random*. Most readers, we believe, find them the best thing in the novel. The Memoirs of Lady Vane and the journalistic account of Mac-Kercher, which helped to popularize this book in 1751, now possess only an antiquarian interest.

Smollett's *Count Fathom*, his third venture in fiction, features in Fathom an unbelievable seducer, impostor, and Iago-like monster, "exhibited to public view," as Smollett informed the reader at the end of Chapter 49, "that mankind may be upon their guard against imposture; so that the world may see how fraud is apt to overshoot itself; and that as virtue, though it may suffer for a while, will triumph in the end, so iniquity, though it may prosper for a season, will at last be overtaken by that punishment and disgrace which are its due." This moral purpose was first stressed in the "Dedication," which contained Smollett's well-known definition of a novel and his apologia for writing criminal biography. He also assured his reader that this novel contained variety in virtuous characters as a contrast to vicious ones, and that he had endeavored "to rouse the spirit of mirth, wake the soul of compassion, and touch the secret springs that move the heart." As all this suggests, Smollett was attempting a novel different in some respects from *Roderick Random* and *Peregrine Pickle*. The monstrous protagonist stands out against the good Renaldo and the angelic Monimia, named after Otway's heroine, but these main characters are too black or too white to be very credible. Neither are the comic type-characters particularly memorable, with the possible exception of the eccentric Sir Stentor Stile, admired by Saintsbury. Furthermore, the comic characters are relatively few, and ludicrous caricature is not often exploited. In general, most of the full-blooded and often coarse vigor of Smollett's earlier satirical portraits has disappeared. Prominent among the type-characters is the sentimental and benevolent Jew, Joshua Manasseh, suggested to Smollett, apparently, by a similar figure in a German novel by Gellert, translated into English in 1752.[15] But Smollett is still satirizing, chiefly through Fathom, many social groups, the medical and legal professions, in particular. Occasionally he resorts to irony, but in this he is obviously inferior to Fielding.

Count Fathom, generally speaking, has for valid reasons never been popular with the common reader or with the critics. Nevertheless, to one interested in the materials and style of the mid-eighteenth-century novel (or in Smollett's own development) this work has a special significance. *Count Fathom* is Smollett's most romantic novel. For example, he introduces many sentimental scenes, as well as his new and remarkable Gothic material in chapters 20 and 21. Moreover, there is found in repeated instances a curiously artificial style, which led the Reverend Henry Francis Cary a century ago to speculate that the novel was translated from another language.[16] Although such a theory is untenable, it is still true that very small sections of a few chapters (see chapter 12) do appear to be adaptations of some drama, possibly of an unpublished fragment written by Smollett himself. In general, the style of this novel, although brilliant, seems more consciously literary and artificial than that of Smollett's other fiction. This im-

[15] See Dr. H. R. S. Van Der Veen, *Jewish Characters in Eighteenth Century English Fiction and Drama* (Groningen, Batavia, 1935), p. 46.

[16] See Henry Francis Cary, *Lives of English Poets, from Johnson to Kirk White* (London, 1846), p. 126.

pression is strengthened by its varied quotations; in addition to some eleven from Shakespeare, pointed out by Professor Kahrl, there is one quotation apiece from Butler, Addison, Armstrong, and Gray.[17] All this goes to show that in *Count Fathom* Smollett was occasionally experimenting in romantic effects and in what for him was a new style. Unfortunately, however, the complete opus does not create a unified and artistic impression.

After an interval of seven years, Smollett wrote *The Life and Adventures of Sir Launcelot Greaves*, the first serial installment of which appeared in January 1760 in the *British Magazine*. This short and hastily written novel is an imitation of *Don Quixote*, and Smollett confessed in the second chapter that his readers might find its scheme "rather too stale and extravagant." For many critics this design has proved an insuperable weakness, leading them to dismiss it as Smollett's feeblest work. It is, however, as Professor Oliver Elton declared, quite easy to forget the incongruity of its scheme and to enjoy this novel's genuine merits, which grow upon one as he rereads it, a fact to which Saintsbury also bore eloquent witness. It is even probable that many non-pedantic readers will enjoy the patent absurdity of its quixotic hero, Greaves. In any event, those who understand the man Smollett will detect in its pages his essential idealism, strong humanitarianism, and capacity for kindly feeling, even though this novel is not as complete an expression of these qualities as is *Humphry Clinker*. Behind Greaves' attacks on corrupt politicians, lawyers, doctors, astrologers, and the then extremely dangerous homes for lunatics lay a quixotic but noble hope for reform. To a certain extent Greaves clearly revealed Smollett's own social idealism.

The characters in *Launcelot Greaves* cannot be numbered among Smollett's memorable creations. The nautical Captain Crowe is not the equal of Trunnion, but he is nevertheless a lively figure, as is Clarke, the lawyer. Aurelia, the very feminine heroine, is more decorative than real. The minor types are average in vitality.

As is already evident, much of the material of this novel had

---

[17] For the quotation from Butler, see Chap. 39; in Chap. 31 Smollett quotes from Addison's *Cato*, v, l. 13; in Chap. 20 we find the line, "stretching their extravagant arms athwart the gloom," from Armstrong's *Art of Preserving Health*, Bk. II, l. 370; in Chap. 17, Smollett utilizes the phrase, "the gates of mercy," which appears to echo the well-known line from Gray's *Elegy*, "And shut the gates of mercy on mankind."

been served up previously, but even so, Smollett contrives to present most of it with vigor and speed. The initial scene of the book has been justly acclaimed. The Yorkshire election-excitement is brilliantly described and satirized with every sign of authenticity. Where can a more graphic, contemporaneous, and Hogarthian account be found in eighteenth-century writing? Smollett's unusual journalistic gift is also illustrated in his description of the scenes in the King's Bench Prison (in chapters 20 and 21) written from personal observation, as was, in all likelihood, the short but delightfully vivid account of the Beef-Steak Club at the beginning of the fourth chapter.

As Professor Martz has pointed out, the prose style of *Launcelot Greaves* is more simple, succinct, and precise than that of *Count Fathom*, this change being due presumably to Smollett's enormous labors as editor and compiler in the 1750's. These stylistic qualities, together with its vivacity and occasional points of topical interest make *Launcelot Greaves* more appealing both to specialists and to amateur readers than one would gather from the overharsh and sweeping judgments of some of Smollett's critics.

The Expedition of Humphry Clinker, Smollett's final work, and a masterpiece acclaimed alike by readers and critics since 1771, convinces all who read it that, had its author been given another decade of vigorous life, possibly he would have surpassed the highest levels achieved in the distinctive creations of Fielding or of Sterne. As it is, there is nothing finer, *sui generis*, in the eighteenth-century novel. This remarkable work is not, as some critics have stated, a rare, unexpected, and inexplicable literary miracle, but rather the logical culmination of the rich maturing of Smollett's art and personality. This conclusion is fairly obvious to one who reads with insight his life and antecedent works. This is not to imply, however, that there are no problems connected with this novel. More light is still needed concerning Smollett's purposes in writing it,[18] and concerning the date of its composition, which seems to have been spread over a considerable period, perhaps from 1766 to 1770.[19] Further-

[18] Prof. Martz conjectures (*op. cit.*, p. 131) that the inspiration for *Humphry Clinker* is to be found in Smollett's desire to make amends to his Scottish readers for his complimentary picture of England in *The Present State of All Nations*, and also to salvage a part of his description of Scotland in that work.

[19] In my unpublished dissertation, "A Study of the Final Period of Tobias Smollett," of which there is a copy at the Yale University Library, I assembled some evidence concerning the probable date of the composition of *Humphry Clinker*.

more, there still remain in its text some unsolved allusions, and other editorial problems.

Certain illuminating observations concerning the general material of *Humphry Clinker* have been recently made. Professor Martz has pointed out that no less than one half of it consists of historical data, either topographical, political, or social; and Professor Kahrl has shown that it contains important elements of travel-data selected by a traveling novelist whose very successful book of travels appeared in 1766. Smollett's device of unfolding the slender plot of *Humphry Clinker* by means of the letters of a family on tour is common knowledge, as is the resultant multiple point of view expressed by the travelers in Matthew Bramble's party on manners, places, and persons in England and in Scotland. This novel extension of Richardson's epistolary method, suggested to Smollett by Anstey's *New Bath Guide*, is very successful in effecting narrative variety and in enriching the setting and the characterization.

In *Humphry Clinker* Smollett created a solid group of pleasing and realistic characters. Jerry and Lydia, the young lovers; Winifred and Tabitha; Humphry; Lismahago; and Matthew Bramble —all of these come to life, especially Bramble, who is often the true image of the author's own self. These central figures are drawn with relatively little distortion, although the old-style caricature of Smollett's early work which inspired Rowlandson and Cruikshank is still visible in Tabitha and Lismahago, and in the short and minor portraits. Bramble, Tabitha, Winifred, and Lismahago, like many of Smollett's characters, are sometimes made ludicrous by farcical practical jokes, but the effect of such hoaxes is more comic because they are applied to characters whom the reader knows well and likes. Accompanying this delectable cluster of fictitious figures are scores of actual persons, many of them considerable celebrities of the 1760's.

For the general reader *Humphry Clinker* provides rich and varied entertainment. As travel literature alone, it is extraordinarily interesting in its accurate and graphic accounts of Ranelagh Gardens and Vauxhall and of London scenes; of Bath in the days of Quin and Derrick; of Harrowgate and Scarborough; and of Edinburgh, Glasgow, Loch Lomond, and the Scottish Highlands. This novel is saturated with colorful and authentic details of all sorts of manners, costumes, and food and drink. Then there is its robust comedy of character tinged with occasional sentiment, which, coupled with a generous quota of ludicrous situations, led Thackeray to call this book the "most laughable story that has ever been written since the goodly art of novel-writing began." Furthermore there is a pleasant appeal for the general reader in the romantic plot, even though it is slightly woven and perfunctorily developed. Moreover, for the reader reasonably well informed about Smollett and the period of the 1760's, *Humphry Clinker* has a special interest in that it embodies in considerable scope his final criticism of that decade, a criticism both satirical and reasonably tolerant, now softened by sentiment and now made incisive by intellectual power. *Humphry Clinker* is notable for Smollett's medical diagnosis of unhygienic conditions in London and in Bath. It also presents through Bramble and Lismahago his political advice on the jury system, and on the freedom of the press, and reveals his vigorous reproof of the extreme political partisanship of that period. Numerous other critical attitudes are expounded directly or may be easily inferred from his scattered satirical portraits of actual persons and from his numerous complimentary references to living celebrities, some of them British, but more of them Scottish. Despite Smollett's warm tributes to friends north of the Tweed, his final novel is distinctly more than what Masson called a "dying Scotchman's farewell to Scotland."[20]

A most winning quality of *Humphry Clinker* is that it conveys a lively sense of Smollett's farewell moods. Although the waves of his violent satire still run high in parts of the book, there is much calm water and serene sunshine. The variety of moods is humanly real and artistically pleasing. On the whole, Smollett is more mellow, more light-hearted, and more reconciled with humanity and with the social scene, and, like Bramble, he can laugh at his own explosive fits of peevishness and misanthropy as well as at the follies that infest the world, follies so ludicrous as to provoke universal laughter. And in generous measure, this final work expresses in artistic form not only laughter but that bitter-sweet quality, which is universal in nature and in the blood and spirit of mankind.

[20] See Masson, *op. cit.*, p. 151.

It avails little to decry Smollett's contribution because he did not develop the dramatic narrative-pattern of Fielding in *Tom Jones*, or did not attain the tragic power of Richardson in *Clarissa*, or failed to exhibit the occasional psychological insight of Sterne. Smollett, with his own rare gifts, vitalized the pages of English fiction by eagle-eyed etchings of eighteenth-century scenes and manners, upon which social historians draw so heavily; by a masterful prose style; by incisive and socially significant satire; by perennially comic characters; and by the piquant flavor of his independent and dynamic personality.

APPENDIX A

Extract from *The Emmet*, Vol. 1, No. 1 (April 5, 1823), pp. 5-6.

Dr. Smollett.

It is pretty generally known that our inimitable Smollet served his medical apprenticeship in Glasgow, but perhaps most people are not aware that the shop was in Gibson's land which lately fell. His first master was Dr. Gordon, whom he afterwards celebrated in Roderick Random, under the name of Potion. His next was Dr. Crawford, the Crab of his celebrated novel. Crawford's shop was the corner one of Gibson's land. The door and one window looked to the Saltmarket, another window fronted Prince's Street. This large land was originally supported on pillars, under which was a sort of long Piazza. It was built by Provost Gibson, in the reign of King William, and consequently was an old house in Smollett's time. In the above shop was displayed the first specimen of that daring humour which afterwards distinguished the illustrious novelist. He was at that time about fourteen years of age, and was seated by the fire along with his fellow apprentice, when, it being a snowy day, a snow-ball was thrown into the shop by some mischievous person in the street. Young Smollett and his companion leaped over the counter to pursue the aggressors, but before they returned, Crawford (Crab) had come into the shop. Smollett stood behind the pillar and let his companion enter and bear the first onset of the doctor's fury. On mentioning the cause of his absence; "Very likely, very likely," said C. with his usual propensity. "Pray, how long might I stand here without being hit by a snow-ball, eh! To the day of judgment I suppose." He had scarcely pronounced these words, when Smollett, who had a snow-ball in his hand, and who, from behind the pillar, saw and heard all that was going on, levelled it at his face, and struck him fairly over his nose, which had exactly the powder-horn shape ascribed to it by his celebrated pupil. Crab, who, with all his irrascibility, was a man of humour, was so pleased with the wit and courage of the lad, that he forgave him on the spot.

Dr. Gordon (Potion) built Lancefield house, near Finnieston. Provost Buchanan of Glasgow, was Squire Gawky; he lived, at one time, in that house almost at the extremity of Anderston, with a front stair and railling leading up to it; the house is in the south

APPENDIX

side of Main street, almost the last house in it, and within a stone
cast or two of Cranston-hill reservoirs. It was then quite in the
country, and was considered a most genteel residence. He lived also
in King street, two or three closes down, on the right hand side.
The honour of being Strap, was disputed between a barber, in
Dumbarton, and Baillie Niven, of Glasgow. It is generally understood to belong to the latter, but whether the worthy Baillie was
ever a knight of the razor, we are uncertain.* Captain Whiffle
was the Earl of Bath, who prosecuted Smollett for ridiculing him
in Roderick Random; and it is said that he only escaped paying
damages, by the following words: "Captain Whiffle," for that was
his name. On these words Smollett's counsel rested their defence,
contending that they sufficiently identified Whiffle as being a
totally different person from the Earl of Bath.

APPENDIX B

The following data were sent to me by my searcher of documents in Spanish Town, Jamaica, British West Indies. They are
presumably accurate, and represent a considerable but not a complete search of pertinent legal records.

1. Charles Lassells, the father of Anne Smollett, died in 1724,
leaving property to the value of £782. Included in this were four
slaves (£140); outstanding debts (£122); and a bond for £120.
(Inventories 13/80)

2. William Leaver, the stepfather of Anne Smollett, died in
1736, leaving property valued at £19,948. This included thirty
pictures; a large quantity of furniture; china and pewter; silver
plate, valued at £100; a wherry; and twenty-four slaves, valued
at £734. (Inventories 18/136)

3. Charles Lassells, brother of Anne Smollett, died in 1752,
leaving property valued at £3,403. He owned fifty-seven slaves,
of whom forty-three were mortgaged along with his cattle to
William Beckford. His house was quite well furnished, and his
china, linen, and books are listed. Among the last were works by

* Since we received the above valuable anecdotes, we have been informed that
Baillie Niven was a knight of the razor, and occupied a house at Barnhill, within a
short distance of Lodge-my-loons, two miles north from Glasgow. The present proprietor of the property in question, has often been visited by the son of the baillie, who
never disputed his worthy father's right to the appellation of Strap. The baillie had
a small house adjoining his mansion, where he prepared the hair for perukes, &c.

Rapin, Locke, Machiavelli, Usher, Swift, and Pope. (Inventories 31/202)

4. Charles Lassells in his will dated October 28, 1746, and proved December 12, 1751, left to his "well beloved Sister Ann the wife of Tobias Smollett," £250 currency to be paid within 12 months of his death. After certain other small deductions, Charles Lassells left the residue of his estate to his daughter Frances with the stipulation that if the latter died without heirs, £750 currency should be paid to Anne Smollett. There were further stipulations by which Anne Smollett may have benefited later. (Wills 28/193)

5. Edward Lassells of St. Thomas-in-the-East, in his will, proved December 11, 1755, left to his sister, Anne Smollett, £50 "it being so much due to her for a negroe I bought of her." (Document-reference not furnished)

6. Charles Lassells, planter of St. Thomas-in-the-East, in his will, proved January 21, 1724, left to his "dear daughter Ann" a bond from Col. James Archbold deceased and his estate to secure the principal sum of £100 and interest to be improved for the use and benefit of his daughter. He also left her two negro girls and provided for her maintenance at the expense of his estate "in decent manner and in proportion with my other children." (Document-reference not furnished)

7. The Parish Register, St. Thomas (Copy), f. 15, contains the record of the baptism of Ann Lassells (later Anne Smollett) on January 4, 1722, when ten days old.

8. On August 21, 1756, Elizabeth Leaver, Tobias Smollett and Anne Smollett, all of Chelsea, gave powers of attorney to John Harvie, Alex Harvie, and Thomas Bontein of Kingston to sell nine men and eleven women slaves and remit the money to Elizabeth Leaver and her assigns. This action was related to an indenture between Elizabeth Leaver and Richard Oswald, merchant of London. (Powers of Attorney 44/102)

9. On March 2, 1763, Anne Smollett and Tobias Smollett appointed Thomas Bontein and Robert Loch of Kingston as their attorneys to sell lands and slaves in Jamaica. (Powers of Attorney 52/51)

10. On September 11, 1773, at Leghorn, Italy, Anne Smollett appointed Angus Macbean her attorney to sell negroes, tenements,

and all her personal estate in Jamaica. (Powers of Attorney 69/145)

11. On February 10, 1753, Elizabeth Leaver, by her attorney, Thomas Bontein, leased to Alexander Dallas, tailor of Kingston, land and house on Water Lane and Harbour Street for nineteen years at £50 per annum, the tenant to pay all taxes. (Deeds 153/107)

12. On July 24 and 25, 1753, Elizabeth Leaver transferred to Richard Oswald and to David Maccullo, surgeon, St. Martins-in-the-Fields, London, three tenements in Harbour Street, Kingston, several plots of ground within or near Kingston, and all her negroes,—all these to go, after Elizabeth Leaver's death, to Anne Smollett. (Deeds 156/70, 72)

13. On January 11, 1764, Tobias Smollett and Anne Smollett sold a lot of land between John's Lane and Duke Street to Anne Bragdon, a free mulatto, for £80 currency. (Deeds 204/59)

14. On March 23, 1764, Tobias Smollett and Anne Smollett sold for £300 currency four lots of footland (each lot 150' by 50') on John's Lane, East Queen's Street, and Upper East Street, Kingston, to Elizabeth Fickle, a free mulatto. (Deeds 204/22)

15. On August 11, 1766, Tobias Smollett and Anne Smollett sold for £80 currency a negro woman to James Nasmyth. (Deeds 221/29)

16. On February 10, 1767, Tobias Smollett and Anne Smollett sold for £80 currency a negro man to Hercules Ross.

APPENDIX C

Extract from *The Emmet*, Vol. II, No. XXVII
(October 4, 1823), pp. 9-10.

Anecdotes of Provost Buchanan, the Squire Gawky of Smollett, &c.

ORIGINAL

In the first volume of The Emmet we gave several authentic anecdotes relating to Smollett, which, we believe, never before appeared in print. These, we have reason to think, gave very general satisfaction, and we have pleasure in again laying a few more of the same nature before the public. Of all novel writers, Smollett was perhaps the least fictitious. Almost all the characters in his Roderick Random, are drawn from life, and many of these in his other works, possess the same advantage. Of the justice of this practice, we are not prepared to speak. We state the fact as it is—and may only remark, that, to this freedom, Smollett, as well as Hogarth, are [sic] greatly indebted for their matchless force and ludicrousness of outline—and for that preception [sic] of the ridiculous in which they have thrown almost all painters and novelists into the shade. Roderick Random, every body knows, is Smollett himself. Strap was Baillie Niven of Glasgow. Crab was Doctor Crawford, whose shop was in Gibson's land, now demolished; and there Smollett served his apprenticeship. His other master, Potion, was a Doctor Gordon, who built Lancefield House, near Finnieston. The Doctor in Peregrine Pickle, was Doctor Akenside, author of the Pleasures of Imagination, a stauch [sic] republican and a violent hater of the Scots; whence Smollett on one occasion represents him having his nose pulled by a Scotch officer. Peregrine Pickle was a gay young nobleman, well know [sic] in the fashionable circles of the day. Indeed there is reason to believe, that almost all his personages were pictures of real life. Squire Gawky was no less a personage than Provost Buchanan of Glasgow. He resided at one time in King Street; then a fashionable part of the town, [sic] he lived afterwards in Virginia Street. His house, we believe, has under-gone a repair, similar to that of the Highlandman's gun, which wanted nothing but a new barrel, ramrod, trigger, and firelock to make it an excellent fowling-piece. That old land which fronted Wilson Street, was Provost Buchanan's, but the whole of the outer shell has been removed, a story added to it, and it has been converted into a part of that fine large land on the west side of Virginia Street. He resided, likewise, at one time, in the Main Street of Anderston. The house is about a couple of stone casts from Cranston Hill reservoirs, on the same side, and has a front stair leading up to the door. He was exactly such a character as he is represented in Roderick Random, so far as personal courage goes. Whether he possessed the other bad propensities, imputed to him in that celebrated work, we are unable, at this distance of time, to say. Smollett had a personal quarrel with him, and probably did not soften matters. As a proof, however, of the estimation in which his personal prowess was regarded by the leiges, we relate the following anecdote.

One day as he was walking before the exchange in his official robes, a poor beggar woman came up to him and solicited charity. In rather rude terms he ordered her to begone; "Aweel my lord," said she, "God bless ye; you have done meikle for me and mine." "What have I done for you and your's?" replied the provost. "O bless you sir, do ye no ken when you were at the battle of Minden, that you ran awa', and my son Archy ran after you and saved his life; if it hadna been for you sir, he would hae stood still and been cut to pieces wi' the rest of his company, but he couldna bide to see his captain running awa' his lane."

The generous character of Smollett himself, is finely illustrated in the following anecdote:—Being solicited charity by a poor man, he gave him by accident a guinea, for a less valuable piece; the beggar immediately hobbled after him and showed him his mistake: "Good Lord," exclaimed the astonished novelist, "what a lodging has honesty taken up with!" So saying, he not only made the beggar keep the guinea, but likewise bestowed upon him another on the spot.

Those readers who wish to know more of Smollett, are referred to the first Number of the Emmet.

APPENDIX D

Archibald Hamilton, Senior (1719-1793), was for many years the printer of the *Critical*, and was also an executor of Smollett's will, but information about him is scanty. At his death in 1793 the *Gentleman's Magazine* (Vol. LXIII [March, 1793], p. 285), ran the following obituary: "At his house in Bedford-row, in his 74th year [died] Archibald Hamilton, esq. many years an eminent printer in Fleet-street, and at Oxford. He will long be remembered as a valuable contributor to the literary interests of his time, and as a man whose social qualities, well-informed mind, and communicative disposition, had endeared him to a numerous circle of friends, and render his death a subject of unfeigned regret. He was the original printer (and, we believe, the projector) of The *Critical Review*. By his only son, who died Oct. 6, 1792 (see vol. LXII, p. 964) he has left several grandchildren and great grandchildren." In the above mentioned obituary of Archibald Hamilton's only son, Archibald II, Hamilton Senior was called "the first establisher of the *Critical Review*." According to John Nichols

(*Literary Anecdotes*, III, 398-99), Hamilton Senior "commenced" the *Critical* with "the assistance of Dr. Smollett and other literary friends." This general tradition is duly preserved in *A Dictionary of the Printers and Booksellers . . . in England, Scotland and Ireland. From 1726 to 1775*, eds. H. R. Plomer and others (Oxford University Press, 1932 [for 1936]), p. 114. Hamilton appears to have been a Scot, having left Edinburgh in 1736 because of the Porteous Riots. For a time he was the principal manager for William Strahan. (See "William Strahan and His Ledgers. A Paper by R. A. Austen-Leigh, M.A. Read before the Bibliographical Society, XVIII December, MCMXXII," p. 13.) In due course Hamilton had his own printing establishment in Chancery Lane (see title page of the bound volumes of the *Critical* from 1758 to 1761) and then in Falcon Court, Fleet Street. Becoming wealthy, he enjoyed his coach before William Strahan felt that he could afford one, a fact which Johnson approved of. Hamilton's residence at one time seems to have been "in the vicinity of Chelsea." (See James Prior, *Life of Oliver Goldsmith, M.B.* 2 vols. [London, 1837], I, 315.) His only daughter, Sarah Hamilton, had "associated much with Johnson, Smollett, Goldsmith, and Garrick," presumably at her father's house. (See Nichols' *Literary Anecdotes*, III, 759.) Archibald Hamilton's huge physique may be inferred from Cuthbert Shaw's satirical portrait of him, written about 1765:

> Foremost, the spite of hell upon his face,
> Stood the Thersites of the Critic Race,
> Tremendous Hamilton! of giant strength,
> With Crab-tree staff full twice two yards in length.

See *The Poems of Cuthbert Shaw and Thomas Russell*, ed. Eric Partridge (London, 1925), p. 57.

Equally large was Hamilton's mentality if we may trust the words of the silversmith, Joseph Brasbridge: "I often spent my evenings at the Globe tavern in Fleet-street. . . . Among the company . . . was Archibald Hamilton the printer, with a mind fit for a lord chancellor." (See Joseph Brasbridge, *The Fruits of Experience; or, Memoir of Joseph Brasbridge, written in his 80th year* [London, 1824], pp. 33-34.)

APPENDIX E

Extracts from the will of Elizabeth Leaver made July 25, 1753, and proved January 19, 1763, from the original document at Somerset House, London.

Mrs. Leaver left to her son, Edward Lassells, £100 Jamaica currency, and to her granddaughter, Frances Lassells, the same sum. To her granddaughter, Elizabeth Smollett, she bequeathed £200 sterling "at her Age of twenty one years" and willed that the "Interest thereof be in the mean time applied towards her Maintenance and Education." She gave his freedom to her negro servant in Jamaica named Charles. All her other property real and personal she bequeathed to Anne Smollett.

APPENDIX F

Letter from Robert Graham to Smollett, August 13, 1771.

London
13th August 1771

Dr Smollett
Dear Sir

A short Time before I left Jamaica, I received your letter from Leghorn, replete with various complaints. If Mr Hamilton has used you badly I heartily condole with you, but at the same [Time?] must begg you will consider that it was not in my power to preserve old houses from decaying or to persuade people to give a high rent for them even when they were in order. Every thing in my power I have done to promote your Interest, but believe me, it is no such easy matter to collect money in Jamaica, as it is in general apprehended[.] more payments are affected [sic] in that Island by discounts by a knowledge of the business of particular people than there is by money or Bills. I have notwithstanding now brought for you about £502 . . 2 . . 6 sterling, which I shall tomorrow settle with Mr Auld & left behind in bonds & papers a principal Sum of £1084 . . 5 . . ¾. Your houses are now all lett, and except the one in harbour Street tenanted by Mr Dallas, all in good order & repair. Your affairs I left in the hands of Mr Angus McBean who was for many years a Clerk to me, & now trades for himself in the town of Kingston. I know his abilitys [sic] in business to be inferior to no man's. I know the Integrity & honesty of his heart, & from a long acquaintance with him & a conviction of his honor & fidelity I have entrusted him with the entire management of my own affairs & for the same reasons put yours into his hands. If my sentiments of M^r McBean & my knowledge of mankind have any weight with you, you will immediately appoint him your attorney, you will serve yourself by making this choice & I will pawn my honor you will never repent you of the trust you place in him.

I believe I have left Jamaica for a few years & if I do not find these northern climes suit my constitution I shall follow your example & steer to the southward. Please let me know how your health is & if you propose soon making a visit to England.

> I am
> > Dear Sir
> > Your most humble servant
> > > R B.

PS.

I have changed my name from Graham in consequence of inheriting Bontine of Ardoch's estate

> > R B.

This letter is printed here from a copy sent to me by R. B. Cunninghame Graham. For a portion of this letter see Graham's *Doughty Deeds An Account of the Life of Robert Graham of Gartmore, Poet and Politician*, London, 1925, pp. 85-86.

APPENDIX G

Inscriptions written for monuments in memory of Smollett.

I. Translation of Dr. John Armstrong's Latin Inscription for the monument in Leghorn.

> Here
> Rest the remains
> of
> TOBIAS SMOLLETT
> A North Briton,
> Who, sprung
> From an ancient and respectable family,
> Shone forth an example
> Of the virtue of former times.
> Of an ingenuous countenance,
> And manly make.
> With a breast animated by the justest spirit,
> He was eminently distinguished
> For great benevolence of temper,
> And a generosity even above his fortune.
> His wit and every character
> Of fertile inventiveness,
> Of true pleasantry,
> Of flexibility to every subject,
> From his aptness and wonderful capacity

For every kind of learning.
The exercise of these talents
Produced a variety of pleasing fictions,
In which
With great exuberance of fancy
And true humour
He laughed at and described
The lives and manners of men,
While
(Shameful to relate!)
This genius
This honour to his country,
Met with nothing
In these abandoned, worthless, insipid times
But what was unfavourable to him
Except indeed
Their abundance of supply to his pen
Of matter of satire;
Times!
In which
Hardly any literary merit
But such as was in the most false or futile taste
Received encouragement
From the paltry mock Mecaenases [*sic*] of Britain!
In honour to the memory
Of this most worthy and amiable
Member of society
Sincerely regretted by many friends
This monument
Was by his much beloved and affectionate wife
Dutifully and deservedly
Consecrated.

Printed from *Plays and Poems written by T. Smollett, M.D.*, London, 1777, pp. xxiv-xxv.

II. Translation of the Latin Inscription written for the monument erected by Smollett's cousin on the banks of the Leven. This inscription was written partly by Dr. George Stuart, partly by John Ramsay of Ochtertyre, and partly by Dr. Samuel Johnson.

Stay, traveller!
If elegance of taste and wit,
If fertility of genius,
And an unrivalled talent
In delineating the characters of mankind,
Have ever attracted thy admiration,

Pause a while
On the memory of TOBIAS SMOLLETT, M.D.
One more than commonly indued with those virtues
Which in a man and citizen
You would praise, or imitate.
Who,
Having secured the applause
Of posterity,
By a variety of literary abilities,
And a peculiar felicity of composition,
Was,
By a rapid and cruel distemper,
Snatched from this world in the 51st year of his age.
Far, alas! from his country,
He lies interred near Leghorn, in Italy.
In testimony of his many and great virtues
This empty monument,
The only pledge, alas! of his affection,
Is erected
On the Banks of the Leven,
The scene of his birth and of his latest poetry,
By JAMES SMOLLETT of Bonhill,
his cousin;
Who should rather have expected this last tribute from him.
Go, and remember
This honour was not given alone to the memory of the deceased,
But for the encouragement of others:
Deserve like him, and be alike rewarded.

Printed from *Plays and Poems written by T. Smollett, M.D.*, London, 1777, pp. xxviii-xxix.

III. An Inscription written in English by Lord. Kames.

No circumstance is trivial in the history of eminent men! Behold, Passenger! the birthplace of TOBIAS SMOLLETT, who by nature was destined to banish spleen, and promote cheerfulness, sweet balm of life! His grave, alas! is in a distant country.

How dismally opposite is an Alexander or a Louis, men destined by nature for depressing the spirits of their fellow creatures and for desolating the earth!

This Pillar, erected by JAMES SMOLLETT of Bonhill, is not for his cousin, who possesses a more noble Monument in his literary productions, but for thee, O Traveller! If literary fame be thy ruling passion, emulation will enliven thy genius: Indulge the hope of a Monumental Pillar, and, by ardent application, thou mayest come to merit the splendid reward.

Printed from Robert Chambers' *Traditions of Edinburgh*, 2 vols. (Edinburgh, 1825), I, 278-79.

IV. Translation of the Latin Inscription written by John Ramsay of Ochtertyre.

Stop, passenger!
If a rich vein of genius and humour,
If exquisite drawings from life,
By the hand of a master,
Were ever admired by thee,
Fondly contemplate for a moment
Yon unadorned mansion.
Under its roof
TOBIAS SMOLLETT, M.D.
Drew his first breath.
In those very fields, on the banks of the Leven,
Did he often play while a boy;
Under the shade of yonder trees
He first courted the rural muse.
After a variety of adventures,
And travelling much in foreign climes,
Having returned for a short space
To his native country,
He was wonderfully refreshed
With the quiet of this sequestered spot,
And with the recollection of his boyish years,
Which alone did not deceive.
Of his character and rank in the literary world
Thou canst not be ignorant,
Nor is it proper to detain thee;
Go then; fare thee well!
Always remembering how sweet and becoming
Is the love of our native soil.

Printed from Smollett's *Miscellaneous Works*, ed. Anderson, 6 vols. (Edinburgh, 1820), I, 101.

APPENDIX H

Through the courtesy of the Rosenbach Company of Philadelphia, I was shown in 1946 an unpublished autograph note signed by Smollett and dated at Chelsea, November 12, 1757. In this note concerning a personal loan, Smollett mentioned a Mr. Colquhoun.

APPENDIX I

Those especially interested in Smollett's manuscript may have noted that his signature was (or is) in the possession of Lady Charnwood, who referred to it in her book, *An Autograph Collection and the Making of It*, London, 1930. In 1932, Lady Charnwood very kindly sent me the following copy of what she described as "a very small piece of paper":

Sealed & delivered
in the presence of us
Urian Leigh
Richard Ellkin
Tobias Smollett

APPENDIX J

In 1919, Dr. Pilatte edited extracts from Smollett's *Travels in France and Italy* in a small volume called *Smollett Lettres de Nice sur Nice et ses Environs (1763-1765) Traduites et précédées d'un Aperçu Biographique*. Nice, Imprimerie de L'Éclaireur. In Dr. Pilatte's prefatory memoir is found the following anecdote of Smollett: "Il [Smollett] defie en duel l'amiral Sir John Mordaunt et c'est à cette occasion qu'en arrivant au rendez-vous il fait la commande restée célèbre chez nos amis les Anglais: 'Pistols for two and coffin for one.' Mais l'amiral se dérobe, poursuit une action légale et Smollett est condamné à 100 livres d'amende et 3 mois de prison pour diffamation."

It is apparent that Pilatte has confused Sir John Mordaunt with Admiral Charles Knowles. However, this anecdote may contain some germ of truth because Smollett, according to his early biographers, offered to give Knowles any satisfaction which he desired. I have been unable to discover the source of the phrase, "Pistols for two and coffin for one." It is possible that Smollett coined it on some occasion or other.

APPENDIX K

Two hitherto unknown letters by Smollett have just been published by Dr. Francesco Cordasco in *Notes and Queries*, CXCIII (1948), 295-96, 364. This material became available to me so recently that I have been unable to study it, or to incorporate it in this biography.

BIBLIOGRAPHY

THIS is a brief and selected list of books and articles, most of which contain biographical material. For an extended list of works on Smollett, the reader is referred to the following pamphlets by Dr. Francesco Cordasco:

Smollett Criticism, 1770-1924: a bibliography, enumerative and annotative, Long Island University Press, 1948. *Smollett Criticism, 1925-1945: A Compilation*, Long Island University Press, 1947.

ANDERSON, DR. ROBERT, "Life" in volume I of his edition of Smollett's *Miscellaneous Works*, 6 vols., Edinburgh, 1820. The best biography by Anderson, who furnished many memoirs of Smollett, the first for his edition of the *British Poets*, London, 1795. Valuable, though vague, incomplete, and superseded.

ANON., "Life" in Smollett's *Plays and Poems*, London, 1777. The first account of any length, incorporating material from the *Westminster Magazine* (1775) and the *Annual Register* for 1775. Valuable because of priority.

BUCK, HOWARD SWAZEY, *A Study in Smollett, Chiefly "Peregrine Pickle,"* Yale University Press, 1925. Valuable for Smollett's quarrels centering in *The Regicide* and in *Peregrine Pickle*. The beginning of modern scholarship on Smollett.

CARLYLE, DR. ALEXANDER, *Autobiography*, Edinburgh and London, 1860. The best edition is that edited by John Hill Burton, London and Edinburgh, 1910. Valuable in its occasional but brilliant illuminations of Smollett and written by a personal friend of the novelist.

CHAMBERS, ROBERT, *Smollett: His Life and a Selection from His Writings*, Edinburgh, 1867. Contains, as does his *Traditions of Edinburgh* (2 vols., Edinburgh, 1825), his *Minor Antiquities of Edinburgh* (Edinburgh, 1833), and his *Biographical Dictionary of Eminent Scotsmen* (4 vols., Glasgow, 1835), careful, pleasing, and original contributions.

HANNAY, DAVID, *Life of Tobias George Smollett*, London, 1887. Valuable for naval background and for its "Bibliography" of Smollett compiled by John P. Anderson of the British Museum.

HANNAY, JAMES, article on Smollett in *Quarterly Review*, vol. 103 (1858), 66-108. Excellent on Smollett's Scottish environment, and pleasingly written.

IRVING, JOSEPH, *Some Account of the Family of Smollett of Bonhill*, Dumbarton, Printed for the Author, 1860. Valuable for its genealogy of the Smollett family and for its data from manuscripts at Cameron House.

BIBLIOGRAPHY

JOLIAT, EUGÈNE, *Smollett et La France*, Paris, 1935. Not primarily biographical, but an important and scholarly work for the student of Smollett.

JONES, CLAUDE E., *Smollett Studies*, University of California Press, 1942. Deals with Smollett's naval experience and with his activities in the *Critical Review*.

KAHRL, GEORGE M., *Tobias Smollett, Traveler-Novelist*, University of Chicago Press, [1945]. Not primarily biographical, but an important and scholarly work for the student of Smollett.

MARTZ, LOUIS L., *The Later Career of Tobias Smollett*, Yale University Press, 1942. Not primarily biographical, but an important and scholarly work for the student of Smollett.

MEIKLE, HENRY W., editor, "New Smollett Letters," in *The Times Literary Supplement* (London), July 24, 1943, and July 31, 1943. Of primary importance for Smollett's life in the 1740's and 1750's.

MELVILLE, LEWIS, *The Life and Letters of Tobias Smollett*, London, [1926]. A cursory and very inaccurate work, to which I have not referred hitherto in this volume.

MOORE, DR. JOHN, "Memoirs," in volume I of his edition of Smollett's *Works*, 8 vols., London, 1797. The only extended account by a friend and acquaintance of Smollett. Valuable, although vague and limited.

NOYES, EDWARD S., editor, *The Letters of Tobias Smollett*, Harvard University Press, 1926. The first and only edition of Smollett's letters as available in 1926. Needs revision and augmentation (some twenty-five more letters have appeared since) but is still invaluable for the student of Smollett.

PARKER, ALICE, "Tobias Smollett and the Law," in *Studies in Philology*, XXXIX (1942). Excellent for Smollett's encounters with, and attitude toward the law.

POWELL, L. F., "William Huggins and Tobias Smollett," in *Modern Philology*, XXXIV (1936). Of prime importance for Smollett's life from 1756 to 1761.

SECCOMBE, THOMAS, article on Smollett in *DNB*, 1898. See also *Errata* volume, 1904, and *DNB*, 1921-22 (vol. 18). A condensed and careful account, with an important reference bibliography.

SMEATON, OLIPHANT, *Tobias Smollett*, Edinburgh, [1897]. A sympathetic but undocumented account, possibly based in part on material still unpublished, or possibly, in places, the product of the author's undisciplined imagination.

WHITRIDGE, ARNOLD, *Tobias Smollett, A Study of his Miscellaneous Works*, Published by the Author, n.p. [1925]. A general and helpful introduction to Smollett.

INDEX

THIS index does not include material in the Preface, the Selective Bibliography, and the Appendix.

Under Smollett are listed his creative writings, certain editions of his collected *Works*, and, for the sake of convenience, all translations traditionally assigned to him. It now appears, however, from a letter of Smollett just published in *Notes and Queries* (August 21, 1948) by Professor Francesco Cordasco that in the translating of *Don Quixote* Smollett received substantial assistance.

Elsewhere in the Index are found the titles of certain translations, periodicals, and other works over which Smollett had some sort of editorial supervision.

INDEX

INDEX

INDEX

graphically and Biographically Considered, 221n.

Scott, William Robert, *Adam Smith*, 17n.

Scottish Medical Degrees, 145-46

"Scrag, Sir Gosling," 127

Seccombe, Thomas, 48n., 59, 124n., 182, 183n., 184, 248, 279n., 295n., 316; *The Age of Johnson*, 168n.

Seilhamer, George O., *History of the American Theatre Before the Revolution*, 201n.

Select Essays, 163

Selection from the Papers of the Earls of Marchmont, A, ed. Rose, 153n.

Series of Letters between Mrs. Elizabeth Carter and Miss Catherine Talbot, A, 95n.

Servandoni, Jean-Nicholas, 88, 89, 90

Shaftesbury, Earl of, *see* Cooper, Anthony

Shakespeare, 320; *Henry IV*, Part Two, 138; *Works*, 249

Sharp, Dr. Samuel, 141, 270, 273; *Letters from Italy*, 270n.

Sharpe, Charles Kirkpatrick, 5, 266

Shaw, Cuthbert, 261; *Poems*, 261n.; *The Race*, 261n.

Shebbeare, Dr. John, 44, 139n., 180, 188-90, 213, 235, 245n., 265n.; *Appendix to the Occasional Critic*, 175n., 180; *The Occasional Critic*, 44n., 180, 185n.; *Third Letter to the People of England*, 173

Sheerness, 31

Shelburne, Earl of, *see* Petty

Shelton, Thomas, translator of *Don Quixote*, 164n.

Shenstone, William, 119, 129; *Letters*, 129n., 217n.; *Poems*, 29

Sheridan, Thomas, *British Education*, 173

Shipborne Church, Fairlawn, Kent, 123n.

Short Vindication of the Proceedings of the Governors of the General Hospital at Bath, A, 147n.

Simpson, Mr., banker, 270

Simpson, John, 60

Simson, Robert, professor of mathematics, 17

Smart, Christopher, 178; *A Translation of the Psalms of David*, 183n.

Smeaton, Oliphant, *Tobias Smollett*, 5n., 43n., 73n., 74n., 90, 116, 124n., 196n., 265, 279n., 308

Smellie, Dr. William, 135n., 137, 139, 140, 219n.; *Collection of Cases*, 139n., 142; *Treatise on . . . Midwifery*, 135, 138

Smellie, Mrs., 139n., 270

Smith, Adam, 268

Smith, J. T., *Nollekens and His Times*, 165n.

Smith, Richard, 42, 100, 177

Smith, Robert, 75, 78-79, 205, 286

Smith, Warren H., 286n., 287 n. 29 and n. 30

Smollett, Anne, 73, 74, 109, 116, 145, 159, 184, 204, 247, 257, 261, 265, 283-86, 293, 295, 296, 298, 299

Smollett, Archibald, 3, 4, 7, 294n.

Smollett, Barbara Cunningham, 3, 4, 160-61, 294

Smollett, Elizabeth, 73, 109, 113, 182, 247, 265n.

Smollett, Captain James, brother of Tobias, 4, 26

Smollett, Commissary James, cousin of Tobias, 5n., 13n., 27, 209, 269, 299, 301n.

Smollett, James, 25

Smollett, Sir James, 4, 7ff., 12

Smollett, Jane, sister of Tobias, 4, 26

Smollett, Tobias, ambition to excel in drama, 57; ancestry, 4; anecdotes, 14, 161, 306, 330; application for medical post in Portugal, 246

attacks on: in *Battle of the Reviews*, 225; by Comber, 188; by Churchill, 241; by Fielding, 131-32; by Grainger, 203, 215; by Reed, 217; by Shaw, 261; by Thicknesse, 273; in *A Vindication*, 132; by Warburton, 149

baptism, 3; birthplace, 3; book-reviewing, first examples of, 134; booksellers, feud with, 119; books subscribed for, 183; books taken to France, 249; boyhood, 7ff.; burial, 298

Chelsea celebrations in honor of: in 1753, 153; in 1761, 237; Chelsea, regard for, 110; Chelsea Old Church, association with, 113

Cleland, Archibald, defense of, 147ff.

coffee-houses frequented by: Don Saltero's, 111; Forrest's, 205; Rainbow, 137

"coma vigil" of, 267-68; consulships, applications for, 246, 271ff.; courtship, 38

death: cause of, 297; false report of in 1769, 281; reports of in 1771, 297n.

doggerel verse concerning, 11

dictator in literature, 168-69; drudgery in writing, 185-86, 219

editing of manuscripts: for Drum-